ANCIENT GREEK DEMOCRACIES

Classical Athenian democracy is rightly famous, but democracy flourished in other parts of the Greek world as well. In this clear and fascinating book, Matthew Simonton traces the emergence, growth, consolidation, and decline of democratic city-states over the millennium down to the fifth century CE. He argues for the widespread and highly participatory nature of democratic constitutions across the Greek world, particularly in the fourth, third, and second centuries BCE. Readers will also learn to appreciate the characteristic ideological, institutional, and material-cultural features of democratic *poleis*. The evidence marshaled includes literary texts, inscriptions, coins, archaeological remains, and monumental art. The book does not shy away from the fact that ancient Greek democracies both empowered lower-class men and rested on a series of exclusions (of women, enslaved people, and foreigners). Nevertheless, *dēmokratia* emerges as a major facet of ancient Greek culture and society.

MATTHEW SIMONTON is Associate Professor of Classics at Princeton University, having previously worked at Arizona State University. His first book, *Classical Greek Oligarchy: A Political History* (2017), received the 2018 Runciman Award from the Anglo-Hellenic League. He is currently at work on a political and cultural history of ancient Greek demagoguery.

KEY THEMES IN ANCIENT HISTORY

EDITORS
P. A. Cartledge *Clare College, Cambridge*
G. Woolf *UCLA*

EMERITUS EDITOR
P. D. A. Garnsey
Jesus College, Cambridge

Key Themes in Ancient History aims to provide readable, informed and original studies of various basic topics, designed in the first instance for students and teachers of Classics and Ancient History, but also for those engaged in related disciplines. Each volume is devoted to a general theme in Greek, Roman, or where appropriate, Graeco-Roman history, or to some salient aspect or aspects of it. Besides indicating the state of current research in the relevant area, authors seek to show how the theme is significant for our own as well as ancient culture and society. It is hoped that these original, thematic volumes will encourage and stimulate promising new developments in teaching and research in ancient history.

Other books in the series
Politics in the Roman Republic, by Henrik Mouritsen
9781 07 03188 3 (hardback) 978 1 107 65133 3 (paperback)

Roman Political Thought, by Jed W. Atkins
978 11 07 10700 7 (hardback) 9781107514553 (paperback)

Empire and Political Cultures in the Roman World, by Emma Dench
978 0 521 81072 2 (hardback) 978 0 521 00901 0 (paperback)

Warfare in the Roman World, by A.D. Lee
978 1 107 01428 2 (hardback) 978 1 107 63828 0 (paperback)

Slaves and Slavery in Ancient Greece, by Sara Forsdyke
978 1 107 03234 7 (hardback) 978 1 107 65889 9 (paperback)

Roman Law in Context (second edition), by David Johnston
978 1 108 47630 0 (hardback) 978 1 108 70016 0 (paperback)

Risk in the Roman World, by Jerry Toner
978 1 108 48174 8 (hardback) 978 1 108 72321 3 (paperback)

The Roman Empire and World History, by Peter Fibiger Bang
978 1 316 51610 2 (hardback) 978 1 009 01372 7 (paperback)

For a full list of titles in this series go to www.cambridge.org/series/key-themes-ancient-history

ANCIENT GREEK DEMOCRACIES

MATTHEW SIMONTON
Princeton University

Shaftesbury Road, Cambridge CB2 8EA, United Kingdom

One Liberty Plaza, 20th Floor, New York, NY 10006, USA

477 Williamstown Road, Port Melbourne, VIC 3207, Australia

314–321, 3rd Floor, Plot 3, Splendor Forum, Jasola District Centre, New Delhi – 110025, India

Cambridge University Press is part of Cambridge University Press & Assessment, a department of the University of Cambridge.

We share the University's mission to contribute to society through the pursuit of education, learning and research at the highest international levels of excellence.

www.cambridge.org
Information on this title: www.cambridge.org/9781108844543

DOI: 10.1017/9781108951586

© Cambridge University Press & Assessment 2026

This publication is in copyright. Subject to statutory exception and to the provisions of relevant collective licensing agreements, no reproduction of any part may take place without the written permission of Cambridge University Press & Assessment.

When citing this work, please include a reference to the DOI 10.1017/9781108951586

First published 2026

Cover image: Bouleutērion (Council House) of Teos, Hellenistic period. Photo credit © Matthew Simonton.

A catalogue record for this publication is available from the British Library

A Cataloging-in-Publication data record for this book is available from the Library of Congress

ISBN 978-1-108-84454-3 Hardback
ISBN 978-1-108-94829-6 Paperback

Cambridge University Press & Assessment has no responsibility for the persistence or accuracy of URLs for external or third-party internet websites referred to in this publication and does not guarantee that any content on such websites is, or will remain, accurate or appropriate.

For EU product safety concerns, contact us at Calle de José Abascal, 56, 1°, 28003 Madrid, Spain, or email eugpsr@cambridge.org

Εἰρήνη

Contents

List of Figures	*page* viii
List of Maps	ix
Acknowledgments	x
A Note to the Reader	xii
Introduction	1
1 From *Eunomia* to *Dēmokratia*, 510–451/0 BCE	6
2 A Contested Existence, 451/0–362 BCE	40
3 The Heyday of Ancient Greek Democracies, 362–146 BCE	96
4 (D)evolutions of Democracy, 146 BCE to Late Antiquity	146
Appendix: Instances of "Democracy" on Stone	175
Bibliographical Essay	180
Bibliography	184
Index Locorum	211
General Index	220

Figures

1.1	Salamis decree. (Photo: Marsyas via Wikimedia Commons, CC BY-SA 3.0).	*page* 23
1.2	Classical Agora. (Photo: American School of Classical Studies at Athens: Agora Excavations. Archive number: 2002.01.0873).	27
1.3	Harmodius and Aristogeiton. (Photo: DEA / G. DAGLI ORTI / De Agostini via Getty Images).	29
2.1	The Pnyx. (Photo: Miguel Sotomayor / Getty Images).	50
2.2	Casualty list IG I^3 1147. (Photo: Lanmas / Alamy).	60
2.3	Athenian ostraka. (Photo: Vita exclusive / Alamy).	70
2.4	Panathenaic frieze. (Photo: Erin Babnik / Alamy).	87
3.1	Law of Eucrates. (Photo: American School of Classical Studies at Athens: Agora Excavations. Archive number: 2012.03.2610).	124
3.2	Teos coin. (Photo: Roma Numismatics / biddr).	125
3.3	Euphron stele. (Photo: George E. Koronaios via Wikimedia Commons, CC BY-SA 4.0).	131
4.1	Smyrnaean agora. (Photo: uskarp / Alamy).	171

Maps

0.1 Greece and western Asia Minor. (Source: *The Cambridge Ancient History* vol. 6) *page* xiii
1.1 The political organization of Attica (after J. S. Traill). (Source: *The Cambridge Ancient History* vol. 4) 30

Acknowledgments

This book received support and encouragement from many sources over the years. I thank Cambridge University Press editor Michael Sharp for approaching me about a potential contribution to the Key Themes in Ancient History series. Series editors Paul Cartledge and Greg Woolf then provided excellent feedback and shepherded the volume through to production. Katie Idle and Bethany Johnson at Cambridge have my eternal thanks for all their help during the production process.

Cédric Brélaz, Mirko Canevaro, and Eric Driscoll read and commented on drafts of individual chapters and saved me from several errors. Portions of the material were presented to the Southwest Ancient Historians reading group, or SWANCies – Denise Demetriou, Denver Graninger, Jeremy LaBuff, John W. I. Lee, and Benjamin Sullivan – whose feedback and conviviality were always so enjoyable; I thank Denise in particular for providing the means of bringing us all together in person on several occasions. Moral support was furnished throughout by Zachary Herz, Danielle Kellogg, and Liv Yarrow; Danielle Kellogg also kindly shared work in advance of publication. As the commonplace goes, any errors that remain are entirely mine.

Whether we talked about the specific arguments of the book or not, I have benefited greatly from conversations about ancient Greek democracies over the years with Scott Arcenas, Geoff Bakewell, Ryan Balot, Henning Börm, Federica Carugati, Alberto Esu, Mark Fisher, Sara Forsdyke, Ben Gray, Jordan Jochim, Demetra Kasimis, James Kierstead, Matt Landauer, Melissa Lane, John Ma, Ingvar Mæhle, Christel Müller, Josh Ober, Nikolaos Papazarkadas, David Polansky, Avshalom Schwartz, Julia Shear, Claire Taylor, and David Teegarden.

This book was conceived and written entirely during my time at Arizona State University. For twelve years I was proud to call ASU home. A Humanities Institute research fellowship in 2023 brought me together with Eugene Clay of the School of Historical, Philosophical, and Religious

Studies, who read and commented on most of the manuscript and was a model interdisciplinary interlocutor. Of all my wonderful colleagues at the School of Humanities, Arts, and Cultural Studies, I single out Charles Eppley, Ilana Luna, and Annika Mann for their collegiality and, more importantly, their friendship. Jenny Dyck Brian, Laurie Stoff, and Alex Young were forever in solidarity. And to Henry Thomson: Thanks for the fellowship.

Arizona is also where I met my wife, Irina Levin, to whom this book is dedicated, whose love and camaraderie I am so fortunate to have every day. I am excited for this next stage of our life together.

A Note to the Reader

Translations of the word *dēmos* in the following text are rendered as "the People," with a capital P, in order both to signal to the reader which term in the original Greek is being translated and to "make the word strange," since an ancient Greek *dēmos* was a much more specific thing than the mundane English word "people." In particular, it was gendered grammatically and ideologically as masculine, and it could be conceived of as a unified actor, a sort of "Mr. The People."

References to ancient authors follow the conventions of abbreviation from *The Oxford Classical Dictionary*, fourth edition, except that I abbreviate Plato as Plat. and his *Republic* as *Rep*. All translations from the Greek are mine unless otherwise noted. Classics journals in the Bibliography are abbreviated according to the style of *L'Année Philologique*, while journals outside the field are spelled out. References to epigraphic evidence can be puzzling if not intimidating, but there is a growing number of websites, some free and some not, that can help readers with the meaning and context of ancient inscriptions. Those who know ancient Greek will find many of the inscriptions cited contained in the Packard Humanities Institute database of searchable Greek inscriptions (epigraphy.packhum.org), while numerous Athenian inscriptions have been translated and annotated at Attic Inscriptions Online (atticinscriptions.com). The website Attalus (attalus.org) has many translated documents from the Hellenistic period. The Collection of Greek Ritual Norms (cgrn.ulg.ac.be) contains translations and commentaries of inscriptions having to do with religion. Those curious about references to *BNJ* and *SEG* should consult with their libraries to see whether they have institutional access to *Brill's New Jacoby* and *Supplementum Epigraphicum Graecum Online*. The Pleiades website (pleiades.stoa.org) can help with the geographical locations of sites.

Map 0.1 Greece and western Asia Minor. (Source: *The Cambridge Ancient History* vol. 6)

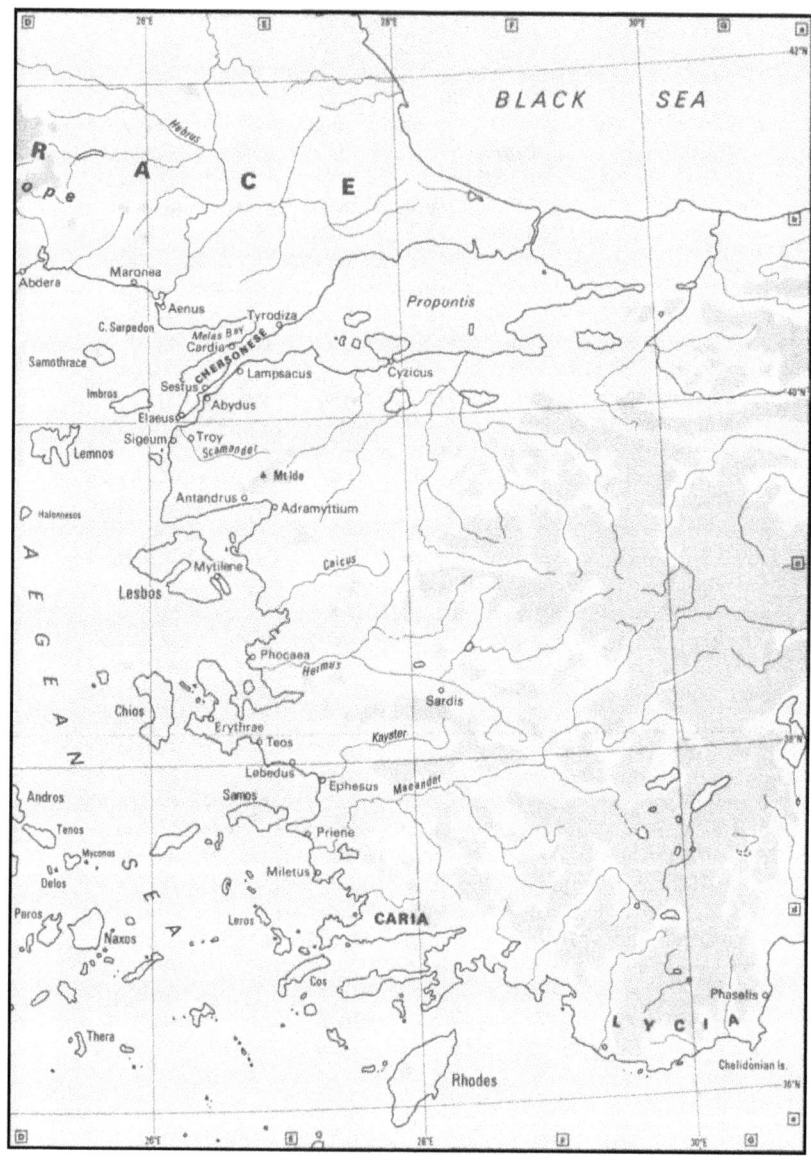

Map 0.1 (cont.)

Introduction

Why another book on ancient Greek democracy? After hundreds if not thousands of books and articles written about it, don't we pretty much get the gist by now? It was direct rather than representative, democratic without being liberal, tied to an outmoded social formation – the autonomous and militaristic city-state – dependent to varying degrees on the labor of enslaved people, and very much an adult free citizen man's affair. Its contributions to our political ideas – about freedom and equality, popular sovereignty, mass and elite, and the very possibility of a "politics" at all (from *ta politika*, "the affairs of the *polis*") – are also well known. It's a well-plowed field – what is new here?

If the present study deserves a place on an already crowded shelf, it is because it offers a *history* of ancient Greek *democracies*, plural. The chronological scope (late sixth century BCE to the second century CE and beyond) and the emphasis on the variety of Greek democracies very much go together. If casual readers of Greek history and political thought know one example of democracy, it is almost certainly that of Athens in the fifth and, to a lesser extent, fourth centuries BCE – the Athens of Pericles, the Parthenon, and the Peloponnesian War. They may be under the impression that this was the regime that most deserved to be called a *dēmokratia* as the ancient Greeks understood the term, or perhaps even the only one that merited the title. They may be aware that other Greek *poleis* claimed the constitutional label for themselves but suspect that this now represented an empty slogan, especially in the period after Alexander the Great's death in 323 BCE. They may think, in line with the opinion of historian J. A. O. Larsen (1954), that the "judgment of antiquity on democracy" was mostly negative. After all, is democracy not a rare and precious thing, a brief experiment that then lay dormant for millennia, neglected when not derided (especially by the elite), until a critical reassessment by modernity?

As this book aims to show, such a picture contains major gaps. While Athens was *especially* democratic, it is true, it was not the only democracy, not even in the fifth century BCE. What is more, "Periclean" Athens does not even represent the apogee of *dēmokratia* in the Greek world. Drawing inspiration from the Athenian example, yes, but also basing themselves on homegrown opposition to the forces of tyranny and oligarchy (the rule of the wealthy few), democrats in countless Greek *poleis* fought – and in many cases died – to see the constitutional form replicated in their own backyards. By about 300 BCE, two hundred years after "people power" first emerged in late Archaic Greece, "democracy" represented the rules of the game for perhaps the majority of Greek cities, even if oligarchs continued to try to pass off their rule under various euphemisms. But these were, from what we can tell, no mere DINOs – democracies in name only – but genuine adherents to forms of *dēmokratia*, ranging from the thoroughgoing to the moderate. In the period labeled by others the "high Hellenistic period" (although this study eschews the usual "Classical" and "Hellenistic" periodization – see later in this introduction), from the late fourth to the mid second centuries BCE, there were hundreds of thousands, perhaps even millions of people in the Mediterranean world and beyond living under democratic constitutional arrangements, distributed among the thousand or so Greek city-states in existence at the time.

Greek "antiquity," then – if we understand the term to encompass more than just the members of the elite who composed our surviving literary texts – did not have so pessimistic a judgment of democracy after all. If we were once inclined to believe it did, it is for a number of reasons: the clout of democracy's critics in the Classical period, including Plato and, to a lesser extent, Thucydides; a "hermeneutics of suspicion" in the scholarship, which has detected "protesting too much" on behalf of *dēmokratia* in most cases outside Athens; the lack of a continuous, contemporaneous historiographical narrative for most of the period between Xenophon and Polybius (fourth through mid second centuries BCE); and a consequent reliance on other forms of historical evidence – epigraphic, numismatic, archaeological, and so on. Recent discoveries and reassessed texts in the last-named body of evidence, however – including pro-"democratic" inscriptions, coins, and monuments, to be discussed in Chapter 3 – have combined with some conceptual reorientations to produce a new near-orthodoxy that *dēmokratia*, it turns out, was actually quite common, at least until the second century BCE. This view remains for the most part the preserve of specialists, though, often working in languages other than English. One purpose of the present book is to make this perspective, along with some of the evidence on which it is based, available to a more general audience.

Ancient Greek-style democracy was not a flash in the pan, then, but an extremely long-lived constitutional form and political way of life. This fact will, it is hoped, be both provocative and discomfiting to a modern readership. Many, probably most, of the readers of this book live in "democracies" of the post–World War II variety – representative, liberal, and social-democratic to varying degrees – while existing in an essentially private-enterprise, capitalist economic system. This constitutional package, touted as representative of the "end of history" following the West's victory in the Cold War, counts as our own current rules of the game. More or less taken for granted for decades, it is now, of course, beset by various forces: the effects of globalization, massive wealth inequality, reactions against multiracial citizenship, the shaking up (if not hollowing out) of traditional political parties, and, perhaps first and foremost in people's minds, the phenomenon commonly called populism, of the left and right varieties. Some worry that our experiment in what we have found fit to label "people power" is coming to an end; others see in antiestablishment movements the promise of a truly democratic renewal. We are, in any case, aware more than ever that the survival of democracy in its present forms is not guaranteed. Democracy has a history, after all. In that regard, it may prove worthwhile to follow the historical trajectory of another nominally democratic culture, one that featured a central, institutional role for non-elite citizens until, one day, it didn't.

A long-term comparative perspective may also open up new views onto the promises and also the limitations of democracy, both ancient and modern. Rather than discuss ancient Greek democracies in terms of what we have "lost" (the intimacy and control of direct participation) or what we have "superseded" (slavery and gender-based exclusion), we can explore the various ways historical forms of democracy, while hinting at a universality of condition, have relied on the maintenance of out-groups of various kinds in order to advance the interests of those fortunate enough to count as "the people." In the Greek case, the claim of the free adult citizen man that his status entitled him to equality of participation and power within a democratic constitution certainly presupposed the existence of slavery. As the late historian Tyler Stovall (2021) showed, however, our own notions of freedom may not be so far off. This is not to say that the likeness between ancient and modern is always, or even often, one to one. Those hoping to find answers to the contemporary conundrum of populism in the ancient Greeks' treatment of "demagogues," for example, are bound to be disappointed. Far from representing an existential crisis facing ancient democracies, demagoguery, understood here as a form of leadership that appealed to the interests of "the People" through mass oratory, was an inescapable feature of any democracy worthy of the name. Extreme demagoguery could be divisive, leading to elite counterreaction in the form of oligarchic subversion, but an ancient Greek democracy without demagogues is practically a contradiction in terms.

This being a history of ancient Greek democracies, not a history of ancient Greece, it is necessarily selective in material and furthermore presupposes some background knowledge on the part of readers. They will know that by the end of the Archaic period (ca. 800–500 BCE) most Greeks lived in *poleis* or city-states of several thousand inhabitants on average, which evolved during the Iron Age (1200–800) after the collapse of the Mycenaean palaces in the late Bronze Age (3000–1200); that Greek communities worshipped numerous gods and heroes in a public capacity through acts of bloody animal sacrifice; that Greeks often went to war against each other using a formation known as the hoplite phalanx; that these communities were primarily agricultural but with increasingly sophisticated commerce and trade as time went on; that they were characterized by a typical premodern demographic regime of high fertility and high infant mortality; and that widespread chattel slavery both supplied the labor by which the elite lived in leisure and, as mentioned, created the distinction between free and enslaved so crucial to the development of an idea of democratic citizenship.

Some works supplying this background, should it be lacking, can be found in the Bibliographical Essay. Important historical developments that directly impacted democracies, such as the Greeks' interactions with the Romans beginning in the late third century BCE, are covered in the opening sections of Chapters 2, 3, and 4. The present work also holds as part of its guiding methodology the assumption that at the confluence of an ideal of citizen freedom contrasted with slavery (the position of democrats) and the notion of a level of "excellence" attainable only by the elite (that of oligarchs) lay the potential for more or less constant conflict between rich and poor, few and many.

This is not an events-based narrative history, which could probably not be written for ancient Greek democracies given the state of the evidence. Instead it aims to trace changes in democratic institutions and ideologies over the centuries by taking a thematic approach within a given time period. And those time periods are, admittedly, weird: not the typical "Classical" (480–323 BCE) and "Hellenistic" (323–31 BCE) eras but instead an initial half century or so of democratic emergence and development (510–451 BCE, Chapter 1); a period of fierce competition with oligarchy for the mantle of political legitimacy (451–362 BCE, Chapter 2); a period of consolidation and spread, within which democratic constitutions reached their apex (362–146 BCE, Chapter 3); and the long, slow decline of popular involvement in politics, for the most part ceasing in the second century CE and finally ending when official assemblies of the people disappeared (146 BCE–ca. 500 CE; Chapter 4). This division stems from my own interpretation of the development of ancient Greek democracies rather than from the standard narrative of a caesura at the death of Alexander the Great, with another following Octavian's defeat of Antony and Cleopatra at Actium in 31 BCE.

CHAPTER I

From Eunomia *to* Dēmokratia, *510–451/0* BCE

1.1 Introduction: Surveying the Political Horizon in 510 BCE

It is nearing the end of what we label the sixth century BCE. In Athens, in the year when Harpactides served as chief magistrate (our 511/10 BCE), the citizens are reeling after what will turn out to be the final deposition of the tyrannical dynasty begun by Pisistratus in 561.[1] Thanks to a crucial intervention by the Spartans (which will later prove inconvenient for Athenian narratives of self-liberation), the tyranny is gone, replaced with a rough-and-tumble intra-elite politics typical of the time. Around the same time, on the island of Sicily, political power in Syracuse lies with the so-called *gamoroi* or land-sharers, a closed caste descended from the original Corinthian colonists of the later eighth century. In Eretria on Euboea, the constitution likewise gives pride of place to an elite group, this time the *hippeis* or horsemen, those fortunate few wealthy enough to be able to rear equids. From what we can glean from epigraphic evidence, Argos in the Peloponnese possesses what we might call elite-led constitutional government, as does its neighbor Elis to the west. Thebes in Boeotia is almost certainly some kind of de facto oligarchy, although the word did not exist yet. Finally, in Ionia, Miletus is controlled by the family of the tyrant Histiaeus, while Erythrae may be governed at this time by the clan known as the Basilidae mentioned by Aristotle.[2]

Across the Greek-speaking world, then, elite political predominance – from a broad-based form to, in rare cases, the most exclusionary regime of all, one-man tyranny – was the norm. Dorians, Ionians, Boeotians – all had

---

[1] Here and elsewhere, slash dates of the style 511/10 indicate an archon year of Athens, distinct from the solar year (the new archon took office in roughly August and served for a year). Sometimes, as with Pericles' Citizenship Law of 451/0, discussed in the next chapter, we know in which archon year an event occurred but not necessarily the calendar year.

[2] Athens: Hdt. 5.66; [Arist.] *Ath. Pol.* 20. Sicily: Hdt. 7.155.2. Eretria: [Arist.] *Ath. Pol.* 15.2; Arist. *Pol.* 5.1306a35–36. Argos: *Nomima* 1.100. Thebes: Mackil 2013: 27–29. Miletus: Hdt. 4.137.2. Erythrae: Arist. *Pol.* 5.1305b18–19.

1.1 Introduction: Surveying the Political Horizon in 510 BCE

largely rid themselves of the tyrannies that had proliferated in the seventh and earlier sixth centuries and settled on various configurations of power-sharing within a socioeconomic upper class, albeit not without some input from the broader adult male citizen community (the *dēmos*). It is therefore remarkable that, despite no prior experience with full popular government, all of the aforementioned cities would be democratic by the chronological endpoint of this chapter, 451/0 BCE. This crucial half century produced the first examples of what the Greeks called *dēmokratia*, the power (*kratos*) of the People (*dēmos*), whence the modern word "democracy" ultimately derives. The institutional experiments and ideological breakthroughs of the period set the tone for all subsequent Greek political developments – developments covered in the later chapters of this book.

But how had this happened? And what did the various Greek communities of the time understand by the word *dēmokratia*, which emerged in the 460s BCE at the latest? These questions remain extremely difficult to answer given the exiguous nature of the contemporary evidence. The first half of the fifth century is in many ways a black box. We must remember that our single greatest source for the late Archaic and early Classical periods, the historian Herodotus, was writing in the later fifth century and likely reconstructing and interpreting the past using contemporary concepts. In composing "constitutional histories" of this period we necessarily rely on a hodgepodge of much later sources, including Aristotle's *Politics* (later fourth century BCE), Strabo's *Geography* (early first century CE), Plutarch's *Lives* (early second century CE), and even Pausanias' travel guide to Greece (later second century CE). Such sources were necessarily written in hindsight, often with the later Peloponnesian War (431–404 BCE) between democratic Athens and oligarchic Sparta in mind. Cities' reactions to the Athenian Empire of the latter three-quarters of the century, one that was not averse to maintaining democratic client states at spear-point, also colored later accounts of the period. What it was like to experience these monumental political changes at the time, with no preconceptions to rely on and no idea how the experiments would turn out, is something of a mystery. Our best and most bounteous contemporary source is actually a poet, Pindar of Thebes (ca. 520–ca. 440 BCE), whose works in various genres – most famously epinician or athletic victory odes, but also hymns, choral dances, and others – provide precious political and ideological testimony.[3] Outside this eyewitness, we possess a few inscribed texts of the period – including, crucially, monuments in stone or bronze

---

[3] See Kurke 1991; Hornblower 2004.

commemorating the Persian Wars of 490 and 480–479 – plus snippets of poets and writers preserved in later sources. The historical accounts in Thucydides' so-called *Pentecontaetia*, covering the "fifty-year period" between 478 and 431, and in the Aristotelian *Constitution of the Athenians* are both later compositions reliant on earlier sources, including Athenian inscribed documents. It used to be thought that earlier fifth-century Athenian history could be more or less accurately reconstructed from such inscribed decrees that survive as well as from the information contained in relevant *Lives* of Plutarch (such as those of Themistocles, Aristides, and Cimon); however, many examples of the former have been systematically redated over the past several decades to the 430s BCE and later, while recent studies have revealed the insurmountable historiographical problems involved with the latter.[4] That may sound bleak, but there is hope beyond the literary sources. Some of our best evidence is actually not textual at all but archaeological: the experiments in political geography and civic reorganization that altered Athens and Eretria, to be discussed in greater detail in Section 1.4. In any case, our reconstructions and conclusions must remain tentative.

This opening chapter, therefore, attempts to do the best it can with the information we have. I first establish what political life was like among the Greek *poleis* in the late Archaic period, before the emergence of the first democracies. It might be tempting, given the rarity of popular government throughout history, to imagine that Greek democracy represented something totally new, a fundamental break with what came before it. That is not entirely right: *Dēmokratia* was in many ways an intensification of existing political trends, particularly as regards the *dēmos* or common people and their role in communal decision-making, officeholding, and legal judgment. "The People" did not emerge in the late Archaic period all of a sudden and fully formed like Athena from the head of Zeus; they had been there all along in political life, albeit with varying degrees of participation across *polis* communities. What changed was people's perceptions of the level of political authority average men could and should hold.

Next we will examine what factors if any were associated with the emergence of democracy. In almost every case a complete causal account is impossible, but some common themes stand out. First, many democratizing *poleis* experienced growth and urbanization in the preceding period. In some cases democratization either depended upon or else brought about

---

[4] On the redating of Attic inscriptions, see Stroud 2006; Rhodes 2008; Papazarkadas 2009; Matthaiou 2010. On Plutarch, see the convincing revisionist account of Zaccarini 2017.

an act of synoecism, the consolidation of several existing communities into a larger city. As Aristotle was later to point out, size favors democracy (even if it is not a sufficient condition in itself for democracy's emergence). Second, political divisions within the elite and social conflict between classes – sometimes causally related to each another – frequently preceded democratization. And finally, the presence of an external threat – more often than not in the later Archaic period, Sparta – sometimes helped trigger and consolidate popular movements, in part by providing the uneasy elite with a reason to support the ascendant democratic regime.

I next survey the institutional changes we can identify as resulting from democratization. In addition to legal reforms known from literary sources, we can also examine how political communities restructured themselves organizationally and spatially. Here the aforementioned archaeological remains from the territories of Athens and Eretria, two *poleis* whose reforms closely resembled and perhaps influenced each other, provide striking evidence for polities remaking themselves according to a new self-image. Such civic reorganization often went hand in hand with changes in cult practice.

Finally, we can try to surmise what changed in Greek political culture following the introduction of democratic rule in numerous cities. What early reactions to democracy do we have? Who expressed them, in what medium, and with what attitude? It has sometimes been argued that democratic practice in Athens and elsewhere provided the impetus for the first exercises in political theorizing, whether in pamphleteering, sophistic teaching, or philosophical dialogue. Those are largely later fifth-century genres – what about in the immediate aftermath of democratization in the first quarter of the century? We will see that democracy provoked an organized opposition early on; in what will be a kind of leitmotiv of the present study, a sign of democracy's vitality in ancient Greece was the violent resistance it incited, beginning with the earliest instances and lasting into the second century BCE and beyond.

1.2 *Eunomia*

By the end of the sixth century BCE numerous Greek communities had lit upon a basic tripartite institutional arrangement that would serve Greek-speaking *poleis* for roughly a thousand years: (1) an assembly of the male citizenry (*ekklēsia*, *agora*, *halia*, or *dēmos*); (2) a council (*boulē*) that prepared business for the assembly; and (3) magistracies or offices (*archai*), which executed the laws. Cities also relied on panels of judges (*dikastai*) empowered to hear and decide legal disputes.[5] It may surprise some readers to learn that decision-making by the community (that is, by the citizens [*politai*] or populace [*dēmos*]) predated the emergence of *dēmokratia* properly so called. After all, when the masses possess "the franchise," are we not looking at a democratic political arrangement? To the Greek way of thinking, no. As we will see, even *poleis* that remained oligarchic occasionally permitted voting on issues by the whole community (albeit in a strictly controlled and arguably manipulative way). This is all to say that we have to be careful in gauging the distance that separates late Archaic politics from fifth-century democracy. Some scholars have argued that the popular element present in Greek communities from as early as Homeric epic renders most *poleis* throughout antiquity democracies or quasi democracies.[6] That would represent an "etic" or "outsider-oriented" definition, however, since it does not track the terminology or mindset that the Greeks themselves employed. Nevertheless, these scholars highlight an undeniable fact: The *dēmos* enjoyed a political role in Greek *poleis* long before the onset of democracy. As two historians have cheekily put it, there was no "long slumber" of "Rip van Demos" down through the Archaic period prior to its sudden awakening in 508/7 in Athens.[7]

But if that participation was not yet democratic, what was its nature? While it varied from community to community, it appears in many cases to have consisted of assembled citizens ratifying, through various voting procedures, prior deliberations of elite magistrates. This staggered process, of having smaller bodies deliberate in advance on proposals to be submitted to a broader audience, was called *probouleusis*, and it seems to have been employed by many *poleis* throughout the period under consideration in this book.[8] What varied was the social makeup of the predeliberating body and its powers, as well as the powers of the assembly. In Archaic Sparta, for example, as we know from the famous document known as the Great Rhetra preserved in Plutarch, the Spartan people (called *damos* in the Doric dialect) were able to vote on proposals of the two kings and twenty-eight elders. The decision, however, remained subject to a veto by the latter.[9]

---

[5] For a recent useful exploration of Archaic Greek politics see Bernhardt and Canevaro 2022. My own thoughts can be found at Simonton 2017: 11–20. Brock and Duplouy 2018 is a thought-provoking revisionist volume largely eschewing institutional approaches to politics.

[6] Habicht 1995; Ruschenbusch 1995.

[7] Harris and Lewis 2022: 254. See also Koerner 1993; Werlings 2010. I do not believe that Greek constitutional development first went through a phase in which possessors of hoplite armor held sovereignty before the *dēmos* as a whole took over political power: See my remarks at Simonton 2017: 41–54.

[8] On *probouleusis* see Andrewes 1954; Rhodes with Lewis 1997: 473–501.   [9] Plut. *Vit. Lyc.* 6.

1.2 Eunomia

What made the Spartan constitution oligarchic (or better, "elite-dominated," since the Greeks did not think in terms of democracy and oligarchy in the Archaic period) was not the presence or absence of "the franchise" for the *damos*. The crucial considerations were instead the following: The predeliberative body in the probouleutic process was composed of unrepresentative and largely unaccountable individuals (the kingship was hereditary, while the elders, as their name implies, possessed a high age requirement and were moreover elected for life). The *damos* could vote only on the proposals, or *probouleumata*, put to it by a presiding annual official, with a strictly up-or-down decision (no amendments permitted), and even then the choice of the assembly was not final but subject to unilateral rejection. Thus, "the People" participated in the Spartan decision-making process, to be sure, but in a highly circumscribed manner. As one scholar has put it, while Spartan *probouleusis* procedures partly resemble those of democratic Athens, they "were marked ... by stronger devices and powerful offices to limit the power of the people, and to keep it in check."[10]

We have good reasons for believing that the Spartans referred to this system, characterized by full participation of the citizenry, but with unequal weights attached to different social classes, as *eunomia*, or good order. The word was not the Spartans' invention: It appears already in the *Odyssey* and *Homeric Hymns* and receives praise from the poet Hesiod and the Athenian lawgiver Solon.[11] That last figure also appears to have implemented it in practice in Athens' political institutions, in a manner not unlike that of Archaic Sparta: While all Athenian citizens were admitted to the assembly – including the poorest census class, the so-called thetes – *probouleusis* proceeded from an elite-dominated Council.[12] Solon was frank in his poetry about the unequal nature of this arrangement: "I gave to the People as much privilege as was *appropriate*, neither taking away honor nor granting it excessively."[13] Elsewhere he insists that Athens will not be characterized by *isomoiria*, "equality of shares."[14] *Eunomia* would suffice.

Everywhere, indeed, *eunomia* seems to have connoted this kind of orderliness, consistency of procedure, guidance at the hands of the city's foremost citizens, and nominal buy-in on the part of the wider community. Its point of contrast was not democracy, which did not yet exist, but tyranny. *Eunomia* later became an oligarchic watchword, but in its origins

---

[10] Esu 2024: 129.
[11] Hom. *Od.* 17.487; *h. Hom.* 30.11; Hes. *Th.* 902; Solon fr. 4.32 West. Cf. Arist. *Pol.* 5.1306b39–1307a1, giving *Eunomia* as the title of a poem by the Spartan Tyrtaeus.
[12] Raaflaub 2006; Canevaro 2022: 378–97.   [13] Solon fr. 5.1 West (emphasis added).
[14] Solon fr. 34.9 West.

it did not stem primarily from fear of or antagonism toward the common people. It came to do so only after the emergence of a competing democratic slogan, *isonomia*, or the equal distribution of political rights (cf. Solon's *isomoiria*).[15] The difference in prefixes is significant: While *eunomia* leaves open the question of the arrangement of political power (after all, a "good" distribution of power might turn out to be unequal), *isonomia* unambiguously insists on equality. Democrats would later claim that their *isonomia* also involved *eunomia*, but the latter was never of foremost concern to them; oligarchs, by contrast, vehemently denied that *eunomia* could ever be secured by democratic *isonomia*. By the same token, the contemporary expression "law and order," while it appeals to goods presumably valued by all citizens of a democracy, often suggests a more authoritarian and antidemocratic approach to politics.

If "eunomic" institutional arrangements are explicitly attested at Athens and Sparta, they are apparent enough elsewhere. Archaic Mytilene had the usual council and assembly, as indicated by a fragment of the poet Alcaeus, who, languishing in exile, longs to hear the *agora* and the *bolla* (that is, *boulē*) being summoned in his hometown.[16] At Chios, a famous inscription now housed in Istanbul mentions a gathering of the *dēmos*, likely for judicial purposes, as well as a special council called the *dēmosiē boulē*. The adjective *dēmosios* can mean belonging to the people in a democratic sense, but it also just means belonging to the community or dealing with public affairs, and I imagine that it signifies the latter here. This council is specified as being composed of fifty men from each of the (three?) civic subdivisions.[17] At Tiryns in the Peloponnese in the seventh century, one clause of a fragmentary inscription says that the magistrates are to carry out an action "as seems good [*dokei*] to the People [*damos*]."[18] This formulation is strikingly close to the so-called enactment formula of later Athenian democratic decrees ("decided by the People": *edoxen tōi dēmōi* – see further Section 1.4), but again, this is but one measure in a multistep process, not a sign of the People's ultimate sovereignty. Officials (and elite-dominated councils) were presumably empowered to take numerous independent decisions in these states without the approval of the *dēmos*. At Corinth, for example, there was a powerful council of eighty, headed by a committee of eight so-called *probouloi*.[19] If Plutarch's testimony for fourth-century BCE practice is any indication, this council transacted most of Corinth's

---

[15] See Chapter 2.4.1 for a further discussion of *isonomia* with bibliography. On oligarchic *eunomia* see Simonton 2017: 8nn22, 59.
[16] Alc. fr. 130b.18 Liberman.   [17] ML 8 with Simonton 2017: 13–14.   [18] *Nomima* I.78.
[19] Nic. Dam. *BNJ* 90 F 60.

business, with little role left for the popular assembly.[20] The point is that *eunomia* could theoretically admit a place for the People, even if it was not a place of primacy. These were not, on the whole, restrictive and authoritarian oligarchies, as they sometimes were in the period after the breakthrough of democracy. This does not mean that the constitutional status quo was accepted as the god-given order of things, or that class conflict was absent (see the next section). But we must be wary of projecting later categories of "oligarchy," "democracy," and so on onto the Archaic period, as Aristotle, Plutarch, and other sources often do.[21]

1.3 Breakthroughs

Given the paucity of narrative history from the end of the sixth century and the beginning of the fifth mentioned earlier, this section is very difficult to write. We have an idea of the "inputs" that went into this tumultuous period (the eunomic arrangements discussed in the previous section), and we know what emerged from the process (democratic regimes in numerous Greek *poleis*), but about the actual alchemical transformation we are largely in the dark. Athens is the best-attested case by far, although the evidence is all after the fact. It will serve as the starting point of the discussion. I will register here my surprise that more constitutional change does not seem to have immediately resulted from the events of the Persian Wars (490 and 480–479), but again our lack of evidence might obscure long-term processes that contributed to democratization.

The Athenian Revolution of 508/7 has been treated many times, and there is not space for another exhaustive discussion here. Readers are encouraged to consult the relevant sections of Herodotus and the Aristotelian *Constitution of the Athenians* for our best narrative accounts.[22] The present analysis follows Herodotus in thinking that Cleisthenes, then the leading member of the elite Alcmaeonid clan of Athens, established democracy at Athens for the first time.[23] I propose to study here not the content of Cleisthenes' reforms (to be described in the following section), but instead

---

[20] Plut. *Vit. Dio* 53.4.
[21] Duplouy 2006 and Meister 2020 are good on the anachronism of our later sources, but they appear to me to downplay or ignore class conflict in the Archaic period and the relatively early onset of constitutional struggle between oligarchs and democrats in the early fifth century BCE.
[22] Hdt. 5.66–78; [Arist.] *Ath. Pol.* 20–22. Among modern studies see esp. Ober 1996, 2007; Osborne 2023: 150–66.
[23] Hdt. 6.131.1. Against the thesis that democracy proper emerged only after the reforms of Ephialtes in 461 BCE ([Arist.] *Ath. Pol.* 25.1–2, 41.2) I follow Zaccarini 2018 in thinking that these reforms were misunderstood by fourth-century authors.

the conditions under which these reforms arose and took hold. These conditions can then be compared with those from other *poleis* where we know that democratization occurred. Such a comparative exercise works relatively well during this period, since Athens was at the time a rather unremarkable *polis* and not yet the *sui generis* powerhouse it would become under its naval empire. In other words, it resembles peers like Eretria, Argos, and Elis at this time to a far greater degree than it later would. To the social scientist, the following will appear an obviously inadequate causal account, not least because it "selects on the dependent variable"; that is, I look exclusively at cases where democratization *did* occur. A genuinely explanatory study would search for cases where the relevant enabling conditions were present but democracy did *not* result; in other words, it would attempt a falsification of the model. I must leave it to others to try this.[24]

For Athens in 508/7, we see the following conditions: first, intense intra-elite rivalry between the aforementioned Cleisthenes and Isagoras son of Teisander, the latter called by the *Constitution of the Athenians* a "supporter of the [Pisistratid] tyrants," for whatever that is worth.[25] Their rivalry may have taken the form of competition over one of the chief magistracies of Athens, the so-called eponymous archonship (the officeholder of which gave his name to the year). All accounts agree that in whatever the traditional political criteria of the time were, Cleisthenes was "getting the worst of it."[26] He therefore made some sort of public appeal to the broader male populace, the *dēmos*, promising political-institutional and civic-organizational reforms that would amount to a transfer of ultimate power away from a tiered (eunomic) system to the citizenry, envisioned as a community of political equals. There is no reason to suppose that Cleisthenes was some sort of dyed-in-the-wool egalitarian bestowing power on the masses out of the goodness of his heart. In a pattern that would repeat itself elsewhere throughout ancient Greek history, he appears to have considered it in his best interest to settle for a position of leadership within a democracy rather than suffer permanent demotion within the constitutional status quo.[27]

---

[24] On early democracies in Greece, see Robinson 1997, although I find his examples prior to the late sixth century for the most part unpersuasive; Robinson 2011 is excellent on the Classical period.
[25] [Arist.] *Ath. Pol.* 20.1.   [26] Hdt. 5.66.2; [Arist.] *Ath. Pol.* 20.1.
[27] Simonton 2017: 21–23. For cases similar to that of Cleisthenes see Diagoras of Eretria (treated in greater detail later in this section); Nicodromus of Aegina, who led an unsuccessful popular uprising on the island (Hdt. 6.88–91); Aristagoras tyrant of Miletus (Hdt. 5.30–37); Proxenus and Callibius of Tegea (Xen. *Hell.* 6.5.7), all with Simonton 2017: 264–65.

In making his appeal to the People, Cleisthenes was likely tapping into interclass grievance and status anxiety, the second of our enabling conditions for democratization. The history of Archaic Athens was replete with class conflict, often over the unequal distribution of land and the extreme instability of social status. In the aftermath of the Pisistratid tyranny there had apparently been a scrutiny of the citizen rolls, with many who had gained citizenship under the tyrants being stripped of their status.[28] Cleisthenes may therefore have promised citizenship to these downwardly mobile groups; in any case, we read in Aristotle's *Politics* that he registered numerous foreign residents and even enslaved people into Athens' new civic subdivisions.[29] Throughout Greek history, intra-elite rivalry and class divisions between rich and poor often had a symbiotic relationship, as rifts between prominent politicians emboldened the onlooking *dēmos* to demand political and social reforms (if not an outright revolution in conditions), with elites then scrambling in anticipation of each other's actions to be the first to become the People's champion (*prostatēs*).[30]

Had Cleisthenes simply carried out his reforms with no further ado, Athenian constitutional history might have been very different. The fledgling democracy likely would have encountered serious skepticism, if not outright hostility and resistance, from the members of Cleisthenes' social stratum, who stood to lose a considerable amount of the power and prestige they had hitherto enjoyed. Here, however, Athens' nascent democratic movement had an unwitting ally: the external threat posed by Sparta, our third enabling condition. Isagoras refused to accept defeat and instead played the biggest trump card he had: guest friendship (*xenia*), a traditional aristocratic institution, with Cleomenes, one of the two kings of Sparta.[31] Cleisthenes fled Athens in anticipation of a Spartan invasion, and Cleomenes entered the city with a small force. When he attempted to install Isagoras and a group of like-minded partisans in power, however – in what would have amounted to a pro-Sparta puppet regime – the Athenians collectively resisted in a three-day siege of the Acropolis.[32] Cleomenes was forced to withdraw, Cleisthenes returned, and the People were now "in firm control of political affairs."[33] By transforming what had

---

[28] Class conflict in Archaic Athens: Canevaro 2022: 393–97; Osborne 2023: 140–43. Scrutiny of citizen rolls: [Arist.] *Ath. Pol.* 13.5.
[29] Arist. *Pol.* 3.1275b35–37.
[30] Aristotle's *Politics* book 5 is replete with examples; see further Simonton 2017: 254–66.
[31] Hdt. 5.70.1. On *xenia* see Herman 1987.
[32] Hdt. 5.72.1–2. On the interesting question of who was remembered as having participated in the uprising see Gottesman 2021a.
[33] [Arist.] *Ath. Pol.* 20.4.

been an internal bout of civil strife into a foreign invasion, the Spartans likely helped consolidate Cleisthenes' democratic revolution by inducing Athens' elite to "rally around the flag." With the new democracy tied to the repulse of an external enemy – one, moreover, bent on regime change – there was now likely little wiggle room for anyone wishing to raise doubts about Athens' experiment in People power. Subsequent Athenian victories over the Boeotians and Chalcidians further solidified Cleisthenes' *dēmokratia* and revealed the extent to which it had unleashed Athens' military potential.[34]

A fourth and final consideration here is that of population growth and urbanization. Athens was simply a much larger city in 508/7 than it had been in the time of Solon.[35] The Pisistratid tyrants had "adorned" the *polis* with great temples and monuments, in the historian Thucydides' words, and the Great Panathenaic festival, instituted in 566 and given firm backing by the Pisistratids, drew not only spectators but, no doubt, a permanent infrastructure of merchants and craftsmen as well.[36] Then as now, growth and "modernization" were no golden ticket to democracy; nevertheless, *dēmokratia* was apparently easier to create and sustain in relatively large cities. As Aristotle explained in the *Politics*, "large *poleis* are comparatively freer of civil strife ... because the middling element [of the population] within them is large"; by the same token, "democracies are more secure than oligarchies and last longer thanks to the citizens of a middling condition, for they are greater in number and participate more in the magistracies in democracies than in oligarchies."[37] In other words (to unpack this rather dense formulation), the growth of the citizen population tended to create a society less polarized between rich and poor, since there was now usually a sizeable middling group that provided stability by mitigating the claims of the extremes. The ability of these people to participate politically to a greater degree in a democracy than in an oligarchy guaranteed the greater stability of the former. The result, Aristotle says elsewhere, is that, "because it has turned out that cities have grown in size, it is perhaps no longer very easy for there to arise any constitution other than democracy."[38] Again, growth was neither a necessary nor a sufficient condition for the emergence of a democratic regime within a *polis*, but it probably made democratization statistically more likely. Aristotle was on to something.

---

[34] Hdt. 5.77–78 with ML 15. [35] Osborne 2023: 39–40. [36] Thuc. 6.54.5.
[37] *Pol.* 4.1296a9–10, 13–16. [38] *Pol.* 3.1286b20–22.

Unfortunately, we cannot see if all four enabling conditions obtained in the case of other early democratizers. There are some suggestive pieces of evidence pointing in that general direction, however. At Eretria, for example, we read in Aristotle that one Diagoras "overthrew the oligarchy of the horsemen [*hippeis*] because he had been mistreated in a marriage arrangement."[39] While a marriage might sound like a trifling thing on which a regime's survival should depend, connections between elite families, cemented among other things by marital ties, were extremely delicate matters of personal honor that might also guarantee an individual access to the highest positions of power within a *polis*. Throughout the Archaic period and beyond, marriages (most often failed marriage proposals) could trigger implosions among the elite and lead to drastic constitutional changes.[40] In the present case, Diagoras' revolution probably fell between 510, the year of the dissolution of the Pisistratid tyranny at Athens (a staunch ally of the Eretrian horsemen), and 499, when Eretria joined with democratic Athens in supporting the revolt of Ionia from the Persian Empire.[41]

That Diagoras' uprising replaced "oligarchy" (or at least, a rather exclusive regime dominated by Eretria's horse-owning elite) with a democracy is suggested by several pieces of evidence. In addition to the *polis*' cooperation with Athens during the Ionian revolt, there is the fact that Eretria's civic reorganization, resulting in a system that would persist throughout its democratic regime of the fifth through second centuries, seems to have occurred shortly after Diagoras' revolution. We will examine this evidence in greater detail in the next section. There is also the testimony of Aristotle's mostly lost *Constitutions of the Eretrians*, a fragment of which tells us that "when Diagoras died at Corinth in the process of being conveyed to Sparta, the Eretrians set up a statue [*eikōn*] of him."[42] Honorific statues of political figures erected at public expense by the community were practically unknown at the time, the only real parallel being the Athenians' statues to the tyrant slayers Harmodius and Aristogeiton in the Agora, also the work of a democratic constitution (see Section 1.4). But it is the mention of Sparta that sparks the greatest interest. Why was Diagoras being conveyed to Sparta? It is likely that the Spartans had summoned him in a less than happy mood. The Spartans prided themselves on being "anti-tyrannical," a stance that conveniently lent itself to supporting pliant, pro-Sparta governments of elites. It was in this spirit that the Spartans had intervened on

---

[39] Arist. *Pol.* 5.1306a35–36.   [40] Simonton 2017: 263–66.
[41] [Arist.] *Ath. Pol.* 15.2 and Hdt. 5.99.1 with Knoepfler 2008: 602–3; Fachard 2019: 175–76.
[42] Arist. fr. 611.40 Rose.

behalf of Isagoras at Athens in 508/7, when they may have suspected Cleisthenes of tyrannical ambitions. The Spartans were likely on good terms with the Eretrian *hippeis*, and they might have wanted to question Diagoras about his (mis)treatment of their friends. The Eretrians' decision to honor Diagoras with a statue would then double as both a rebuke to Sparta and an assertion of their independence. This reconstruction must remain speculative, but if true it resembles the Athenian situation quite closely.

In other cases we are even less well informed. Elis and Mantinea in the Peloponnese may have seen democratization attendant upon so-called synoecism or the amalgamation of existing regional settlements into a single, larger *polis*; on the other hand, a democratic revolution could have initiated or completed the act of synoecism rather than resulted from it. In any case, the cities were democratic by the outbreak of the Peloponnesian War in 431, and there is no reason to believe they were not so already in the earlier fifth century; Aristotle writing in the later fourth century mentions Mantinea as an example of a moderate democracy of the old-fashioned type.[43] Argos is a more peculiar case: The city definitely saw constitutional change after its devastating loss to Sparta at the Battle of Sepeia circa 494 BCE, but the nature of this change is contested. Herodotus says that the city had become so depopulated from military casualties (said elsewhere to be six thousand men) that slaves briefly took over the *polis*, while Aristotle says these newcomers were neighboring peoples; their legal status (enslaved or free) remains unclear.[44] It is important to bear in mind that if Herodotus' informants in the later fifth century were Argives, they would have been citizens of a democratic regime at the time. Thus the "slave" label for those who briefly controlled the city after Sepeia might be scurrilous, an attack on nonnative elites from other communities. Whatever happened after Sepeia, Argos was almost certainly democratic by the time of its alliance with Athens in 462, since it buried its dead after the Battle of Tanagra in 457 in the Athenian (democratic) fashion (see next chapter); epigraphic evidence from the second quarter of the fifth century reinforces the picture.[45] The origins of the Argive democracy must remain shrouded in mystery, but its democratic bona fides as attested by institutions and political culture is strong, as we will explore in greater detail in the next chapter.

---

[43] See the treatments in Robinson 2011: 28–33, 34–40; Frullini 2023.
[44] Hdt. 6.83; Arist. *Pol.* 5.1303a6–8. For a recent overview of the problem see Frullini 2021.
[45] OR 126, ll. 44–45 and *SEG* 13.239; on Argive democracy see further Robinson 2011: 6–21; Piérart 2020.

It is worth noting that in the cases of Elis, Mantinea, and Argos we are looking at Peloponnesian *poleis* regularly threatened by Sparta, the regional hegemon. All of these cities would have been aware of the kind of treatment to which Tegea in Arcadia had been subjected when it capitulated to Sparta in the sixth century, known from a treaty preserved in a fragment of Aristotle. One clause of the treaty amounted to constitutional interference in Tegea on the part of Sparta, since it mandates that the Tegeans not be allowed to make certain Messenians citizens of their *polis*. That is, the Tegeans were being prevented from increasing the number of potentially anti-Sparta citizens among their ranks (since the Messenians were the age-old enemies of Sparta since the time of the eighth- and seventh-century Messenian Wars).[46] As we have seen elsewhere, the Spartans had a penchant for encouraging pro-Sparta puppet governments; this practice would continue during and after the Peloponnesian War. Many of these *poleis*, then, geographically ringing Sparta and aware of its military and political ambitions, might have developed their democracies in part as a defensive measure, either anticipating or reacting to Spartan constitutional interference. This would fit the model of the Athenians strengthening their new democracy in the wake of Cleomenes' failed invasion.

I have sought out examples that resemble the best-known case of Athens in 508/7, but that is to restrict myself to democracies that developed more or less endogenously – homegrown movements. In numerous cases, however, democracy was installed through external interference. If we are to believe Herodotus, after the failure of the Ionian revolt from Persia in 494, the Persian governors of the area changed the constitutions of these cities from tyranny to democracy as a means of placating them and preventing future disorder.[47] Scholars have questioned Herodotus' term "democracy" here, preferring to see something more like "non-tyrannical constitutional government," but we will see that democracy in, for example, Ephesus was likely real enough. The democratic regimes of Thebes and the other cities of Boeotia probably resulted from the Boeotians' military loss to Athens at Oenophyta in 457 BCE and the Athenians' ensuing decade-long hegemony over the region.[48] Other examples, like Miletus and Erythrae in Ionia, probably had their own democratic traditions, but these were "hijacked" and accelerated, as it were, by the Athenian Empire.[49] Indeed, the

---

[46] Arist. fr. 592 Rose with Bolmarcich 2005: 12–17.   [47] Hdt. 6.43.3.
[48] Arist. *Pol.* 5.1302b27–30; [Xen.] *Ath. Pol.* 3.11; cf. Thuc. 1.108.3; Robinson 2011: 53–54.
[49] There was a brief period of *isonomia* at Miletus after the tyrant Aristagoras abdicated: Hdt. 5.37.2. By 434/3 BCE Miletus had a constitutional structure modeled after the Athenian one: OR 143. For Erythrae see OR 122 with OR 121 (Athenian regulations).

hardening positions of the Greek superpowers, Athens and Sparta, as the premier purveyors of democracy and oligarchy, respectively, would make the *stasis* or civil strife of the ensuing period, covered in the next chapter, especially fierce.

1.4 Early Democratic Institutional Developments

What institutional difference did the emergence of *dēmokratia* make in a *polis*? The magistracies (*archai*) are a good place to start. We tend to think of ancient Greek democracies as dominated by a boisterous and powerful assembly of the citizens, and they were; nevertheless, the fifth-century Greeks themselves may have thought of constitutional differences mainly in terms of who had access to the city's political offices. All we have are later formulations from the second half of the fifth century onward, but they are instructive: According to a speaker in Herodotus, democracy (or rather, *isonomia*) is the constitution in which "the masses [*to plēthos*] hold the offices."[50] For the crotchety Athenian pamphleteer known as the Old Oligarch, writing in the final quarter of the fifth century, it was characteristic of the Athenian democracy that "the *dēmos* is the one that participates in the offices."[51] According to Socrates as depicted in Xenophon's *Memorabilia*, where the magistracies (*archai*) are filled according to a property requirement (*ek timēmatōn*), there the constitution (*politeia*) is a "plutocracy" (the rule of the wealthy, that is, oligarchy), but where they are filled "from all [the citizens]" (*ek pantōn*), there it is a democracy.[52] Indeed, the simplest and most common definition of oligarchy among the ancient Greeks, if our extant sources are representative, was the limitation of officeholding to those who fulfilled a property requirement. As I will argue in greater detail in a moment, this stricture represented a reactionary response to democracy on the part of oligarchs in the earlier fifth century; it had not been particularly common practice in the Archaic period.

It is not clear whether access to the magistracies was always so important to the Greeks or instead became so only after constitutional struggle between democrats and oligarchs emerged in the fifth century. What seems undeniable is that democratization brought a major expansion in the number of citizens participating in *archai* year in and year out. In Athens this is especially clear in the case of Cleisthenes' new Council of

---

[50] Hdt. 3.80.6. The full passage declares the masses hold the magistracies "by lottery"; we will explore this phenomenon in the next chapter.
[51] [Xen.] *Ath. Pol.* 3.13. For this author see Lenfant 2017.   [52] Xen. *Mem.* 4.6.12.

1.4 Early Democratic Institutional Developments

Five Hundred, with fifty men serving from each of the ten new tribes (we will return to the details of this council in a moment). Representation from each of Attica's 139 demes or districts, with a quota system based on population, necessarily diversified the members of this Council. Furthermore, while we do not know the specifics of limits on officeholding during the early democracy, it would be unusual by Greek standards if individual citizens were allowed unlimited iterations on the Council. By the fourth century participation was limited to two nonconsecutive terms in a lifetime, but even with laxer rules in place during the early fifth century, the number of Athenian citizens cycling through the Council must have been enormous.[53] Contrast the Council of oligarchic Corinth mentioned in Section 1.1, comprising only eighty members (ten from each of the eight civic subdivisions) and almost certainly limited by a property qualification during the fifth century.

The differences are instructive: In oligarchies such as Sparta and Corinth, the council had considerable agenda-setting powers and could manipulate the assembly in various ways; its members, moreover, came exclusively from the city's elite. In a democracy like Athens, on the other hand, the Council prepared business for a more powerful assembly and was a representative cross-section of the citizenry, a kind of microcosm of the *polis*.[54] Council and assembly would later return to a more stratified relationship, as representing the elite and the masses, respectively, but not until the high Roman Empire (see Chapter 4). We know of few other democratic councils in the period under review, but in (probably) the late 450s Athens mandated a *boulē* of 120 men for the Ionian *polis* of Erythrae, where the councilors were to be men over thirty years of age selected by lottery (literally "by the bean" – see Chapter 2.3.7) and forbidden from serving twice within a four-year period.[55]

In addition to the Council there were numerous other magistracies at Athens, not just military ones (general, taxiarch) but financial and administrative ones, as well. By the middle of the fifth century, thanks to the growth of the city and its empire, there may well have been about seven hundred, *not including the Council of Five Hundred*, as the *Constitution of the Athenians* states.[56] In good democratic fashion, they tended to be collegial (with power shared by boards, not concentrated in individuals) and had short terms of office, usually one year. (Oligarchies preferred

---

[53] Fourth-century term limits: [Arist.] *Ath. Pol.* 62.3. [54] Schol. ad. Aeschin. 3.4.
[55] OR 121. Elsewhere in the same decree the Athenians force the Erythraeans to swear loyalty to the *plēthos* (here, "masses") of Athens in ideologically charged language.
[56] [Arist.] *Ath. Pol.* 24.3 with Hansen 1980.

fewer, individualized magistracies with greater powers for longer terms.[57]) The vast majority of these posts became sortitive, or selected by random allotment, by the middle of the fifth century if they were not so already from the beginning. As we will see in the following chapters, sortition, with its belief in the political competence of the average citizen, was particularly reflective of democratic ideology, but it was not actually a necessary condition for *dēmokratia*. Nor was payment for officeholding (receiving a compensatory wage called *misthos*), although it was initiated by Pericles at Athens probably in the 450s BCE and became characteristic of numerous democratic regimes subsequently.[58]

Some scholars have argued that ancient Greek democracies were genuinely democratic only when the poorest citizens of a *polis* were able to participate to the greatest possible degree through sortition and payment; one might alternatively say that the "promise" of *dēmokratia* was fulfilled only through this arrangement.[59] We can concede that such a system was *more* democratic than a payment-less alternative, but it would be wrong to say that Athens of the earlier fifth century was not yet a democracy. When we consider (1) the sheer number of magistracies, (2) the likely limitations placed on iteration of office, and (3) the fact that, as far as we know, the Athenians never failed to fill the mandated posts, we see that the constitution was so participatory, with such a high percentage of non-elite citizens passing through the *archai*, that it deserves the title of *dēmokratia* as the Greeks understood the term. This was truly a society where the citizenry, in the words of Aristotle, experienced "ruling and being ruled in turn."[60]

If *dēmokratia* was the *politeia* where the members of the *dēmos* participated in the *archai*, it was also obviously a constitution where the *dēmos* made political decisions – in the form of laws and decrees passed in the popular assembly, the *ekklēsia*.[61] This by itself was not the *differentia specifica* of democracy, however, since, as we have seen, Archaic constitutions sometimes allowed the community as a whole to decide on issues; it was the *conditions* of this decision-making that made the difference. What changed from the eunomic arrangements of the earlier period were (1) the regularity and finality of the assembly's decisions (with what appeals that were permitted being referred to judicial panels made up of average citizens), (2) the scope of business handled, (3) the legal protection and indeed encouragement of debate and amendments, extending to all

---

[57] Arist. *Pol.* 6.1317b17–1318a10, 1320b18–20 with Simpson 2011.   [58] [Arist.] *Ath. Pol.* 27.3–4.
[59] Raaflaub 2007.   [60] For this phrase, see Arist. *Pol.* 3.1277b13–16.
[61] In fifth-century Athens there was no distinction between permanent laws (*nomoi*) and temporary decrees (*psēphismata*); this changed, however, at the end of the fifth century (see next chapter).

citizens, and (4) the assembly's ability, within the scheme of *probouleusis* discussed in Section 1.2, to reject the recommendations of the Council, which prepared all business for the *ekklēsia*, including preliminary decrees. (Contrast again Sparta, where the kings and elders could veto decisions of the assembly of which they did not approve.) The power and centrality of the popular assembly were also such that its method of decision-making became normative within democratic thought: The more decisions that could be made by groups of average citizens employing majority rule, the better.[62] In a democracy, says a speaker in Herodotus, the masses "refer all deliberations [*bouleumata*] to decision-making in common [*es to koinon*]"; "in the many is everything [*en gar tōi pollōi eni ta panta*]," says the same speaker in a somewhat enigmatic comment. The latter statement seems to mean both that majority rule suffices for rendering decisions legitimate and that all one could want out of politics lies with *hoi polloi*.[63]

At Athens the centrality of the assembly shines through in an exceptional document, a decree concerning arrangements on the island of Salamis inscribed on a marble post (Figure 1.1).[64] Based on a combination of letter forms and content, scholars have dated this, apparently the earliest extant Athenian decree on stone, to the period just after Cleisthenes' revolution – and it is no coincidence that the young democracy would choose to memorialize its collective decision in this novel way. The beginning of the inscription confronts the viewer with a formulation that will become utterly banal but is nothing short of revolutionary for the time: *edoxen tōi dēmōi*, decided by the People.[65] This represents the first time we know of that a decree was enacted

Figure 1.1 Salamis decree. (Photo: Marsyas via Wikimedia Commons, CC BY-SA 3.0).

[62] Arist. *Pol.* 4.1298a28–31, 6.1317b28–30.   [63] Hdt. 3.80.6.   [64] *IG* I³ 1.
[65] I have regularized the spelling of the transliteration from the old Attic script to the Ionian alphabet so as not to confuse the reader.

(and an inscription made to begin) in the name of the *dēmos*. In other words, the *dēmos* has ceased to play the bit part assigned to it in Archaic *eunomia* and has taken the production into its own hands. And if anything, this decree is even more "democratic" than its brethren during the height of the imperial democracy in the later fifth century, since it lacks any reference to the Council. The normal "enactment formula" of an Athenian decree then was "decided by the Council and the People," reflecting the fact that the normal procedure of *probouleusis* had taken place and the assembly had agreed with the Council's recommendations.[66] Either this was an instance when the assembly made a decision different from the recommendation of the Council, or else the secretary who drafted it for the stonecutter neglected to include the Council's role (perhaps for the ideological purpose of highlighting the role of the People).

These nominally democratic enactment formulae become so widespread in the ensuing fourth through second centuries BCE as to cease to prove the existence of genuine democracy taken on their own (see Chapter 3). It is significant, however, that they do not appear in the epigraphic record until the age of democracy, and in their earliest instances they are surely politically meaningful. They are rare outside Athens but appear also at Argos, where several decrees of the second quarter of the fifth century are "decided by the *halia*" (the Doric word for an assembly) and name the chairman of the Argive council (*bola*) who presided over the session.[67] A decree of Eretria from, at the earliest, circa 450 BCE begins "decided by the Council and the People," although the democratic regime responsible for this inscription had probably been in existence since the revolution of Diagoras (see Section 1.3).[68] An Eretrian decree from later in the century is a nice example of the phenomenon whereby a *polis*' enactment formulae might change with a change of political regime: Stemming from a period when Eretria's democracy had been overthrown by Athenian oligarchs and replaced by an oligarchy, the decree begins "decided by the Council," with no mention of the People.[69] The appearance of the Council alone in a decree is sometimes indicative of oligarchy, starting as early as a law recording confiscations of land in the famously oligarchic city of Chios circa 470 BCE.[70] In general, oligarchies inscribed far fewer political decisions than democracies, a fact that must be reflective of ancient Greek

---

[66] Rhodes 1972: 64.   [67] OR 126, ll. 44–45; *SEG* 13.239.
[68] *IG* XII *Suppl.* 549 with the comments of D. Knoepfler at *BE* 2014 no. 219.
[69] OR 175; for the historical context see Thuc. 8.48, 64, 95–96.
[70] OR 133, where we read of a Council and a small executive committee called the Fifteen. For the constitutional history of Chios in the Archaic and early Classical periods see Christesen et al. 2024.

1.4 Early Democratic Institutional Developments

democracies' greater devotion to publicity and to the involvement of the citizenry.[71]

The empowered assemblies of early democracies sometimes made controversial decisions. The Athenian institution of ostracism, devised by Cleisthenes but first used in 488/7 BCE, did not take place in a normal assembly on the Pnyx Hill in Athens but was certainly conceived of as an act of the entire citizenry. Certain critical observers came to consider it one of the most notorious practices of the Athenian democracy. It and Syracusan "petalism," also dating to the first half of the fifth century, will be discussed in greater detail in the following chapter, but we can note here that they were both instances of the democratic community taking the all-important power of exile into its own hands.[72] Meanwhile, the regime of the Ionian *polis* of Ephesus of the early fifth century, probably one of the democracies installed by the Persians in 493 after the failed Ionian revolt (see Section 1.3), came under criticism from the philosopher Heraclitus, a citizen of the city, for its decision to exile his friend Hermodorus. A quotation of the infamously obscure philosopher, preserved in both Strabo and Diogenes Laertius, actually reads as a quite straightforward denunciation of the community's decision and is, furthermore, a precious piece of evidence for democracy during a very ill-attested quarter century:

> The Ephesians are all worthy of being hanged, starting with the youth, and the city left to those who have not yet come of age, since they exiled Hermodorus, the worthiest man among them, saying, "Let there not be one who is worthiest among us, or if so, let him be elsewhere and with other people."[73]

Heraclitus not only attests to the democratic power over exile in Ephesus at the time – he also ascribes to the Ephesian masses ("all" the Ephesians) the kind of popular resentment against outstanding individuals that critics of the Athenian democracy saw in an institution such as ostracism.[74] We will encounter further antidemotic sentiments on the part of Heraclitus (his nickname in antiquity was *ochloloidoros*, "mob-reviler") in the next section.

Popular participation in the courts of justice was a feature of democracies from the mid fifth century onward, and we see evidence for that in our period in the form of the so-called Teian *Dirae*, public curses from Teos and its colony Abdera dating to the second quarter of the fifth century,

---

[71] See Chapter 2.4.5. For oligarchies' tendency not to inscribe, see Simonton 2017: 145n138.
[72] Forsdyke 2005.
[73] Heraclitus DK 22 B 121. On this evidence see also Robinson 2011: 172–73.
[74] Cf. Plut. *Vit. Arist.* 7.2.

perhaps the 470s. The second of these two texts requires a quorum of two hundred men at Teos and five hundred men at Abdera in order for a court (or the assembly acting as a court) to carry out certain punishments.[75] The relatively high numbers suggest a desire to involve a large and representative portion of the male citizenry.[76]

A final institutional development to explore is that of building projects and civic reorganization. The two are interrelated, since constitutional change in ancient Greece was often accompanied by a change in the nomenclature of civic subdivisions (*phylai*, usually translated as "tribes"), which could affect which ancestral heroes received prominence in cult. Newly ascendant regimes might also obliterate the building projects of their predecessors and embark on their own. This is clearest at Athens, where literary sources and archaeology tell us a lot about Cleisthenes' reforms. He dispensed with the four traditional Ionian *phylai* and instituted ten new ones, asking the god Apollo at Delphi (through the medium of the Delphic Oracle) to choose ten out of a preselected one hundred – one could think of this also as the god offering his imprimatur to the new democracy.[77] The resulting ten tribes were named after the so-called Eponymous Heroes of Attica, figures from myth such as Erechtheus (mentioned in Homer's *Iliad*) and Pandion: They were (in official tribal order) Erechtheis, Aigeis, Pandionis, Leontis, Akamantis, Oineis, Kekropis, Hippothontis, Aiantis, and Antiochis.

We will return to the composition of these tribes in a moment. What I wish to stress here is that the reshaping of Athens at this time extended to a physical reshaping of the city and its territory. The new democracy shifted its civic center of gravity, as it were, from the Archaic Agora (located to the east of the Acropolis and containing the Prytaneum, or town hall, as confirmed recently by an inscription) to the site of the Classical Agora, the one visited today (Figure 1.2).[78] A new *bouleuterion* or council house was constructed to accommodate Cleisthenes' Council of Five Hundred; what is more, recent research has shown that the *bouleutērion* and the assembly space on the Pnyx Hill above the Agora were purposefully oriented to be in each other's sight lines.[79] Meanwhile, if the same author's interpretation is correct, Cleisthenes' democracy deliberately tore down the Archaic temple on the Acropolis (called the Bluebeard Temple) and began construction on the Older Parthenon (the one later destroyed in the Persian invasion

---

[75] Adak and Thonemann 2022: Document 3A, ll. 13–22. [76] Robinson 2011: 140–45.
[77] Hdt. 5.66.2; [Arist.] *Ath. Pol.* 21.6.
[78] Inscription: Kavvadias and Matthaiou 2014; see further *SEG* 64.29. [79] Paga 2020: 166.

1.4 Early Democratic Institutional Developments

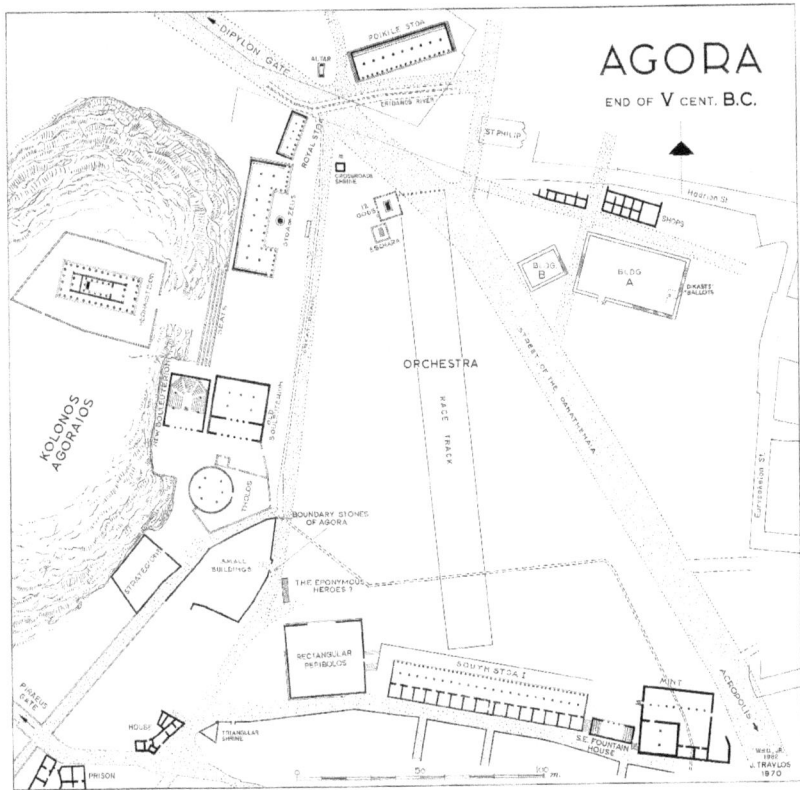

Figure 1.2 Classical Agora. (Photo: American School of Classical Studies at Athens: Agora Excavations. Archive number: 2002.01.0873).

of 480) early in the regime's history.[80] We will return in the next chapter to the Athenian democracy's building program during its height, while further acts of destruction and reconstitution of monuments receive treatment in Chapter 3. Manipulating the civic landscape turned out to be a fairly common political tactic, not limited to democratic regimes.

Also in the wake of Cleisthenes' revolution came the first public statues to the Athenians' "tyrannicide liberators" Aristogeiton and Harmodius. This duo, comprising an older male lover (*erastēs*) and his young beloved (*erōmenos*) respectively, had chafed under the Pisistratids' rule and assassinated Hipparchus, the younger brother of the reigning tyrant Hippias, at

---

[80] Paga 2020: 49–50, 65–66.

the Panathenaic festival of 514 BCE.[81] This was not the end of the tyranny but rather its intensification, as the surviving Hippias ruled in a much more paranoid and authoritarian fashion. It would take a Spartan intervention in 510 – again a Panathenaic year – to rid Athens of Pisistratid rule for good. Despite or perhaps because of this inconvenient history, Harmodius and Aristogeiton were re-remembered as the liberators of Athens from tyranny and founding fathers of democracy. Poems were sung in their honor, in one case claiming that the two had killed the tyrant and "made Athens *isonomos* [a place of *isonomia*]."[82] A bronze statue group was erected in the Agora at (presumably) public expense, an exceptional honor not to be replicated by the Athenians until the early fourth century. This group was taken from Athens by Xerxes' forces during the Persian Wars in 480, but a second, more famous group by the sculptors Critius and Nesiotes replaced it, known from depictions and copies in multiple media (Figure 1.3). The statues' poses, with the older, bearded Aristogeiton striding forward and the younger, beardless Harmodius raising his sword arm for the death blow, would come to serve as a sort of instruction manual for resisting threats to the democracy.[83]

If the city center of Athens was altered in quite visible ways, the countryside received no less of a transformation, albeit of a more conceptual and institutional kind. The new, fundamental building block of Cleisthenes' constitution was the deme (Greek: *dēmos*, the same word as "the People"), settlements throughout the territory of Attica where citizens were registered. Demes, which can be thought of as neighborhoods or villages, predated the Cleisthenic reforms, but they achieved a new centrality under the democracy.[84] Each of the roughly 139 total demes was allocated to one of the three regions of Attica, the *astu* (the city center surrounding the Acropolis), the *paralia* (coastal area), or the *mesogeia* (inland area). Each of the ten new tribes in turn was composed of clusters of demes from each of the three regions, the clusters being called *trittyes* or thirds (Map 1.1).[85] The tribes were responsible for sending fifty councilors each to Cleisthenes' Council of Five Hundred every year, as we have already seen, with each deme within a tribe providing a set number of men based on population totals at the time of the first registering under Cleisthenes' new dispensation. (We call these numbers bouleutic quotas.) The demes therefore differed in

---

[81] Hdt. 5.55–57; Thuc. 6.54–58; [Arist.] *Ath. Pol.* 18. [82] Athen. 15.695a–b.
[83] Statues: Azoulay 2017. Pose: Ober 2003. One scholar has identified a monumental stepped base in the center of the Athenian Agora along the Panathenaic Way as the site of the Critius and Nesiotes group: Baltes 2020.
[84] Osborne 1985; Whitehead 1986. [85] Traill 1975.

1.4 Early Democratic Institutional Developments

Figure 1.3 Harmodius and Aristogeiton. (Photo: DEA / G. DAGLI ORTI / De Agostini via Getty Images).

size but were more or less equitably distributed throughout the new tribes – the deme of Acharnai, for example, north of the *astu*, was very large, providing twenty-two councilors every year and serving as the lone deme of the inland *trittys* for the tribe Oineis.

Cleisthenes' tribal reorganization achieved several objectives. The much larger scale and greater intricacy compared with the old system of four tribes with three subsections each constituted a thorough "mixing" of the citizenry, according to the *Constitution of the Athenians*: "[Cleisthenes] wished to mix them up in order that more people might partake of the constitution [*politeia*]."[86] Not only would more citizens than previously

---
[86] [Arist.] *Ath. Pol.* 20.2.

1 From *Eunomia* to *Dēmokratia*, 510–451/0 BCE

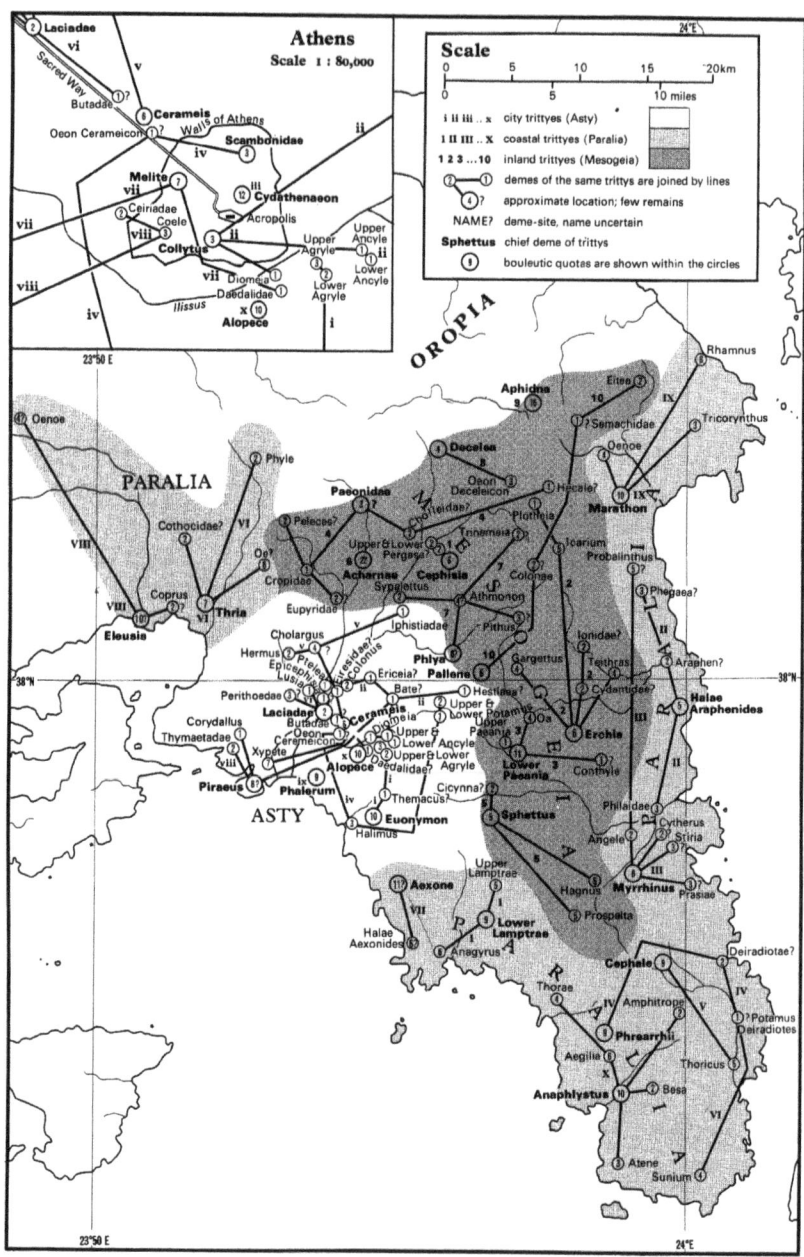

Map 1.1 The political organization of Attica (after J. S. Traill).
(Source: *The Cambridge Ancient History* vol. 4)

participate on the Council, since 139 different demes now had to be represented year in and year out by different men, but the grouping of fifty councilors in each tribal contingent was guaranteed to come from the different regions of Attica. Those regions had served as the power bases for different factions in the period prior to Pisistratus' tyranny; now they were neutralized.[87] The cooperation of the members of the tribal contingents was no theoretical matter, either: For a tenth of the year, called a *prytany*, each fifty-man group served as the executive officers of the Council, presiding also over sessions of the assembly that fell within their *prytany*; they were called *prytaneis* (presidents). In getting to know each other and work together, the *prytaneis* no doubt brought relevant knowledge from – and political concern for – the different constituencies of Attica, being attuned to local conditions.[88]

Subtler transformations were at work in Cleisthenes' tribal reforms as well. Neighboring demes that had constituted regional centers during the Archaic period – often centers of cult – were sometimes "broken up," if only conceptually, and redistributed among Cleisthenes' *trittyes* and tribes. The most famous example is that of the so-called Marathonian Tetrapolis from northeast Attica, comprising, as its name implies, four sites, Marathon, Oenoe, Tricorythus, and Probalinthus. Under Cleisthenes' reforms, the last-named site was carved off from the other three, which belonged to the coastal *trittys* of the tribe Aiantis, and made to belong to Pandionis. Presumably these sorts of decisions were intended to undercut any local prestige and authority a man might derive from connection with the traditional cults administered by the Tetrapolis.[89] This is in keeping with Aristotle's advice on civic reorganization in the *Politics*, citing Cleisthenes as an example: When establishing a thoroughgoing democracy, "Different and more numerous tribes and brotherhoods [*phratriai*] must be created, and private cults must be collected into a few common ones, and one must contrive in everything so that all [citizens] are mixed together to the greatest degree, while the former associations are dissolved."[90]

Athens' civic reorganization may appear unique, but similar things transpired at nearby Eretria on Euboea not long afterward, perhaps in direct emulation of the Athenian model. We have seen that a revolution by one

---

[87] Hdt. 1.59.3; [Arist.] *Ath. Pol.* 13.4 with Osborne 2023: 151.   [88] Ober 2008.
[89] Lewis 1963, who also unconvincingly argues that Cleisthenes strengthened the political position of his family the Alcmaeonids through his reforms.
[90] Arist. *Pol.* 6.1319b23–27. As it turns out, Cleisthenes did not in fact dissolve the old *phratries* of Attica but left them in place: [Arist.] *Ath. Pol.* 20.6. Cleisthenes' revolution was thus not as thoroughgoing as Aristotle in the *Politics* suggests.

Diagoras overturned the old oligarchy of the horsemen there, probably after 510 BCE. The resulting democracy was then responsible for a thorough reorganization of the city's tribal structure, which modern scholars have pieced together largely from later epigraphic evidence. The system was definitely in place by the end of the fifth century, since it is attested in an unpublished inscription recently discovered at the important cult site of Amarynthus, which shows Eretria incorporating into itself the preexisting Euboean *polis* of Styra. Styra likely gave up its autonomy in order better to guard itself against the threatening Athenian fort at Rhamnous situated opposite the bay in Attica.[91] The closeness to the Athenian example probably means the tribal organization had already been in existence by then for a long time, from the period immediately after Diagoras' revolution.

Like Attica, the Eretriad (territory of Eretria) was made up of demes in addition to the city center of Eretria itself; there were fifty to sixty of them. The demes were distributed among five territorial subdivisions called *chōroi* (regions), and demes from each of the five *chōroi* came together to make the city's six tribes. As in Attica, therefore, there was regional "mixing" in the tribal reorganization of the Eretriad.[92] Furthermore, the Eretrian tribes were, like Cleisthenes', named after "epichoric" or local heroes: Narkittis for Narkissos, Mekistis for Mekistos, Admetis for Admetos, and so on. In fact, our knowledge of the tribe Admetis comes from a third-century inscription showing members of the constituent demes of the tribe making financial contributions for the construction of a sanctuary to the hero Admetos – civic organization and cult intertwining once again.[93] Eretria thus constitutes a remarkable democratic peer to Athens, evolving around the same time and with similar organizational ramifications. As one expert on Eretria has aptly put it, "the isonomic wind of change [represented by Cleisthenes' reforms] was not only blowing over the Athenian Acropolis but over Eretria as well."[94]

1.5 Democracy and Greek Culture

We know that democracy has been rare historically. We assume that its first emergence in ancient Greece must have registered like a thunderbolt. But what impact can we detect in contemporary sources? What difference did *dēmokratia* make to Greek culture and political thought at the time? How did poets, artists, and intellectuals react to it? (Remember, again, that

---

[91] Knoepfler 2018: 920. [92] Fachard 2012; 2019. [93] Knoepfler and Ackerman 2013.
[94] Fachard 2019: 179.

1.5 Democracy and Greek Culture

we are dealing with a period before the height of Athenian imperialism, which colored subsequent views of democracy considerably.) One thing we can be sure of is that democracy heralded a revolution in Greek constitutional thinking. By about 470, we have the latest possible date for the emergence of the notion, fundamental to all subsequent Greek thought, that constitutions could be defined primarily by what portion of the citizen body controlled them: the one, the few, or the many. The poet Pindar, in a victory ode for the tyrant Hieron of Syracuse, states gnomically: "The man of straight tongue prospers in every political arrangement [*nomos*]: in a tyranny [*turannis*], and when the boisterous host [*labros stratos*] or the wise [*hoi sophoi*] watch over a city."[95]

Several things are at stake here. For one, the concept of political participation has changed. Under Archaic *eunomia*, as we have seen, the primary contrast was between a community that ruled itself and one that was controlled by a tyrant. Within the former, there were differential roles based on one's social position in society: Elites predominated in the magistracies, which had considerable powers, but some matters were still referred to the male citizenry as a whole (the *dēmos*), assembled for the purpose. It would not have made sense to ask which portion of the city ruled it to the exclusion of the others, even though everyone knew that elites played outsized parts. If anything was tripartite in the social system, it was the socioeconomic schema of high, middle, and low, with the "middle" more a conceptual space representing the avoidance of extremes than an actual class position; "mass" and "elite" better describe the distribution of wealth.[96] It was, paradoxically, the insistence of the early democracies that all should rule equally that created constitutional divisions and a much different way of conceiving of politics. For against the claim that *dēmokratia* represented the rule of the whole in equal apportionments (*isonomia*), critics of democracy insisted that the purported wholeness of the term *dēmos* in fact concealed a partisan reality: the rule of the poor majority, in its own interest, to the detriment of all who were truly "good" or "worthy" (*chrēstos*) – that is, the rich. Politics gradually came to be viewed as a matter of which self-interested part of the city controlled the *polis*, in the process metaphorically "enslaving" the others.[97] As Plato would later say, the usual trio of regimes – tyranny, oligarchy, and democracy – were not so much "constitutions" (*politeiai*) as "dictatorships of one

---

[95] Pind. *Pyth.* 2.86–87.
[96] On "middling" ideology in the Archaic period, see Morris 1996 and Kurke 1999 with the criticisms of Hammer 2004. For the distribution of wealth in fifth- and fourth-century Athens, see Kron 2011.
[97] See Xen. *Mem.* 1.2.40–46, discussed further in the next chapter.

faction over the others" (*stasiōteiai*, formed from *stasis* or civil strife).[98] Oligarchs maintained their exclusive control over the constitution by instituting property requirements for officeholding; tyrants obviously arrogated powers to themselves alone. "Participating in political life" now had a different meaning: Whereas even the *thetes* had participated, to some degree, in the Solonian constitution, "partaking of the constitution" (*metechein tēs politeias*) was now a matter of which group had access to the institutions that would grant them exclusive or at least dominant control over the city (allow them to "watch over" it, in Pindar's words).

The possibility of constitutional opposition also meant that the different factions developed different normative justifications for their rule, with concomitant condemnation of the others. In Pindar's formulation, oligarchy is the rule of "the wise"; by necessity, he is denying that wisdom resides in the "boisterous host" of democracy. There had always been an elitist and anti-egalitarian streak in Greek thinking. The *dēmos* could represent all that was "common" and therefore "vulgar."[99] The seventh-century poet Archilochus had even insulted someone as a prostitute by calling them "*dēmos*."[100] These prejudices now took on a more virulent and reactionary cast as elites recoiled from the experience of democracy. Heraclitus, to return to the "crying philosopher" of Ephesus, said of some unnamed targets, "What reason or mind have they, who obey the singers of the People and make use of the crowd [*homilos*] as a teacher, not knowing that 'the many are bad, the few good'?"[101]

What Heraclitus means by "the singers of the People" is unclear – perhaps he means rhapsodes at public festivals – but the phrase he quotes is actually a repurposing of an old maxim by Bias of Priene, one of the "Seven Wise Men" of Archaic Greece.[102] In Bias' usage it probably meant that most people are incapable of attaining virtue; Heraclitus, however, gives it new meaning by applying it to democracies such as the one he lived under at Ephesus.[103] No regime in which the crowd was the central protagonist could possibly be good. In fact, *dēmos* became something of a dirty word for oligarchically minded elites. I find it significant that Pindar used the word, so far as we can tell, in poems for victors from democracies and tyrannies only.[104] He and his contemporary Bacchylides celebrated

---

[98] Plat. *Leg.* 8.832c.   [99] Donlan 1999: 225–36; Rose 2012.   [100] Archil. fr. 242 West.
[101] DK 22 B 104.   [102] Diog. Laert. 1.87.
[103] Not all pre-Socratic philosophers were hostile to democracy, however: Empedocles of Acragas was remembered as a champion of democracy against the local oligarchy there (on this tradition, see Horky 2016).
[104] For example, for tyrannical Acragas (*Ol.* 3) and democratic Argos and Camarina (*Nem.* 10 and *Ol.* 5).

1.5 Democracy and Greek Culture

a different set of qualities for notoriously oligarchic *poleis* like Thebes and Aegina, in both of which they detected "moderate good order" (*sōphrōn eunomia*).[105] On the other hand, the declaration of the poet Simonides in a song for Athens on the occasion of the military victory at Marathon in 490, namely that "the *dēmos* of the Athenians alone accomplished this," may show the Athenian democracy embracing the term as a badge of honor.[106]

Not every Athenian was pleased with *dēmokratia*, however. As the democracy amassed cultural, material, and military capital – building walls, erecting statues for Harmodius and Aristogeiton in the Agora, minting the first examples of the city's distinctive owl coinage, taking the initial steps on the road to what would become the Athenian empire – there were those who already found the power of the People overweening.[107] In the 460s the tragic playwright Aeschylus could mention in a drama, in a circumlocution, the "ruling hand of the People," *dēmou kratousa cheir*. This is our earliest explicit attestation in the sources of a concept, *dēmokratia*, that must have developed earlier still.[108] The People's "ruling hand" was most obviously felt in the votes of the assembly on the Pnyx Hill by show of hands (*cheirotonia*), but to some members of the elite it may have felt like the heavy hand of a master.

People also debated, already in the 460s and 450s, the quality of the city's political leadership, a topic that became an even sorer subject during the Peloponnesian War years (see next chapter). Here we have to exercise caution, since the later sources often introduce serious distortions when it comes to early fifth-century political history, from the late fourth-century Aristotelian *Constitution of the Athenians* to Plutarch's Roman-era *Lives*. In particular, we must resist a picture of openly democratic and oligarchic factions in Athens during this period, or a schematic view (popularized by the *Ath. Pol.*) according to which there was a single great champion of the people and countervailing champion of the notables at any given time.[109] In fact, everyone was, at least outwardly, working for the good of the Athenian *dēmos*.[110] And yet there were definitely differences of style and substance among politicians.

We can rely on the testimony of an eyewitness, the poet Ion son of Orthomenes, whose home city, Chios, despite being a tribute-paying

---

[105] Pind. fr. 52a.10 S-M; Bacch. 13.149. For epinician poetry as advice for oligarchic stability, see Kurke 2007; Simonton 2017: 198–206.
[106] Simon. fr. 86 West.
[107] Walls: See discussion of the Long Walls that follows. Statues: See Section 1.4. Coins: I follow Aperghis 2013 on owl coins postdating 510 (I think 508/7).
[108] A. *Suppl.* 604.   [109] [Arist.] *Ath. Pol.* 28.2.   [110] Mann 2007: 73–74, 184–85.

member of Athens' empire, was allowed to retain an oligarchic constitution. Ion himself seems to have shared some of the prejudices of the ruling elite of his *polis*.[111] Ion died in 420, but not before leaving behind a set of memoirs, portions of which are selectively quoted by surviving ancient sources. Born in the early fifth century to a prominent family from an illustrious island, he interacted with several famous Athenian figures from the first half of the 400s. In particular, he informs us, he met the Athenian commander Cimon when he (Ion) was still a young man. Cimon was later remembered as a crypto-oligarch, an opponent of the more "radical" democracy that resulted from the acquisition of the empire. In reality he seems to have served the democracy loyally (as well he might – his father, Miltiades, was the victor of the near-mythical Battle of Marathon against Persia in 490), even if he promoted cooperation rather than competition with Sparta, which in a memorable turn of phrase he labeled Athens' "yoke-mate" (as though they were a team of draft animals).[112]

Ion recalls a banquet of the 460s at which Cimon, present, was praised for his skill at singing to the lyre. The guests then declared him cleverer than Themistocles – architect of Athens' navy, brilliant commander in the Persian Wars, victim of ostracism in 471 – who "admitted he never learned how to sing or to play the kithara, but knew how to make a *polis* great and wealthy."[113] In other words, the snobbish guests had a laugh at the expense of Themistocles' rather gauche materialism and lack of aristocratic politesse.[114] Cimon, meanwhile, is described elsewhere by Ion as "harmonious, supple, and educated" (*memousōmenos*, that is, trained in the arts of the Muses).[115] Another contemporary, a rather eccentric pamphleteer named Stesimbrotus from the island of Thasos, likewise praised Cimon as "free of all Attic shrewdness [*deinotēs*] and blathering [*stōmulia*]."[116] Both words are applied in other sources to politicians who are too clever by half and rely on half-truths and blowing smoke. A true gentleman would simply not deign to do such things. The famous tragedian Sophocles was like that, again according to Ion: ready with a bon mot while in his cups, but "when it came to politics he was neither skilled nor active, but like one

---

[111] On Ion of Chios see Jacoby 1947; Geddes 2007.
[112] Plut. *Vit. Cim.* 16.8 = Ion of Chios *BNJ* 392 F 14.
[113] Plut. *Vit. Cim.* 9.1 = Ion of Chios *BNJ* 392 F 13.
[114] My analysis here differs from that of Mann 2007: 179–82 in that I am focused less on the communicative styles of the politicians and more on the elite community at Athens critical of democratic leadership already in the 460s.
[115] Plut. *Vit. Per.* 5.3 = Ion of Chios *BNJ* 392 F 15.
[116] Plut. *Vit. Cim.* 4.5 = Stesimbrotus *BNJ* 107 F 4. On Stesimbrotus' politics see Pownall 2020.

of the good [*chrēstos*] Athenians."¹¹⁷ A "good" Athenian was not skilled or active in politics because politics had become a rogues' gallery populated by rank rabble-rousers like Themistocles and the young Pericles. A century and a half later, Aristotle's pupil Theophrastus composed a playful character sketch of an "oligarchic personality type." The figure declares, among other things, "I'm amazed at people who enter politics – what can they want?"¹¹⁸ The sentiment is already found in Ion of Chios' memoirs.

Antidemocratic feeling at Athens grew to a boiling point in the early 450s, when the Athenians both openly antagonized the Spartans in the First Peloponnesian War (460–446) and began work on the Long Walls, the fortifications that connected the Athenian city center or *astu* with the ports of Piraeus and Phalerum. The city had for several decades been benefiting from its powerful fleet, an institution that existed in a symbiotic relationship with the democracy itself, growing in strength step by step one with the other. Conservatives in Athens believed that the successful "island-ization" of the city, if the *astu* were to be given an impregnable walled artery to the sea, would mark a point of no return toward thoroughgoing democratic radicalism.¹¹⁹ They therefore plotted, in the words of Thucydides, "to put a stop to the People and the construction of the Long Walls," presumably by staging a revolution and replacing democracy with oligarchy.¹²⁰ In the event the insurrection failed to materialize, but the threat had been real enough. The Athenians managed to stave off *stasis* for another forty-plus years, thanks in large part to the ability of the empire to secure elite buy-in to the constitution through the promise of spoils and positions of leadership. The conspiracy of 457, however, shows that "democracy-versus-oligarchy" was very much a live issue already in the first half of the century.

Athens was precociously (and provocatively) democratic, but we can see resistance to democracy elsewhere too, if we know where to look. In Elis, a vase from around 460 BCE bears on its foot the inscription "*philagoria kakiston*," perhaps "love of speaking in the assembly [the agora] is the basest thing."¹²¹ One scholar has interpreted this as a negative commentary on the current political scene, meant for elite consumption: "a programmatically terse critique of demagogic politics in the notoriously democratic polity of Elis."¹²²

---

¹¹⁷ Athen. 13.604d = Ion of Chios *BNJ* 392 F 6. ¹¹⁸ Theophr. *Char.* 26.4.
¹¹⁹ For the association of the Long Walls with naval democracy and empire see Xen. *Hell.* 2.2.20.
¹²⁰ Thuc. 1.107.4, the historicity of which claim is doubted by Badian 1993: 213n50, but see Hornblower 1991 *ad loc.*
¹²¹ Siewert and Taeuber 2013: no. 341. ¹²² Ma 2014.

In Thebes, on the other hand, onomastics, or the study of names and naming practices, can come in handy. We know that by 413 at the latest, there had emerged at Thebes a fiercely pro-Sparta faction committed to oligarchic politics and headed by, among others, one Astias and Koiratadas. These are significant names: Astias means something like Mr. Urbane. One historian has recently pointed out the connection between oligarchic politics and ambitions to monopolize the city center of the *polis*, or *astu*, to the exclusion of the *dēmos*; Astias' parents would then have "showed remarkable class consciousness in naming their son."[123]

The extremely rare name Koiratadas, meanwhile, means Mr. Son-of-a-Ruler, basing itself on the old Homeric term *koiranos*, ruler or master.[124] Now, *koiranos* and related words eventually became wrapped up in debates between democrats and oligarchs. The latter claimed that when Homer's Odysseus said, "multiple rulership [*polukoiraniē*] is no good thing; let there be one ruler [*koiranos*], one king," he had democracy in mind when referring to multiple rulership (as anachronistic as this argument might be).[125] It seems highly likely that Koiratadas' name is already reflective of oligarchs' embrace of this ideological view. If Astias and Koiratadas were at least thirty by the time of their first mention in the sources, in the year 413 BCE, they would have been born probably in the 450s or 440s, when Thebes was either still experimenting with democracy or had recently rid itself of it. Recall that this democracy had likely been imposed by the Athenians after the Boeotians' defeat at the Battle of Oenophyta in 457. Aristotle says that it disintegrated when the well-resourced elite [*hoi euporoi*] came to despise its "disorder and anarchy," while the Old Oligarch mentions a brief period when the Athenians consented to supporting an oligarchy in Boeotia; the result was that within a short time the common people in the Boeotian cities were "enslaved."[126] Astias and Koiratadas were presumably born in or around this tumultuous milieu. Just as Hamilcar Barca would later force his young son Hannibal to swear never to be a friend to the Roman people, so, it seems, some fathers in Thebes reared their sons to be inveterate haters of the *dēmos*, beginning with their very names.[127]

*

---

[123] Papazarkadas 2022: 12n56 ("Astias" and "astu" are derived from the same root).
[124] Koiratadas: two entries in LGPN. For Homeric *koiranos*, see, e.g., *Il.* 7.234.
[125] Hom. *Il.* 2.204–205 with Arist. *Pol.* 4.1292a13–15; Theophr. *Char.* 26.2; Nepos *Dio* 6.4; cf. Xen. *Mem.* 1.2.58–59, quoting the lines just previous in the *Iliad*.
[126] Arist. *Pol.* 5.1302b27–30; [Xen.] *Ath. Pol.* 3.11.   [127] Hannibal story: Polyb. 3.11.7.

1.5 Democracy and Greek Culture

The present chapter is bound to be frustrating on several fronts: not enough material about political developments in the earlier Archaic period; too little evidence from the first half of the fifth century; the lack of an event-based historical narrative. With any luck, however, the reader has by now picked up on some key themes that will be explored in much greater detail in the following chapters. Even with a fragmentary evidence base, we can see that the earliest ancient Greek democracies were already grappling with the extent to which they wished to involve non-elite men of the citizen community – members of the *dēmos* – in the most important decisions of the city. That a democratic *polis* was in some sense governed by the *dēmos* as a group of political equals was not in doubt – what would continue to be debated were the depth and thoroughness of that governance. How political participation might be guaranteed through funding and the distribution of political offices was also an open question. Furthermore, with the power and privilege that accrued from being a democratic (male) citizen came newfound concerns on the part of average men as to how they were counted as *politai* and with whom their status could be contrasted. Members of the *dēmos* developed a series of answers as to why they should exercise rule: They were free, they were men, and they were native to their land (or naturalized). As we will see, the deepening of democratic practice in ancient Greece would prove impossible without the hardening of boundaries between insiders and outsiders in all these categories. But there was also the reaction of those who considered themselves superior even to these criteria: the elite of birth, wealth, and education. We have seen numerous times already their uneasy if not outright hostile attitude toward the *dēmokratiai* they encountered. Those doubts, inflamed in many instances to the level of virulent hatreds, would only increase over the near century from 451/0 to 362 BCE. It is to this period of existential struggle between democracy and oligarchy that we now turn.

CHAPTER 2

A Contested Existence, 451/0–362 BCE

2.1 Introduction

The present chapter spans the period for which we have the richest and most copious evidence from the ancient world for democracy in action. That profusion stems from the fact that texts covering the Athenian democracy of the later fifth and earlier fourth centuries have survived in greater numbers. In some cases this has to do with ancient readers' preference for Athenian authors already considered classics by the later fourth century BCE; in others it is a result of Athens' monumental record of publishing inscriptions on stone – its "epigraphic habit" – which has been documented through centuries of antiquarianism and excavations. Athens' particular brand of "People power" thus emerges from sources in all sorts of genres: a (rare!) continuous historiographical tradition in the form of Thucydides and Xenophon, covering 431–362 in detail; inscribed decrees and other epigraphical evidence, particularly that pertaining to the Athenian Empire circa 454–404 BCE; tragedy and, especially, the political plays of Aristophanes and other Old Comic poets (the latter surviving in fragments); Attic oratory, and in particular Antiphon, Andocides, and Lysias;[1] archaeological remains; and the philosophical dialogues of Plato and Xenophon, which not only depict events of our time span but were largely composed during it as well. This period encompassed, at least down to 404, the apex of Athens' Aegean-wide empire, the Age of Pericles with its accompanying building projects, the Peloponnesian War (431–404), and Athens' brief experiments (in 411 and 404) with oligarchic regimes, after which its democracy took on a slightly modified but stable form for nearly

---

[1] The later Attic orators, especially Aeschines and, above all, Demosthenes, supply detailed information about the Athenian democracy of the latter half of the fourth century. However, I do not devote a separate chapter to "the Athenian democracy in the age of Demosthenes" (so Hansen 1999), since the political institutions under which Aeschines and Demosthenes operated were for the most part already in place by 362.

a century. If the general reader knows anything about Athens and the Athenian democracy, it likely originates from the era in question.

Athens, therefore, will be the focus of much of this chapter. But Athens, in keeping with trends surveyed in the previous chapter, was far from the only democracy of the period. Its influence could be felt in cities that adopted, whether voluntarily or under special pressure from Athens' empire, democratic institutions along Athenian lines. However, there were also numerous homegrown democracies throughout the Greek world, evincing remarkable variety within a common democratic framework. Of these we will pay especial attention to Syracuse, Argos, Erythrae, and Thasos, but these represent just a small fraction of the total number of democratic regimes.[2] Furthermore, despite (or, perhaps, because of) the domestic might and imperial ambition of Athenian *dēmokratia* at this time, democracy as a whole in Greece was never more embattled and precarious. Opposition to the power of the People hardened into conspiracies on the part of those who favored an alternative constitutional setup, oligarchy or the rule of the (wealthy) few. Conflicts between democrats and oligarchs, in episodes of what the Greeks called *stasis* or civil strife, while present already in the first half of the fifth century (see the previous chapter), probably reached their peak over the course of the near century between 451/0 and 362.

At the midway point, the period of Spartan hegemony (404–379), it looked as though the Greek experiment with democracy might have been dealt a fatal blow. Spartan errors, however, along with the ever-growing appeal of democracy to average citizens within the *poleis*, meant that *dēmokratiai* gained a renewed lease on life in the later fourth century, cementing themselves as the sole legitimate constitutional form in Greece (see the next chapter). Thus, in a divergence from standard histories of ancient Greek democracy, I am going to spend no more time on the golden age of Athenian democracy than on the regime type's efflorescence in the ensuing centuries. We cannot understand the latter except in comparison with the exceptional surviving information about the former, and so the present chapter will reconstruct, in as detailed a form as space permits, the chief institutions and ideological preoccupations of fifth- and early fourth-century Athens. But we must always bear in mind that in a history of Greek democracies in general, there is no obvious reason why we should focus more on the experience of the sixty thousand or so adult male citizens

---

[2] See the numbers collected in Hansen and Nielsen 2004, Robinson 2011, and Teegarden 2013: appendix.

of fifth-century Athens than on that of the (perhaps) millions of Greeks who lived under democratic regimes in subsequent ages.[3]

The structure of the chapter is as follows. In what will be a common feature of the next three chapters, I first provide a brief historical overview of the period covered, highlighting milestones in the history of democracy in the process. The chapter then builds up a sketch of the Classical Athenian democracy as though it were a human individual, from the inside out, beginning with the institutional "skeleton" of assembly, magistracies, law courts, and ostracism, on which I then overlay the ideological "flesh" of ideas, concepts, values, and aesthetic representations.[4] In outlining Athens' key formal institutions, I proceed in the order in which one would have encountered them across the life cycle of an Athenian male citizen; women's lives, and female citizenship compared with that of men, appear here briefly as well. Other *poleis'* institutions crop up throughout as points of comparison. The ideological section, in addition to exploring the positive democratic values of freedom and equality, also catalogs some negative images (slave, foreigner, woman) against which the average Athenian citizen male defined himself and without which ancient Greek democracies in general were probably impossible. These will be examined in greater detail in the next chapter. An excursus explores democracy and the democratic citizen's relationship to material culture. Finally, having completed my picture of "the democrat," I place him in conflict with his chief ideological competitor of the time, "the oligarch." This last section of the chapter discusses the proliferation of *stasis* during our period and the often violent forms it could take, with oligarchic reactionaries precipitating or in some cases being anticipated by populist "demagogues." Looming over both regimes was the specter of the tyrant, who occasionally emerged out of democratic dissolution. Given all these threats facing democracies, their survival and even flowering across the fourth, third, and early second centuries BCE were anything but preordained. If, in contrast to certain traditional accounts, I argue against the notion of the death of Greek democracy in the later fourth century, this is not to suggest that the triumph of *dēmokratia* was inevitable.

---

[3] For fifth-century Athenian demography see Akrigg 2019.
[4] In employing this metaphor, I do not mean to suggest that the formal institutions were somehow more fundamental than ideology or were temporally prior to it. As in the growth of a living organism, the systems developed in tandem and could not function apart from each other.

2.2 Historical Overview

Historians refer to the span between the end of the Persian Wars (479 BCE) and the outbreak of the Peloponnesian War (431) as the *Pentecontaetia*, or Fifty-Year Period, during which time the Athenians, as Thucydides put it, "increased in power."[5] This increase took the form of an *archē*, first and foremost "command" or "rule" but conventionally translated as "empire," which began its existence as a voluntary association of cities sworn to in 478/7. By 451/0, when our story begins, Athens had greatly expanded its influence, bringing much of the Aegean Sea and beyond under its control.[6] Outside of a few token states (Chios, Samos, and the *poleis* of Lesbos), it supplied the bulk of the ships for its nominally defensive alliance, for which it compelled its "allies" to pay tribute (*phoros*) in what to an outsider might resemble a protection racket. Recalcitrant *poleis* like Naxos and Thasos – major city-states proud of their Archaic-era traditions – had by 451 been forcefully humbled and brought back into the fold, in the latter case with grave misgivings by Sparta. Although still allies in the 470s, the Spartans had grown wary of Athenian assertiveness and in the mid 460s severed ties irrevocably by dismissing the Athenians from a campaign against a rebellion by their slaves, known as the helots, in Messenia. Thucydides says the Spartans suspected the Athenians' "revolutionary spirit" (*neōteropoiia*), a reference to their democratic way of life.[7] Free to pursue their interests unchecked, the Athenians embarked on an ambitious expedition against Egypt, which ended in spectacular failure.[8] Beginning in 454/3, they transferred their imperial treasury from the sacred island of Delos to Athens itself and inscribed the first Tribute-Quota Lists, enumerating the portions set aside for Athena: Their power was taking on an even more monumental and aggressive cast.[9] Wars on multiple fronts, including against Sparta itself, continued down to 446/5, when the so-called Thirty Years' Peace reaffirmed Athens' control over the massive island of Euboea, an important source of grain.

The year before, the Athenians had kick-started their famous midcentury building program (on which more in this chapter's excursus), laying the foundations for their new temple to Athena, today known as the Parthenon. Within a few decades the Athenian Acropolis, left in ruins since the 480s as

---

[5] Thuc. 1.89.1.
[6] On the Athenian Empire: Meiggs 1972; Low 2008; Ma, Papazarkadas, and Parker 2009; Driscoll 2018; Lazar 2024. For the expansion of Athenian power prior to 478/7, see Kallet 2013.
[7] Thuc. 1.102.3.   [8] Thuc. 1.110.   [9] Meritt, Wade-Gery, and McGregor 1939–49; Stroud 2006.

a reminder of Persian hubris, would be completely transformed into a celebration of imperial grandeur.[10] The Athenian democracy, to the great chagrin of its growing number of detractors, had proven itself resilient almost beyond belief. Here was an expanding maritime imperial power, flush with more cash than any *polis* had ever seen, and constantly innovating in the realms of politics, architecture, culture, and the economy. Its citizens were paid to participate in government (a development, as we have seen, begun in the late 450s), its theater of Dionysus hosted the productions of Aeschylus, Sophocles, and Euripides, and its port, the Piraeus, welcomed heaps of Egyptian papyrus and Syrian frankincense. Under Athens' "tutelage," wanted or not, dozens of imperial subject cities were experimenting with democratic institutions of their own.[11] To the average Greek, Athens must have appeared the most revolutionary place on earth.

A generation later, most of that was all over. One evening in 405 BCE, the Athenian state galley, the *Paralus*, arrived in the port, announcing the destruction of the rest of the fleet. In Xenophon's words, "a loud wail proceeded up from the Piraeus through the Long Walls [Athens' defenses linking harbor and city] to the center of town, one person conveying the news to another."[12] Except for its walls, Athens was now defenseless; a bitter winter siege would follow. Upon capitulation, the victorious Spartan commander, Lysander, had the Long Walls demolished to the music of women playing the pipes. Returning Athenian exiles, many of them undoubtedly of oligarchic sympathies, rejoiced at the thought that the day marked the beginning of "freedom" (*eleutheria*) for Greece.[13]

What had happened? Twenty-seven years of on-off struggle known as the Peloponnesian War (431–404).[14] In the influential phrasing of Thucydides, who began working on a history of the conflict at its outset, this was "the greatest upheaval known to the Greeks and to a portion of non-Greeks – almost a majority of humankind."[15] In a decision that continues to fascinate scholars of international relations, the Spartans opted to check ever-growing Athenian power, not (supposedly) because of any technical treaty infractions, but out of pure fear and self-interest.[16] Still, they had the good sense to call it a war of liberation for Athens' imperial subjects.[17] The Athenians, for their part, continued to innovate, this time in warfare: Rather than face the Spartan-led hoplite army in

---

[10] Shear 2016.
[11] Athens did not enforce democracy across the board (so Brock 2009), but it did encourage democracy ([Xen.] *Ath. Pol.* 1.14; Thuc. 8.64.1; Xen. *Hell.* 3.4.7).
[12] Xen. *Hell.* 2.2.3.   [13] Xen. *Hell.* 2.2.23.   [14] Cawkwell 1997; Lendon 2010; Roberts 2017.
[15] Thuc. 1.1.2.   [16] Thuc. 1.23.6 with de Ste. Croix 1972; Lebow 2012.   [17] Thuc. 2.8.4–5.

a potentially decisive pitched battle, they withdrew behind the Long Walls and relied on the Piraeus for supplies, leaving the Attic countryside to destruction. It is a sobering thought that our first substantial contemporary reflections on Athenian life, in the form of Aristophanic comedies beginning in 425, do not predate these exceptional circumstances. Indeed, some scholars have speculated that the cramped urban conditions – not to mention the need to deal with a deadly plague, on top of an insecure empire – encouraged the more "demagogic" politics of the period, particularly after the death of the senior politician Pericles in 429 (see further Section 2.3.3).[18] In any case, while the Athenian democracy continued to hold its own, there was no lack of *stasis* throughout the rest of the Greek cities, as the great powers encouraged their local partisans: The Greek "third world," as one scholar has labeled it, suffered as the Athenians backed democrats and the Spartans oligarchs.[19] It would be a mistake, however, to assume that, because many of these democracies had been maintained at the barrel of a gun, so to speak, they lacked popular support. The Spartans, much as they might prefer to work with oligarchies, learned that they often had to respect democratic constitutions if they wanted Athens' subjects to agree to revolt.[20]

A period of peace beginning in 421 was punctured when the Athenians, as with their Egyptian campaign of almost fifty years prior, bit off more than they could chew with an attempted conquest of Sicily in 415. The Spartans were soon back in Attica, this time with a permanent occupation of the deme of Decelea north of Athens. The failure of the Sicilian expedition in 413, followed by a vigorous (and unprecedented) Spartan naval campaign against the imperial subjects of the Ionian coast in Asia Minor, sowed self-doubt and a concomitant willingness to reform within the Athenian democracy. In 411, for the first time in almost a century, the Athenians abandoned democracy on the promise of increased Persian aid against the Spartans – the ironies here abound.[21] The ensuing oligarchic regime, centered around a council calling itself the Four Hundred, quickly discredited itself and sparked the reestablishment of democracy after an interim regime that lasted about eight months; for the oligarchs who

---

[18] This was already the diagnosis of Aristophanes: *Pax* 632–48.
[19] "Third world": Gehrke 1986. *Stasis*: Price 2001; Arcenas 2020.
[20] De Ste. Croix 1954 sparked an immense debate on the popularity of the Athenian Empire. I can find no case where a *dēmos* agreed to revolt from the Empire without being assured in advance they would retain their democratic constitution. They preferred to be autonomous, all else being equal, but appear to have opted to remain in the empire if it meant avoiding oligarchy. See now also Canevaro and Lewis 2024.
[21] Thuc. 8.53, 67–69.

survived, the lesson seems to have been that an even narrower, more ruthless junta was required if democracy was going to be kept down.

After six more grueling years, at the conclusion of the winter siege, they got their chance: With Lysander's approval, a government of thirty men took power. Not only did the Thirty Tyrants, as they came to be known, oppress citizens and foreigners indiscriminately, going so far as to expel average Athenians from the city center, they relied upon a Spartan occupying force to maintain their rule.[22] A democratic resistance movement based out of the northern deme of Phyle, led by Thrasybulus the son of Lycus of Steiria, snowballed into a major threat to the Thirty (with support, ironically, from the oligarchic Thebans, who since the conclusion of the Peloponnesian War wanted to see the Spartans' power checked). Eventually the Spartan king, Pausanias, with the approval of the home government, considered it in Sparta's interest to see the Athenian civil war cease: fifteen men were dispatched to swear the two sides to the great Amnesty of 403 BCE.[23] Democracy would reign uninterrupted at Athens until 322 (see next chapter), while any open advocacy of oligarchy ceased. The experience of the Thirty more than any other cemented in the Athenians a fiercely democratic identity, given expression in numerous decrees and monuments around the turn of the century (see excursus).

Other states were not so fortunate. The period of peak Spartan hegemony (404–394) saw the dissolution of numerous democracies throughout Athens' former imperial holdings and the installation of decarchies or governments of ten men, handpicked by (and therefore fiercely loyal to) Lysander.[24] Here as in so many other instances the Spartans allowed themselves to act without any consideration for their subjects' interests, discrediting not just narrow cliques but oligarchy more generally in the process. When the Spartan fleet was smashed by Persian forces commanded by the exiled Athenian general Conon off Cnidus in 394, the cities of Asia Minor appear to have genuinely welcomed the restoration of democracy: Erythrae, for one, voted Conon the first epigraphically attested honorary statue.[25] Sparta was further challenged on land by the Corinthian War (395–387), which saw democracy introduced at Corinth in cooperation with already-democratic? Argos.[26]

---

[22] On Athenian oligarchs and the oligarchic regimes: Brock 1989; Rhodes 2000; Shear 2011; Caire 2016. Expulsion: Xen. *Hell.* 2.4.1.
[23] Xen. *Hell.* 2.4.38; [Arist.] *Ath. Pol.* 39. Amnesty: Loening 1987; Wolpert 2002; Dreher 2013.
[24] Spartan hegemony: Ruzé 2017.   [25] RO 8 with Ma 2006.
[26] Corinthian War: Hamilton 1979. Democracy at Corinth: Robinson 2011: 22–23.

The peace reached in 387, with King Artaxerxes of Persia as its enforcer (thus its title of the King's Peace), consigned the Greeks of Asia Minor to pro-Persian regimes and allowed the Spartans once again to throw their oligarchic weight around, humbling the Mantinean and Phliasian democracies within the Peloponnese.[27] But arrogance cost them once more: The occupation of the Theban acropolis and the installation of a narrow pro-Spartan regime precipitated a democratic revolution in Thebes in 379, led by the generals Epaminondas and Pelopidas.[28] The Athenians, meanwhile, reconstituted their own alliance one hundred years after the first, in 378, although they were careful in the league charter to specify that their allies would remain constitutionally autonomous.[29] A massive Spartan defeat at Leuctra in 371 at the hands of the Thebans revealed the structural weaknesses of this once proud power, which had allowed itself to dwindle to about one thousand full citizens.[30] The Spartans could only look on in horror as the Thebans liberated the Messenian helots and (re)founded the city of Messene in 369; the contemporaneous establishment of the super-city of Megalopolis in Arcadia, at the head of an Arcadian League of democratic cities, compounded Sparta's problems.[31] Opposition to a single hegemon, however, once again made for strange bedfellows, as the Spartans and Athenians allied with others to take on Thebes at the Battle of Mantinea in 362.[32] With that inconclusive engagement, the historical narrative of Xenophon, and the period under review here, come to an end.

2.3 A Life Cycle of Political Institutions in Democratic Athens

2.3.1 Childhood and Citizen Enrollment

What was it like to navigate the formal institutions of the Athenian democracy during our period?[33] It might be illuminating to approach the question by imagining the life of a male citizen growing up in this milieu. (I will discuss female citizens briefly in Section 2.3.5 and at greater length in Chapter 3.7.1 – here we must acknowledge that women did not participate in most of the

---

[27] For oligarchy in Asia Minor after 387, see, e.g., RO 56 (honors of the oligarchic regime of Erythrae for Mausolus of Caria). Spartan interference: Xen. *Hell.* 5.2.1–10, 5.3.10–25.
[28] Xen. *Hell.* 5.4.1–12 with Robinson 2011: 56–57.   [29] RO 22; Cargill 1981.
[30] Xen. *Hell.* 6.4.3–16; Hodkinson 2000: ch. 13.
[31] Roy 2000; Luraghi 2008; Robinson 2011: 41–44.   [32] Xen. *Hell.* 7.5.14–27.
[33] For more detailed overviews of Athenian political institutions during this period, see especially Hansen 1999; also Ober 1989: 75–103; Sinclair 1991.

institutions that follow, at least on the present author's understanding of political institutions.)[34] In 451/0, our upper chronological boundary in this chapter, the Athenian politician Pericles the son of Xanthippus of the deme Cholargus, a scion of the illustrious Alcmaeonid family and a leading general and statesman of the time, successfully carried a proposal that a man would have to be born from citizen parents on both sides if he was to enjoy citizenship in the democracy.[35] Before this, many Athenians – particularly upper-class ones like Pericles' rival Cimon the son of Miltiades – were born to non-Athenian mothers.

The reasoning behind Pericles' citizenship law remains obscure – the Aristotelian *Constitution of the Athenians* says simply it was "due to the great number of citizens" – but it may have gone hand in hand with the greater social and economic benefits that were accruing to citizens both through the empire and through increasing redistributive measures within the democracy. Citizenship needed to be a more exclusive club, given the number of "membership goods" to which a citizen was entitled.[36] Furthermore, whether a cause or an effect of the legislation or both, the Athenians increasingly came to see themselves as a kind of collective aristocracy of blood, a community that was one big *genos* (clan).[37] (See Section 2.4.1 on the myth of autochthony.) Patrolling the boundaries of citizenship therefore intensified. A man's acknowledgment of his children by a citizen wife was a major milestone in an Athenian child's life and an important piece of information in his biography going forward, of interest to both friends and enemies.[38]

If the father's confidence in a son's legitimacy persisted through the latter's childhood, the next critical moment came during the son's eighteenth year, when the father presented him to his fellow demesmen to be registered as a member of the deme and therefore a full citizen. This was no perfunctory exercise: If the demesmen rejected a candidate and the verdict was upheld by an appeals court, the miserable individual was sold into slavery outside Attica.[39] This appears to have been a rare occurrence, but the danger was real. Most Athenian fathers also enrolled their sons at the annual Apatouria festival in the so-called phratries or brotherhoods, membership in which was probably not required for citizenship

---

[34] For a reinterpretation of Athenian citizenship, downplaying political institutions and emphasizing complementary gender roles in religious cult, see Blok 2017; I address this argument at greater length in the next chapter.

[35] [Arist.] *Ath. Pol.* 26.3.

[36] Azoulay 2014a: 81–83. By contrast, Aristotle reveals that in some other democracies, a man might become a citizen if he was born from a citizen father or mother alone; at times even illegitimate children were enrolled (*Pol.* 3.1278a27–29). See also Davies 1977 on Athens' decision.

[37] Blok 2009; Lape 2010. [38] Scafuro 1994; Osborne 2010: ch. 12. [39] [Arist.] *Ath. Pol.* 42.1.

but could serve as further evidence that one was a citizen in good standing.[40] With all the centralization that the creation of the Athenian democracy entailed (see previous chapter), it comes as a surprise to the modern reader to see so many crucial functions of government delegated to the sub*polis* level, to what were in some cases voluntary associations. It may be that the Athenians trusted these smaller, more tight-knit bodies to have the local knowledge necessary to adjudicate citizenship claims.[41] Deme-level associations also replicated the format of city politics with assemblies and decrees of their own, as well as numerous communal religious rituals (documented by extant deme calendars of sacrifices). They thus prepared young citizens for participation in the city center, to which we now turn.

2.3.2 The Assembly

Once enrolled in a deme, an Athenian male citizen was eligible to attend the citizen assembly, or *ekklēsia*.[42] This was an open-air meeting on the Pnyx Hill in Athens, in an area above the Agora, which in the fifth century could accommodate between six thousand and thirteen thousand people (Figure 2.1). In the fifth century, a mass of citizens sat in the natural theater formed by the slope of the Pnyx facing downhill toward the speaker's platform, the *bēma*.[43] Athens was hardly alone in holding citizen assemblies: As we saw in the previous chapter, this had been a regular feature of the Greek *poleis* since Archaic times, as numerous literary sources and inscribed laws attest.[44] Where the Athenian and other democracies differed was in broadening the scope of the assembly's power and its constitutional authority. As we saw in the last chapter, decisions of the Spartan assembly, for example, could be vetoed by its elders and kings, a substantial check on the power of the people there; the Athenian *ekklēsia* had no such stricture. Its decisions were carried by a simple majority show of hands, the only precondition being that agenda items had been set for debate by the Council (on which more in a moment). It is unsurprising that at Athens and elsewhere the assembly was often simply called the *dēmos*, since it represented – if it was not strictly speaking coterminous with – the citizen

---

[40] Lambert 1993. [41] Kierstead 2019.
[42] Hansen 1983, 1989. In the later fourth century the two years before age twenty would be taken up by service in the youth training program, or *ephebeia*: [Arist.] *Ath. Pol.* 42.2–5. On Athenian and other ephebates see Chapter 3.2.
[43] Shear 2011: 177–78. [44] Simonton 2017: 11–20.

Figure 2.1 The Pnyx. (Photo: Miguel Sotomayor / Getty Images).

body as a whole, in its decision-making capacity.[45] As the Framers of the United States Constitution recognized, the presence of a citizen assembly was perhaps the defining characteristic of an ancient-style, direct democracy. The author of *Federalist* 63 claims that the true distinction between ancient and modern self-government "lies in the total exclusion of the people, in their collective capacity, from any share in the latter"; Americans instead allow themselves to be governed by their representatives.[46]

What would one see and hear at the Athenian assembly? We overlook much of what made ancient democracy distinct if we neglect the ritual aspects of these meetings. At Athens, a session began with an official named the *peristiarchos* carrying a sacrificed piglet around the space in an act of purification.[47] The herald (*kēryx*) of the assembly then offered a customary prayer soliciting the gods' aid and cursing tyrants and anyone plotting with the Persians – a custom so old-fashioned by the 410s that Aristophanes could poke fun at it as being obsolete.[48] Agenda items previously

---

[45] Simonton 2021. On this "representative" aspect of ancient democratic assembly meetings, see below, Excursus.
[46] Hamilton, Madison, and Jay 2014: no. 63.
[47] Ar. *Ecc.* 128; Aeschin. 1.23; Istros *BNJ* 334 F 16.
[48] Aeschin. 1.23; Dem. 19.70; Ar. *Thesm.* 295–351 with *Vesp.* 488–99 and Raaflaub 2003.

deliberated on by the Council (*probouleumata*) were then presented to the assembly by the presiding officers (*prytaneis*), who were current members of the Council.[49] *Probouleumata* were of two main types, open and closed, the former ones in which the Council staked no particular position on a question but left it to the assembly to debate, the latter ones in which the Council declared a firm opinion in advance. It was possible through a procedure known as *procheirotonia* or a preliminary vote for the assembly to approve closed *proboulemata* with no debate if they garnered unanimous consent. The great historian of the Athenian democracy P. J. Rhodes estimated that roughly half of all fourth-century decisions were made this way.[50] Thus while we tend to think of the assembly as a prime example of ancient Greek talkativeness, some of its business was carried out in silence.

Nevertheless, debate was of course a major feature of Athenian and other democratic assemblies, and it could be ferocious. All open *proboulemata* and any closed ones that had been rejected required comment. At Athens the herald recognized those who desired to address the assembly; his opening question was simply, "Who wishes to speak?"[51] The open-ended nature of the question, tacitly acknowledging that any male citizen who wanted could come forward (see Section 2.4.1 on the importance of *isēgoria*), indicates the lack of agenda control on the part of the elite at Athens and the concomitant democratization of deliberative authority. It seems that in oligarchies – or at least, in those that permitted popular assemblies of any sort – it was typically an official, and therefore a member of the ruling class, that addressed the *ekklēsia*, with popular feedback prohibited.[52] In the Athenian democracy, by contrast, it was a conversation among the People. The sitting generals and other military officials might naturally be turned to on matters of war, but although they enjoyed some forms of procedural priority, they did not have agenda-setting abilities or veto power over debate.[53]

And the speakers might indeed originate from the non-elite: Plato's Socrates claims that when the Athenians deliberate about the administration of the *polis*, the man who stands up and advises his fellow citizens might equally be a blacksmith or a cobbler, a merchant or a ship captain, a man of illustrious or obscure birth.[54] By the same token, the audience

---

[49] In the fourth century the role played by the fifth-century *prytaneis* fell to the *proedroi* or chairmen, one from each of the nine tribes not currently serving as *prytaneis*: [Arist.] *Ath. Pol.* 44.2–3.
[50] Rhodes 1972: 68–81.   [51] Ar. *Ach.* 45, *Eccl.* 130; Dem. 18.170.   [52] Aeschin. 3.220.
[53] For deference toward the generals, see OR 150, ll. 54–56; OR 162, l. 5.   [54] Plat. *Prot.* 319d.

was socially diverse, with poorer men predominating. Once again, Socrates – in Xenophon's depiction this time – provides us with evidence, along with some editorializing. "Who are you ashamed of speaking before?" he asks a young protégé. "Fullers and leatherworkers? Builders and smiths and farmers? Those bartering goods in the Agora and calculating how they can buy cheap and sell dear? For the assembly is composed of all these sorts of men." And they, Socrates adds, constitute "the least intelligent and least powerful."[55] The critics' dismissiveness notwithstanding, these common men might let their displeasure at what was being proposed be known, with a silencing effect, through *thorubos*, raising a ruckus at the speaker. Such outbursts could hardly be controlled by the presiding officials and often led politicians to change their tune lest they be heckled off the speaker's platform. Frequently criticized by earlier generations of historians as an expression of pure mob rule, *thorubos* has come to be recognized as a democratic mechanism that empowered average assembly goers and steered speakers toward proposals that commanded the greatest level of consensus.[56]

In any case, it is not as though the average members of the assembly, by dint of their shared class position alone, necessarily held identical opinions about policy. Nor did speakers simply tell the audience *qua dēmos* what "it" wanted to hear, despite what Plato has Socrates say to a habitual speechifier: "In the assembly, if, when you are speaking, the *dēmos* of Athens says it is not of that opinion, changing course you say what it wishes."[57] The assembled crowd was not a monolith, and the articulation of a democratic will required a dialogical process of back-and-forth false starts and compromises. All the same, *thorubos* remained a powerful tool in the hands (or rather, the throats) of non-elite Athenians. It disciplined men who often thought themselves superior to their lower-class citizen counterparts. As a mere eighteen-year-old, our hypothetical Athenian would probably not have put himself forward as a speaker – although the ambitious Alcibiades son of Cleinias, for one, had few scruples about entering politics in his twenties – but he could have felt comfortable joining in the heckling.[58]

---

[55] Xen. *Mem.* 3.7.5–6. [56] Tacon 2001; Villacèque 2013a; Canevaro 2019.
[57] Plat. *Gorg.* 481e; cf. *Rep.* 6.492c and the echo of this passage in Dio Chrys. 34.31, writing in the first century CE: discussion in Chapter 4.5.
[58] Alcibiades' youth: Thuc. 5.43.2. Cf. Xen. *Mem.* 3.6.1: Glaucon wishes to be leader despite not being twenty yet.

2.3 A Life Cycle of Political Institutions in Democratic Athens

2.3.3 Political Leadership: The Rhētores

Strictly speaking, any male citizen in good standing was allowed to address the assembly, and the rate at which average citizens availed themselves of this right appears to have been considerable.[59] There developed, however, a de facto cohort of regular speakers who, while holding no official title, constituted the political leadership class of the democracy: the *rhētores* (singular: *rhētōr*). Experienced (sometimes formally trained) in persuasive speech, they attempted to scale the greasy pole of politics at Athens with little more than their words to aid them. Their preeminence in the assembly could be fleeting, only as secure as their last successful proposal.[60] Unfortunately, we have very few contemporary testimonials of what these speakers were like prior to the Peloponnesian War.[61] The aforementioned Pericles' skills were formidable: He is said "alone of the *rhētores* to have enchanted his listeners and left behind a sting in them"; on other occasions his thunderous authority earned him the sobriquet "Olympian."[62] Pericles was the rare politician whose ascendancy was unshaken for a relatively long period of time. Elected one of Athens' ten generals fifteen straight times between 444/3 and 430/29, he was also the foremost speaker in the *ekklēsia*, and his policies were generally followed.[63] But again, he did not run a "government": His proposals had to find approval with a majority of assembly goers in every instance.[64]

After Pericles' death from the plague in 429, our sources have very few good things to say about the next generation of *rhētores*.[65] Cleon the son of Cleaenetus of the deme Cydathenaeum in particular is assailed as a liar, thief, slanderer, and conspiracymonger; his snobbish detractors threw in that he couldn't be considered a proper, landed gentleman because he engaged in commerce (he owned a successful

---

[59] Barbato 2023.
[60] *Rhētores*: Ober 1989; Yunis 1996. On rhetorical training by so-called sophists see Robinson 2011: 210–16. The ability to speak well was considered especially important in a democracy: Ant. fr. 1a.1–17 Nicole; Vassallo 2013 (republishing a fragmentary Socratic dialogue on papyrus). The *rhētores* on the whole could afford to participate in politics full-time – i.e., they were wealthy.
[61] Contemporary sources include Ion of Chios (*BNJ* 392) and Stesimbrotus of Thasos (*BNJ* 107), discussed in the previous chapter.
[62] Eup. fr. 102 K–A; Ar. *Ach.* 530 with Azoulay 2014a: ch. 3.
[63] Plut. *Vit. Per.* 16.3. On Pericles' life and career, see Azoulay 2014a; Martin 2016; Samons 2016; and review by Simonton 2018c.
[64] Contrast Thucydides' famous statement that under Pericles Athens was "nominally a democracy, but in reality the rule by the foremost man" (2.65.9) – an exaggeration.
[65] On Athenian political leadership in the later fifth century, see Finley 2019: ch. 2; Connor 1992; Mann 2007; Rhodes 2016. For ancient critical assessments see Thuc. 2.65.10–11; [Arist.] *Ath. Pol.* 28.1–3.

slave-staffed tannery).[66] Nipping at Cleon's heels were other would-be "champions [*prostatai*] of the People," similar in style: Hyperbolus "the lamp-maker," Cleophon "the lyre-seller," Lysicles "the sheep-dealer," and various other (supposedly) unsavory types.[67] Concurrent with the emergence of these men, it seems, comes the first appearance of a word that would haunt the subsequent history of democracy: "demagogue." *Dēmagōgos* is neutral in its literal meaning, signifying simply a leader of the people. Almost immediately, however, it took on a negative coloring, implying one who *mis*leads the *dēmos*. To democracy's opponents, the system was so based on ignorance, vice, and prejudice that it could only ever devolve into screaming matches among contending demagogues, each one willing to go lower than the next if it meant winning the support of the "mob" – and each one equally ready to parlay that popular mandate into a tyranny should the opportunity arise.[68]

Demagogues really could destabilize democracies, mainly by precipitating violent oligarchic reaction on the part of a city's elite. We will return to the danger of demagoguery in the following chapter, where it will become apparent just how ubiquitous it was in the democratic cities of ancient Greece. For now it is worth bearing several factors in mind, in particular as regards the most famous crop of demagogues, those of Classical Athens.[69] First, our picture of them comes almost exclusively from two problematic sources: the historian Thucydides, whose admiration for Pericles and contempt for Cleon are explicit, and the Old Comic poets (Aristophanes, but also, in fragmentary form, Cratinus, Eupolis, Plato Comicus, and others), whose currency was satire and vitriol.[70] We have little sense of the actual speaking styles of the demagogues or of their sources of appeal, which were considerable.

---

[66] [Arist.] *Ath. Pol.* 28.3 and Ar. *Eq.* with Lafargue 2013; Saldutti 2014. Cleon appears as a villain in the 2018 Ubisoft video game *Assassin's Creed Odyssey*, spouting the not-so-subtle slogan "Make Athens Great Again."

[67] See the discussion by Rosenbloom 2004. For a recent defense of these figures see Lafargue 2022, but the tradition goes back to the British liberal historian George Grote (1794–1871): Kierstead 2014.

[68] On demagogue and demagoguery see Saldutti 2015; Caire 2019. On demagoguery and tyranny, see the pronouncement of the great nineteenth-century Swiss cultural historian Jacob Burckhardt: "[I]n every talented and ambitious Greek dwelt a tyrant and a demagogue" (2013 [1898]: 56).

[69] We read of demagogues from multiple other Greek *poleis*, however: from Mantinea, "grievous" to the elite (Xen. *Hell.* 5.2.7); from Syracuse (Diod. Sic. 11.87.5, 13.34.6); and from Argos (Diod. Sic. 15.57.3–58). Elsewhere they might be known as the *prostatai tou dēmou* (champions of the People): at Corcyra (Thuc. 3.70.3, 4.46.4; Aen. Tact. 11.15); Megara (Thuc. 4.66.3); Syracuse (Thuc. 6.35.2); Elis (Xen. *Hell.* 3.2.27); Argos (Aen. Tact. 11.7); and Heraclea Pontica (Aen. Tact. 11.10b).

[70] Thuc. 2.65.8–9, 5.16.1. On the politics of Old Comedy, a vast subject, I agree most with those who see the comic poets as conservative and opposed to the demagogues: see Sommerstein 1996; Cartledge 2020.

Second, standing up for the People's interests, however defined, could be a dangerous business: There were men who hated to see the democracy succeed, and indeed of the aforementioned leaders, Hyperbolus and Cleophon were murdered by oligarchic conspirators, as was a third "champion," Androcles.[71]

Third, despite worries about demagogues becoming tyrants, their competition and turnover rate were such that they were rarely prominent long enough to consolidate personal power. The eighteenth-century Swiss philosopher Jean-Jacques Rousseau, typically considered one of modernity's most radical democrats, actually denied the label "democracy" to Classical Athens, which he deemed a "very tyrannical aristocracy, governed by philosophers and orators."[72] While orators no doubt played an indispensable role in the Athenian democracy, it would be wrong to think they dominated it. They were as much governed by their audiences as they governed them.

Fourth, while Thucydides' narrative has suggested to some that the period of the "bad Athenian demagogue" lasted only until the end of the Peloponnesian War, the type clearly persists into the fourth century in men like Cephalus, Agyrrhius, Epicrates, and Callistratus. According to the Aristotelian *Constitution of the Athenians*, down to the author's time "popular leadership [*dēmagōgia*] has been handed down among those most willing to be over-bold and to please *hoi polloi* with an eye towards immediate gain." Demagogues were thus more mundane and less an existential threat than we might at first believe.[73]

And finally, it is difficult to conceive on what normative grounds a people in a democracy could be prohibited from choosing whatever leadership they wish. The twentieth-century American critic and satirist H. L. Mencken once wrote that "democracy is the theory that the common people know what they want and deserve to get it good and hard."[74] Elitism aside, there is truth to the idea that a democratic people must live with the results of their free choices; in the Athenians' case, their collective wisdom, and not a little good fortune – attributed by the comic poets to an almost irrational favoritism on the part of the gods – meant that, most of the time, the system worked out for them.[75]

---

[71] Thuc. 8.65.2, 73.3; Lys. 13.12. We know of oligarchic assassination attempts (some successful) on democratic leaders from Elis (Xen. *Hell.* 3.2.27), Megara (Thuc. 4.74.3), and the Arcadian League (Xen. *Hell.* 7.4.3), as well. See further Simonton 2017: 114–18, and later examples in Chapter 3.5.
[72] Rousseau 1973: 122.
[73] [Arist.] *Ath. Pol.* 28.4; cf. Theopompus *BNJ* 115 FF 85–100; Idomeneus *BNJ* 338 FF 2, 11–15 for fourth-century Athenian demagogues, and see Simonton 2022: 45–46.
[74] Mencken 1916: 19.   [75] The gods' favor: Ar. *Nub.* 588–89, *Ecc.* 473–75; cf. Dem. 19.256.

2.3.4 Military Service, Liturgies, and Status Distinctions

A young man in his twenties in Athens was not yet eligible to hold a magistracy, but he did not lack for opportunities to interact further with the city's political institutions. From age eighteen to fifty-nine he was liable for military service. If he was wealthy enough to equip himself as a hoplite, in the fifth century he might be conscripted through one of several lists (*katalogoi*) drawn up by the city's military officials (we see once again the lack of a centralized bureaucratic register).[76] As we learn from Aristophanic comedy, lists were posted beneath the statues of the tribal Eponymous Heroes in the Agora, ten in total.[77] Poorer men could offer to row in the empire's fleet, where they would have toiled alongside enslaved men and metics.[78] All military positions were paid in the Athenian democracy, at tremendous cost.[79] If wounded in battle to the point where he was unable to work, or if a man had a disability that prevented him from laboring for a living, he could apply to the Council for a small pension. While more generous than nothing, it would not have guaranteed an easy existence.[80]

At the other end of the economic spectrum, a young man from a wealthy family who came into his inheritance might have to pay so-called liturgies, *leitourgiai* or "works for the people" (from *leōs*, the Attic equivalent of the Homeric *laos* or "host"). These were personal expenses, falling exclusively on the wealthy, that paid for certain public goods, of which two were the most onerous: the equipping of a trireme and the financing of a festival chorus (on which see Section 2.3.5). While an opportunity for amassing personal prestige, liturgies were mandatory, and, along with direct taxes like the so-called *eisphora*, they amounted to a form of economic redistribution within the city.[81] Elites might buckle under them to the point of revolt.[82] Regardless of his wealth, daily life would also have driven home to our hypothetical citizen the vast gulf between status groups in the city – after all, the maintenance of existing property relations and status

---

[76] Christ 2001. [77] Ar. *Pax* 1183–84. [78] Strauss 1996.
[79] Gabrielsen 1994; Pritchard 2015: ch. 4.
[80] [Arist.] *Ath. Pol.* 49.4; Lys. 24 with Rose 2017. There was also what was perhaps a welfare fund in the form of the *diōbelia* or "two-obol payment": Blok 2015. For wealth, poverty, and public services in Classical Athens see Taylor 2017, exploring previous analyses of Athens' distribution of property in Ober 2010 and Kron 2011.
[81] Whitehad 1983; Wilson 2000; Christ 2007; Fawcett 2016; Keim 2018. Athens' liturgical class numbered twelve hundred male citizens in the fourth century, or 4 percent of a total of thirty thousand.
[82] Thuc. 8.48.1, 63.4; cf. Theophr. *Char.* 26.5.

2.3 A Life Cycle of Political Institutions in Democratic Athens

distinctions (including, crucially, enslavement) is one of the most political institutions there is.[83] The man would learn that while free men and enslaved sometimes worked side by side and even earned similar rates of pay, the city's laws punished the former with fines, the latter with corporal punishment in the form of repeated lashings.[84] Not only enslaved people, but also the city's resident foreigners (metics) were liable to torture during judicial proceedings, while the citizen body (physical as well as metaphorical) was considered inviolate.[85] We will explore the issue of the democratic citizen's honor, or *timē*, in greater detail shortly.

2.3.5 Public Cult

At the very blurry boundary between politics and culture in Athens were the city's religious festivals. Any public ritual, as both a model of and a model for a community's ideal ordering of itself, is inherently political, but Athens' festivals were even more political than this.[86] First, there was their connection with imperial power. At the City Dionysia every spring, the city literally put on display its blood and treasure: The sons of those who had died in war, maintained at public expense until they reached the age of majority, were paraded in the theater in arms, while the tribute of the empire, extracted from Athens' subjects, was similarly exhibited, talent by talent.[87] Second, the production of festivals, as a liturgy (see Section 2.3.4), meant that they represented yet another form of transfer from the wealthy to the community as a whole. The critic known as the Old Oligarch grumbled that "the common people think they deserve to get paid for singing, running, dancing, and sailing in the fleet [note the conflation of festival and military liturgies], in order that they come to possess wealth and the rich grow poorer." Elsewhere he observed that the Athenians held more festivals than any other Greek city.[88] For some, Athens' cultural production, today considered a milestone in the history of the arts, was a tax at the expense of the wealthy. Third, religious rituals constituted one

---

[83] On status in Athens see Kamen 2013; Davies 2017.
[84] RO 25, ll. 30–32. For slaves and free working side by side see Vlassopoulos 2007 and Sobak 2015, with comments by Canevaro 2018a: 102.
[85] Akrigg 2019: 134.
[86] On this view of ritual see Christesen 2012: 221. For the debate on the political nature of Athens' festivals, particularly the Dionysia, see Goldhill 1987; Rhodes 2003; Carter 2004a; Wilson 2009. On the Panathenaea see Shear 2021.
[87] Isoc. 8.82.   [88] [Xen.] *Ath. Pol.* 1.13, 3.2; cf. 2.9–10.

of the prime venues for the expression of citizenship by Athenian women. While they were barred from all forms of political decision-making (what Aristotle called *krisis* and *archē*, "judgment" and "office holding"; see next chapter), Athens' *politides*, its female citizens, played crucial roles in public cult.[89]

Finally, there was the actual content of the artistic output at festivals, particularly drama. Old Comedy, as we have seen, was thoroughly political.[90] Aristophanes' prize-winning entry at the winter Lenaea festival of 424, the *Knights*, brought on stage the personified Mr. Demos of Pnyx, a kind of Athenian John Q. Public. Demos, a "crotchety, half-deaf little old man," lets his household slaves, including one purchased from faraway Paphlagonia (a parody of the politician Cleon), compete sycophantically for his favor in a domestic allegory of public life.[91] In a fanciful conclusion, Demos, magically restored to his state from the earlier fifth century (the "good old days"), vows to put aside demagogues and war and enjoy some much-deserved peace. The comic stage was clearly a forum for thinking through pressing public issues. But tragedy could be no less topical. In his *Suppliant Women* of 423, Euripides has a character inveigh – anachronistically, since he is supposed to inhabit the mythological Greek past – against the flaws of democracy, including the demagogue who,

> puffing up his audience with speeches, twists things this way and that for his personal profit, at one point pleasant to them and providing much delight, then in turn harming them; then with fresh slanders he conceals his previous faults and evades justice.[92]

As he cheered and booed as he saw fit – as in politics, audiences in ancient Greek drama did not tend to sit in polite silence – our young Athenian would have further learned how to think and speak about democratic citizenship.[93]

2.3.6 *The* Epitaphios Logos

Another important political ritual a young man might attend was the annual public burial of the war dead and the pronouncement of a funeral oration (*epitaphios logos*) over the grave by a leading citizen. Thucydides tells us that this was an "ancestral custom" (*patrios nomos*) of the

---

[89] Blok 2017. [90] Harvey, Wilkins, and Dover 2000; Rosen and Foley 2020.
[91] Quotation: Ar. *Eq.* 42–43. [92] Eur. *Suppl.* 412–16.
[93] For more on the theater and democracy, see Winkler and Zeitlin 1990; Roselli 2011; Villacèque 2013b.

2.3 A Life Cycle of Political Institutions in Democratic Athens 59

Athenians, but it was one that probably went back only to the earlier fifth century.[94] In exchange for dying in war on behalf of his *polis*, the Athenian democracy buried a man at public expense and reared his children (now considered orphans once their father was dead) to adulthood, as we saw. The public cemetery of the city, the *dēmosion sēma*, was located in the Kerameikos neighborhood or Potters' Quarters located northwest of the Classical Agora; many private grave monuments have been excavated there as well.[95] The dead were memorialized in casualty lists drawn up tribe by tribe, several of which have survived to the present day. Except for the military officers, no distinctions are drawn among the dead, not even their patronymics; thus, in one list, there is no way to distinguish two men, both named Lysias, listed six lines apart. Such was the somewhat anonymizing price one paid for a collective public burial (Figure 2.2).[96]

The Athenians, Thucydides says, choose on each occasion a man "who would appear to be not unintelligent in judgment and foremost in estimation" to deliver the eulogy.[97] The funeral oration Thucydides attributes to Pericles, delivered in the winter of 431/0 at the conclusion of the first year of the Peloponnesian War, is the single most famous statement about the Athenian democracy that has come down to us from antiquity.[98] What we have to remember, which would have been taken for granted by our young man, especially as life went on and he experienced additional years of war, is that such *epitaphioi logoi* were delivered on numerous occasions. Six have survived in whole or in part, some mere rhetorical exercises, however, and one, contained in the dialogue *Menexenus* by Plato, a rather cutting parody.[99] The vast majority that were pronounced have been lost to us. As numerous scholars have recognized, the funeral oration was an opportunity for a leading citizen to articulate a vision of the city and its values, thereby instilling a collective sense of civic identity and social memory among the Athenians.[100] Although they were ideologically colored and factually distorted

---

[94] Thuc. 2.34.1 with Clairmont 1983.   [95] Arrington 2015.
[96] *IG* I³ 1147, ll. 93, 99. The Athenians granted the democratic Argives a similar casualty list after the Battle of Tanagra in 457 (ML 35 with a new fragment published by Papazarkadas and Sourlas 2012, who discuss the democratic aspects; OR 111 is a combined edition), and the Argives continued the practice themselves down through the fifth century: *SEG* 29.361. Casualty lists were not limited to democratic regimes (Low 2003), but the absence of patronymics in Athenian and Argive lists is a democratic feature.
[97] Thuc. 2.34.6.   [98] Thuc. 2.35–46.
[99] They are: that of Thucydides; Gorgias DK 82 B 6; Lys. 2; Plat. *Menex.*; Dem. 60; Hyp. 6.
[100] Loraux 1986; Steinbock 2013: 49–58; Barbato 2020: 58–66; Pritchard 2024.

Figure 2.2 Casualty list IG I³ 1147. (Photo: Lanmas / Alamy).

(see Section 2.4.1 on the myth of autochthony), few would question the historical value of the speeches for understanding Athenian society; one might compare the State of the Union address delivered annually by the president to the United States Congress. Athens seems to have been unique in offering funeral orations, but as we will see in the next chapter, it was considered good democratic practice throughout the Greek world to bury the war dead at public expense and support their children.

2.3 A Life Cycle of Political Institutions in Democratic Athens

2.3.7 The Council and the Other Magistracies

At age thirty, an Athenian man was now eligible to hold a magistracy (*archē*, also the word for "rule" more generally).[101] Although the assembly and other massed bodies of average citizens (see Section 2.3.8) held sovereignty in Athens, in the sense of unappealable authority, the officeholders were the closest thing to its "government," with the power of command – to varying degrees – over fellow citizens. For the Greeks in general, historically quite suspicious of power, the question of who would exercise it and how it would be apportioned occupied no small part of their constitutional thinking; the answers the various cities came up with often meant the difference between democracy and oligarchy. Oligarchic regimes, says Plato's Socrates, set "an amount of property, greater where the constitution is more oligarchic, less where it is less so, and they decree that he is not to partake of the magistracies whose property does not equal the stated requirement."[102] In oligarchies, in other words, one portion of the citizenry – the wealthy – did all the ruling, while the other was permanently ruled. In democracies, by contrast, the *politeuma* – that is, the circle of the citizenry that was eligible for office holding – comprised the entire *dēmos*.[103] There could be occasional exceptions – treasurers in Athens, for example, were supposed to belong to the highest Solonian property class (although this stricture became a dead letter) – but the major offices were supposed to have low or nonexistent property requirements.

This basic setup tells us *who* could rule, but not necessarily *how* they came to occupy office. Most famously in Athens, but also in other democracies, the majority of magistracies were distributed randomly, by lottery (also called sortition), rather than by election.[104] It was not mandatory, as in modern jury duty; instead, citizens put forward their names, which were then selected by some mechanism (at Athens it was the drawing of a white bean rather than a black one).[105] Hundreds of offices were apportioned in this fashion every year in Athens, but we know other *poleis* had similar arrangements. The democratic constitution of Erythrae in Ionia, mandated by a decree of the Athenian Empire in (perhaps) the late 450s, specified that the city's council was to consist of one hundred and twenty men over the age of thirty selected by lot (the bean again).[106] The

---

[101] See already the discussion of magistracies in Chapter 1.4.   [102] Plat. *Rep.* 8.551b.
[103] Simonton 2017: 40.
[104] See Sintomer 2023 for a history of this political mechanism and Malkin and Blok 2024 for its history in Archaic and Classical Greece.
[105] The bean: Hdt. 6.109.2; Thuc. 8.66.1; Ar. *Av.* 1022; *Dissoi Logoi* DK 90 B 7; Xen. *Mem.* 1.2.9; [Arist.] *Ath. Pol.* 24.3.
[106] OR 121, l. 9. Papazarkadas 2009: 78 suggests a date of the 420s rather than the 450s.

prevalence of sortition in democracies meant the two came to be closely associated. In one of our earliest descriptions of democracy, in Herodotus, we read that where the majority rules, offices are distributed by lot; numerous subsequent authors speak of democracies in a similar way.[107] Certainly selection by lottery was the most democratic mechanism available, but it was not a necessary condition for democracy, nor was it used exclusively by popular regimes. Oligarchies could also distribute offices by lottery, just among the wealthy elite alone, and elections were considered democratic so long as every citizen was eligible for office and the entire *dēmos* did the electing.[108] (We will see several examples of election in democracies in the following chapter, although sortitive offices persist.)

Some sources even questioned, if rather sophistically, the democratic bona fides of sortition. An anonymous treatise known as the *Dissoi Logoi* or Double Arguments, for example, composed around 400 BCE, observes that while the lottery is considered impeccably democratic, in fact in all of the cities of Greece there are men who despise the common people (are *misodēmoi*, "People haters"). If such men are elected by lot for office, they will dissolve the democratic constitution from within. The author proposes that the People should elect officials known to be loyal to democracy.[109] His hypothetical outcome does not seem to have occurred in reality, since, as we will see in the discussion of ideology, sortition tended to increase the number of people in government who were prodemocratic. If anything, the adoption of sortitive offices was thought to deepen existing democracy, as when a politician named Diocles convinced the Syracusan *dēmos* to select their officials by lottery in 412/11 BCE.[110]

At Athens one of the most important magistracies was membership on the Council (*boulē*).[111] As we saw in Chapter 1, councils were a common feature of ancient Greek constitutions stretching back to the Archaic period. The *gerousia* or council of elders of Sparta is a prime example, but Solonian Athens probably had its own Council of Four Hundred (with one hundred men drawn from each of the four pre-Cleisthenic tribes).[112] Councils throughout the Greek world had as one of their primary tasks the formulation of recommendations to be introduced to the popular assembly; as noted in the previous chapter, we call this process *probouleusis*, or "deliberation in advance," resulting in *probouleumata*.[113]

---

[107] Hdt. 3.80.6; cf. Plat. *Rep.* 8.557a; Arist. *Rhet.* 1.1365b32.
[108] Oligarchic sortition: Simonton 2017: 39. [109] DK 90 B 7; cf. Isoc. 7.26.
[110] Diod. Sic. 13.34.6 with Arist. *Pol.* 5.1304a27-29. [111] Rhodes 1972. [112] [Arist.] *Ath. Pol.* 8.4.
[113] Andrewes 1954; de Laix 1973; Esu 2017.

2.3 A Life Cycle of Political Institutions in Democratic Athens 63

At Athens the character of the Council was democratic insofar as it was meant to be a sort of *polis* in miniature whose members constituted a representative cross-section of the city.[114] This representation was not only geographic (through the bouleutic quotas of the different demes, discussed in the previous chapter) but socioeconomic as well: the stricture that no one could be a councilor for more than two nonconsecutive terms of one year each, combined with regular payment (*misthos*) for office holding after the mid-fifth century BCE, meant that councilors necessarily came from a wide swath of the citizenry and not primarily from the wealthy elite.[115] (On the ideological coloring of *misthos* see Section 2.4.4.) Democratic councils, therefore, were intended to be one more venue for the involvement of the *dēmos* as a whole and not, as in the Roman Senate or in the Greek *boulai* of the Imperial Period (see Chapter 4.4), the exclusive preserve of an elite. *Probouleusis* was, however, a limitation on the power of the assembly, since there was a law at Athens and elsewhere that nothing could be discussed in meetings of the *ekklēsia* that was *aprobouleutos*, not deliberated on in advance by the Council; this constraint prevented ambitious *rhētores* from simply saying what they thought would be most popular on any given occasion, no matter how unconnected with current agenda items.[116] The Council had many other duties as well, and its standing committee, which slept for a third of a given tribe's prytany in the Tholos building in the Agora, served as a kind of round-the-clock guard for the city.[117]

Membership on the Council was not the only magistracy, however: Athens had hundreds, from the ten commissioners of the Agora (*agoranomoi*) to the ten commissioners of the city (*astynomoi*, whence the modern Greek word for police) to the eleven administrators of the prison. As becomes readily apparent, officeholders tended to serve on boards rather than singly, one from each of Athens' ten tribes.[118] Almost all of these offices were sortitive – the main exception were the military offices, which

---

[114] Schol. ad. Aeschin. 3.4 with Hamon 2001.
[115] [Arist.] *Ath. Pol.* 62.2 with Taylor 2007. In other democratic *poleis* some offices' terms were only six months, as at Argos (Kritzas 2006: 421 [see further below]), and see the example of Rhodes, discussed in the following chapter. Aristotle thought six-month terms were especially democratic: *Pol.* 5.1308a14–16.
[116] [Arist.] *Ath. Pol.* 45.4; Dem. 22 with Giannadaki 2020. For a complaint that demagogues violated this norm and introduced decrees not deliberated on advance in a context as late as the second century CE, see Chapter 4.5, discussing Dio Chrys. 56.10.
[117] [Arist.] *Ath. Pol.* 44.1.
[118] Theophrastus' Oligarchic Man, by contrast, prefers there be just a single magistrate, "provided he is a real man" (*Char.* 26.2).

were elected from all the citizenry by the assembled *dēmos* in special sessions of the *ekklēsia*.[119] Detractors of democracy like the Old Oligarch sneered that this was a matter of the *dēmos* exempting itself from offices that brought more risk than profit, and it is true that elected officials tended to come from the elite.[120] But the main consideration was that these offices required skills crucial to the city's existential survival, and while the socioeconomically privileged did predominate among them, the lack of property requirements attached to them allowed poorer but meritorious individuals like Iphicrates of the deme Rhamnous (the son of a shoemaker) to ascend their ranks. In fact, Aristotle's pupil Theophrastus cited Iphicrates as an example of why property requirements for military office were old-fashioned, since they would exclude many people qualified to serve their *polis*.[121] Furthermore, although an influential line of modern argument, basing itself on the Greek example, views election as inherently aristocratic and sortition as the truly democratic selection mechanism,[122] competition for elective office in Athens could be fierce, with candidates making all sorts of populist claims to get a leg up on their rivals. It is unsurprising when Aristotle notes that where offices are elective, with no property requirements, and the *dēmos* does the electing, those eager to hold office will "play the demagogue" to the masses during their electoral campaigns.[123]

It might be useful here to introduce the evidence of another democracy of the period, that of Argos, as a point of comparison.[124] The workings of its institutions have been further clarified recently through the discovery and decipherment of inscribed bronze tablets from the sacred treasury of Athena, which probably served as the state treasury; the texts have yet to be published in full.[125] Argos had a citizen assembly, the *halia* (the Doric equivalent of *ekklēsia*), open to all adult male citizens, as well as a council (*bōla*) of indeterminate number but with representation from the city's four tribes.[126] The bronze tablets have revealed to us the existence of eight

---

[119] [Arist.] *Ath. Pol.* 61.1.   [120] [Xen.] *Ath. Pol.* 1.3 with Taylor 2007: 338.
[121] Keaney and Szegedy-Maszak 1976.
[122] On election as aristocratic, see most prominently Manin 1997. The thought goes back to Aristotle (*Pol.* 4.1294b7–9, where he is talking about tendencies, however, not hard and fast rules) and rests on the assumption that elections favor those who are already prominent in society.
[123] Arist. *Pol.* 5.1305a28–32 with Simonton 2025.   [124] Robinson 2011: 6–21; Piérart 2020.
[125] Kritzas 2006. The present author saw a fine exhibition of a selection of them, expertly annotated, at the Epigraphical Museum of Athens in the summer of 2022.
[126] Argos had originally used the three traditional Dorian tribes (Hylleis, Dymanes, and Pamphyloi), but after a democratic revolution of the earlier fifth century new citizens were enrolled in a fourth tribe, the Hyrnathioi: see Piérart 2020: 114, 124–25.

2.3 A Life Cycle of Political Institutions in Democratic Athens

sunepignōmones ("fellow arbiters"), two from each tribe, who dealt with state revenues. There was a further Council of Eighty, attested in Thucydides, probably twenty men from each tribe, that had judicial and economic authority in some matters.[127] In one of the bronze plaques we see these Eighty and a board of officials called the *artynai* withdraw several talents from money belonging to the goddess Hera "for the campaign in Corinth" – that is, the Corinthian War. The phrase *hai artynai* seems to have referred to the magistrates in office and is the equivalent of the Attic wording *hai archai*, "the magistracies." In some inscriptions representatives of the different boards of magistrates are listed as present, as we read of presiding officers of the council, of the Eighty, of the military officials called the polemarchs, and so on. The boards also had secretaries attached to them.[128] As mentioned, most of these magistrates were semestral, or limited to half the year, a good democratic measure.[129] The precise record-keeping exemplified by the bronze tablets shows that the Argive democracy no less than the Athenian wished to keep its finances in order and its magistrates honest. Unfortunately, we do not know whether officials were elected or allotted, and there is so far no evidence for payment for office (*misthos*). The six-month term limits, however, must have guaranteed constant fresh blood and high participation among the citizenry. Although Argos has been called a more moderate democracy when compared with Athens' "radical naval" variety, it was no less capable of producing demagogues and civil strife (see Section 2.5).[130]

2.3.8 The Law Courts

Reaching the age of thirty also opened the doors of the *dikastēria*, or law courts, to the male citizen of democratic Athens.[131] Again, the administration of justice was something central to all Greek *poleis* (as it is to nearly all societies), and not just to democracies. It is in its scope, powers, procedures, and participation rates that we find the specifically democratic aspects of Athenian justice. As with the *ekklēsia* and large-scale magistracies, the *dikastēria* were sites for the involvement of large, representative groups of citizens; the judges (*dikastai*) assembled in the courts could even be conceived of as the *dēmos* itself. Panels of judges ranged from several hundred to fifteen hundred for special cases. The panels for a given day

---

[127] Thuc. 5.47.1, where the council and the *artynai* are also mentioned.
[128] Kritzas 2006: 414–22.   [129] Kritzas 2006: 421.   [130] More moderate: Piérart 2020.
[131] Harrison 1968–71; MacDowell 1978; Todd 1993; Lanni 2006, 2016; Phillips 2013; Gagarin 2020.

of cases were established from a pool of six thousand potential judges, constituted by, once again, a sortitive procedure that involved a *klērōtērion* or randomization mechanism.¹³² The judges, sworn to a special judicial oath, heard arguments from the litigants involved, the prosecution speaking first. All documentary evidence was submitted in advance to a presiding official. There was a norm that judges should listen dispassionately to both sides before casting judgment, but *thorubos* could erupt in court no less than in the assembly.¹³³ As in the assembly too, persuasive speech was crucial. Although the venue had as its official aim truth and justice rather than what was beneficial for the city (it required "dicastic" as opposed to "symbouleutic" rhetoric),¹³⁴ those famous for their oratory, like the politician Demosthenes, often sold their skills as speechwriters (*logographoi*) to litigants, or they might speak as their supporters (*synēgoroi*) in court.¹³⁵ There were no professional lawyers, however, and a man was expected to speak on his own behalf – if he employed a logographer, he memorized the latter's composition ahead of time. If a litigant could not afford a speechwriter, he might have recourse to what today strikes us as a surprising tactic: magic. Binding spells (*defixiones*), known from numerous inscribed lead curse tablets, were often aimed at one's opponents in court. "I bind my enemy Demetrius, and Phanagora, in blood and ashes, with all the dead," states a recently published curse tablet from what the editor argues is a judicial context.¹³⁶

Speeches in the Athenian courts could be quite impassioned, with elements that strike the modern reader as extraneous or manipulative (but of course contemporary lawyers train in these techniques as well). Aristotle suggests that nondemocratic regimes conducted judicial proceedings differently: "Slander, pity, anger, and other such emotions of the soul have nothing to do with the judicial question but are meant for [affecting] the judge. Thus if in the case of all judgments it was like in some cities now – and particularly in those that are well-governed [*eunomoumenais*, places that employ *eunomia* or 'good order,' a byword for oligarchy] – the speakers would have nothing to say."¹³⁷ After listening to both sides, judges cast a secret ballot into a voting urn rather than employ show of hands; the ballots were counted, and the majority position prevailed. Verdicts of *dikastēria* were unappealable and could result in immediate punishment, which in some cases was also voted on by the judges. In Socrates' trial for

---

¹³² [Arist.] *Ath. Pol.* 24.3, 63–69.   ¹³³ Bers 1985.   ¹³⁴ Arist. *Rhet.* 1.1358b6–28.
¹³⁵ Rubinstein 2000.   ¹³⁶ Lamont 2023: 193. See also Papakonstantinou 2021.
¹³⁷ Arist. *Rhet.* 1.1354a16–21.

2.3 A Life Cycle of Political Institutions in Democratic Athens 67

impiety in 399, for example, his opponents successfully argued for the death penalty, while he claimed his "punishment" ought to be public maintenance for life, since by his lights he had benefited the city.[138]

If we are to believe Aristophanes, judges in the later fifth century tended to be older men, who sometimes supplemented whatever income they had in old age with a *dikastēs*' daily wage of a triobol, or half a drachma.[139] The comic poet satirically depicts them as irascible and prejudiced against wealthier litigants, and some critics charged that the law courts were nothing more than a vehicle for political persecution of men considered insufficiently democratic, or even an excuse for the *dēmos* to expropriate private wealth for public use.[140] The courts enjoyed a similar reputation in other democracies as well, as when the city of Phlius fined certain of its wealthy citizens for seeking aid from the Spartans; the latter considered the Phliasian *dēmos* to have committed hubris.[141] In Athens during the fifth century a category of litigator known as a sykophant arose (*sukophantēs*, literally "fig revealer," and different from our current understanding of sycophant as toady). This figure was said either to threaten wealthy men with frivolous lawsuits in order to extort hush money from them or to prosecute defendants they thought the common people would be biased against in order to amass political prestige.[142] The propensity for such lawsuits supposedly grew out of an old Solonian law that allowed a volunteer prosecutor, "whoever wished" (*ho boulomenos*), to take up the case of any other citizen.[143] "This city is unlivable thanks to the sykophants," says a figure in Theophrastus' collection of Athenian character types, tellingly labeled the Oligarchic Man.[144] Predictably, the oligarchic regime of the Thirty that came to power in 404 "abolished the political authority of the dikasts" and had many men accused of sykophancy put to death.[145] The system was revived with the restoration of democracy, however, and remained vibrant down through the fourth and third centuries (see next chapter).

---

[138] Plat. *Ap.* 36d. The reward of *sitēsis* or public maintenance was rare and confined to the city's main benefactors; Cleon may have been awarded it in 425: Ar. *Eq.* 280–81 with Domingo Gygax 2016: ch. 5 and Blok and van 't Wout 2018.
[139] Ar. *Vesp.* with [Arist.] *Ath. Pol.* 62.2.   [140] [Xen.] *Ath. Pol.* 1.13, 16–18.
[141] Xen. *Hell.* 5.3.13. On oligarchs' antipathy toward what they saw as the hubris of the lower classes, see Canevaro 2024.
[142] Christ 1998. Sykophants are known from other democracies: Syracuse (Diod. Sic. 11.87.5) and Tenos (Eupolis fr. 245), for example.
[143] [Arist.] *Ath. Pol.* 9.1.   [144] Theophr. *Char.* 26.5.
[145] [Arist.] *Ath. Pol.* 35.2; cf. Xen. *Hell.* 2.3.12.

2.3.9 Ostracism

If our hypothetical citizen were born at the very beginning of the period in question, following the passage of Pericles' Citizenship Law in 451/0, he would have been around thirty-five years old when the final Athenian ostracism was carried out around 416. The practice, however, would have technically remained on the books throughout his life, even if the Athenians did not avail themselves of it. *Ostrakismos* ("the use of *ostraka*," or potsherds) was supposedly devised by Cleisthenes and presented to the People as part of his package of reforms in 508/7, but it was first used twenty years later, in 488/7, and about fifteen times subsequently down to the late fifth century.[146] In the sixth of ten political periods or prytanies of the year, the *dēmos* voted in the assembly whether an ostracism was required; a simple majority vote sufficed.[147] Again, for the vast majority of years down to 416, and ever thereafter, the People voted no. The next two prytanies were spent, no doubt, with much campaigning for and against different prominent politicians. In the eighth prytany, the People assembled by tribe in the Agora and carried with them an inscribed potsherd (*ostrakon*) with the name of a citizen on it. These were deposited in the center of the Agora in an act of *ostrakophoria* and counted; a quorum of six thousand was required, and (it seems) whoever garnered a plurality of votes among those six thousand was ostracized. He had to leave Attica for ten years, although his property was left untouched, and he could continue to draw revenues from it. At the end of the ten years (if he had not died in the meantime) he was reincorporated into the community.[148]

The purpose of ostracism has been endlessly debated. Several ancient authors label it a safeguard against tyranny, and indeed the first person ostracized was Hipparchus the son of Charmus of the deme Collytus, who was a relative of the former tyrant Pisistratus. After an initial run of pro-Pisistratid figures, however, the *dēmos* switched to ostracizing prominent politicians: Xanthippus, the father of Pericles, in 485/4; Aristides the son of Lysimachus, "the Just," in 483/2; and Themistocles the son of Neocles in (probably) 471.[149] For one ostracism of the late 470s we actually possess most of the votes in the form of an enormous deposit of more than nine

---

[146] [Arist.] *Ath. Pol.* 22. [147] [Arist.] *Ath. Pol.* 43.5. For the prytanies, see previous chapter.
[148] Philoch. *BNJ* 328 F 30; Poll. *Onom.* 8.19.
[149] [Arist.] *Ath. Pol.* 22.4–8. For Aristides' ostracism, see the amusing anecdote (probably apocryphal) preserved at Plut. *Vit. Arist.* 7.5–6: Aristides helped an illiterate man, who was unaware he was speaking with Aristides, to write the latter's name on his potsherd. When asked why he was voting to ostracize Aristides, the man replied, "Because I'm sick of hearing him called 'The Just' all the time!" thus revealing his own pettiness and confirming that Aristides deserved the nickname.

2.3 A Life Cycle of Political Institutions in Democratic Athens 69

thousand *ostraka* found in the Kerameikos, painstakingly studied and published over a long process between 1966 and 2018.[150] Plutarch, looking back at the institution from a much later time period, thought that it arose from an envious leveling impulse on the part of the common people, who could not tolerate any single individual rising too high in prominence.[151]

Among modern scholars, for their part, some have speculated that ostracism aided in resolving disputes between two or more prominent elites that might otherwise end in civil strife. Others have thought it was the appropriation and domestication on the part of the *dēmos* of the tendency of Archaic aristocrats to violently drive their opponents into exile. A recent analysis emphasizes its ritualistic aspects.[152] All these arguments are plausible, and they have helped explicate a form of banishment that often appears arbitrary and even authoritarian from a modern point of view. The nineteenth-century Swiss liberal Benjamin Constant, for example, in a celebrated essay on "the liberty of the ancients compared with that of the moderns," noted that ostracism, "which appears to us, and rightly so, a revolting iniquity, proves that the individual was much more subservient to the supremacy of the social body in Athens, than he is in any of the free states of Europe today."[153] The rudimentary state of the centralized bureaucracy in Athens, however, meant that often physical removal was the surest way to prevent bloody social breakdown. It was also, uncontestably, a further example of the power the common people of Athens held over their leadership.

The excavated *ostraka* themselves are rare and crucial evidence for the *vox populi* or "voice of the people" of fifth-century Athens; they constitute a mass repository of non-elite voices from a very early period of the democracy's existence (Figure 2.3). They sometimes contain biting commentary against the "candidates": to take poor Themistocles alone, he is called "cheap" in one, "the recipient of anal sex" (*katapygōn*) in another. One sherd mysteriously asserts, "Themistocles from the deme Phrearrhioi, on account of honor [*timē*]."[154] In this regard *ostraka* served almost like contemporary "mean tweets" directed by average people against politicians and celebrities. Athenians also sometimes cast ballots for abstract concepts, in what was conceivably an act of attempted magical banishment: "hunger"

---

[150] Brenne 2018.
[151] Plut. *Vit. Arist.* 7.1–2. See also Heraclitus' criticisms of the Ephesians for exiling his friend (DK 22 B 121), discussed in the previous chapter.
[152] Ostwald 1988; Forsdyke 2005; Kosmin 2015; Wecowski 2023.   [153] Constant 1988: 316.
[154] Sickinger 2017: no. 38; *SEG* 46.80; Brenne 2018: no. 8463 with Barbato 2021.

Figure 2.3 Athenian ostraka. (Photo: Vita exclusive / Alamy).

(*limos*) appears several times, perhaps signaling the everyday anxieties of the average person.[155]

Controversy surrounding the final ostracism, that of the populist politician Hyperbolus the son of Antiphanes around 416, might also provide a glimpse of Athenian social attitudes and ideology. Supposedly, either Nicias or Alcibiades – two of Athens' most prominent generals and fierce opponents – was set to be expelled during this ostracism, but they colluded along with their followers to have Hyperbolus selected instead.[156] Thucydides, for his part, calls Hyperbolus a "wretched creature" and says he was ostracized, not due to fear of his power or prestige (perhaps normal grounds for ostracism), but because of his disgusting nature (*ponēria*) and the shame he brought on the city.[157] Whatever the reality, the Athenians never held an ostracism again, perhaps a sign that they had grown exasperated with the practice, which was no longer targeting the high-status men for whom it was devised. "He [Hyperbolus] has suffered things worthy of his ways," said Plato the Old Comic poet (not the philosopher), "but

---

[155] Kosmin 2015: 133.
[156] Plut. *Vit. Nic.* 11.3–4, *Vit. Alc.* 13.3–5. For the date, see Rosenbloom 2004, who argues, however, for 415.
[157] Thuc. 8.73.3, describing Hyperbolus' murder on Samos in 411 BCE. The historian Theopompus added that his corpse was tied up in a sack and cast into the sea (*BNJ* 115 F 96a), a ritual act.

unworthy of him and his tattoos; for ostracism was not invented for the sake of such individuals."[158] All the same, as has been mentioned, the Athenians of the fourth century continued to ask themselves in the sixth prytany if they desired an ostracism, always choosing no.

The Athenian variety of ostracism is the best known, but it was not the only instance. Ancient sources tell us that the Argives, Milesians, Megarians, and Syracusans carried out versions of ostracism, in the last case inscribing names on flower petals in a process called *petalismos* or "petalism"; inscribed *ostraka* have also been excavated at places as far flung as Cyrene in North Africa, Chersonesus on the Black Sea, and Naxos and Thurii in Magna Graecia.[159] We know that petalism was similarly discontinued by the Syracusans, albeit earlier than Athenian ostracism. The historian Diodorus Siculus, in an entry under the year 454/3 BCE, says that the threat of petalism caused the Syracusan elite to withdraw from political life, leading to an efflorescence of demagogues, sykophants, and civil strife. The Syracusans therefore rescinded the law and the problems ceased, at least for the moment.[160] Ostracism, petalism, and similar mechanisms thus appear to be rather controversial democratic measures that did not outlast the fifth century.

2.3.10 Retirement in the Deme

We now move to our hypothetical Athenian's golden years. He could of course continue to participate in the central political organs of the city as long as he lived. At age fifty-nine he would have become exempt from military service but compelled to serve for one year as an arbitrator (*diaitētēs*) in disputes concerning property valued at ten drachmas and above. Arbitrators tried to clear as many cases as possible by arriving at a settlement acceptable to both parties, although their judgments were not binding. Many low-level citizen disputes must have been settled this way, without recourse to a *dikastērion*.[161] Let us assume that after our man completed his service as arbitrator he decided, due to increasing mobility issues in his old age, that he would devote more time to the civic life of his deme. The demes had their own assemblies and officials, most notably the

---

[158] Plat. Com. fr. 203 K–A. The "tattoos" refer to the tattooing of slaves, since elites often denied that the demagogues were citizens, ascribing servile origins to them. Andocides claimed Hyperbolus' father was a tattooed slave working in the city's silver mint (fr. 5 Dalmeyda) – obviously false.
[159] Schol. ad Ar. *Eq.* 855; Diod. Sic. 11.87.3; Kosmin 2015: 122n 4 with archaeological bibliography.
[160] Diod. Sic. 11.87.3–6.   [161] [Arist.] *Ath. Pol.* 53.2–6 with Kapparis 2018: 225–27.

demarch or mayor, as well as local liturgies and festivals.[162] As with modern neighborhoods and suburbs, the demes could have particular (and peculiar) reputations: the demesmen of Aixone were said to be blasphemers, while the Potamians were mocked for welcoming illegally registered (and so fraudulent) citizens.[163] We have indeed seen, at the outset of this general section, that the demes played a crucial gatekeeping role in admitting individuals to Athenian citizenship.

Scholars have wondered about the broader relationship of center to periphery in Athens: Did the demes replicate the political dynamics of the *astu* on a smaller scale, or might they instead have provided solace to conservatives fleeing the democratic hothouse that was the area within the Long Walls?[164] The state of our evidence for the demes makes these questions difficult to answer. Intriguing recent research suggests that within elite families, anyway, only one branch tended to participate in city politics while another might remain in the deme, safeguarding the family's ancestral assets there.[165] As an Athenian male citizen approached death, he would prepare his will and divide property among his heirs; the life cycle would then continue in a new generation.

2.4 Democratic Ideology

We have reviewed the formal institutional "skeleton" of democracy as encountered by the male citizen during the life cycle. We can now attempt a fleshing out of the ideological system – the blood, muscle, and nerves, as it were – that animated the institutions and kept them functioning. By ideology I mean often informal sets of norms, assumptions, slogans, attitudes, and reflexes that manifest in everyday political life – a decent Greek translation for such a notion might be *nomos*, which encompasses both law and custom. In addition to the specifically democratic civic ideology covered here, we can also identify as ideological, in a more Marxist sense, the set of principles that justified the political economy of the Greek *poleis* more broadly. This was founded on the distinction between the free person, who might (potentially) enjoy various rights of

---

[162] Whitehead 1986. Other *poleis* also saw extensive activity at the deme level: We have already seen the demes of Eretria (see previous chapter), while from the third century we possess multiple decrees on stone from the deme of Halasarna on the island of Cos.
[163] Harp. s.v. *Aixōnēsin, Potamos*. Studies of individual demes, which varied considerably from one to the next, are growing: Kellogg 2013; Ackermann 2018.
[164] Osborne 1985, 2010: ch. 2 for the first position; contra N. Jones 1999, 2004.
[165] Kellogg forthcoming.

citizenship, and the enslaved, whose labor was the key source of enrichment for the elite and whose unfree legal status served as the negative image against which the free population formulated their own identity. In fact the two sets of ideologies permeated each other and are not so easily separated. We will also see that these ideologies were not watertight monoliths but admitted of dissenting voices, some of them radically dissenting.

2.4.1 Freedom and Equality

In contemporary political philosophy, it is often supposed that there is a distinction and in fact a tension between freedom and equality: Should the government be arranged so as to allow for the maximal amount of individual liberty among citizens, or should it sacrifice some of that liberty in the name of more equal outcomes for all? The Greeks also argued about freedom and equality, but on somewhat different grounds.[166] The justification for democracy originated, according to Aristotle, from the fact that all people who were free (*eleutheros*), in the specific sense of not enslaved, should have a say in the administration of their community (which was "naturally" a *polis*).[167] For democrats, the beginning and end of the discussion lay in this criterion of freedom: Since all men within the *dēmos*, rich and poor alike, were equally free, they were all equally entitled to the same powers of citizenship.[168] (By contrast, oligarchs believed power should be distributed according to worth rather than according to freedom – it just so happened, in their view, that their unequal wealth and outsized contributions to the *polis* sufficed to establish their greater worth.[169]) Democracy therefore represented the ideal expression of

---

[166] For an intellectual history of the Greek notion of freedom see Raaflaub 2004. For interesting recent discussions that attempt to transcend the modern categories of positive and negative liberty (for which see, most influentially, Berlin 2003, drawing on Constant 1988), see Liddel 2007; Edge 2009; Hansen 2010; Campa 2024.

[167] Arist. *Pol.* 3.1280a24–25; cf. 5.1301a28–30. An absence of being enslaved was the most fundamental meaning of *eleutheria* in the Greek world. This comes through clearly in Patterson 1991, influenced by Finley 1981. The recent study of freedom by de Dijn (2020) rightly stresses the communal, participatory aspect of sustaining freedom in the ancient Greek world but downplays the free/slave distinction. See, however, Nyquist 2013; Gourevitch 2015: ch. 1; Stovall 2021.

[168] A crucial addendum here is long-term residency or other factors (like birth from two citizen parents at Athens) that distinguished the citizen from the resident foreigner, who was also free. Another important issue was whether equality of birth entailed equality of goods besides political power – property, for example. Despite occasional acts of confiscation and redistribution, few ancient democracies appear to have considered material equality necessary for justice. As we have seen, however, democracies did readily distribute some wealth through liturgies and other taxes; they may have believed some minimal baseline of public goods provision was needed to ensure citizen dignity (Ober 2012).

[169] Arist. *Pol.* 5.1301a31–33, b35–40.

the notion of *isonomia* encountered in Chapter 1, "equal distribution" of political rights (with the *-nom* root deriving originally from the verb *nemein*, "to distribute," and not primarily from *nomos*, or "law," which would render the meaning "equality of law").[170]

Scholars have wondered if the term *isonomia* predated *dēmokratia* and could apply to certain broad-based, self-governing oligarchies no less than full democracy.[171] Perhaps it did historically, but by the later fifth century *isonomia* was associated closely with democracy and was in fact assumed of it; the burden of proof was on oligarchies, by contrast, to show that they qualified as *isonomos*.[172] As Thucydides' discussion of civil war in the Greek world reveals, however, many believed that democrats' championing of *isonomia politikē*, which ought to mean "equality of powers for the citizen," masked the domination of the poor majority over the wealthy few.[173] Certainly democrats could use the notion to try to discipline men they perceived as insufficiently democratic. A Syracusan "demagogue," Athenagoras, addressed his opponents in the assembly in 415 BCE this way: "Do you not want to enjoy equality of political rights [*isonomeisthai*] with the majority? And how would that be right, if men who are the same were not deemed worthy of the same privileges?"[174]

In any case, this equality of powers extended to the equal ability of any interested male citizen to speak in the assembly, called *isēgoria* ("equality of political/public address").[175] Democrats contrasted their openness to hearing from all citizens with the tendency of oligarchic regimes to reserve speaking powers for the presiding official – a pattern followed by the Roman Republic, we may note. Because power was distributed equally, it was "fair" (another meaning of *ison*, in addition to "equal") that what seemed best to a majority should be authoritative – a supermajority requirement would de facto entail the rule of a minority.[176] Thus the decision rule in the assembly was technically just over 50 percent: if it came down to it, the votes would be counted and the preference given to a bare majority, as happened when the Athenians debated destroying the

---

[170] Vlastos 1953; Schubert 2021. Whatever its etymological origins, *isonomia* did, in any case, become associated with equality before the law.
[171] Raaflaub 1996.
[172] Hdt. 3.80.6; Thuc. 3.62.3 (where it is denied that the Theban regime of the earlier fifth century was an *isonomos oligarchia*, while *dēmokratia* is listed with no such qualifier – *isonomia* would thus appear to be assumed in its case); Isoc. 7.20; Plat. *Rep.* 8.561e.
[173] Thuc. 3.82.8.   [174] Thuc. 6.38.5.
[175] Hdt. 5.78; [Xen.] *Ath. Pol.* 1.12; Dem. 20.16. The recent discussion in Gottesman 2021b considers *isēgoria* apart from its assembly setting.
[176] Arist. *Pol.* 5.1310a30–31; Schwartzberg 2014.

city of Mytilene in 427.[177] In practice, however, the Athenians, like other Greeks, placed a high priority on *homonoia*, or unanimity, and the procedural and discursive norms of the assembly encouraged coordination around proposals that garnered something nearing consensus. In the *dikastēria*, by contrast, where debate among the judges was not allowed and ballots were secret, close votes were normal.[178]

The Athenian belief in citizen equality was reinforced by a notion that differentiated the *dēmos* of Athens from communities elsewhere: "autochthony," or the belief that every Athenian was descended from a primordial indigenous group that had literally been born "from the earth itself." Such a civic myth granted the Athenians, or so they claimed, an irrevocable right to their "motherland," from which they had sprung, while also serving to make the Athenians into an exclusive, impermeable kind of collective clan (*genos*). They were no rabble collected from abroad, as later Romulus' Rome was explicitly and proudly said to be, but of pureblooded ancient stock. This exclusionary racial ideology was intimately connected with Pericles' Citizenship Law, passed in 451/0 and examined previously in this chapter, which limited citizenship to the children of two Athenians. While a chauvinistic belief on the part of the Athenians, it was also one more mechanism that placed the masses of the *dēmos* on the same level as the elite in civic ideology, since no Athenian was "purer" than any other. The funeral oration or *epitaphios logos* was a prime locus for the promulgation of the belief in autochthony.[179]

2.4.2 *Personal Freedom*

From the equality (*isotēs*) of citizen freedom (*eleutheria*) arose civic ideals that remain more obscure to us. Aristotle and other elite sources claim that it was a principle of democratic regimes that a man "live as he wishes" – the closest approximation to this in contemporary parlance might be social libertarianism, in which there is no legal stricture against private activities that do not harm others. According to Aristotle, democratic citizens demanded this laxity because to be told what to do was the mark of a slave.[180] Some scholars have pointed out that in democratic discourse as

---

[177] Thuc. 3.49.1. [178] Canevaro 2018b, 2019. On *homonoia*, see Chapter 3.5.
[179] On autochthony see Loraux 1986, 2000; Rosivach 1987; Blok 2009; Barbato 2020; Canevaro forthcoming.
[180] Arist. *Pol.* 5.1310a25–36, 6.1317a40–b13; cf. Plat. *Rep.* 8.557b; Thuc. 2.37.2 (Pericles' Funeral Oration), 7.69.2 (in an exhortation to his troops the Athenian general Nicias reminds them of "the ability of all [in Athens] to order their life subject to no control").

revealed in the assembly and the law courts, speakers never claim a citizen can do anything and everything he wants, since that would amount to lawlessness.[181] Democrats did indeed emphasize their ordered living and their adherence to the laws – but the relevant question here is, "libertarian" relative to *what*? In oligarchies, where, as we have seen, one portion of the citizenry did all the ruling, while the other was permanently ruled, lower-class life seems to have been more strictly regulated. This greater "oversight" (*epimeleia*) stemmed not only from the need for oligarchs to control the movement of the *dēmos*, which constantly threatened to overthrow the ruling class, but also from oligarchs' belief that they knew better than the ignorant and irrational commoners how to order one's life virtuously.[182] Democrats rejected this view, prompting elite critics to charge that the common people in a democracy abused language to justify their disordered lifestyle: license (*akolasia*) was called "freedom" (*eleutheria*), anarchy "happiness" (*eudaimonia*), and slander "free speech" (*parrhēsia*).[183] In reaction, philosophically minded oligarchs developed the notion that to be "truly free" (*eleutherios*, not merely *eleutheros*) one had to exhibit a certain level of self-mastery, to free oneself from "servile" appetites that made a member of the *dēmos* no better than a slave.[184] The idea of a "true freedom" that distinguishes "gentlemen" from the common "herd" persists to this day, as in the history of the term *artes liberales*, the "liberal arts" or "arts befitting a truly free person" of higher education, which originally served to validate the ruling classes of Europe.[185]

2.4.3 Freedom of Speech

The last-named Greek term in the trio listed in the foregoing paragraph is *parrhēsia*, literally "saying everything," another somewhat ambiguous term politically.[186] In its earliest usages it might have applied to a fearless willingness to stand up to figures in authority, particularly tyrants. It thus made sense that in a democracy *parrhēsia* was something every citizen

---

[181] Liddel 2007; Filonik 2019; contra: Campa 2024.   [182] Simonton 2017: 71, 97, 168–85.
[183] Isoc. 7.20; Plat. *Rep.* 8.560e–61a; Theophr. *Char.* 28.6.   [184] Raaflaub 1983.
[185] The postliberal political philosopher Patrick Deneen (2018), in his autopsy of why liberalism supposedly "failed," claims repeatedly (see, e.g., pp. 99–100) that in ancient Greece liberty was not understood as freedom to do what one wanted but instead self-mastery through virtue – but this is to repeat Plato and Aristotle's side of the story only.
[186] Carter 2004b; Saxonhouse 2005. The concept was a major preoccupation of the French philosopher Michel Foucault toward the end of his life: See his posthumously published lecture on *parrhēsia* (2019). It should not be confused with the modern notion of freedom of speech as enshrined in a constitutional right.

could safely employ, since they had no social and political superiors other than themselves. In practice, however, *parrhēsia* was claimed over time as a special attribute of the city's socioeconomic elite, who now required fortitude, they argued, if they were to stand up to the collective tyrant that was the *dēmos*.[187] "I know," asserts the rhetorician Isocrates in an address to the Athenians, "that it is an uphill battle to oppose your intentions, and that although we live under democracy, there is no *parrhēsia*, except here [in the assembly] for the most crazed speakers."[188] "I think," says Demosthenes to the assembly, "that when deliberating about matters of such importance you ought to grant *parrhēsia* to each of your advisers," as though they had a predilection not to.[189] We will see in Chapter 4 that speakers continued to talk this way as late as the second century CE.

2.4.4 Sortition and Misthos

The "equal distribution of political powers" in Athens and elsewhere could be ensured to differing degrees. As we have seen, the Athenians chose to apportion authority randomly, through sortition rather than election. In its origins, the lottery may have been intended as an effective means of preventing men or groups of men from amassing too much personal power, in line with Greek suspicions about centralized authority more generally.[190] It clearly came to reflect, however, a belief on the part of democrats that citizens all equally possessed the civic virtue necessary to carry out magistracies with at least a minimum of competence. This attitude contrasts strongly with modern practice, in which the dynamics of election tend to engender a belief that political representatives are differently endowed with the ability to handle the complexities of government.

Growing dissatisfaction on the part of voters with the "political class" or "establishment," however, has encouraged more participatory experiments in which lottery and direct democracy feature.[191] The sentiment is found already in the 1963 remark of the conservative commentator William F. Buckley Jr., that he would "sooner live in a society governed by the first two thousand names in the Boston telephone directory than in a society governed by the two thousand faculty members of Harvard University."[192] In this the godfather of modern American conservatism

---

[187] Landauer 2019. For the People as tyrant see further below. [188] Isoc. 8.14. [189] Dem. 15.1.
[190] Davies 2003. [191] Landemore 2020; Waxman and McCulloch 2022.
[192] Buckley 1963: 134.

finds surprising company in the twentieth-century Trinidadian Marxist C. L. R. James, who, in a 1956 essay on the Athenian democracy entitled "Every Cook Can Govern," noted that the Athenian method represented a "refusal to hand over [political power] to experts, but to trust to the intelligence and sense of justice of the population at large, which meant of course a majority of the common people."[193] For James, the Athenians' well-roundedness provided a blueprint of sorts for a postcapitalist society in which everyday people would administer both politics and the economy.[194]

Certainly the Athenian *dēmos* and other ancient democrats worked hard to guarantee that the language of politics and of the legal system would be accessible to the citizen amateur. Extemporaneity and lack of polish were extolled; an opponent sneered that Demosthenes' speeches "smelled of the lamp" (that is, were carefully composed in writing by oil lamp on previous evenings).[195] Payment for office (*misthos*), a regular feature of Athens and some other democracies after the mid fifth century BCE, helped ensure that the average man not only was allowed to participate in politics but actually did so.[196] After all, if politics were not a paid position, only the well-to-do would have the time and leisure necessary to participate in it.

Critics claimed that unscrupulous politicians dangled the possibility of ever-greater wages in front of the noses of voters in order to lead them astray.[197] Outside of a few rare instances, however, *misthos* appears not to have been manipulated by individual politicians; it was a depersonalized system. Still, the opponents of democracy grumbled that the *dēmos* had come to feel itself entitled to other people's money.[198] Payment and sortition also combined to encourage socially "worse" individuals to staff

---

[193] James 1956, accessed at www.marxists.org/archive/james-clr/works/1956/06/every-cook.htm. James does not say so but the title of his piece is based on a supposed remark of Vladimir Lenin.

[194] By contrast, the philosopher Friedrich Nietzsche, writing in the 1880s, thought that the democratic spirit of Athens was already apparent in the United States and Europe of his day: "The individual becomes convinced that he can do just about everything and *can manage almost any role*, and everybody experiments with himself, improvises, makes new experiments, enjoys his experiments; and all nature ceases and becomes art" (*The Gay Science* no. 356 = Nietzsche 1974: 303; emphasis in original). The philosopher Hannah Arendt, for her part, admired the civic-minded, participatory spirit of the ancient Greeks but thought the political and economic realms should be kept separate: Arendt 1958.

[195] Plut. *Vit. Dem.* 8.4. Gagarin 2020: ch. 1 notes all the ways the Athenian legal system was accessible to amateurs. Kallet 2008, by contrast, argues that politicians' specialized knowledge of matters like finance gave them an advantage over average people.

[196] [Arist.] *Ath. Pol.* 27.4.   [197] Ar. *Eq.* 51, 1352; [Arist.] *Ath. Pol.* 28.3.

[198] [Arist.] *Ath. Pol.* 27.4 records a saying of Pericles' advisor, the musical theorist and sophist Damon of Oe, to the effect that *misthos* was not taken from others but was "the People's own." On this figure see Wallace 2015.

the magistracies, as detractors saw it, thus further empowering the *dēmos* (indeed, one might say reinforcing the democratic system as a whole).[199] The Aristotelian author of the *Constitution of the Athenians* says that, once Pericles instituted pay for the *dikastēria*, "some people complained that they grew inferior, since average people always took greater care than the upper classes to be allotted the position."[200]

2.4.5 Publicity and Accountability

If the *dēmos* of Athens was taking advantage of political participation at every opportunity, they did not, for all that, let officeholders off the hook when it came to scrutiny and accountability. One plank of democratic ideology was a commitment to radical transparency. In Athens, this had something to do with keeping tabs on the massive income of the empire, but a desire to itemize, calculate, record, store, and publicize in order to prevent corruption and keep the powerful in check was no less important.[201] This process began with the recruitment and exit review of the officeholders, all of whom had to undergo an initial screening procedure called a *dokimasia*, followed by an audit or *euthynai* ("straightening") upon completion of their one-year tenure.[202] Herodotus connects these procedures with democracy early on, having a character say in his Constitutional Debate that the majority (*plēthos*) is able to scrutinize its officeholders after their term of office (the latter are *hypeuthynos*, "subject to audit").[203] Most of these scrutinies went without incident, but especially after the period of oligarchies in the late fifth century the *dokimasia* might be used to shine a light on a man's activities during the Four Hundred and the Thirty.[204] *Euthynai* could also result, if there was a discrepancy in the funds, in a man's being fined and declared a public debtor if he could not pay, stripped of his citizenship (experiencing *atimia*) in the meantime.[205] *Dokimasiai* and *euthynai* have been shown to be procedures of numerous Greek cities, democratic and oligarchic alike.[206] Where democracies differed was in ultimately settling these disputes through judicial panels staffed with average members of the *dēmos*.

Evidence at an audit might come from the numerous inventories the Athenians kept cataloging their income and expenses. They also maintained copies on file of every decree passed by the assembly (in the fourth

---

[199] For a comparison of the social profiles of allotted and elected magistrates, see Taylor 2007.
[200] [Arist.] *Ath. Pol.* 27.4.   [201] Roberts 1982.   [202] [Arist.] *Ath. Pol.* 48.3–5, 55.
[203] Hdt. 3.80.6.   [204] Lys. 16, 26, 31.   [205] Hunter 2000.
[206] Fröhlich 2004; Feyel 2009; Oranges 2021.

century these were stored in the Old Bouleuterion, which had become a sanctuary to the Mother of the Gods), so that any citizen could consult them; Athens' laws were likewise on permanent display.[207] The hundreds of public inscriptions that littered the Acropolis, the Agora, and other locations further laid bare Athens' political business.[208] Scholars have debated Athens' indisputable "epigraphic habit," its tendency to inscribe its decisions on stone and other materials. Were these for the benefit of the average citizen? Or did they instead provide an additional outlet for the traditionally aristocratic values of competition and display? Or might they have been meant for the gods' consumption first and foremost?[209] So-called formulae of disclosure in some inscriptions, providing the rationale behind the act, usually state that the information is being recorded "so that those who wish [*hoi boulomenoi*]" might know their contents. In some cases the point seems to be purely informative, in others a form of encouragement for the *dēmos*' well-wishers, who will enjoy similar honors to the ones recorded in the inscription should they benefit the city. Both scenarios presuppose a system in which an informed citizenry is authoritative in taking decisions and bestowing rewards, and so they can, in the present author's opinion, be taken as evidence for a "democratic" aspect to Athens' culture of inscribing.[210]

"We must cease courting the political offices," says Theophrastus' Oligarchic Man, "and thereby allowing ourselves to be mistreated [*hubrizomenous*] or honored [*timōmenous*] by these men [that is, the *dēmos*]."[211] We have just seen that one purpose of all the recordkeeping at Athens was so that the People could reward its benefactors and punish its enemies, a prerogative that the Oligarchic Man laments.[212] Whether the justice meted out by the *dēmos* amounted to hubris was often in the eye of the beholder. The populace could certainly inflict drastic punishments. In

---

[207] Rhodes 1991, 2001; Sickinger 1999; Pébarthe 2006; Faraguna 2017. Similar administrative documents have been discovered from democratic Argos, in the form of more than one hundred bronze plaques recording transactions of the state treasury of the *polis* (discussed in Section 2.3.7 and previewed in Kritzas 2006). The bronzes reveal numerous aspects of Argive politics, bureaucracy, and finance, including the names of civic subdivisions like phratries and villages. When published, these documents will no doubt constitute a major advance in our knowledge of ancient Greek financial administration.

[208] For Athens' "decree culture" see the monumental work of Liddel 2020.

[209] Hedrick 1999; Sickinger 2009; Meyer 2013; Lambert 2017: ch. 3. Many scholars now agree that Athenians were decently literate for a premodern people: Pébarthe 2006; Missiou 2011.

[210] Athens' system of recordkeeping and accountability was also likely part of an attempt to aggregate "useful knowledge" among the citizenry, as argued extensively by Ober 2008.

[211] Theophr. *Char.* 26.3.

[212] For the development of a system of benefactors and honors in the Greek cities, see Chapter 3.8.

one year during the fifth century (we do not know which), an entire board of the treasurers of the Athenian Empire, known as the Hellenotamiae, were accused of embezzlement, with nine out of ten of them put to death before exonerating evidence appeared.[213] We have already seen that many of the most prominent politicians of the fifth century were ostracized, and a worse fate, in the form of property confiscation or death, could befall generals perceived to have let the People down. After a military defeat in Aetolia, the fifth-century general Demosthenes (not the more famous politician of the fourth century) refused to return home to Athens, fearing the Athenians' wrath.[214] If we are to believe Plutarch, the general Paches publicly killed himself in the courtroom rather than face the verdict of the *dēmos*.[215] Then there is the notorious case of the generals after the Battle of Arginusae in 406 BCE, in which six of eight charged with negligence were executed, a decision the Athenians came to regret.[216] Plutarch in the passage just cited tantalizingly mentions "all those [authors] who survey the offenses committed by the [Athenian] *dēmos* against the generals," as though it were a well-worn topic. Nonmilitary politicians could also be put on trial for "deception" of the *dēmos*.[217] One scholar showed that, out of a sample of forty-one politicians, only nineteen "avoid[ed] some kind of political catastrophe at the hands of ... their fellow citizens."[218]

Rough treatment of its political class was not limited to the Athenian democracy either: When an Argive general returned home after making an agreement with the Spartans without consultation of "the masses" [*to plēthos*], the Argives began to stone him to death. He survived by seeking refuge at an altar, but the democracy confiscated his property.[219] In 410, shortly after the reforms of Diocles that had made the offices sortitive (see Section 2.4.4), the Syracusan *dēmos* deposed and exiled three of its generals in a move heavily criticized by many of the troops in the field.[220]

2.4.6 Democracy and the Rule of Law

Democrats believed that their vigilance was necessary to keep politicians honest. Their (arguably) heavy-handed treatment of elites, however, brings us to the question of democracy and the rule of law. Did Athens and other democratic regimes apply the laws equally to all citizens, or was democracy the rule of only a part of the citizenry, and in its own narrow class interests at that?

---

[213] Ant. 5.69–70. [214] Thuc. 3.98.5. [215] Plut. *Vit. Arist.* 26.3.
[216] Xen. *Hell.* 1.7 with Asmonti 2006. [217] On deception in Athens see Hesk 2000.
[218] Knox 1985: 143. See also Allen 2000 on democratic punishment. [219] Thuc. 5.60.6.
[220] Xen. *Hell.* 1.1.27–31 with Diod. Sic. 13.34.6.

The school of Aristotle thought that most democratic regimes were biased in favor of the common people, and that the act of the Athenian *dēmos*, when it agreed to repay loans taken out by the Thirty, was the exception that proved the rule: "In other cities, the victorious People not only do not spend their own funds, they also carry out a redistribution of the land [*sc.* to the detriment of the wealthy few]."²²¹ A young Alcibiades, according to a smart piece of oligarchic propaganda related by Xenophon, attempted to trick his guardian, Pericles, into agreeing with him that "when the great mass [*plēthos*] passes a decree, overpowering the holders of property rather than persuading them, it constitutes an act of force rather than law," just as when tyrants and oligarchs oppress their populations.²²²

Historians have noted that the Athenians professed adherence to the rule of law as an ideal, just as all Greek *poleis* tended to do, and some have argued that institutional guidelines and norms were such as to encourage procedural regularity, respect for the letter of the law, and the avoidance of bias or caprice. This would amount to a kind of democratic judicial review.²²³ Scholars also point to the Athenians' decision in the late fifth century to reform their law code and create a system whereby temporary decrees (*psēphismata*) henceforth would have to be in conformity with the permanent laws (*nomoi*) or face repeal.²²⁴ So-called *nomothesia*, the process of creating new laws, however, remained in the hands of the People themselves.²²⁵ Did this setup amount to the "rule of law" rather than "popular sovereignty"?²²⁶ The frustrating truth is that we do not possess sufficient data to test the claims of ancient democrats against the reality of the situation. It is no answer to point to the longevity and thus the (apparent) legitimacy of the Athenian democracy, since the regime may have been so efficient at promoting the interests of the common people as to reduce its elite critics to demoralized inaction.²²⁷

---

²²¹ [Arist.] *Ath. Pol.* 40.3; cf. Arist. *Pol.* 3.1279a17–21; Plat. *Rep.* 1.338e; [Xen.] *Ath. Pol.* 1.4, 6–8.
²²² Xen. *Mem.* 1.2.40–46, with quotation at 45.
²²³ Canevaro 2017a; Esu 2024; Gagarin 2020: ch. 8; Carugati, Weingast, and Calvert 2023. By contrast, see Carawan 2020 for the position that Athenian devotion to the rule of law was rather more inconsistent.
²²⁴ The eighteenth-century Anglo–Irish statesman and thinker Edmund Burke (1986 [1790]: 327), in the course of formulating the philosophy of modern conservatism in his *Reflections on the Revolution in France*, claimed that "[t]he vice of the ancient democracies, and one cause of their ruin, was, that they ruled ... by occasional decrees, *psēphismata*." For complaints in ancient authors, see Arist. *Pol.* 4.1292a23–25; [Arist.] *Ath. Pol.* 41.2.
²²⁵ Canevaro 2013; Canevaro and Esu 2018.   ²²⁶ Thus posed by Ostwald 1986.
²²⁷ The Old Oligarch acknowledges that opponents of the Athenian democracy ca. 420 BCE have few options: [Xen.] *Ath. Pol.* 3.12–13 with Ober 1998: 14–27. Gagarin 2020: ch. 1 argues from stability that the Athenian justice system enjoyed legitimacy. Herman 2006 is a thoroughgoingly optimistic picture of Athenian society; see Christ 2006a, 2006b for a corrective.

2.4 Democratic Ideology

Perhaps it is worthwhile to ask whether Athens' upper class was "dominated," using the definition of the term promoted by neorepublican political theorists. On this understanding, which distinguishes itself from the conception of liberty utilized by liberal theories, domination occurs not merely when one actor actively oppresses another, but when one actor is in a *structural position* potentially to oppress another and face no repercussions. Living under the cloud of this potential oppression can strongly influence the behavior of the dominated, causing them to do and say things they otherwise would not.[228] What sort of evidence would suffice to be able to state that the elites of Athens were not dominated under the democracy?[229] From a more normative angle, is a system in which the majority dominates the few preferable on utilitarian grounds to one in which the few dominate the many, since more people enjoy freedom under the former than the latter? In this regard Athens and other ancient democracies might continue to provide food for thought in contemporary theoretical debates.[230]

*

Modern historians have gone back and forth on whether ancient Greek democrats formulated their own, "bottom-up" political ideology and culture or instead internalized existing aristocratic values like honor, competition, and display.[231] My own reading of the cumulative evidence has always suggested the former, but pinpointing a single text that shows this "popular culture" in action is difficult. One place to start, but also a place to finish this section, is with Theophrastus' portrait of the Friend of Scumbags (*Philoponēros*). The philosopher's *Characters* is a difficult text whose import for the historian is anything but straightforward: The characters are parodic, and therefore extreme and distorted, but also

---

[228] See Pettit 1997; Skinner 1998.
[229] Certainly the elite could speak of themselves as being "enslaved" by the democracy (Tamiolaki 2013), and many did retire into *apragmosynē*, "quietism," rather than run the gauntlet of public life in Athens (Carter 1986). In all these cases, however, the language of "domination" and "slavery" was parasitic on the actual institution of enslavement, which remained the primary form of domination in Greek society (Lewis 2018); I examine in greater detail how this domination enabled democracies in the following chapter.
[230] For instance, the neorepublican understanding of liberty as nondomination has recently been used to argue for "socialist republicanism," in which material advantages are to be regulated if the poor are to escape domination by the rich (O'Shea 2020; Muldoon 2022). It seems worth asking at what point the socioeconomic elite, if that category has not been eliminated through equalization of property, might be dominated by the majority in such a setup. Cartledge (2018: 1, 265, 287), on the other hand, has suggested that the Athenian democracy was a kind of Leninist "dictatorship of the proletariat."
[231] E.g., Ober 1989; contra Wilson 1992. On "popular culture" at Athens, see Canevaro 2017b.

meant to pick out recognizable types.²³² The Friend of Scumbags is described as follows:²³³

> [He] is the sort of man who falls in with people who have been defeated in the law courts and have lost public cases, and supposes that if he associates with them he will learn the tricks of the trade and become a man who is not to be trifled with. He says of honest men [*chrēstoi*] that [the text is corrupt] ... and that there is no such thing as an honest man, because people are all similar [*homoioi*], and he will say sarcastically "What an honest man he is." He describes the scumbag [*ponēros*] as "a man of independent character" [*eleutheros*]. ... He supports him when he is speaking in the assembly or when he is on trial in court. He is apt to say to the jury "You must judge the case, not the man." And he describes him as the People's guard-dog [*ho kuōn tou dēmou*] (because he barks at offenders) and claims "We shall have nobody willing to trouble their heads on our behalf if we throw away people like this."²³⁴

We must recognize right off the bat that the whole thumbnail sketch is replete with politically charged language. *Ponēros* does not just mean scoundrel or scumbag, but is the regular term, especially when coming from the mouths of the elite, used to castigate vociferously prodemocratic *rhētores* and their constituents. Cleon, Hyperbolus, Cleophon, and others are repeatedly called *ponēroi prostatai tou dēmou*, "scumbag champions of the People," in fifth-century texts.²³⁵ The opposition between *ponēros* and *chrēstos* utilized here is the same the Old Oligarch deployed in his late-fifth-century screed.²³⁶ The *Philoponēros*, as the description makes clear, is a fierce partisan of politicians who claim to speak on behalf of the People's interests. He agrees with the central "demagogic" conceit that the People require a "guard dog" against the would-be encroachments of the elite – that without the *ponēros*' help, "offenders" (*hoi adikountes*) will triumph at the expense of the *dēmos*.²³⁷ As for the pretensions of the elite, these count for nothing: Who is this man to say

---

²³² Lane Fox 1997; Millett 2007; Ebner-Landy and de Nicolay 2023.
²³³ Given the notorious difficulties of this Greek text, I use Diggle's 2004 edition and translation, slightly modified.
²³⁴ Theophr. *Char.* 29.2–5.
²³⁵ Eur. *Suppl.* 243; Ar. *Pax* 684, *Eccl.* 176–77; cf. Thuc. 6.89.5. See further Rosenbloom 2004.
²³⁶ E.g., [Xen.] *Ath. Pol.* 1.4. Lane Fox (1997: 131–32) argues that the word *ponēros* here describes people who are bad "in a moral sense" and not in the Old Oligarch's "social sense," but this is to take Theophrastus' portrait as an objective description of reality and not as potentially reflecting political biases and ideologies (i.e., the Theophrastean narrator labels as "bad men" those who in another's description would be "defenders of democracy").
²³⁷ "Guard dog of the People" seems to have been applied by Cleon to himself: Ar. *Eq.* 1017, *Vesp.* 835–42; cf. [Dem.] 25.40, likely a later forgery but inspired by fifth- and fourth-century discourse. Theophrastus' language about a champion of the People protecting it from evildoers recalls Hdt. 3.82.4.

he is *chrēstos* and therefore special? Does he not know that social distinctions of this sort are false – because all people are deep down similar (*homoioi*)? The person the elite call a scumbag this fellow calls "a man of independent character," using the word that unites all participants in a democracy and serves as the basis of their equal political rights: *eleutheros*, the fact that they are all equally free and not enslaved. As we have seen, actions justified by democrats under the label "freedom" (*eleutheria*) were viewed by critics of democracy as no better than "anarchy." Our *Philoponēros* would presumably reject that interpretation.

In sum, we have here an Athenian citizen, in however distorted a form, who refuses to bow to the political and ethical pronouncements of his social "betters," and who in fact sees them as conspiring against him; to stave off their attacks, he is happy to embrace an aggressive champion whom his elite enemies view as no better than trash. To the extent the portrait contains any truth, whatever this is, it is not a worldview that has simply adapted elite language and values for its own purposes.

Excursus: Democracy and Material Culture

In the previous chapter we examined the spatial and organizational changes made to the communities of Athens and Eretria following the introduction of democracy. The building projects of the fifth century arguably represented an even greater transformation of the Athenian civic landscape. First there were the Long Walls, the construction of which began in the late 460s, slightly before the starting point of this chapter. The Walls connected the fortified Piraeus port with the *astu* or city center of Athens, which had been walled on the proposal of Themistocles in the aftermath of the Persian Wars.[238] Beyond their obvious defensive function, the Long Walls were intimately connected with Athens' democratic constitution. In bringing city and port together to the relative neglect of the countryside, they effectively made Imperial Athens an island that could not be defeated so long as it imported its needs via overseas trade. They also "pointed" the city toward the true source of its might: its imperial fleet, manned, as we saw in the previous chapter, by lower-class citizen men, and which brought in the empire's tribute.

---

[238] Thuc. 1.89–93, 107.1 with Conwell 2008; Theocharaki 2019.

(cont.)

Themistocles, Thucydides tell us, was "the first to dare to tell [the Athenians] that they must cleave to the sea," making them into a naval power, and the Long Walls solidified this relationship.[239] They were so emblematic of Athens' transformation into a maritime democracy, it seems, that their construction sparked resistance among Athenian conservatives: There were men around the time of the Battle of Tanagra in 457 "who hoped to put a stop to the democracy and the building of the Long Walls."[240] This conspiracy went nowhere, however, and the Walls were completed. In the 440s, Pericles proposed a Middle Wall, in a speech that Plato's Socrates claims to have heard personally.[241] Socrates was not very impressed with the fifth-century empire's material assets, nor with the politicians who proposed them: "With no consideration for moderation or justice, they have filled the *polis* with harbors, shipyards, walls, tribute, and other such nonsense."[242] To the average Athenian, however, these were all sources of pride.

Around the same time as the construction of the Middle Wall, after the conclusion of the so-called Peace of Callias with Persia, the Athenians launched their monumental building program.[243] The massive Acropolis structures known as the Propylaea (the "Initial Gates" leading to the Acropolis), the Erechtheion, and, most famously, the Parthenon (called in Classical antiquity the Hekatompedon or Hundred-Footer, a typical name for a Greek temple) all resulted from this initiative, as did the Odeion music hall further down the hill. The program is often attributed wholly to Pericles, but it seems he was most directly involved with proposing the Odeion. He likely served on boards of overseers (*epistatai*) for the other structures, but always as part of a team.[244] The *dēmos* of Athens was the ultimate authority for the project.

The structures undeniably served as a testament to Athens' imperial power and wealth, but scholars have debated just how "democratic" they were meant to be. The Parthenon, in particular, remains an "enigma," as one scholar has put it in a famous discussion.[245] The iconic structure, which housed the sculptor Phidias' enormous "chryselephantine" (gold and ivory) statue of Athena, appears never to have served as an actual temple where cult sacrifices

---

[239] Thuc. 1.93.4, discussed in the previous chapter.
[240] Thuc. 1.107.4; cf. Plut. *Vit. Cim.* 17.3–4.   [241] Plat. *Gorg.* 455e.   [242] Plat. *Gorg.* 519a.
[243] Hurwit 1999; Shear 2016. On the controversial Peace of Callias see Badian 1993: ch. 1.
[244] Pericles and the Odeion: Plut. *Vit. Per.* 13.5, quoting Cratinus fr. 73 K–A. Overseer: Philoch. *BNJ* 327 FF 37, 121; Strabo 9.1.12.
[245] Connelly 2014, a sustained argument attempting to show that the Parthenon frieze does not depict a historical Panathenaea festival (as many scholars have argued) but a scene from Athenian mythology.

2.4 *Democratic Ideology* 87

(cont.)

Figure 2.4 Panathenaic frieze. (Photo: Erin Babnik / Alamy).

were carried out.²⁴⁶ Its sculptural program, and specifically the long Ionic frieze that runs below the roof above the inner colonnade, which probably shows the Athenian community assembled for the Panathenaea festival to Athena, further contributes to the notion that it was a monument as much to the Athenians themselves as to the goddess.²⁴⁷ (Figure 2.4) The square sculpted metopes on the four exterior sides, showing an Amazonomachy, Gigantomachy, Trojan War, and Centauromachy, have been interpreted as showing the forces against which the Athenian male citizen defined himself: the female, the old order of the Titans (opposed to the reigning Olympian gods), the foreigner, and the animal world, respectively.²⁴⁸

For all of the fifth century, the only statues of human beings in the Athenian Agora remained those of Harmodius and Aristogeiton, whom we encountered in the previous chapter. The influence of the statues, however, and of the tyrannicidal ideology they embodied, could be felt far from Athens. During the period of the empire, for example, the city of Cyzicus on the Propontis minted coins showing the tyrannicides standing on top of a tuna fish, the official symbol of the *polis*! As two specialists of Athenian coinage have put it, the Cyzicene coins "advertise a solidarity with Athens that could hardly be expressed more vividly";

---

²⁴⁶ Statue: Thuc. 2.13.5; Philoch. *BNJ* 328 F 121; OR 135. No cult: Höcker 2006.   ²⁴⁷ Neils 2001.
²⁴⁸ Hurwit 1999: 242; cf. Shear 2016: 117–21. For the importance of these polarities for male citizens within democracies, see further Chapter 3.7.

they also spread knowledge of the statue group and its message, almost turning it into a "meme."[249] We read in Plutarch that when the Syracusan tyrant Dionysius asked what the best kind of bronze was, a subversive courtier replied, "that from which they fashioned the statues of Harmodius and Aristogeiton," a remark that cost the unfortunate man his life.[250] The statue group was thus a potent symbol, and, for a time, a rarity. After the Battle of Cnidus in 394, however, the Athenians authorized statues of the naval commander Conon, an Athenian citizen, as well as the Cypriot king Evagoras of Salamis. Further monuments to the generals Chabrias, Iphicrates, and Timotheus followed, in line with what one scholar has termed a campaign to transform the Athenian Agora into the "space of the democratic citizen."[251] Honorific statues for living human beings proliferated in other *poleis*, as well, in what we will see in the next chapter was a veritable explosion of images during the later fourth through second centuries.

The Athenians' reluctance to honor people with monuments had changed following the oligarchic interludes of the Four Hundred and the Thirty in the late fifth century. The city now saw numerous decrees and statues go up honoring the defenders of democracy, many of them expressly mentioning *dēmokratia*.[252] After the fall of the Four Hundred, the restored democracy passed a decree proposed by one Theozotides that extended the city's existing support for war orphans (see Section 2.3.6) to the children of men who died under the oligarchy. "As many of the Athenians as died a violent death during the oligarchy, coming to the aid of the democracy," it begins, "to the children of these men" were to go the benefits.[253] A list of names follows, among which number the sons of one Androcles, probably the "demagogue" murdered by oligarchs.[254] The response to the reign of terror of the Thirty was even more vociferous. The men who returned to the Piraeus from Phyle with the general Thrasybulus and overthrew the oligarchy were honored with a monument in the Agora. The fragments of the inscription were identified thanks to an epigram cited in a speech of Aeschines: "The indigenous [*palaichthōn*] People of Athens honored these men with crowns for their excellence, who first initiated the overthrow of men ruling the city with unjust laws, at great personal risk."[255]

An additional fragment of this inscription has recently been published, the dimensions of which reveal that the monument was a statue base and not a thin

---

[249] Kallet and Kroll 2020: 141.   [250] Plut. *Mor.* 68a–b.   [251] Shear 2011: ch. 9.
[252] The decrees expertly collected and commented on in Liddel 2020 make clear the sheer number of decisions issued in the wake of the Thirty, especially.
[253] OR 178, argued (persuasively, in my opinion) by Matthaiou 2011: 71–81 to belong to the period after the Four Hundred rather than after the Thirty, as Stroud 1971 argued.
[254] Thuc. 8.65.3.
[255] *SEG* 28.45 with Aeschin. 3.190. The epithet "indigenous" is a reference to the Athenians' belief in their autochthony; see Section 2.4.1.

stele. One scholar has proposed that it would have supported an image of – deified – Demokratia (or less likely Demos); if correct, this would represent one of the earliest instances of depicting personifications like these.[256] The Athenians also collectively swore an oath at this time that was later inscribed on stone. It established that anyone attempting to overthrow the democracy could be killed with impunity.[257] We will see numerous additional oaths along such lines in the next chapter.

When we move beyond Athens, the evidence for democracy and material culture between 451 and 362 becomes much rarer. Other democracies, certainly, published inscriptions on stone, in some cases influenced in their "decree culture" by the Athenian example.[258] They might also institute monuments, honors, or festivals directly tied to democracy. The fifth-century Syracusans, for example, established a festival for Zeus Eleutherios ("of Freedom") after overthrowing their tyranny and establishing democracy.[259] In the fourth century, the populace of Sicyon in the Peloponnese interred the populist politician Euphron, labeled a "tyrant" by Xenophon, in their agora, on the grounds that his introduction of democracy made him a new "founder" of the city. Presumably his public tomb, the recipient of hero cult, served as an important site of collective democratic memory going forward.[260] We will see a profusion of democratically themed festivals and monuments throughout the Greek world in the following chapter. As for building programs, Eric Robinson has studied the public spaces fifth- and fourth-century democracies constructed for their assembly meetings. Reviewing examples from Argos, Acragas, Mantinea, Megalopolis, and Syracuse, he finds that their meeting places, like the Pnyx in Athens, could hold large numbers of citizens, but that none of them was designed to house the entire *dēmos*.[261] Except in some very small *poleis* like those known from Asia Minor, it was never an expectation that the full (male) citizen population had to meet collectively in order for the "power of the People" to be a reality. By the same token, the assembly audiences that took decisions on behalf of the community in ancient Greek democracies were to some degree "representative" of the broader citizenry.[262]

---

[256] *SEG* 62.50. The new fragment confirms that the proposer was the important post–Civil War politician Archinus ([Arist.] *Ath. Pol.* 40.1–2). For images of personifications along these lines, see Chapter 3.6.

[257] Lyc. 1.122–27 with Andoc. 1.96–98 (placing the oath in 410, but argued by Canevaro and Harris 2012 to be a spurious document).

[258] Lewis 1997; Liddel 2010.   [259] Diod. Sic. 11.72.2.

[260] Xen. *Hell.* 7.3.12 with Lewis 2004 and Simonton 2018b. We will see another monument, this time associated with Euphron's homonymous grandson, in Chapter 3.6.

[261] Robinson 2011: 229–30.   [262] Cammack 2021; Simonton 2021.

2.5 Conclusion: Constitutional Conflict in the Classical Age – Could It Be Overcome?

Asking whether certain elites were justified in rejecting democracy becomes at some point a purely academic exercise for the historian, who discovers that, whatever the rightness or wrongness of the situation, reject democracy they did, often through violent means. At the same time, lower-class men living under oligarchic regimes frequently rose up and overthrew their wealthy overlords. The incompatible ideologies of democracy and oligarchy increasingly made *stasis* or civil strife a fact of life for the Greek cities of the fifth and fourth centuries.[263] One historian has recently argued that we have in fact underestimated the total number of *staseis* from the time period: Cities were likely to experience them more than once every decade.[264] Scholars, unsurprisingly, have differing thoughts on the causes of *stasis* – was it primarily about social conflicts between rich and poor? About opposed political ideologies? Or were constitutional labels largely a smokescreen for intra-elite rivalries?[265]

It seems obvious to the present author that it made a difference to average Greeks whether, at the conclusion of a bout of *stasis*, their city was now under a democratic or oligarchic regime. It seems equally obvious that common people tended to favor democracy, elites oligarchy.[266] Even the Athenian democracy of the high empire, which has often been presented as an exceptional case whose wealth and power allowed it to "transcend" the *stasis* usually endemic to the Greek *poleis*, had its dissenters. Thucydides tells us that the "reasonable" (*sōphrones*) men of Athens preferred that the populist politician Cleon be killed rather than achieve a military victory against the Spartans, and Alcibiades is depicted as telling the Spartans that "we prudent people" (*hoi phronountes*) at Athens always recognized democracy for what it was: "acknowledged foolishness." The only reason they did not subvert it was because the Spartans' hostility made any talk of changing the constitution impossible.[267] Alcibiades' speech is self-serving and meant to flatter a Spartan audience, but he cannot be far wrong: As we have seen, the *Dissoi Logoi*

---

[263] On competing notions of justice, fairness, honor, and hubris among contestants, see Fisher 2000; Cairns, Canevaro, and Manzouranis 2022.

[264] Arcenas 2020.

[265] Lintott 1982; Gehrke 1985; Berger 1992. Börm 2019 carries Gehrke's emphasis on intra-elite rivalries into the Hellenistic period; see next chapter.

[266] Cf. Finley 1983: 9. The French political philosopher Pierre Manent (2013) sees the struggle between the few and the many as the central, structuring dynamic of the ancient Greek city; cf. Pont 2020, drawing on Manent, who does not see this way of life ceasing until the fourth century CE (see Chapter 4.6).

[267] Thuc. 4.28.5, 6.89.6.

2.5 Conclusion

thought there were men in every *polis* who "hated the *dēmos*," while the Old Oligarch says that "throughout the world the 'good set' [*to beltiston*] is opposed to democracy."²⁶⁸ While it is true that democratic leadership tended to come from the ranks of the elite, among men who in some cases fought to the death for democracy, it is no less true that many people who acquiesced for the moment in having to jump through democratic hoops, seeing no viable political alternative, later proved themselves capable of killing in the name of oligarchy. As in all revolutionary times, there was also a large, multifarious set of people in the middle who might be swayed either way depending on the circumstances.

The proclivity toward class hatred and violence in the period under review can be shocking to the modern reader, for whom representative democracy and its nominal respect for all citizens is (probably) taken for granted.²⁶⁹ In fact, the frank political language of the ancient world, and in particular elite disdain for the "ignorant mob," has been the norm in history, in many cases taking its cue from Classical Greek examples.²⁷⁰ "Among the 'best' [*beltistoi*]," says the Old Oligarch, "there is the least license and injustice ... but among the common people there is the greatest amount of ignorance, disorder, and wickedness [*ponēria*]: for the need to work [*penia*] inclines them more towards shameful practices, and some people suffer from lack of education and ignorance due to want of resources."²⁷¹ It is a surprisingly materialist analysis, one which of course does not question the unequal distribution of goods that makes the tendencies identified by the author supposedly inevitable. The goal for the aristocrat in this situation appears to the Old Oligarch as obvious:

> If you seek *eunomia* ["good order," a euphemism for oligarchy], first of all you will see the cleverest men laying down the laws for the others; then the good [*chrēstoi*] will punish the scum [*ponēroi*] ... and will not allow insane people to serve on the Council or make proposals or gather in assembly. From these excellent practices the *dēmos* would quickly fall into slavery [*douleia*].²⁷²

Aristotle likewise tells us of oligarchs in his own time who swear an oath amongst themselves to "be hateful toward the *dēmos* and devise whatever

---

²⁶⁸ DK 90 B 7; [Xen.] *Ath. Pol.* 1.5.
²⁶⁹ The sociologist Michael Mann (1986: 217) observed that Greece "is the first known society to ... exhibit[t] to us *symmetrical, political class struggle*" (emphasis in original).
²⁷⁰ Cf. Hill 1965 for the people as a "many-headed monster" in sixteenth- and seventeenth-century elite sources (cf. Plat. *Rep.* 9.588c). G. E. M. de Ste. Croix (1981: 74, 77), in a monumental work that won the 1982 Isaac Deutscher Memorial Prize for writing in a Marxist tradition, argued that Aristotle's analysis of class antagonism in the ancient Greek world was proto-Marxian.
²⁷¹ [Xen.] *Ath. Pol.* 1.5.   ²⁷² [Xen.] *Ath. Pol.* 1.9.

evil against them that I can."²⁷³ What other approach was possible when faced with the common people, regularly likened to a hubristic, out-of-control horse or a ferocious beast?²⁷⁴ In this dehumanizing environment violence perhaps became inevitable. When the Mantinean democracy was overthrown by the Spartans in 385, the presence of Lacedaemonian troops was the only thing that kept the aristocrats of Mantinea from killing sixty prodemocratic politicians, now deposed from power.²⁷⁵ In other cities the democrats were not so lucky: If we are to believe Plutarch, the Spartan commander Lysander allowed the oligarchs of Miletus to murder eight hundred defenders of democracy. The number, if accurate, is so high that it must have included many average people.²⁷⁶

This is not to say democrats lacked for violent partisanship. The democrats of Corcyra, over the course of the infamous bout of *stasis* analyzed by Thucydides in the third book of his *History*, did not stop until they had wiped out every last conceivable oligarch: "The *stasis* that had become so great came to an end ... for there was no longer any opposing element left worth speaking of."²⁷⁷ Then there was the so-called *skytalismos* or clubbing in Argos in 370 BCE, called by Diodorus Siculus "a bout of *stasis* and slaughter such as has never been reported among the other Greeks." Within the Argive democracy, "demagogues" whipped up the populace against certain members of the elite, who decided in desperation to band together to put down the democratic constitution. Thwarted in their plot, twelve hundred supposed oligarchs were eventually killed in a citywide hunt for subversives. Their method of execution, being cudgeled to death by a *skytalē* or staff after a perfunctory trial, gave the *skytalismos* its name. Eventually, the *dēmos* turned on the demagogues themselves, who in a panic were trying to dial back the bloodshed. "So these men," says Diodorus, "as though an avenging spirit were involved, met a fitting end, and the People, ceasing its mad rage, was restored to its previous state of goodwill."²⁷⁸

Restoring civic harmony after such paroxysms of violence could be extremely difficult, and we possess reconciliation agreements inscribed on stone that show the attempt in action. Most, it should be noted, come from democratic regimes.²⁷⁹ One from early fourth-century Thasos

---

²⁷³ Arist. *Pol.* 5.1310a9–10.
²⁷⁴ Com. Adesp. fr. 700 K–A with Plut. *Vit. Lys.* 21.4; Plat. *Rep.* 6.493a–b.   ²⁷⁵ Xen. *Hell.* 5.2.6.
²⁷⁶ Plut. *Vit. Lys.* 19.2; cf. [Xen.] *Ath. Pol.* 3.11.   ²⁷⁷ Thuc. 4.48.5.
²⁷⁸ Diod. Sic. 15.57.3–58. Evidence for the *skytalismos* has reportedly been found in the administrative texts on bronze discussed earlier in this chapter (mentioned by Kritzas 2006: 424) but has not yet been published.
²⁷⁹ See, e.g., *IG* XII.7 3 (Arcesine on Amorgos, first half of the fourth century); RO 39 (Iulis on Ceos, 362); RO 85 (Mytilene, ca. 334); *SEG* 51.1075 (Chios, ca. 334). *SEG* 57.576, from Dicaea ca. 364, is

seems to have a clause demanding that certain participants in a previous oligarchic regime have their houses torn down. The fragment ends with the mention of an oath that all Thasians must swear, "except for those who established the oligarchy."[280] A leitmotif of these inscriptions, going back to the Athenian Amnesty of 403, was the injunction *mē mnēsikakein*, "not to remember past wrongs," which often proved hard to uphold in practice as revolutionaries lay in wait for opportunities for revenge.[281]

As acrimony between oligarchs and democrats within cities intensified, goodwill between cities of the same regime type increased. The so-called Quadruple Alliance of 420 BCE involved four democracies – Athens, Elis, Argos, and Mantinea – and we read expressly that two of them were attracted to each other's democratic constitution (Argos and Mantinea: Thuc. 5.29.1).[282] Around the same time, the oligarchic Boeotians and Megarians found Sparta's *politeia* more conducive to their interests than the Argive democracy.[283] When the Athenian democratic fleet off Samos was engaged in *stasis* with the home government of the Four Hundred in 411, ambassadors from the Argive democracy arrived with news that "they would aid the People of Athens at Samos," thus acknowledging the naval democrats as the legitimate government.[284] At the end of the Peloponnesian War, when the Athenians' allies were deserting them in the aftermath of the Battle of Aegospotami in 405, the Samian *dēmos* remained loyal, "slaughtering the elite and keeping possession of the *polis*": For this they were effusively praised by the Athenians afterward and even awarded Athenian citizenship.[285] In the fourth century, Argos played an important role fostering democracies in the Peloponnese: at Corinth during the Corinthian War, as we saw; at Mantinea; and at Sicyon, for example.[286] The reconstituted Boeotian League under newly democratic Thebes and the similarly democratic Arcadian League played a comparable role, at one point overthrowing oligarchic regimes in all of the Achaean cities and replacing them with democracies. The exiled oligarchs from the different cities, however, banded together and restored each other to power.[287]

---

ambiguous regarding the city's constitution (see further Driscoll 2016). On such reconciliation agreements, see Dössel 2003; Gray 2015.
[280] *I. Thasos* 111.1. For similar civic oaths see Chapter 3.5.   [281] Loraux 2002.
[282] By the same token, the Syracusans presented the greatest challenge to the Athenian *dēmos* precisely because they were a dynamic and powerful democracy, just like the Athenians: Thuc. 7.55.2.
[283] Thuc. 5.31.6.   [284] Thuc. 8.86.
[285] Xen. *Hell.* 2.2.6 with OR 191 and RO 2; on the inscription see especially Elsner 2015.
[286] Robinson 2011: 22–23; Xen. *Hell.* 5.2.6, 7.1.44.   [287] Xen. *Hell.* 7.1.43.

Thus, even though cities might overthrow existing regimes for purely cynical reasons of state, it would not be an exaggeration to speak of a growing "Democratic International" (with its oligarchic counterpart) during the earlier fourth century.[288] And even if states of differing constitutions found themselves in an alliance with each other, their treaties often made a point of safeguarding the constitutional status quo: When the Athenians allied with democratic Phlius and oligarchic Achaea, Arcadia, and Elis in 362/1, the terms of the alliance specified that the democracies of Athens and Phlius would be protected, as would the "constitutions" (speaking euphemistically) of the other parties.[289] We will encounter numerous later instances of this phenomenon in the following chapter.

In attacking each other, democrats and oligarchs drew on the traditional language of opposition to tyranny and tyrannical hubris. When the Spartans were soliciting support at the outset of the Peloponnesian War, they depicted the Athenian democracy as a kind of collective tyrant, and it became common to think of the Athenian and other *dēmoi* as tyrants whose needs were catered to by demagogic "flatterers."[290] The Athenian oligarch Critias, killed at the Battle of Munychia in 403 during the Athenian civil war, had as his grave monument a depiction of personified Oligarchia setting fire to Demokratia, with the epitaph, "This is the tomb of good men, who for a short time checked the accursed *dēmos* of Athens in its hubris."[291] Oligarchs could also point to the occasional emergence of actual tyrants from democratic regimes, who often began their careers as "demagogues." Dionysius of Syracuse, Euphron of Sicyon, and a popular leader named Philoxenus from an unknown city were said to be instances of this phenomenon; Dionysius served as one of Aristotle's favorite historical examples.[292] The Athenians feared this might happen with Alcibiades, with whom they were paradoxically infatuated at the same time.[293] On the other hand, it was comparatively easy for democrats to equate their opponents, being by nature few in number, with tyrants or narrow tyrannical cliques.[294] A democratic uprising at Rhodes in 395 saw the ringleaders rally their fellow citizens against the "tyrants" of the city, in reality an

---

[288] Despite this growing tendency, ancient democracies definitely went to war with each other on occasion, in an exception to the modern "democratic peace thesis": Robinson 2006.

[289] RO 41. Arcadia had become an oligarchy since the actions just mentioned. Oligarchies did not refer to themselves as such in official documents, while democracies did; this suggests the waning legitimacy of oligarchy already in the first half of the fourth century.

[290] Thuc. 1.122.3. See Hdt. 3.81.2; Ar. *Eq.*; Arist. *Pol.* 4.1292a12–23 with Kallet 2003; Landauer 2019.

[291] DK 88 A 13 with Madson and Smith 2024.

[292] Diod. Sic. 13.95; Xen. *Hell.* 7.1.44–46; Phainias *BNJ* 1012 F 4; Arist. *Pol.* 5.1305a26–27, 1310b30–31.

[293] Thuc. 6.15.4 and Ar. *Ran.* 1422–25 with Wohl 2002. [294] Simonton 2017: 60–61.

oligarchy spearheaded by a prominent family.[295] The liberation of the Theban Cadmea from Spartan occupiers and a local puppet government in 379 also transpired under the banner of opposition to "tyrants."[296]

As we will see in the next chapter, for various reasons this democratic conflation of oligarchs with tyrants eventually triumphed, but it could not be taken for granted in the period under review. If anything, the near century from 451/0 to 362 was, as I have argued elsewhere, the golden age not of democracy, but of oligarchy: It was during this time that oligarchic ideology developed and oligarchic partisans stood their best chance of putting down democratic experiments once and for all.[297] It is to the failure of these efforts and the broad spread of democracy during its own golden age that we can now turn.

---

[295] *Hell. Oxy.* 18.1–3 Chambers with Simonton 2015.   [296] Xen. *Hell.* 3.4.9.
[297] Simonton 2017: Afterword.

CHAPTER 3

The Heyday of Ancient Greek Democracies, 362–146 BCE

3.1 Introduction

The chronological boundaries of this chapter, and the historiographical and conceptual assumptions behind them, require some initial comment. In the study of ancient Greek democracies, once we get beyond the question of whether genuinely democratic regimes existed beyond fifth-century Athens, the next big dividing line is undoubtedly that between the Classical and Hellenistic periods (conventionally 480–323 and 323–31 BCE, respectively). An old and influential tradition in scholarship held that while many *poleis* were free to experiment with democracy so long as the city-states remained autonomous, the "death of the *polis*" following the campaigns of Philip II of Macedon and his son Alexander the Great meant that talk of "democracy" (or of any kind of free government) beyond about 338 BCE was, in essence, a sham.[1] This view has been replaced, over the past forty years or so, with a new near orthodoxy that the early Hellenistic cities retained much of their earlier vitality, in some cases even getting a new lease on life thanks to the decline of traditional great-power politics in mainland Greece.[2] Nevertheless, debate persists about the democratic bona fides of these polities: While some speak of a golden age of *dēmokratia* in the earlier Hellenistic period, others remain skeptical, either because the evidence is too scanty to make informed judgments or because the term "democracy" is thought to have been evacuated of all substantive content and left a largely meaningless slogan.[3] Thus, while many would now have difficulty

---

[1] Already the British historian George Grote (1794–1871) could write, in the preface to his twelve-volume *History of Greece*, that "after the generation of Alexander, the political action of Greece becomes cramped and degraded" (Grote 1849: xv). Green 1990 continues in this vein.

[2] Robert 1969; Gauthier 1984 (to which this entire chapter owes much); Fröhlich 2004 (the trend is predominately but by no means exclusively francophone); Ma 2013. For summaries of the current state of research see Fröhlich forthcoming a and b.

[3] "Golden age": Heller 2009: 341; Azoulay 2014b: 391; Müller 2014: 536n15. Skeptical: Chaniotis 2010; Mann 2012.

3.1 Introduction

arguing against Eric Robinson's demonstration that there were numerous instances of "popular government in the Greek Classical age," they may still have their doubts about "Hellenistic democracy."[4]

As the chronological scope indicated by the title of this chapter should make clear, I find such a division between "Classical" and "Hellenistic" democracy deeply misleading. This periodization is, as almost all are, a modern invention, stemming from the nineteenth-century scholar J. G. Droysen's notion of a "Hellenizing" period following Alexander the Great, during which Greek ideas and institutions spread to new locations.[5] While the ancient Greeks themselves certainly understood that Alexander's conquests entailed enormous ramifications for their world, they had no conception – something modern scholars sometimes appear in danger of forgetting – that one way of life came to an end and another began in 323 BCE. If anything, following Alexander's death the cities may have hoped for a return to "normalcy." Many *poleis* continued to use their democratic institutions uninterrupted, while others gained experience of them for the first time. Demagogues harangued; assemblies deliberated; would-be oligarchs and tyrants occasionally attempted to overthrow popular regimes – these were societies that Aristotle, whom we will discuss in greater detail shortly, would likely have recognized as "democratic," albeit of a moderated variety. To treat as fundamentally different the antityranny legislation of Eretria (ca. 340) and Cyme's democratic regulation of its generals (ca. 270) – on both of which see further below – because they fall on opposite sides of the year 323 is, to the present author, anyway, worse than arbitrary: It hinders us from tracing genuine changes in ancient democratic practice over time. Rather than assume, then, that a post-323 date ipso facto means we are potentially in the presence of a democratic imposter, we should approach the whole body of evidence for ancient Greek democracy as free as possible from the habits of mind that modern periodization can instill, in order to see with fresh eyes what patterns emerge.[6]

Thus the present chapter: Although the start date (the final event covered by Xenophon's *Hellenica*) is a bit arbitrary, it allows for a period of more than a century in which democracy first emerged and democratic norms were consolidated – that covered for the most part by the previous two chapters. From 362 BCE onward, however, democracy was a fact of life in the Greek world. It must have been clear that no force existed, as Sparta

---

[4] Robinson 2011. [5] Droysen 1836–43.
[6] The chronological boundaries of Gray 2015 (ca. 404–146 BCE), an inspiration to the current study, are similar.

had once fleetingly appeared after 404, capable of rolling it back entirely. Furthermore, the trend noted in the previous chapter, whereby democrats lumped together oligarchy with tyranny as equally illegitimate constitutions, accelerated over the course of the fourth and third centuries. From the time of the Battle of Mantinea, as we will see, an increasing number of Greek *poleis* not only adopted formally democratic institutions – they also appear to have fulfilled their promise through robust participation by average citizens in the business of governance, for a period lasting more than two hundred years.

The reader must bear in mind at all times, however, that, while the argument speaks in terms of general trends, there were always exceptions and reverses. Similarly with the chosen ending point of this chapter: In many ways, the sack of Corinth in 146 following its defeat in the Achaean War, and the imposition of census-based oligarchic regimes thereafter by the victorious Roman general Lucius Mummius, represent a turning point in ancient Greek constitutional history. The Greek cities were also already undergoing transformations at the time that saw the rise of the "big benefactors," a kind of hereditary elite praised in new and increasingly inegalitarian language (see next chapter), so that the Romans were in effect beating a dying democratic horse. But even still, the year 146 is not a sharp caesura, merely characteristic of broader trends. There would be sparks of demotic collective action subsequently, even as the language of "democracy" faded from the extant public documents of the period. The chief point is that we cannot allow modern categories to obfuscate what appears, in my view, at any rate, to be a long democratic arc reaching from the fourth to the second century, with a peak, perhaps, in the first half of the third century BCE.

3.2 Historical Overview

With its leading politician Epaminondas killed at the Battle of Mantinea in 362, Thebes' hegemony was in disarray.[7] Into the vacuum created by the exhaustion of the rival mainland Greek powers stepped the kingdom of Macedon, led by its endlessly ambitious king Philip II (r. 359–336). Philip (and later Macedonian kings) doubtless preferred oligarchies to democracies, on both ideological and pragmatic grounds: Handpicked client regimes were easier to control and more likely to remain loyal to

---

[7] The reader who wants a more thorough historical overview should consult Shipley 2000 and Hornblower 2011.

Macedon, in addition to elevating the more elite members of the community. That said, while Philip and his successors did sometimes install oligarchic or tyrannical regimes among the Greek *poleis*, a less confrontational approach to Macedon on the part of politicians does not necessarily mean they were crypto-oligarchs. Philip benefited from Athens' preoccupation with the so-called Social War (357–355), a revolt of several key allies from the Second Athenian Confederacy, which involved a constitutional change from democracy to oligarchy on the part of such rebels as Rhodes and Chios. Although Athens and Philip agreed to a peace treaty in 346, it proved deeply unpopular to the Athenian *dēmos*, and the politicians who had been appointed the city's peace negotiators fell out among themselves.

Athens aided the Euboean city of Eretria in 341, putting down a tyrant installed by Philip and restoring the city to the Eretrian People. As we will see, the constitutional vicissitudes at Eretria during this period produced some forceful declarations on the part of restored popular regimes in favor of democracy and against oligarchy and tyranny. War between Athens and Macedon broke out again shortly thereafter, culminating in the Battle of Chaeronea in 338, where Philip decimated a military coalition led by Athens and Thebes. An influential line of scholarly thought has considered this moment the effective "death of the *polis*" (as we saw previously).

If this was the death of the Greek city, its zombified corpse remained quite vigorous. In reality, participants at the time hardly saw this as the end of the line, and political wrangling continued much as before. While the defeated Thebans were forced to accept an oligarchic regime of three hundred returning exiles, the Athenian democracy was left unscathed. Most Greek cities, though, with the exception of the Spartans, had little choice but to accept a common peace and to enroll in Philip's alliance, the League of Corinth, which safeguarded its members' constitutional status quo.

Philip's assassination in 336 brought to the throne his twenty-year-old son Alexander III (the "Great"), who in six short years managed to invade the Persian Empire and defeat the last Achaemenid Great King, Darius III (r. 336–330). In liberating the Greek *poleis* of the East from Persian rule Alexander set up democratic regimes, establishing a precedent whereby cities paid considerable honors to monarchs in exchange for constitutional protections. This must count as a major milestone in the history of Greek democracy, when the greatest king the Greeks of the time had ever known gave his imprimatur to popular government rather than rule by the few.

Alexander's premature death in Babylon in 323 famously led to the dissolution of his kingdom, as the *diadochi* or "successors," men like Ptolemy, Seleucus, and Antigonus Monophthalmus ("the One-Eyed"), fought it out among themselves for a substantial piece of the pie. The democratic gains in the Greek East were offset during this period (323–281) by constitutional chaos on the mainland, as the *diadochi* alternatively put down and raised up again democracies and oligarchies as suited their immediate political needs. The Athenian democracy was the most famous victim: After the uprising called the Lamian War was quashed in 322, Athens entered a long period of constitutional uncertainty, including two census-based oligarchic regimes in 322–318 and again in 317–307.

The city then came under the thumb of Demetrius I Poliorcetes ("the Besieger"), son of Antigonus the One-Eyed, but a citizen uprising in 287 restored "the democracy of *all* the Athenians," as a later inscription says (to distinguish this constitution from the compromised regime that preceded it).[8] The anti-Macedonian venture known as the Chremonidean War ended in defeat in 262/1, with Macedonian control of Athens subsequently secured through the presence of garrisons. The situation would not change until 229, when the last garrison commander agreed to dissolve his post in exchange for a huge payment. Thereafter Athens charted a largely isolationist and quiescent path, standing aloof from many of the conflicts in mainland Greece, but in 199 it made the momentous decision to ally with the Romans (on whom more in a moment) against Philip V of Macedon in the Second Macedonian War (200–197).

While Athens' democracy underwent several important alterations during this long period, scholars are now largely in agreement that Athens' political institutions constituted a moderate form of democracy down through the end of the period surveyed in this chapter, at least during bouts of independence.[9] Indeed, at several points after 318/17 the city could be more vocal than it had ever been about the importance of democracy – whether this was protesting too much, however, we will examine elsewhere.

In the Greek-speaking world beyond Athens, the third century saw the spread and entrenchment of democracy as the sole legitimate form of government, the instability of the period of the *diadochi* notwithstanding. Especially in the East, we find multiple civic oaths inscribed on stone from this century specifying that the citizens will do their best to uphold democracy and not admit any competing kind of *politeia*, the threat of which remained real (see further Section 3.5). In general, the cities of the Aegean and Asia Minor increasingly communicated with each other on

---

[8] *IG* II³ 911, ll. 82–83.
[9] That it was a more moderate form of democracy than in the fifth and fourth centuries is not in doubt: See, for example, Lambert 2017: ch. 9, which shows that the assembly exhibited far less independence from the council.

common terms, through such institutions as proxeny bestowal, *isopoliteia* agreements (the bilateral offer to grant citizenship to the citizenry of two different *poleis*), and the sending of panels of so-called foreign judges to adjudicate sensitive legal cases.[10] This "peer–polity interaction," documented by an overall increase in epigraphic production starting in the fourth century, tended to assume a constitutional backdrop of democracy; as the historian Philippe Gauthier put it, the cities spoke a sort of "democratic lingua franca."[11]

Internally, many *poleis*, beginning with Athens in (probably) the 330s BCE, developed an ephebate (*ephēbeia*) or training program for young men, which, over several years, taught not only sons of the elite but also a broad swath of the male population how to comport themselves as responsible soldiers and citizens.[12] In keeping with this focus on producing well-trained local militias, freedom of action in foreign policy did not necessarily diminish, either, despite the looming presence of the successor kingdoms. *Poleis* still went to war with each other using citizen armies, swore to alliances, and submitted to third-party arbitration.[13] The "freedom, autonomy, and democracy" that recur again and again as qualities of the *polis* to be respected by outside powers were not necessarily empty slogans in our period, although cynical actors could and did exploit them.

The situation on the mainland is less clear, especially for the Peloponnese in the first half of the third century, where tyrannies proliferated. In 251, however, the politician and general Aratus of Sicyon consolidated multiple Peloponnesian cities into the expanding Achaean League (*koinon*), a federated constitutional form popular with mainland Greek communities in the third and second centuries.[14] As we will see in Section 3.4, while the

---

[10] Proxeny: Mack 2015. *Isopoliteia*: Saba 2020. Foreign judges: Robert 1973; Crowther 1992; Hamon 2012; Magnetto 2016.

[11] Peer–polity interaction: Ma 2003. "Democratic lingua franca" ("*koinè* démocratique"): Gauthier 1993: 218; see also Ma 2018 on the "great convergence" of the Hellenistic period. Note that in a treaty between Miletus and Heraclea under Latmus from the earlier second century, the two *poleis* agree that any arbitration between them will be presided over by a "free and democratic city" (*Syll.*³ 633, ll. 84–85).

[12] For the Athenian ephebate, see Friend 2019 and Henderson 2020. Perrin-Saminadayar 2007 focuses on the period of 229–288. Chankowski 2010 examines the ephebate during the Hellenistic period in Athens and beyond. For the relatively inclusive nature of the *ephēbeia*, see Hin 2007, who cautions, however, that the costs involved in many cities "will definitely have excluded lower-class boys" (152). The ephebate would thus be one of a number of institutions in democratic cities that failed to benefit the very poorest citizens. We will return to the Imperial incarnation of this institution in the following chapter.

[13] War: Ma 2000a; Chaniotis 2005; Boulay 2014. Alliances: Schmitt 1969; Errington 2020. Third-party arbitration: Ager 1996.

[14] See the contributions to Beck and Funke 2015.

politician and historian Polybius (ca. 200–ca. 118) called the League a "true democracy," its structure granted the elite considerably more authority than in a small, democratically governed *polis*, although there were no formal property requirements for office holding. In Magna Graecia, Syracuse was ruled by a series of tyrants for most of our period, beginning with Dionysius II in the fourth century and continuing through Hiero II and his grandson Hieronymus in the late third, but other communities like Tarentum were (famously) democratic.[15] The Italian and Sicilian Greek *poleis* were some of the first to encounter the expanding Roman Empire, thanks to geographical proximity.

Indeed, Polybius records an Aetolian politician, speaking before an audience at Naupactus in 217, as having warned the Greeks of the "clouds appearing from the west."[16] He refers to the Romans and Carthaginians, at that time engaged in the Second Punic War (218–201) but predicted by the speaker to expand and settle upon Greece, whichever one should win the conflict. In the Romans the Greeks encountered a fiercely militaristic people with imperial ambitions on a Mediterranean-wide scale; it was also a society with – for all its seeming popular elements – much greater ideological and institutional deference toward a narrow political elite, the so-called *nobiles* of the Senate, than Greek democracies were used to.[17]

The Romans' growing importance, appreciated by the Sicilian historian Timaeus of Tauromenium, was felt in their war of the 270s BCE against the democratic Tarentines of Southern Italy and their ally King Pyrrhus of Epirus. In a series of wars against Greek monarchs – first Philip V of Macedon, then Antiochus III of the Seleucid Kingdom – the Romans expanded their influence on the foreign policy and constitutional trajectory of the Greek cities. The aftermath of the Battle of Cynoscephalae in 197, in which Philip V was defeated, saw the Greeks bestowing godlike honors on a Roman, Titus Quinctius Flamininus, for the first time. Beginning with the Peace of Apamea in 188, but accelerating after the defeat of the Macedonian Perseus at Pydna in 168, some communities began referring to the Romans as the "common benefactors" of the Greeks, an unprecedented title.[18]

---

[15] See, e.g., Arist. *Pol.* 6.1320b11–14; Strab. 6.3.4; Plut. *Vit. Pyrrh.* 13.2. Theopompus *BNJ* 115 F 233 criticizes the number of Tarentine festivals, a common complaint by conservatives against ancient democracies.

[16] Polyb. 5.104.10.

[17] For Roman imperialism see the recent survey of Burton 2019. The revisionist thesis of Millar 1986, that Rome was a kind of direct democracy, has in turn been resisted by, among others, Hölkeskamp 2010. My position is that whatever we wish to label the Roman Republic, it was far less democratic than the average Greek *polis*.

[18] Erskine 1994.

A failed uprising by the Achaean League in 146 spelled the end of the autonomy of the mainland Greeks. The victorious Roman commander Mummius was careful to put down democracies and install oligarchic governments based on property requirements in their place, at least for a time.[19] Elsewhere, however, constitutional interference was not so blatant, although the Romans clearly preferred dealing with oligarchies and could impose them on occasion. But by the mid second century BCE the Romans were pushing at an open door: As we will see in the next chapter, processes largely endogenous to the *poleis* were encouraging the rise of an ever more entrenched class of office-hogging "notables," with a concomitant decline in the power of the average citizen. The Roman penchant for elitist government accelerated a deformation of *dēmokratia* already underway.

3.3 Understandings of Democracy

In the preceding section I did not yet specify what was understood by "democracy" during the period in question. Unfortunately we will never have a complete picture of the different attitudes toward and understandings of ancient Greek democracy, given the state of our sources. However, what we can do is take two authors' contemporary treatments from around 330 BCE and compare their assessment of democracy with the historical evidence of literary texts, inscriptions, and archaeological remains. Those individuals are the philosopher Aristotle of Stagira (384–322) and the rhetorician and historian Anaximenes of Lampsacus, who is almost certainly the author of a text known as the *Rhetoric to Alexander* included among the works of Aristotle. The two wrote at a time when democracy had been developing for more than one hundred and fifty years (since 508/7, let us say) and thus could draw on a wealth of historical examples as well as theoretical reflections. Indeed, Aristotle's *Politics* represents the fruit of his school's systematic investigations into the constitutional histories of various *poleis*, in the form of 158 separate *politeiai*, only one of which, that of Athens, survives. I hope to convince the reader in what follows that these texts are not the last gasp of a period of "*polis* freedom" that was snuffed out before the ensuing centuries of the Hellenistic period: They remain good guides to the politics of the Greek cities in the later fourth, third, and second centuries. This is decidedly not a case where the owl of

---

[19] Paus. 7.16.9.

Minerva, as the philosopher Hegel put it, takes flight only at dusk (that is, understanding comes only after a phenomenon has petered out).

Aristotle's *Politics* is the most important document on ancient Greek political life that has come down to us. While its worth as a source for political history is priceless, it cannot truly be understood apart from Aristotle's greater logical, psychological, and metaphysical projects, adequate discussion of which lies outside the scope of this project. What I would emphasize is the sheer usefulness and learnedness – his idiosyncratic philosophy notwithstanding – of Aristotle's text. Simply put, Aristotle's school recorded more about Greek constitutional development than we can ever know. Whatever we think of Aristotle's influence on the history of political thought, we cannot ignore him. And here is what he says about democracy: For Aristotle, democracy was one of the three "deviant" forms of constitution, including also tyranny and oligarchy, to which corresponded three "legitimate" forms: monarchy, aristocracy, and, in the case of democracy, so-called *politeia* or "constitutional government." These distinctions are rarely found in historical or rhetorical texts, which speak simply of democracy and oligarchy without qualification and use "aristocracy" as a mere euphemism for oligarchy. Aristotle does acknowledge, however, that most *poleis* of his day lie somewhere on the spectrum between democracy and oligarchy (4.1296a22–23), and he notes the greater stability (5.1302a8–11) and moderation (4.1289b4–5) of democracies compared with oligarchies and tyrannies. He also suggests that their numbers are on the rise. Intriguingly, at one point he writes that, "since it has turned out that *poleis* have grown greater in size, it is perhaps no longer very easy for a constitution other than democracy to emerge" (3.1286b20–22).[20] Clearly, for Aristotle writing in the later fourth century, democracies were very common, they were proving themselves better than oligarchies at spreading and surviving, and their future looked assured.[21] Democracies also best fit Aristotle's influential definition of citizenship, according to which the male citizen (*politēs*) in the "absolute sense" was one who partook of *archē* (political office) and *krisis* (legal judgment).[22] But what, for Aristotle, were democracies?

---

[20] See already Chapter 1.3.
[21] As the historian Philippe Gauthier (1984: 86) put it forty years prior to the time of this writing, "Recorded on the threshold of the Hellenistic period, this remark looks like a prediction, which the assertions of the authors of later decrees appear precisely to confirm."
[22] *Pol.* 3.1275a22–23 with 1275b5–7. For this definition, recently subjected to critical scrutiny, see Section 3.7.

3.3 Understandings of Democracy

The philosopher provides the shortest, clearest list of traits in Book 6 of the *Politics*, although we must note that elsewhere in the treatise he views democracy as comprising four subtypes, from least to most radical.[23] In summary form, though, he says that democracies are characterized by the following features (6.1317b17ff.): that all citizens should select magistrates [*archai*] chosen from a pool comprising all citizens; that either all or as many offices as do not require experience and skill should be selected by lot (be *klērotai* – but Aristotle admits elsewhere that election, so long as it is "by all from all," is just as "popular," *dēmotikon*: 4.1300a32); that iteration of office should be limited and magistracies confined to a short amount of time; that all citizens should be eligible to serve as judges (*dikastai*) who have competence over all legal decisions; that the assembly [*ekklēsia*] should be authoritative in most matters; and that most officeholders should receive pay. These were apparently the features that Aristotle and his school both encountered frequently and considered to be reflective of what they saw as the core tenets of democracy, freedom and equality (6.1317b1–7). Elsewhere in the text the philosopher explains that democracies' greatest source of weakness was their tendency to produce demagogues who antagonized the wealthy to the point of *stasis* (4.1292a15–30, 5.1304b19–1305a7).

Alongside this particular understanding of democracy we can set the evidence of the contemporary *Rhetoric to Alexander*, a text that is invaluable in that it is both non-Aristotelian and non-Athenocentric in nature.[24] Indeed, a recent study of the *Rhetoric* has shown that it presupposes a world of smaller, rather more moderate democracies than Athens, in which its author considered skill in rhetoric to be useful.[25] The relevant section on democracy ([Arist.] *Rhet. ad Alex.* 1424a13–38) is worth quoting in full:

> In democracies it is necessary to make the smaller offices [*archai*], which constitute the majority of them, chosen by lot [*klērotai*] (for this reduces the risk of civil strife), but the greatest [offices] should be elected by the masses [*plēthos*]. For in this way the *dēmos*, being authoritative in bestowing honors on whomever it wishes, will not resent those who receive them, and the more prominent [citizens] will cultivate gentlemanly behavior [*kalokagathia*] more,

---

[23] I cannot dwell on the legitimacy of Aristotle's subtypes – historians have found it difficult to apply a subtype designation to any given *polis* – but they are important evidence that he believed there were regimes that were obviously democratic without, however, matching the "extreme" Athenian democracy point for point.
[24] For its worth as evidence for democracy and oligarchy see Hansen and Nielsen 2004: 83; Simonton 2017: 88.
[25] Piepenbrink 2021. By "moderate" I mean using a mixture of election and sortition for office holding and relying on little or no payment for office.

knowing that having a good reputation among the citizens will not be unprofitable for them. . . . As to the remaining administration [of democracies], it would be a great task to go through each thing one by one, but in short it is necessary to take care that the laws will avert the masses [*plēthos*] from plotting against the owners of property and will implant in the rich a sense of rivalrous zeal [*philotimia*] for spending money on the community's public services [*leitourgiai*]. One might produce this situation in the following way, if there are certain honors specified by the laws for the owners of property in exchange for their expenditures for the community, while, as for those who labor, the laws hold in higher honor those who work the land and sail in the navy rather than the people of the marketplace [*hoi agoraioi*]. For in this case the wealthy will willingly carry out public services for the *polis*, while the *plēthos* will desire hard work rather than vexatious litigation [*sykophantia*]. It is also necessary, in addition to these matters, that powerful laws be laid down that prevent the redistribution of land and the confiscation of the possessions of those who carry out public services, as well as serious penalties for those who contravene these strictures. There must be set aside, for those who die in war, a public plot of land in a fine spot in front of the city for the purposes of burial, and their children are to be given support at public expense until they come of age.

The two texts touch upon democratic themes – payment for office, sykophancy, liturgies – that we have encountered before, but they also contain new developments. In particular, compared with the evidence for the close association between democracy and sortition that we have seen in such authors as Herodotus, the Old Oligarch, and the *Dissoi Logoi*, Aristotle and Anaximenes are much more open to the officials being elected under democracy – the *Rhetoric to Alexander*, in fact, advises this method for the "greatest" offices on prudential grounds. Both authors have also had enough experience with democracies to recognize their chief source of instability: demagogic politicians who convince the masses to confiscate the property of the wealthy, thus leading to civil strife.

The two texts, but especially the *Rhetoric to Alexander*, serve as a kind of practical guide for keeping democracies on an even keel. Anaximenes is particularly concerned that democracy be able to strike the right balance between empowering the majority and respecting the property and honor of the elite. As we will see, keeping the wealthy and powerful loyal to the constitutional status quo through a robust regime of honors and privileges was one of the central concerns of Greek democracies in their heyday. These governments, it seems, were not expected to overcome the social differentiation of the citizenry into the wealthy and the laboring classes – the poor they would always have with them. Economic inequality was compatible with democracy and did not qualify as oligarchy so long as average citizens had access to the magistracies (or at least were not legally barred from the highest ones by a property requirement) and their power in the assembly and law courts was preponderant.

3.4 Democracies during the "Heyday": An Institutional Overview

In the previous chapter we reviewed the key features of the Athenian democracy in "the age of Pericles": a powerful assembly in which amendments were possible and "demagogic" rhetoric likely; a probouleutic council selected by lot; numerous other magistracies selected by lot and granted an allowance (*misthos*); short terms of office, sometimes with limits on iteration; the rendering of accounts by officeholders to the People; the empaneling of very large law courts with judges, again chosen by lot and paid; a strong system for compelling wealthy men to engage in liturgies; and the burial of the war dead at public expense and the rearing of "war orphans" until they reached the age of majority. This arrangement, for many scholars, represents the gold standard of ancient Greek democracy against which all others must be measured. And we must admit right at the beginning that, while the state of our documentation means that we will probably never have as clear an institutional picture for any other ancient Greek *polis*, it is unlikely that many of them could top Athens when it came to the democratic total package. But as we have just seen with Aristotle and Anaximenes, a city did not have to match Athens absolutely on every point in order to be reckoned a genuine democracy. What follows is not exhaustive but instead meant to suggest the range of constitutional setups considered sufficiently democratic in the period in question.[26] In all cases we must go beyond the bare evidence supplied by the enactment formulae of decrees, the prosaic "decided by the *boulē* and the *dēmos*" found in literally thousands of inscriptions from the Greek world – a formula that can be misleading – in order to try to drill down to the real workings of power.

We can start with the offices. As we saw already in Chapter 1.4, for the ancient Greeks the composition and selection of the magistrates was central for classifying a regime as democratic. A regime that limited its councilors, according to a property requirement, for example, was considered oligarchic, and the more oligarchic the higher the requirement. We

---

[26] Obviously, each *polis* was unique, with its own institutional history, but recent work has highlighted constitutional similarities within specific regions of the Greek-speaking world, for instance Fröhlich 2019 on the cities of Aeolis, demonstrating the common role of the *stratēgos* within them.

see census-based regimes like this in Athens in 322 and 317, in Cyrene in the late fourth century, and in the Achaean League after the failed Achaean War of 146.[27] Some democracies matched Athens' penchant for choosing councilors by lottery: In the antityranny law of Eretria from around 340, we read that no council is to be considered legitimate unless it is "selected by lot from out of [all] Eretrians."[28] In a treaty of *isopoliteia* between Miletus and Heraclea under Latmus from around 180, we learn that Miletus had a "law on the council" (*bouleutikos nomos*) that almost certainly specified that councilors were to be chosen by sortition.[29] At Magnesia on the Maeander around 200, there were some officeholders selected by election and some by lot, just as in the scheme advocated by Anaximenes.[30] As late as the first century BCE, the Roman politician Cicero says that the Rhodians' council was made up of the same people as the assembly (and so probably chosen by sortition) and received *misthos*; they also served for the short term of six months.[31] (Rhodes, as we will see, had numerous democratic features remarked on by ancient writers.) In many cities it would have been typical for the councilors to be chosen by election. It is a truism in studies of the ancient world that election was a "more oligarchic" method of choosing magistrates than allotment, but that does not mean that it signaled an oligarchic regime per se. As long as there were no property requirements for office and all citizens could participate in elections, this was democratic. And while election did favor the already prominent (the nondemotic notables), it was no guarantee that the people would not choose a "rabble-rouser": in late fourth-century Syracuse, elections were likely to result in "any chance demagogue" holding office, since "the majority [*plēthos*] was opposed to the preeminence of men who dared speak frankly to them" and preferred populists.[32]

When it came to setting the agenda for the assembly, a probouleutic council was considered normal, and indeed many democracies limited themselves to deliberating only on such matters as the *boulē* had approved for discussion. What was undemocratic was an official or a board limited by a property qualification that could unilaterally dictate what the assembly could discuss or veto decisions of the assembly that went against its wishes. Aristotle says that officials called *probouloi* and *nomophylakes* (guardians of the laws) performed such a function in oligarchies, and indeed Xenophon says that in "well-governed states" (a euphemism for

---

[27] Diod. Sic. 18.18.4, 74.3; *IGCyr*010800; Paus. 7.16.9.
[28] *SEG* 51.1105a, ll. 19–20, with "all" convincingly restored by the editor of the inscription.
[29] *Syll.*³ 633, ll. 52–53.   [30] *Syll.*³ 589, ll. 37–38.   [31] Cic. *Rep.* 3.35.48.
[32] Diod. Sic. 20.79.3 with Simonton 2025.

3.4 Democracies during the "Heyday"

oligarchies) the *nomophylakes* ensure that the citizens "obey the laws," probably by vetoing unwanted legislation. In Sparta this was one of the prerogatives of the *gerousia*, or council of elders, which had the right to "set aside crooked measures" of the assembly. Under the oligarchy of Demetrius of Phalerum in Athens between 317 and 307, a panel of *nomophylakes* could do just that.[33] Strabo alerts us to officials called *epiklētoi* who worked with a *gerousia* to administer affairs at Ephesus under an oligarchy imposed by Lysimachus in 302.[34] These bodies appear in two decrees of the period that show that they enjoyed agenda-setting power.[35] Such measures were clearly intended to limit the range of decisions available to the assembly and to prevent the rise of demagogic politicians who worked against the elite's interests. As we will see, in many of the *poleis* under consideration excessive demagoguery remained a serious problem from the fourth to second centuries, and so the regimes where they appeared probably did not employ *probouloi* or *nomophylakes*.[36] There are subtler cases, however, where we see boards of magistrates seemingly predominating, but their exclusivity is difficult to measure. In Miletus beginning around 180, magistrates called *prytaneis* appear to be able to make policy at the expense of the assembly.[37] Roberta Fabiani has recently argued for a similar dynamic at Iasos, but even earlier, beginning in the second half of the third century. There the board of (again) *prytaneis*, appearing on prosopographical grounds to belong to the city's elite, seems to have enjoyed agenda control.[38] I find it unlikely that the office of *prytanis* had a formal property requirement, but such a de facto takeover by the notables of an important magistracy is one of the biggest problems facing those who believe in thriving democracy in the Hellenistic period, and requires further study.

Anaximenes, quoted previously, predicted that the legal system might prove an opportunity for democratic abuse of the wealthy, and he advised that strict laws be laid down to protect the property of the notables from confiscation.[39] Aristotle certainly knew multiple examples of democratic courts of law (*dikastēria*) expropriating the elite, usually at the instigation of demagogues.[40] I believe that the tiny island *polis* of Telos had such

---

[33] Philochorus *BNJ* 328 F 64. [34] Strab. 14.1.21. [35] *Syll.*³ 353; *i. Ephesos* 1470.
[36] Democracies of this period also continued to exhibit *thorubos* or the ability of the crowd to "raise a ruckus" in an attempt to put pressure on speakers: see, e.g., Polyb. 38.12.4–5. This continued in the Imperial period, albeit under altered constitutional circumstances, as the orations of Dio Chrysostom show: see Chapter 4.5.
[37] Müller 1976: 55–56. [38] Fabiani 2012, disputed by Fröhlich 2021.
[39] On the legal systems of Hellenistic democracies see esp. Walser 2012; also Hamon 2009: 364–66.
[40] Arist. *Pol.* 5.1304b20–24, 1305a5–7, 6.1320a4–6.

courts, and such demagogues, as I will examine in greater detail in the next section. Certainly elsewhere *dikastēria* could be large, they could be allotted, and they could be paid positions. There is considerable evidence for Rhodes' legal panels, which were filled by allotment, and Athens continued to have strong "people's courts."[41] (Most of the *klērotēria*, or allotment machines, that survive and supply evidence for Athens' legal system actually date to the Hellenistic period.[42]) In a *sympoliteia* agreement of the second century between Stiris and Medeon in Phocis – a process whereby two cities politically merged – we read that *dikastēria* should be selected by lottery.[43] When Miletus adjudicated a dispute between Messene and Sparta in the second century, it empaneled a court (*kritērion*) of six hundred men "selected by lot from the entire People, the largest allowed by the laws."[44]

We can now turn to the assembly. In order to show that many cities during this time remained democracies, it was necessary first to establish that the magistracies (*archai*) could and did remain in the hands of ordinary citizens. The mere existence of an assembly of the people was not a sufficient condition for democracy, as we will see in the next chapter when we examine the survival of assembly politics in the Imperial era. That said, given the democratic nature of the magistracies surveyed just now, it is no surprise that we also have plenty of evidence for well-attended, even boisterous *ekklēsiai* during the period 362–146. Citizens continued to listen to fierce debates between speakers, as in the Rhodian assembly of 168 BCE labeled "extremely turbulent" by Polybius, in which the two sides argued for and against allying with the Macedonian king Perseus.[45] Similar debates accompanied the Tarentines' confrontation with the Romans in the 270s.[46]

In general, when crises and "disturbances" (*tarachai*) gripped the cities, when their inhabitants were "in dire straits" (*thlibomenoi*), it was the assembly of citizens that attempted to rectify the situation, often by electing military commanders or sending embassies.[47] Thus the assembly of Istria (from the mouth of the Danube River in modern Romania) elected a certain Agathocles commander of a squad of archers when neighboring Thracian "barbarians" were harassing the city around 200.[48] When the Abydenes were besieged by Philip V of Macedon, also in 200, the male citizens met in the assembly and resolved "with unanimity" to

---

[41] For Rhodes, see Thomsen 2020: 21–22. [42] Papazarkadas 2021; cf. *IG* II² 1163.
[43] *Syll.*³ 647, ll. 32–33. [44] *Syll.*³ 683, ll. 47–49. [45] Polyb. 29.11.2. [46] Plut. *Vit. Pyrrh.* 13.2.
[47] See, e.g., *SEG* 24.1095, l. 9 (*tarachē*); *I. Erythrai* 28, l. 38 (*thlibomenoi*). [48] *SEG* 24.1095.

take a series of measures to withstand the siege and to kill themselves collectively, along with their wives and children, should the inner wall of the city be taken by the enemy.[49] Here we see the assembly endowed with the ultimate power, that over life and death.

The typical assembly meeting would of course have also covered much more mundane matters, such as deciding on domestic policy and honoring benefactors. Many *poleis* had in addition special sessions of the *ekklēsia* set aside for the election of the magistrates. Assemblies in Greek democracies during our period seem to have met fairly regularly, on average at least once per month. Fourth-century Athens, with its forty sessions annually, may have been special.[50] Attendees to the assembly were also paid in some *poleis*: Athens made payments from the 390s down to 322, and there is epigraphic evidence for a similar procedure at Iasos in the early third century.[51] In sum, the *ekklēsia* remained the central expression of the *dēmos' kratos* in Greek democracies of this period, much as it had before.

Finally, we come to the last measure Anaximenes mentions, the public burial of the war dead and the rearing of their children. At first glance, we might consider this a generalization based on the specifically Athenian practice of the *patrios nomos*, examined in the previous chapter. In fact, Anaximenes' remark is in line with democratic practice from multiple *poleis*. The Rhodians, under siege by Demetrius Poliorcetes in 305, decreed that they would "bury the bodies of the war dead at public expense and support their parents and children, taking up the task by recourse to the public treasury; they would also offer dowries for the maiden daughters at public expense and honor the sons with a full set of arms in the theater at the Dionysia when they reached the age of majority."[52] A recently published second fragment of an inscription from mid fourth-century Thasos shows that, in addition to the parents and children of the war dead receiving such special privileges as front seats at the games and a suit of arms (awards known already from a preexisting *stēlē*), the war orphans would receive material support (*trophē*) on the community's dime.[53] Sometimes *poleis* awarded these sorts of gifts to the descendants of men who had fought specifically on behalf of democracy. In Athens, we have

---

[49] Polyb. 16.31.1–5. See further Section 7 of this chapter on the decision to kill the women.
[50] Rhodes with Lewis 1997: 503–504; for cities in Ionia and Caria, see Bernini 2023: 61–74 with table 2.
[51] Athens: [Arist.] *Ath. Pol.* 41.3. Iasos: RO 99 (with the redating of Fabiani 2015), and see further de Ste. Croix 1975.
[52] Diod. Sic. 20.84.3. For the freeing of slaves during this episode see Section 3.7.
[53] Fournier and Hamon 2007 = *SEG* 57.820b; see also *I.Thasos* 111.5. For this decree's treatment of metics, see Section 3.7.

seen that the decree of Theozotides, probably dating to the period after the oligarchy of the Four Hundred and so in 410 or thereabouts, granted *trophē* to the children of Athenians (but not metics) who "died a violent death in the course of defending democracy during the time of oligarchy."[54] This example is followed by the antityranny law of Eretria from around 340, which prescribes honors for the sons and daughters of those who might die "killing a tyrant or the leader of an oligarchy."[55] This system of public honors makes sense in a democratic constitution rather than an oligarchic one: In the latter, while there could certainly be rewards for informants and other incentives that kept members of the *dēmos* invested in the constitution's survival, it would have been folly to publicize non-elite benefactors of the regime, since it would have meant opening up the whole social and political question of what was owed to the *dēmos*, a slippery slope for an oligarchy.

The foregoing evidence ought to go some way toward assuaging the suspicion, often voiced in the past by historians, that "democracy" after the death of Alexander meant little more than "republican self-government," and that these so-called democracies were in reality oligarchies.[56] In favor of this interpretation scholars have pointed to Polybius, who labels as a "true democracy" the elite-dominated Achaean League.[57] But Polybius' use of the word "true" suggests special pleading: He is using the language and ideology of his time, which saw democracy alone as legitimate, in order to try to show how his beloved *koinon* was truer to democratic principles than the more egalitarian constitutions that also (primarily) went under that name.[58] Thus he declines to apply the term "democracy" to Athens, for example, which seems to have possessed a moderate but – in Polybius' eyes – still quite populist democratic constitution in the later third and second centuries.[59] Polybius' language of "true" democracy indicates that there were many contemporary cities which, precisely because they empowered the People to a degree Polybius found unacceptable, the historian considered not "democratic" but rather "ochlocratic" or "run

---

[54] SEG 28.46, ll. 4–11; see already Chapter 2, Excursus. On this decree and the treatment of metics in Athens, see Section 3.7.
[55] SEG 51.1105a, ll. 10–15.   [56] Larsen 1954: 9; de Ste. Croix 1981: 322; O'Neil 1995: 119.
[57] Polyb. 2.38.7. However, despite the fact that policy at the federal level was directed mostly by leaders from elite families (O'Neil 1984–86), the Achaean League did have popular features, since poor men could attend the assembly (and on rare occasions apparently tip the *koinon* in the direction of populist policies: Polyb. 38.12.4–5); also, as we have seen, a census-based constitution was established in it only after 146: See further Walbank 1995: 213–16.
[58] See Grieb 2013; Thornton 2019.
[59] Reestablishment of moderate democracy after 229 BCE: Worthington 2020: 190.

by the mob."⁶⁰ And indeed his own history furnishes many examples of highly participatory regimes, some of which go so far as to devolve into demagoguery and tyranny. As the next section makes clear, the citizens of these constitutions might legitimately fear the imposition of an unwanted oligarchic regime down through the second century. The protestations of Polybius on behalf of Achaea are therefore not evidence for the thesis that *dēmokratia* had been emptied of all substantive content by the third and second centuries but rather the precise opposite.

3.5 Threats to Democracy and Their Solutions

Ancient Greek democracies, like other *politeiai* of the period, constantly had to be on the lookout for *stasis*, or civil strife, even if, as we have seen, Aristotle considered democracies less prone to this destructive menace than oligarchies and tyrannies. This holds for democracies on either side of Alexander the Great's death in 323: As a recent study has shown, the Hellenistic period no less than the Classical was replete with episodes where intra-citizen violence led to a *metabolē tēs politeias*, a "change in constitutional type."⁶¹ Because oligarchical and tyrannical coups d'état by definition involved groups representing a minority of the total citizen population of a *polis*, their revolutionary tactics tended to unfurl in ways that accounted for their smaller numbers. The monopolization of central civic space and the exclusion of the broader *dēmos* from the acropolis, agora, or defensive walls was one such measure. We have already seen how the Thirty Tyrants at Athens expelled the majority population from the *astu*, or city center; they were not the last oligarchs to do so.⁶² The author of a handbook for surviving sieges, Aeneas Tacticus, probably writing in the 350s BCE, recounts how conspirators at Argos waited for the community to celebrate a festival outside the city walls. They then attacked civic officials at the festival, hoarded the citizenry's weapons, and retreated within the walls, locking the *dēmos* out of the city and effecting an oligarchic coup.⁶³ The Eretrian law against tyranny and oligarchy of the 340s, discussed previously, likewise imagines a scenario in which

---

⁶⁰ Polyb. 6.57.9.   ⁶¹ Börm 2019.   ⁶² See Chapter 2.2.
⁶³ Aen. Tact. 17.2–4. The event may date to 417, in a revolution mentioned by Thucydides (5.81.2). Coincidentally, Aeneas' text indicates the existence of democratic regimes throughout the Greek world in the fourth century: at Argos again (11.7–10), at Heraclea Pontica on the Black Sea (11.10b), and at Corcyra off the western mainland (11.13–15). Oligarchic subversives mentioned in these cases are frequently referred to as "the rich."

"the *dēmos* is shut out of the walls."⁶⁴ (For the practical intent underlying such antityranny legislation, see later in this section.) The fourth-century tyrants of Eresus on Lesbos were also remembered as having done this.⁶⁵

The seizure of the acropolis or city center was often accompanied by the introduction of a garrison that secured the antidemocratic regime's power. Thus, in a letter to the Carian *polis* of Mylasa in the 230s BCE, the local dynast Olympichus claims that upon initially occupying the city, hitherto garrisoned, he "led away the garrison from the acropolis [*akra*] and restored the *polis* [to the citizens] in a free and democratic state."⁶⁶ A late fourth-century decree from Eretria, recorded by the Renaissance traveler Cyriac of Ancona but since lost, says somewhat cryptically that during the festival of Dionysus "the garrison departed and the *dēmos* was freed and recovered its ancestral laws and democracy."⁶⁷ We must imagine a similar moment of liberation in an honorific decree from third-century Erythrae in Ionia praising the citizen Phanes because "he contributed money at no interest for the dismissal of the mercenary troops and the demolition [*kataskaphē*] of the acropolis fortifications."⁶⁸ There was thus a close connection in the minds of ancient Greeks between the occupation of the acropolis, the presence of a garrison, and the imposition of nondemocratic rule. This association was so strong that a local historian of Erythrae, probably writing in the first half of the third century, could imagine that in the eleventh century BCE his *polis* had been taken over by "oligarchic tyrants" who took advantage of an extramural festival of Artemis to seize the city center and establish their own personal rule, with the help of a Chian garrison force; they admitted no commoners within the walls. There is probably nothing genuinely historical in this account, but it nicely reflects the democratic mindset of the time period.⁶⁹

How to guard against such insurrections? The Eretrian law against tyranny and oligarchy provides practical advice: Counseling against resigning oneself to the fait accompli presented by an oligarchic or tyrannical takeover of the walled city, the law enjoins well-wishers of democracy to "seize some location in Eretrian territory which should appear advantageous as a place to gather for

---

⁶⁴ *SEG* 51.1105b, l. 26.   ⁶⁵ RO 83B, ll. 2–3.   ⁶⁶ *I. Labraunda* 8.B, ll. 13–15.
⁶⁷ *IG* XII.9 192, ll. 3–5. The garrison may have been bribed or paid to leave (cf. *IG* II³ 1 918 [Strombichus in Athens, 287, likely bribed]; Plut. *Vit. Arat.* 34.4 [Diogenes at Athens, 229]; *I. Erythrai* 21 [Phanes of Erythrae, earlier third century; see just below]), but if so the decree is silent about it.
⁶⁸ *I. Erythrai* 21, ll. 7–10. Note the charge of the populist politician Heraclides against Dion of Syracuse that the latter did not "demolish [*kataskaptein*] the acropolis [*akra*]" that had served as a bulwark for the tyranny of Dionysius the Younger: Plut. *Vit. Dio* 53.1.
⁶⁹ Hippias of Erythrae *BNJ* 421 F 1 with Simonton 2018a.

3.5 Threats to Democracy and Their Solutions

all those coming to the aid [of the People]."⁷⁰ Another approach was to threaten civic officials who would betray a democratic city in this fashion and to praise those who preserved the democracy in times of crisis. A decree from Aeolian Cyme from the second quarter of the third century warns that "if one of the men whom the *dēmos* elects for its generalship and security should not hand over the city in a state of freedom and democracy, or should surrender the keys [of the city walls] to those putting down the democracy ... or should allow someone to propose that we must hand over the city to someone or to receive a garrison or to surrender the keys," he is to be liable to a charge of treason and subversion of the democracy.⁷¹ Less reliant on sticks and more on carrots, Erythrae praised its board of generals sometime in the first half of the third century for "guarding the democracy for the *dēmos* and handing the *polis* over in a state of freedom to those who served as generals after them."⁷² A contemporary decree from Cos, giving thanks for the repulsion of the Galatians from Delphi in 279, instructs sacred ambassadors to Delphi to sacrifice to Apollo on behalf of the salvation of the Hellenes, but also to pray "that there be good things for the People of Cos and that they conduct their political life in unanimity [*homonoia*], in a state of democracy."⁷³ The Coans were likely worried about the possibility of treason in the face of a hostile invasion, even if they were far away from the Greek mainland. Clearly, civilian and military officials sometimes found themselves in situations where they faced pressure, whether from internal subversives or from external enemies, to betray the city and its democratic constitution, and the *poleis* felt the need to guard against such an outcome.

Another defensive mechanism against tyranny and oligarchy was the mass swearing of citizen oaths. These ceremonies, often undertaken in the aftermath of an abortive or briefly successful overthrow of the constitutional status quo, attempted (how successfully we cannot know) to establish the aforementioned *homonoia* or "unanimity" among the citizenry.⁷⁴ They stem almost exclusively from self-professed democratic regimes.⁷⁵ An

---

⁷⁰ *SEG* 51.1105b, ll. 26–28.   ⁷¹ *SEG* 59.1407, ll. 11–23 with Hamon 2008.
⁷² *I. Erythrai* 29, ll. 12–14. Cf. the language of *IG* ii³ 1 985, ll. 38–39 (Athens, mid third century); *I. Rhamnous* 404, ll. 16–18 (Athens, 260s BCE).
⁷³ *IG* xii.4 68, ll. 25–28.
⁷⁴ On *homonoia*, an ideal often important enough to receive cult worship, see Thériault 1996. A reconciliation agreement from Mytilene ca. 334 in support of democracy makes pledges to personified "Homonoios and Homonoia" (RO 85a, ll. 7–8).
⁷⁵ An exception is *Syll.*³ 526, from Itanos on Crete, an oligarchy; the citizenry swear that "I will not carry out a redistribution [*anadasmos*] of the land or of houses, nor a cancellation [*apokopē*] of debts," both well-established sources of elite anxiety. As we saw in Chapter 2.5, Aristotle notes that in his day oligarchs would swear to "be hostile towards the People and counsel whatever evil [against them] I am able" (*Pol.* 5.1310a9–10).

important precedent here was the Athenian ephebic oath, a version of which survives on stone. The orator Lycurgus called the oath, which in his day the ephebes swore after being registered as citizens, as "that which secures the democracy." In it the ephebes swear not to yield to anyone who puts down the established laws, using the verb for acquiescence (*epitrepein*) that will become standard in such pledges.[76] As for later examples, a dossier of decrees from late fourth-century Telos, a tiny island *polis* neighboring Cos in Asia Minor, includes a citizen oath to the effect that "I will abide by the established constitution [*politeuma*] and guard over the democracy ... nor will I bear arms against the *dēmos* nor take counsel with someone who has seized the acropolis [*akra*] nor knowingly yield to anyone plotting against or putting down the democracy."[77] A similar oath, this time dealing with the political absorption of Calymna by Cos in the late third century, has a section proclaiming, "I will not establish an oligarchy or a tyranny or any other constitution [*politeuma*] outside of democracy on any pretext ... nor will I seize the acropolis [*akra*]."[78]

These oaths highlight the importance of guarding the commanding heights of the city, but others, without mentioning the acropolis, still enshrine democracy and reject competing constitutional forms. We possess not one but two oaths of this type from Chersonesus on the Black Sea, the first of which, from the earlier third century, states, "I will not dissolve the democracy, nor will I yield to anyone betraying and dissolving it nor join in covering this up, but I will report it to the [civic officials]." The citizens are also made to swear that they will carry out the magistracies with justice and cast their ballots as judges "according to the laws"; this is clearly a community with broad civic participation. The inscription was discovered during excavations of the Chersonesitan agora, revealing that it was erected in the central space of the city in order to increase visibility and notoriety; we will return to these spatial dynamics shortly.[79] A *sympoliteia* agreement between Smyrna and Magnesia under Sipylus of around 245, whereby the latter was absorbed into the former, contains the following oath for the new citizens: "I will join in preserving autonomy and democracy ... should I learn of someone plotting against the *polis* ... or putting down the

---

[76] RO 88, ll. 11–16; Lyc. 1.79.
[77] *IG* XII.4 132. Cf. *SEG* 57.1409, from early Hellenistic Sagalassos in Pisidia, although it is unclear if this was a democratic regime.
[78] *IG* XII.4 152, ll. 21–24.
[79] *IosPE* I² 401, ll. 13–17, 22–36. The second oath (*IosPE* I² 402), from one hundred years later, likewise mentions preserving democracy but also, tellingly, "the friendship with the Romans" (l. 3). On oaths and civic space see Williamson 2013.

3.5 *Threats to Democracy and Their Solutions*

democracy and the equal distribution of power [*isonomia*], I will inform the People of Smyrna."[80]

Closely related to these oaths and sometimes overlapping with them are laws we can class within the category "antityranny legislation." The strategic logic underlying these measures has been established by the penetrating study of David Teegarden: They were meant to create common knowledge of commitment to democracy among the assembled citizenry and thus to facilitate collective action in defense of the constitution in the face of attempted coups.[81] The first such piece of legislation may have been imposed by Athens on one of its imperial subjects in the fifth century, but Athens would soon pass its own laws, beginning (probably) in the aftermath of the Thirty Tyrants. There was a renewal in 336, in the famous Law of Eucrates (see further Section 3.6 on the iconography of this monument).[82] As we saw, Eretria enacted such a law around 340, which provided for public support of the orphans of a tyrannicide who died in the act. A relevant section states: "Should someone set up a tyranny or oligarchy and maintain it with force, all the citizens are immediately to come to the aid of the People and to join battle with those preventing the assembly ... from meeting."[83] A law from early third-century Ilium likewise fiercely denounces both tyranny and oligarchy, stating that anyone who became tyrant or leader of an oligarchy was to suffer a kind of *damnatio memoriae*, with his name erased wherever it might appear in public documents.[84]

A final means of guarding against tyrannical or oligarchic subversion was to build protection of one's democracy into an interstate military alliance. We have seen that Athens did this already in its *symmachia* with Arcadia, Achaea, Elis, and Phlius in 362/1.[85] We see further examples from *poleis* as far afield as Sinope on the Black Sea, Telos among the Doric Sporades, Cibyra in southwest Asia Minor, and Pisidian Termessus.[86] The last

---

[80] *OGIS* 229, ll. 65, 67. See also *I. Ilion* 45 (first half of the third century); *I. Labraunda* 47 (Mylasa, second century); *SEG* 47.1563, ll. 41–43 (*sympoliteia* of Heraclea under Latmus and Pidasa, late fourth century – but the cited oath portion as it survives on the stone does not explicitly name democracy as the constitution).

[81] Teegarden 2013.

[82] Malouchou, publishing a second facsimile of *IG* I³ 14, argues that one section of this Athenian imperial decree for Erythrae represents the first antityranny legislation (*SEG* 64.30, ll. 31–32). The oath of Demophantus as found at Andoc. 1.96–98 is probably a forgery, but a genuine one existed, which was likely passed after 404 rather than after 411 (Canevaro and Harris 2012). Law of Eucrates: RO 79.

[83] *SEG* 51.1105b, ll. 20–23. [84] *I. Ilion* 25, ll. 116–28. On this *damnatio* technique see Section 3.6.

[85] RO 41, ll. 24–26; see Chapter 2.5.

[86] *I. Sinope* 1, ll. 27–28 (ca. 350); *SEG* 25.847 (Telos, early third century [relevant passage restored]); Meier 2019: no. 2 (Cibyra, first half of the second century); *TAM* III.1 2, ll. 14–15 (Termessus, second century).

example states, "should anyone attack the city or the territory of the Termessians in war ... or put a stop to the laws or the revenues or the established democracy [*dēmokrateia (sic)*] in either of the *poleis* [that is, Termessus or Adada, the alliance partner], they are to come to each other's aid as best they are able."

After about 200 BCE, the word "oligarchy" drops out of our sources almost entirely, although talk of democracy continues, as we will see in the next chapter.[87] "Tyranny" of one sort or another, whether truly run by a single individual or by a narrow clique, remained a valid threat. By this time there were probably few left who would try to establish a rigid oligarchy of the fifth-through-third-century type, which had progressively been discredited and become impracticable.[88] But it was likely also the case that elites no longer needed to establish an alternative set of institutions to secure their interests, since they were finding creative ways of doing just that through existing, nominally democratic structures. In any case, constitutional struggles and debates about what constituted genuine democracy continued, but seemingly without the vocabulary of *oligarchia*. (A new epigraphic discovery could of course change this picture completely.)

As we saw in the previous chapter, antidemocratic revolutions were often preceded by the assassination of the *prostatai tou dēmou*, the "champions of the People," whether in Athens, Elis, or Megara, among others.[89] This tactic persisted through the period under review. In Corcyra in 361/0, oligarchic plotters framed the *prostatai* of the People for the wounding of Athenian garrison soldiers, condemning them to death before staging a takeover of the *polis*.[90] According to Demosthenes, the democratic politician Euphraeus of Oreus on Euboea was similarly imprisoned in the 340s by pro-Macedonian oligarchs on a trumped-up charge of "disturbing the peace of the city" (*suntarattonta tēn polin*, 9.60), after which the oligarchic faction easily dominated the city because the populace was terrified.[91] Dion of Syracuse,

---

[87] In the 210s BCE Messene experienced a revolution from oligarchy to democracy (Polyb. 4.31.2, 7.10.1; Plut. *Vit. Arat.* 49.2–3), after which attestations decline.

[88] Some oligarchies already in existence, however, like that of Massalia, continued: Note the presence of the aristocratic Council of the Six Hundred at *Syll.*³ 591, ll. 45–49 (decree of Lampsacus ca. 196).

[89] See Chapter 2.3.3.   [90] Aen. Tact. 11.13–15 with Diod. Sic. 15.95.3.

[91] The ensuing oligarchy was overthrown by the Athenians in 341 and democracy restored: Charax *BNJ* 103 F 19. Euphraeus had in the meantime killed himself: Dem. 9.62. On "disturbance" (*tarachē*), see also Aen. Tact. 11.7–10, where the *prostatēs* of the People at Argos, despite learning of a revolutionary plot (as Euphraeus had done), did not divulge it to the populace for fear of the city's being plunged into a state of disturbance (*tarachē*); instead, he assembled the citizens under arms, thus foiling the oligarchic scheme.

intending, around 354, to alter his city's constitution from a democracy to an oligarchy, ordered his popular rival Heraclides killed in his own home.[92]

These episodes bring us to the Janus-faced figure of the *prostatēs tou dēmou*, sometimes also called the "demagogue" – "Janus-faced," because while democracies required their defenders, these men might sometimes turn out to be too much of a good thing. So far in this section we have examined antidemocratic threats to the constitutional status quo as though they were a completely exogenous variable, but in reality they existed in a dialectical relationship with processes internal to democracy, particularly popular leadership. As Aristotle and, indirectly, Anaximenes indicated in the passages cited in Section 3.3, democracies could be destabilized from within by popular, indeed *populist* politicians who antagonized the elite to the point of *stasis*. So long as the notables did not fully control the political agenda in the assembly, the possibility remained that enterprising *rhētores* would egg on the People to enact policies disapproved of by the majority of the elite. The result could be antidemocratic reaction on the part of would-be oligarchs or the establishment of a demagogic tyrant.[93]

As the previous chapter mentioned, the paradigm case for Aristotle of a popular leader who seized absolute power was Dionysius the Elder of Syracuse.[94] Plenty of usurpers, however, followed his example in the fourth and third centuries. Clearchus of Heraclea Pontica was actually recalled from exile by the ruling oligarchs of his city in order to put down a popular uprising, but he turned the tables on his minders by becoming champion of the people (*patronus plebis*) and, subsequently, the founder of a tyrannical dynasty around 364.[95] Agathocles of Syracuse rocketed to power in 317 following a playbook suspiciously close to that of Dionysius the Elder before him; whatever the exact truth of the matter, without a doubt he parlayed his popularity into tyrannical authority.[96]

Finally, Polybius describes the descent of the city of Cius in Mysia around 203 BCE into civil strife, confiscations, and murder under the "demagogic and greedy" politician Molpagoras. He put the wealthy at the mercy of the "mob" and, by expropriating the rich's property and redistributing it to "*hoi polloi*," earned himself "monarchical power."[97] The language of Polybius'

---

[92] Plut. *Vit. Dio* 53.2–3.
[93] On the relationship between ancient demagogues and modern populists (of both the left and right varieties), see Simonton 2024.
[94] Chapter 2.5.   [95] Justin 16.4.1–10; Diod. Sic. 15.81.5.
[96] Diod. Sic. 19.6 with de Lisle 2021. Cf. Phaenias of Eresus *FGrH* 1012 F 4, on the (undated) demagogue-turned-tyrant Philoxenus, an account featuring similar clichés.
[97] Polyb. 15.21.1–2.

account betrays its bias, but we need not question the fundamentals of the story. In the face of persistent economic inequality and debt, there were always politicians willing to take advantage of the social tensions arising therefrom; the temptation was too great not to "indulge" the masses in their desire for the property of the elite.[98]

Elsewhere demagoguery precipitated oligarchic resistance or simply devolved into paroxysms of violence, as we saw in the case of the *skytalismos* at Argos in 370.[99] The aforementioned Heraclides of Syracuse, prior to his assassination at the hands of agents of Dion, had induced Hippon, another of the city's politicians, to propose a redistribution of land (*gēs anadasmos*), one of the calling cards of the demagogue. Political instability and, eventually, Heraclides' murder followed.[100] Aristotle lists a number of other fourth-century examples in Book 5 of the *Politics*, where he is discussing the characteristic sources of instability in democracies and oligarchies. In both Cos and Rhodes demagogic politicians so provoked the notables that they caused them to combine and to dissolve the democratic governments in place.[101]

In this connection we should consider a remarkable dossier of decrees from the tiny island of Telos, sandwiched between Cos and Rhodes, dating to around 300. The dossier records that several members of the elite had been prosecuted in the courts on charges they considered unjust. It seems that some of their property had been confiscated, sparking an attempted antidemocratic coup on their part. Whatever the exact details, the Telians have brought in Coan arbitrators to deal with the issue of the property and to reintegrate the citizen body within a democratic constitution (see the citizen oath discussed earlier in this section).[102] I have argued elsewhere that we should understand the situation as one of "demagogic" persecution of at least some of the elite, in a manner conforming to Aristotle's generalization that "the demagogues of the present day, in order to ingratiate themselves with the common people, often carry out confiscations by means of the law courts."[103] The Telian politicians in question may even have learned "best practices" from their similarly demagogic neighbors on Rhodes and Cos.[104]

---

[98] Note Polybius' praise of the politician Philopoemen of Megalopolis, who supposedly "conducted his political life for the most part not with a view to pleasing [his fellow citizens] but through frank address [*parrhēsia*] to them; one would find that this occurs rarely [in a democracy]": 23.12.8.
[99] Chapter 2.5.   [100] Plut. *Vit. Dio* 37.3.
[101] *Pol.* 5.1304b25–31; cf. 1302b23–24 (Rhodes again). For possible dates for these events, see the discussions at Robinson 2011: 152–55, 168–69.
[102] *IG* XII.4 132.   [103] *Pol.* 6.1320a4–6 with Simonton 2019, esp. 197–201.
[104] Intriguingly, both Telos and nearby Cnidus issued coins with "*damokratia*" stamped on them around this time; Telos' coinage also copied that of Cos iconographically. See further Section 3.6.

3.5 Threats to Democracy and Their Solutions

Here, then, is "Classical"-style demagoguery present in a "Hellenistic" democracy. There is no shortage of further examples, in fact.[105] It was a *topos* in writing about democracies during this period that they were periodically "disturbed" by demagogues in the same way that the sea was whipped into a fury by the winds. The language of "disturbance" goes back to Aristophanes' depiction of the Athenian demagogue Cleon, and Demosthenes uses similar wind imagery as well.[106] As Dionysius of Halicarnassus intones, writing (probably) about the demagogic politicians at Tarentum in the lead-up to the Pyrrhic War of the 270s, "democratically governed cities undergo something similar to the seas. For the latter are disturbed [*tarattetai*] by the winds, although they have it in their nature to be calm, while the former are stirred up [*kukōntai*] by the demagogues, even though they are not in themselves wicked."[107] Clearly, populist champions of the masses could disrupt civic life during the period in question.[108]

Were there democratic means, however, of avoiding this quintessentially democratic problem? As we have seen, Anaximenes recommended establishing laws that protected the property rights of the elite; Aristotle counsels a similar approach. It was also a mark of "responsible" democratic politics that nothing should be discussed at meetings of the assembly that was not previously put on the agenda by the council; a *rhētōr* could not urge a decree that was "*aprobouleuton*."[109] It may be that the phenomenon of sending so-called foreign judges to adjudicate sensitive court cases in other *poleis* was in part designed to preempt demagoguery, by taking litigation out of the hands of local politicians.[110] Intriguingly, a decree of

---

[105] I have discussed Hellenistic demagogues in Simonton 2022; cf. Scholz 2012; Urso 2019. For the fifth and earlier fourth centuries, see Chapter 2.3.3 and the references discussed by Robinson 2011: 227–28.
[106] Ar. *Eq.* 66, 214, etc.; Dem. 19.136.
[107] *Ant. Rom.* 19.7.2. On the Tarentines' politicians see also Plut. *Vit. Pyrrh.* 13.2–5; Dion. Hal. *Ant. Rom.* 19.4–5; App. *Samn.* 16. For "stirred up" compare Ar. *Eq.* 692. Polybius attributes an almost identical simile to Leon son of Kichesias of Athens, speaking on behalf of the Aetolians in 189: 21.31.9–13. We will see this language used even in the Imperial period in the next chapter.
[108] See also Agatharchides *de mari Erythraeo* fr. 18 Müller (author of the second century BCE; the context is unclear): "Whenever a demagogue addressed the masses [*hoi polloi*], putting himself in the position not of a friend but of a flatterer [*kolax*], the impulse of the mobs [*ochloi*], taking as its advisor a guarantor of error, ruined the city."
[109] [Arist.] *Ath. Pol.* 45.4, and see Chapter 2.3.7. Contrast the "demagogues" of Dio Chrys. 56.10, who introduce *aprobouleuta* decrees. Control of the agenda by officials selected according to a property requirement, however, was oligarchic: see Section 3.4.
[110] On foreign judges, which first emerge at the end of the fourth century, see Robert 1973; Crowther 1992; Magnetto 2015. As Crowther notes, recourse to foreign judges remained exceptional, and most cases would have been heard by citizen *dikastēria*.

Priene for Alexandria Troas from the second century describes a situation in which Prienian judges heard cases about violence and unconstitutional measures at Alexandria. The purpose of sending the judges, according to the degree, was "so that fair and just results obtain for all the citizens, by which measures democracy is best preserved." The phrasing suggests that a democracy might be "disturbed" if judicial dealings were considered to be politically partial.[111]

I have dwelt at length in this section on threats to democracy in order to establish that *dēmokratia* could not be taken for granted during the period in question. These governments could and did collapse, whether through foreign interference or internal breakdown, to be replaced by alternative, nondemocratic regimes. Whatever the precise institutional setup or balance of power within these governments, which varied from city to city, the citizens of Greek democracies time and again evince concern for their preservation, as well as a real sense of anxiety that enemies, whether foreign or domestic, might subvert them. As time goes on, we see fewer indications in the evidence that Greeks were worried that "democracy" in particular (as opposed to, say, "freedom," a perennial concern) was in existential danger, but in our heyday the unease, and the democracy to which it applied, were genuine.

3.6 The Space and Stuff of *Dēmokratiai*: Aspects of Democratic Culture

The meaning(s) of ancient Greek democracies were not exhausted by their formal institutions. They also had a culture, as expressed through (among other things) citizen activities in the central, public spaces of the *polis* and the creation and manipulation of material objects. We already saw how in the late sixth century the Athenian and Eretrian democracies, among others, ushered in a radical reconceptualization of civic space through reforms to their political geography and their investment in often massive public building programs.[112] In this section I examine what texts, objects, and archaeological remains can tell us about the space and material culture of Greek democratic societies in their heyday. In particular, I survey statues, reliefs, and coins; political festivals and the cult worship of political

---

[111] *I. Priene* B-M 119, ll. 14–15.
[112] See Chapter 1.4. The growth of political architecture exploded during the period under review in the present chapter: see Bernini 2023.

3.6 *The Space and Stuff of* Dēmokratiai

personifications; and the ways engagement with monuments in the civic landscape could strengthen democratic regimes.

In the previous chapter we met Mr. Demos of Pnyx, Aristophanes' personified People of Athens from his play *Knights* of 424. The representation of "*dēmos*" and "democracy" would continue at Athens through the fourth century and beyond. There were paintings of the Athenian People by Euphranor in the Stoa Basileios (along with Theseus and Demokratia), by Aristolaus, and by Parrhasius, the last of which supposedly showed the People in all its variegated moods: "irresolute, irritable, unjust, inconstant, but also easily moved, gentle, merciful," and so on, according to the elder Pliny.[113] Demos and Demokratia also appear in so-called document reliefs, the sculptures in relief adorning certain inscribed decrees of the People. The most famous instance is the Law of Eucrates of 337/6, discovered in 1952, which shows a seated Demos, represented as a bearded older male, being crowned by Demokratia (Figure 3.1).[114] There was also a statue of Demokratia in the Agora, probably the recipient of cult, which may have been erected after the restoration of democracy on the twelfth day of the month of Boedromion in 403, following the fall of the Thirty (on these sorts of cults and festivals see later in this section).[115]

The third century witnessed the expanded use of monumental statues of the People, particularly in interstate diplomacy. The decree quoted in the manuscripts of Demosthenes' speech *On the Crown*, section 91, according to which the democracies of Byzantium and Perinthus voted to erect a statue group of the Peoples of their two cities crowning the People of Athens, has long been known to be a Hellenistic forgery; nevertheless, it attests to what was by its time fairly common practice.[116] When Rhodes was hit by a terrible earthquake in 228/7, Hiero and Gelon, the tyrants of Syracuse, were not content to contribute money to the suffering city but also had constructed in the marketplace of Rhodes a statue group with the People of Syracuse crowning the Rhodian People.[117] A decree of Mylasa in

---

[113] Paus. 1.3.3; Plin. *NH* 35.137, 35.69. I have argued elsewhere that because the Athenian People, as a real entity (the thirty thousand or so adult male citizens of Athens), rarely if ever actually did anything collectively involving every last one of its constituent members, it had to be "represented" constantly, not just by artists but by speakers in the assembly: Simonton 2021.

[114] Lawton 1995; Glowacki 2003; Blanshard 2004; Simonton 2020.

[115] Raubitschek 1962 = *SEG* 21.679. By contrast, it was difficult if not impossible to depict the *oligoi* or "ruling few" of oligarchies using a single representational figure, although the gravestone of the Athenian oligarch Critias supposedly depicted Oligarchia setting fire to Demokratia (DK 88 A 13), and the playwright Heniochus put on stage a character called Aristocratia paired with Demokratia (fr. 5 Kassel-Austin: Classical era; exact date unknown).

[116] Dem. 18.91 with Canevaro 2013: 261–65.   [117] Polyb. 5.88.5–8.

124 3 The Heyday of Ancient Greek Democracies, 362–146 BCE

Figure 3.1 Law of Eucrates. (Photo: American School of Classical Studies at Athens: Agora Excavations. Archive number: 2012.03.2610).

Caria from the second half of the third century establishes a festival on the thirteenth of an unknown month, to mark the day when "the People recovered its freedom and democracy." In order to extol the benefactor responsible for this recovery, the neighboring dynast Olympichus, the decree orders the construction, not just of a statue of Olympichus, but also of a larger-than-life statue of the People crowning him.[118]

We are normally in the dark as to what these statues, which do not survive, looked like, except perhaps their crowning posture. However, a remarkable new decree from Abdera in Thrace contains a precise (and priceless) description. Abdera had been sacked by a Roman army under the praetor Lucius Hortensius in 170, during the course of the Third Macedonian War (171–168 BCE), for putting off his inordinate demands for provisioning.[119] The city reached out to others for support during the difficult rebuilding process, including its colonial mother city, Teos. When the latter responded generously to the request, the People of Abdera decreed that they would "erect a colossal bronze statue of the *Dēmos* of the [Teians], on the agora in the

[118] *SEG* 58.1220, ll. 5–8.   [119] Livy 43.4.8–13.

3.6 The Space and Stuff of Dēmokratiai

Figure 3.2 Teos coin. (Photo: Roma Numismatics / biddr).

most prominent spot, pouring a libation with a kantharos with the right hand, and with the left hand/arm leaning on the *stēlē* on which this decree shall be inscribed; and let there be a small column standing by on the left-hand side, [on which] let there be placed a Nike crowning the *Dēmos* of the Teians with an ivy-wreath."[120] This image of the People seems to be modeled on the cult statue of Dionysus at Teos, the appearance of which is known from contemporary coins (Figure 3.2).[121]

Numismatics, we should note in this connection, occasionally furnishes evidence for cults to Demokratia as well. A silver coin from Metapontum in Italy, dating to the second half of the fourth century, shows on the obverse the laureate head of a woman adorned with earrings and a necklace; she is labeled "Damokratia" (in the Doric dialect). The image probably refers to a cult statue of Democracy at Metapontum that was the recipient of sacrifice.[122] Coins from Cnidus and Telos, both dating circa 300, likewise display female heads identified as Damokratia, implying cult worship.[123] (On *stasis* at Telos from this time, probably brought on by demagogic activity, see Section 3.5.) Finally, the Demos itself received

---

[120] Adak and Thonemann 2022: Document 1B, ll. 56–61 (translation of Adak and Thonemann).
[121] Adak and Thonemann 2022: 214–23. For a monumental image of the People (in this case, *le peuple*) proposed but never completed by Jacques-Louis David during the French Revolution, see Rosanvallon 2006: 80–81.
[122] Unpublished; Classical Numismatic Group Triton VIII, Lot 34.
[123] Hansen and Nielsen 2004: no. 903, p. 1124; Stefanaki 2008: nos. 15–17. There was also a statue of Demokratia in the council chamber at Pergamum in the latter half of the second century: *Syll.*³ 694, ll. 31–32.

worship in numerous cities: The Athenians instituted a cult to Demos and the Graces following their liberation from a Macedonian garrison in 229, and we know of worship of the Demos at Cos, Telos, Erythrae, and Delos, to name just a few other instances.[124] (Interestingly, despite the existence of these cults, personifications of the People on coins do not begin until the high Roman Imperial period, when they proliferate.[125]) It had been normal in the fourth and earlier third centuries, at Athens and elsewhere, to pray and sacrifice *on behalf of* the People or on behalf of its salvation; for a community to, in effect, *worship itself* represents a fascinating development in the history of Greek politics and religion.

Several examples surveyed just now brought to our attention the institution of festivals marking the anniversary of liberation or of the recovery of democracy. Critics had long identified Greek democracies as having an intimate and excessive relationship with festival activity: As we have seen, the Old Oligarch complained that the Athenian *dēmos* exacted festivals from the rich as a kind of tax, while elsewhere in his pamphlet he noted that the Athenians held more festivals than any other Greek *polis*.[126] The fourth-century historian Theopompus of Chios (no fan of democracy), in his account of events between 360/59 and 336 called the *Philippica*, likewise harped on the profligacy of such democracies as Athens and Tarentum when it came to holding public sacrifices.[127] Beginning at the very end of the fifth century, these festival activities expanded from being (among other things) opportunities for the common people to have a good time to explicitly celebrating the existence of democracy itself.[128]

As noted, the Athenians commemorated 12 Boedromion (in what was roughly our September) as the day in 403 when Thrasybulus and his partisans reinstituted democracy following the tyrannical oligarchy of the Thirty.[129] Other democratic regimes also clearly used festivals as occasions on which to observe the importance of freedom and democracy. The year 341 was an *annus mirabilis* for the *polis* of Eretria on Euboea, which saw it freed from the tyrannical rule of Cleitarchus and its democracy restored by Athens, as we have seen (Section 3.2). The Eretrian law against tyranny and oligarchy followed soon after (Section 3.5), but we also possess a decree from this period arranging for the celebration of the Artemisia festival based out of the goddess'

---

[124] Habicht 1997: 180–82; Adak and Thonemann 2022: 224–26.   [125] Fernoux 2011: 48.
[126] [Xen.] *Ath. Pol.* 2.9–10, 3.2. See already Chapter 2.3.5.   [127] *BNJ* 115 FF 100, 233.
[128] For the proliferation of such political festivals in the Hellenistic period, see Chaniotis 1995. As we will see, they were not limited to that period, and there were important changes in the later Hellenistic era.
[129] Plut. *Mor.* 349f.

sanctuary at Amarynthus. The brief motivation clause at the beginning of the inscription states that the purpose of the decree was to ensure "that we celebrate the Artemisia as finely as possible and that the *greatest number of people sacrifice*"; the conclusion of the text instructs that the decree be written up on a stone *stēlē*, "so that the sacrifice and musical contest for Artemis happen on these terms for all time, *seeing that the Eretrians are free and fortunate and in charge of their own affairs [autokratores]*."[130] The jubilant democratic atmosphere that accompanied this festival is palpable.

A later decree from Eretria, celebrating the dismissal of an armed garrison and the recovery of democracy, specifies that, "in order that there be a memorial [*hypomnēma*] of this day, it was decided by the Council and the People that all the Eretrians and inhabitants of the city will wear crowns of ivy at the procession of Dionysus," presumably in perpetuity.[131] Similarly at Priene in Ionia: We can piece together from several disparate sources that a man named Hiero seized tyrannical power in the *polis* around 301. Democratic partisans fled the city and eventually returned, spearheaded by the recipient of the honors outlined by a later inscription, whose name is now lost to us. The inscription states that "in order that there should be a memorial ['*hypomnēma*' again, albeit restored] of the struggle that occurred on behalf of our autonomy and freedom … the citizens present and all free people are to wear crowns every year in the month of Metageitnion on [x] … on which day the People's recovery of autonomy took place." The festival would be called the Soteria, the celebration of Salvation.[132] In the same decree in which the People of Mylasa order the construction of a colossal statue crowning a statue of its benefactor Olympichus (see earlier in this section), it is also specified that the community should "carry out a procession and a sacrifice each year on the fourteenth of the month of [x], on which day the People recovered its freedom and democracy."[133]

---

[130] RO 73, ll. 2–4, 42–45 (emphasis added). With this clause on being free we may compare a series of decrees from early Hellenistic Priene proclaiming it autonomous at the time (*I. Priene B-M* 16–19).

[131] *IG* XII.9 192, ll. 5–8. Cf. *IG* II³ 1 877: The Athenians in 283/2 honor the poet Philippides because, among other things, he was the first to institute a contest for Demeter and Kore in 284/3 (shortly after the restoration of the "democracy of all the Athenians" in 287 – see Section 3.2) that served as a "memorial [*hypomnēma*] of the freedom of the People" (ll. 44–45).

[132] *I. Priene B-M* 6, ll. 16–25. For Hieron's tyranny, see also Paus. 7.2.10; *I. Priene B-M* 132; *Syll.*³ 363. We will revisit the language of "struggle." For another Soteria festival, see the burial of Aratus of Sicyon in his hometown in 213: "[the Sicyonians] carry out a sacrifice to him on the fifth day of the month of Daisios, when he released them from tyranny, and they call this sacrifice the Soteria" (Plut. *Vit. Arat.* 53.4.).

[133] *SEG* 58.1220, ll. 11–14. Compare the situation in Miletus, where a tyrant named Timarchus ruled for a period in the mid third century until put down by the Seleucid king Antiochus II, who then received the epithet Theos ("God") from the grateful Milesians; I find it likely (although it cannot be proved) that the Milesians celebrated a festival in honor of this recovery of their freedom and democracy (App. *Syr.* 65; *I. Didyma* 358).

Such festivals were no mere pageantry, an excuse for feasting and intoxication. Gathering en masse in the city center; worshipping at the tomb of a founder, tyrannicide, or freedom fighter; hearing the patriotic narratives of local historians[134] – all of these actions would not only have strengthened individual citizens' commitment to the democratic constitution, but they also served as a kind of staging ground for collective action on the part of the People in defense of the regime and as a deterrent to would-be tyrants and oligarchs.[135] The festivals were also frequently part of a larger back-and-forth contestation over monuments and collective memory waged between democracies and their enemies. Both sides would attempt to erase all traces of the other from the civic landscape upon coming to power, typically by tearing down or otherwise altering material objects.[136] The Thirty at Athens in 404, to start with an example from an earlier period, removed the laws of Ephialtes and Archestratus from the Areopagus and destroyed multiple *stēlai* recording proxenies decreed by the democracy. After returning to power the *dēmos* proudly reinscribed the decrees; we also read that the Athenians confiscated the property of the Thirty and refashioned it as implements to be carried in their festival processions.[137] When oligarchs staged a coup in Ephesus shortly before Alexander the Great's campaign in Asia Minor, they "dug up from the agora the grave of Heropythus, who had liberated the city." This Heropythus remains a shadowy figure, but the location of his grave, conspicuously placed in the agora, suggests heroic honors, perhaps in exchange for a tyrannicidal act. By attacking it the Ephesian oligarchs were signaling that a new symbolic order was coming into being; they also likely intended to intimidate the population into acquiescence by highlighting its failure to stop the desecration from occurring.[138] Sometime in (probably) the second quarter of the third century, an oligarchic regime

---

[134] I have argued that the sole surviving fragment of the local historian Hippias of Erythrae is practically a how-to manual when it comes to fending off oligarchic and tyrannical attacks, written in the context of an early third-century BCE democracy: Simonton 2018a, esp. 520–29.
[135] Simonton 2018b.
[136] Culasso Gastaldi 2003; Flower 2006 (who uses the term "memory sanction").
[137] Laws of Ephialtes and Archestratus: [Arist.] *Ath. Pol.* 35.2. Decrees destroyed by the Thirty: ML 94; *IG* I³ 229, II² 6, II² 9. Confiscated property: Philochorus *BNJ* 328 F 181. The tyranny of Hiero at Priene in the early third century (see above) seems also to have torn down some proxeny decrees awarded by the democracy, since we possess a proxeny from the period shortly thereafter that has expressly been "reinstated" (*I. Priene B-M* 27, l. 8). Oligarchs in Iulis on Ceos knocked down *stēlai* from Athens upon coming to power shortly before 362: RO 39, ll. 27–33.
[138] Arr. *Anab.* 1.17.11 with Simonton 2018b. Compare Xenophon's negative reaction toward the heroic honors paid to Euphron of Sicyon, whom the democrats buried in the agora and considered their city founder, as we saw in the previous chapter (Xen. *Hell.* 7.3.12). For political conflict concerning heroic burial see Fröhlich 2013: 238–44.

3.6 *The Space and Stuff of* Dēmokratiai

briefly came to power in Erythrae. A decree of the restored democracy states that "those in the oligarchy removed the sword from the statue of Philites the tyrant-killer, considering its stance to be entirely aimed against them." The People decrees that the sword be restored and the statue crowned at the festival of the new moon and at the other festivals, "so that the People should be seen clearly taking great care of and holding in memory forever its benefactors, both living and dead."[139] Here we have a nice confluence of the ideological import of monuments and a festival context.

Democrats could, of course, also subject their opponents to a kind of *damnatio memoriae*.[140] We saw this already in the case of the antityranny legislation from Ilium from the first half of the third century, where the tyrant or oligarch's name was to be erased from all dedications and other inscriptions (Section 3.5). The Syracusan democracy, under the direction of Timoleon, destroyed the tyrant Dionysius' acropolis citadel and even razed his house and tomb in 343, constructing courts of law on the spot.[141] When Demetrius of Phalerum's oligarchy at Athens came to an end in 307, the People supposedly melted down his more than three hundred statues erected throughout the city, in some cases converting them into chamber pots.[142] Again in 199, the Athenians passed a law consigning the memory of the Antigonid house of Macedon to oblivion: Livy says that they "passed a motion that all statues of Philip [V], all representations of him, and their inscriptions, and also those of his ancestors, male and female, should be removed and done away with, [and] that all the feast-days, sacred observances and priesthoods which had been established in honor of him or his ancestors should be abolished," among other strictures.[143] We can see the effects of this *damnatio* in the chiseling out of Antigonid names from Attic inscriptions; the main exceptions are decrees where the Antigonids are plainly depicted as enemies of Athens, as in the honors for Callias of Sphettus.[144] Livy (likely echoing Polybius, his source) chides the

---

[139] *I. Erythrai* 503, ll. 4–9, 15–16, with Gauthier 1982 and Teegarden 2013: ch. 5. The statue was to be tended by the officials of the marketplace, indicating that it stood in the agora.
[140] Savalli-Lestrade 2009 has a useful discussion of the Hellenistic period. Luraghi (2019: 123) notes that while democracies might have dishonored individuals by overturning their monuments, they did not admit to erasing the facts of the past.
[141] Plut. *Vit. Tim.* 22.1–3. Recall the use of acropoleis by tyrants and oligarchs for keeping themselves in power, discussed in Section 3.5.
[142] Diog. Laert. 5.77 with Azoulay 2009.
[143] Livy 31.44.4 (trans. Sage). Knoepfler 2019 argues for Livy's date of 199, against Byrne 2010, favoring 200.
[144] Byrne 2010; *IG* II³ 1 910.

130 3 The Heyday of Ancient Greek Democracies, 362–146 BCE

Athenians for being goaded into action by "tongues ready to incite the mob"; concluding his discussion of the episode, he sniffs that the unwarlike Athenians conducted their campaign against Philip "by means of letters and words, which constitute their sole strength."[145] Democracies had perhaps something of a reputation for impulsively inflicting this kind of *damnatio*: when the Rhodians, in the midst of being besieged by Demetrius Poliorcetes in 304, declined to tear down the statues they had previously erected for Demetrius and his father Antigonus, our source, Diodorus Siculus, notes that this was an (uncharacteristically) wise decision by a democracy.[146]

We can conclude this survey of struggles over monuments and memory with a brief look at one of the best studied cases. In 323, in the wake of Alexander the Great's death, the Athenians were seeking out military allies against Macedon. Euphron the son of Adeas, a politician from Sicyon in the Peloponnese and the grandson of the man given heroic honors in the agora there, reported his *polis'* commitment to the alliance, for which he and Sicyon received praise from the Athenian assembly. When the ensuing Lamian War ended with the defeat of the alliance at Crannon in 322, the Macedonian general Antipater installed an oligarchic regime in Athens, which promptly tore down the honors for Euphron. We know this because a further decree of the restored democracy from 318 explains these circumstances, in the process republishing Euphron's earlier honors. The later decree was moved by the fiercely democratic politician Hagnonides of the deme Pergase, who would be put to death by the oligarchy of Demetrius of Phalerum a year later (this was the vexed constitutional period at Athens mentioned in Section 3.2). In Hagnonides' telling, Euphron had played a role in liberating his city just prior to announcing its military alliance with Athens in 323: "Euphron returned from exile and cast out the garrison from the acropolis with the Sicyonians' support, and, having liberated his *polis*, he made it a friendly ally of the People of Athens."[147] Then, when the Macedonians reasserted their power in the cities following the Lamian War, "he chose to die struggling [*agōnizomenos*, convincingly restored in a gap on the stone] on behalf of the democracy so that he not look upon his own fatherland or the rest of Hellas enslaved." Meanwhile, "those ruling in the oligarchy [at Athens] rescinded his honors and tore down the *stēlai* [recording them]"; but "now, since the People has returned and has

---

[145] Livy 31.44.3, 9.   [146] Diod. Sic. 20.93.6–7.
[147] Recall the importance for democratic regimes of expelling occupying forces from the *akra* or acropolis, discussed in Section 3.5.

3.6 *The Space and Stuff of* Dēmokratiai

Figure 3.3 Euphron stele. (Photo: George E. Koronaios via Wikimedia Commons, CC BY-SA 4.0).

regained its laws and democracy," the honors can be renewed and reinscribed, as they duly were.[148] Yet there is still more to this intriguing monument, currently housed in the National Archaeological Museum in Athens (NAM 1482). Its apex features one of the most striking "document reliefs" yet found (see earlier in this section for this phenomenon), a sculpted scene depicting, from left to right, Athena, the personified Athenian Demos in larger-than-life proportions, Euphron himself, equipped with sword, and what is probably a page tending to Euphron's horse (Figure 3.3). We can guess that this relief was an innovation of the decree of 318 and not original to 323, since Euphron's sword picks him out as the sort of tyrannicidal figure depicted in the later decree who "struggles on behalf of democracy" to the point of death.[149]

The Euphron *stēlē* concretizes ("marbleizes"?) a number of the issues we have surveyed. It represents an attempt to remedy the misdeeds of a preceding oligarchic regime, but also to fix for all time a specific vision of the past. In the latter respect it has succeeded; after all, it is thanks to the

---

[148] See the aforementioned parallel cases of oligarchs tearing down *stēlai*.
[149] *IG* II² 448, ll. 45–48, 53–56, 60–64. The earlier decree is now *IG* II³ 1 378.

later decree that we have purported evidence for the constitutional histories of Athens and Sicyon at the time. But we have to be careful when writing history from the motivation clauses of decrees. As Philippe Gauthier once pointed out, "the exaltation of the merits of a benefactor [as with Euphron here] led to remembering the past and the values to which the city was attached, in short to publishing a sort of official version of civic history."[150] This history was of course not disinterested; it resulted from an emotional moment in the civic assembly, in which an orator drew up an account of the past that his audience wanted to hear – this was history as approved by the People.[151] It was also, as another scholar has put it, "history in hindsight": In this regard, we see that the second decree contains a much more passionate and partisan version of Euphron's actions than the first, highlighting his liberation of Sicyon and heroic death.[152] Finally, the *stēlē* is both a monument in its own right and a kind of ideological and political playbook: It proclaims the inevitability of democracy's triumph over adversity ("since the People has returned and has regained its laws and democracy"), but it also suggests that one may have to imitate the actions of Euphron (struggling and dying) in the course of that restoration.[153] But whatever the outcome, the People can be counted on to reward its benefactors, just as the personified Demos of the document relief is perpetually in the act of honoring Euphron.[154]

The Euphron *stēlē* is thus in many ways exceptional, but it is also just one more instance of a phenomenon, the honorific decree, that littered the agoras, acropoleis, and sanctuaries of the Greek cities. As numerous historians have pointed out, the fact that we tend to discover these objects reused or buried and not in situ means that we must mentally reconstruct a landscape now lost to us, in which these *stēlai* filled civic space like so many gravestones. Although numerous laws, regulations, and inventories were also inscribed, out of all public documents honorific decrees predominate in our period.[155] Their functions and meanings were manifold, but

---

[150] Gauthier 1985: 91. [151] Luraghi 2010, 2019; cf. Lambert 2012. [152] Wallace 2014.
[153] Several other inscriptions praise the honorand for "struggling" (*agōnizesthai*) on behalf of the *dēmos*, democracy, freedom, etc.: *IG* II² 457, ll. 16–17 (honors for the deceased Athenian politician Lycurgus, Athens, 307/6); *IG* II³ 1 911, ll. 28–29 (honors for Callias of Sphettus, Athens, 270/69); *SEG* 59.1407, ll. 16–18 (threats against generals who would betray democracy, Aeolian Cyme, second quarter of the third century); *SEG* 63.645, l. 4 (posthumous honors for Astyanax, Rhodes, third century); *I. Priene* B-M 6, ll. 2, 17 (establishment of Soteria festival, Priene, early third century).
[154] Simonton 2018a: 531–35. The irony of the decree's vehemently prodemocratic stance is that the reimposition of oligarchy under Demetrius of Phalerum was looming at the time. For whatever reason, that regime did not destroy the monument.
[155] Liddel 2020: table 1.

a central purpose was to publicize the People's honors for its benefactors both foreign (the great majority) and domestic, in order to keep the benefactions coming and to encourage others to do the same. Greek democracies increasingly required these benefactors to function and, in situations of existential threat, to survive, as we will see in Section 3.8.

3.7 *Dēmos* and Others

The foregoing sections have surveyed the travails of the *dēmos* in its struggles against its fiercest enemies. I have tried to show that democratic regimes could not be taken for granted and that their citizens had to remain on alert against the possibility of subversion, at least down to the end of the third century. Thus I do not believe that "democracy" was important only to those members of the elite who adopted it as a slogan in their competition with rivals. To the extent that democracies remained quite distinct from oligarchies and tyrannies, they bolstered the civil rights and political power of average male citizens to a significantly greater degree than their alternatives. While it can never be known for certain, it seems probable that in most of the communities so far surveyed decision-making and control were largely in the hands of the citizenry and not an elite subset thereof. This granting of power by Greek democracies to men who had to work for a living, and even to men who owned no real property and labored for others, remains an exception to the rule for much of world history.

But of course, not everyone who resided in a *polis* belonged to the *dēmos*. Comprising (in most cases) the freeborn adult native males of citizen parentage, the *dēmos* necessarily represented a minority of the total population of a city-state. There is no *polis* from Greek antiquity that was not constituted by various modes of categorization and exclusion along these lines. This section is concerned with the question of to what extent and by what means these categories of exclusion made possible a democratic identity. It examines the intersecting categories of gender, status, and ethnicity, particularly as they were embodied in the figures of the female citizen, the noncitizen resident foreigner, and the enslaved person. We will in effect move down a pyramid of power and privilege at the apex of which sat the citizen male.[156] Since I cannot hope to explore these issues in the space they deserve, I will limit myself to intervening in some recent debates in the scholarly literature. In line with one of the aims of this chapter, I also wish to suggest how evidence of the third and second centuries can contribute to these debates.

---

[156] Of course, within the apex of the male citizenry there was a further pyramid of wealth and privilege.

3.7.1 Citizen Women

The generic Greek term for "citizen" is the noun *politēs*, whence arises the complex word *politeia*, meaning simultaneously "citizenship," "constitution," and "policy." As we saw in Section 3.3, for Aristotle in *Politics* Book III the mark of the (male) *politēs* in the "absolute sense" is the fact of partaking in judicial decision-making and office holding (*krisis* and *archē*, respectively).[157] We also saw in Section 3.4 how democracies in the period in question made such forms of participation available to a broad swath of the male citizenry at any given time. In recent years, multiple scholars have found Aristotle's definition of the citizen to be one-sided or defective in crucial respects. In a groundbreaking book, Josine Blok has drawn attention in particular to the importance of female citizenship in Classical Athens, a citizenship that cannot be defined by *krisis* or *archē*.[158] While previous historians have noted that freeborn Athenian women enjoyed numerous rights denied to metics and enslaved people[159], Blok's achievement has been to emphasize and illustrate all the ways these women were legally defined *citizens* no less than were their male counterparts.[160] Yet she has also proffered a new understanding of what citizenship entails, one that moves us further away from Aristotle's definition and grants complementary roles to male and female citizens in Athens. For Blok, citizenship is participation in the *hiera kai hosia* of the *polis*, that is, the "sacred and sanctioned," or, as Blok glosses it, "the human gifts to the gods and conduct towards gods and humans showing proper respect for the gods."[161] On this model, women and men equally perform their citizenship vis-à-vis the gods, albeit in differing and sometimes mutually exclusive ways.

As it pertains to the Greek democracies we have been studying, I would suggest that this redefinition picks out citizenship in a *marked sense*. Since it is true that both men and women were citizens (*politai* and *politides*, respectively) who belonged to the same *politeia*, if one were asked to explain what it is those groups have in common to the exclusion of noncitizens, one could point to their shared participation in the *hiera kai hosia*. Blok's formulation thus succinctly expresses the criteria for belonging to a citizen community as contrasted with groups excluded from that community. In the *unmarked sense*, however, "*politeia*" in the ancient Greek world was primarily about the exercise of power. In the canonical

---

[157] Arist. *Pol.* 3.1275a22–23.   [158] Blok 2017; see also Blok 2005, 2013.   [159] Schaps 1998.
[160] For the effect of Pericles' Citizenship Law of 451/0 (see Chapter 2) on citizen women, see already Osborne 2010: ch. 12.
[161] Blok 2017: 99.

3.7 Dēmos *and Others*

trifold division of regimes, the three different types of *politeia* are not concerned with what group in the *polis* partakes of the *hiera kai hosia*, but rather with what group exercises *kratos* (power) or *archē* (rule): *monarchia* (the rule of one), *oligarchia* (the rule of the few), or *dēmokratia* (the power of the *dēmos*/many). In Athens, the constitution was not characterized as the "rule of the citizens" (which would be "*politokratia*" – a word that in any case does not exist in ancient Greek), but as *dēmokratia*, the "rule of the *dēmos*" – and the *dēmos* was gendered, grammatically and conceptually, as male.[162]

Thus, when we look for the language of citizenship in historiography and inscriptions, what we typically find is "citizen" and "citizenship" in the unmarked sense – that is, in the sense that reflects the male-dominated nature of ancient Greek society. Consider a decree of Priene dating from just after the Galatian migration into Asia Minor in 278 BCE. This was a tumultuous period that saw fighting between the Galatians and the settled communities of the area. A Prienean citizen man named Sotas is praised in the decree for his actions during this difficult time: He first "gathered together the strongest of the citizens [*hoi politai*] and those people from the countryside who desired to join in the danger with them against the barbarians." The group had as its mission to "save the citizens [*hoi politai*] in the countryside," that is, "[the citizens] themselves, their wives, their children, and their possessions in the countryside."[163] Note that *hoi politai* here, which, in its masculine plural form, can encompass both men and women as the situation requires, turns out to mean male citizens only, and that the woman are referred to not as *politides* (female citizens) but as *gunaikes*, "wives." "Citizens" are citizen men, with power over a household containing a wife, children, and "possessions" (which might of course include slaves). The noun *politis*, furthermore, is rare in all ancient Greek sources, whether poetry or prose, literature or epigraphy. Much more common are phrases like "the sacred herald is to pray ... on behalf of the safety of the *polis* and the countryside and the citizens and their wives and children."[164] Similarly, in an inscribed *sympoliteia* agreement between Miletus and Pidasa, we read, "the Pidasans are to be citizens [*politai*] of Miletus, as are their children and wives, that is, as many [wives] as are Pidasans by birth or are citizens [*politides*] of a Greek *polis*." It is men who are marked by default as citizens, while the women are referred to as

---

[162] See Section 3.6 for representations of the *dēmos*. As always, translation matters: it is somewhat misleading to render *dēmos* as "people," especially because English does not gender nouns and the word "people" might lead readers to think *dēmos* has a more capacious meaning than it does.

[163] *I. Priene* B-M 28, ll. 19–23.   [164] *Syll.*³ 589, ll. 22–28 (Magnesia on the Maeander, 197/6 BCE).

"wives" until their legal status becomes important – that is, until the *marked* sense of "citizen" becomes relevant.[165]

This primacy of the male citizen was not an academic distinction. Because men and men alone partook of *krisis* and *archē*, they were in a position to enforce their political decisions on the female citizen population (and many others), willing or not. This imbalance comes through clearly in an inscription from the city of Teos in Ionia from the second half of the third century.[166] The *polis* had been raided by pirates, who kidnapped numerous inhabitants, both enslaved and free. The pirates demanded that a large sum be raised as a means of ransoming the prisoners. The assembly of Tean men therefore decreed that all citizens should be invited to contribute whatever they could to the effort, on the promise that they would be repaid with interest. The acquisition of certain luxury items, furthermore, like gold and silver drinking cups and female clothing embellished with purple dye, would be illegal and subject to punishment until the funds were raised and the prisoners ransomed. Citizen women thus had their options even further restricted – their husbands would normally have had the ultimate say over whether they got new clothes – by a political decision in which they had no say.[167]

The stakes were even more extreme in the case of Philip V of Macedon's siege of the *polis* of Abydus on the Hellespont in 200. When the situation looked dire, the all-male assembly decided that they would fight to the death; a select group of elder men would swear to see out their pledge to kill the women and children rather than allow them to be taken alive.[168] The citizen women of Abydus may have shared the men's convictions in this case – the text does not indicate one way or the other – but, having no choice about this issue of life and death, they can fairly be designated the subjects of male citizen domination.

3.7.2 Free Resident Foreigners

We now move from the citizen in-group to out-groups both free and enslaved: resident foreigners (metics) and chattel slaves. Our best evidence

---

[165] See already the arguments of Fröhlich 2016: 124–25 along similar lines; also I. Savalli-Lestrade at *BE* 2019 no. 40. For a critical response see Sebillotte-Cuchet 2017; but note also Farioli 2020.

[166] The latest edition is Hamon 2018; see further *SEG* 67.792.

[167] Still, it is worth noting that the Teans' decision would mainly have affected wealthy women. For male-dominated Greek democracies favoring lower-class women over those of the elite, see, e.g., [Plut.] *Mor.* 842a: the fourth-century Athenian politician Lycurgus passed a law forbidding women from traveling to Eleusis for the Mystery rites there via carriage, "so that commoner women wouldn't be belittled by rich women."

[168] Polyb. 16.31.1–6; see already Section 3.4. The gruesome pledge was eventually carried out.

3.7 Dēmos *and Others*

for metics comes from fifth- and fourth-century Athens. Foreigners – some of whom might be citizens of other Greek *poleis* – who decided to take up residence in Athens for longer than a month were required to register with a citizen sponsor (*prostatēs*); they could then live and work in Athens (but not own real property) so long as they paid the metic tax (*metoikion*) of one drachma per month for men. Wealthy metics were required to pay extraordinary taxes (*eisphorai*) and, if they had hoplite arms, to serve in the army. Some metics did make spectacular fortunes at Athens if they were not already rich, but there were clearly also working-class metics. Metics might also be non-Greek. Freed slaves (*apeleutheroi*) who remained in Athens after manumission were required to register as metics as well.[169]

Athenian attitudes toward metics can never be fully recovered, but they were no doubt complex. Scholars have argued over whether citizens viewed metics with contempt or embraced them with open arms – but surely it depends on the metic in question, since there might be different attitudes toward, say, the "millionaire" Syracusan metic Cephalus (a friend of Pericles) on the one hand and a working-class non-Greek freedperson on the other.[170] Critics of democracies charged them with adopting too indulgent a position toward metics (and slaves, as we will see), in line with democracy's supposed laxity and disorder. Thus the Old Oligarch complains that the Athenian *dēmos* has granted *isēgoria* (equality of political speech) to metics because the latter are needed for their skills and for participation in the fleet; Aristotle says that Cleisthenes enrolled metics as citizens after the revolution of 508/7.[171] The first of these views is plainly false, the result of antidemocratic ideology, while the second highlights the exception to the rule. In reality, the Athenian democracy was quite stingy when it came to enfranchising metics.

The privileges of belonging to the citizen "club," especially during the high empire of the mid fifth century, led the Athenians to patrol the boundary between *politēs* and metic quite scrupulously, even ferociously on occasion. During the same period, as we saw in the previous chapter, the development of the ideology of autochthony at Athens, that is, the belief that the Athenian citizenry represented the descendants of primordial occupants of the land literally sprung from the earth, created what one scholar has called a racial identity among the Athenians, with concomitant anxiety about the "contamination" of the pure citizen group by outsiders.[172] Far from letting metics pass undetected as citizens (something

---

[169] Whitehead 1977. [170] Contrasting views on metics: Wijma 2014; Akrigg 2019: 134.
[171] [Xen.] *Ath. Pol.* 1.10–12; Arist. *Pol.* 3.1275b35–37. Cf. Isoc. 8.88.
[172] On autochthony, see the sources cited in Chapter 2.4.1. Racial identity: Lape 2010.

Aristotle thought inevitable in a large city like Athens), the Athenians had strict measures in place to root out metics who dared usurp citizen privileges.[173] A legal procedure called the *graphē xenias* (charge of foreign status), if successfully prosecuted against someone claiming to be a citizen, resulted in death or slavery. A metic caught living without a sponsor (and so living "off the grid," as it were, and potentially mingling among citizens as though a citizen him- or herself) likewise faced enslavement.[174] But metic-focused paranoia also sometimes claimed citizen victims. Athenians whose family members performed "servile" jobs associated with metics, such as wet nurse or ribbon seller (both female professions), or even spoke with a non-Attic accent, had to worry about accusations of metic status if a scrutiny of the citizen registers (*diapsēphisis*) occurred, as they occasionally did in Athenian history.[175] There may have been pressures on lower-class Athenians to "perform" as "proper citizens," namely by disguising traits that could be associated with metics (or slaves).[176]

In any case, because democratic citizenship in Athens and elsewhere was highly valuable and could be dangled in front of metics as an incentive or disciplining device, metic populations in the Greek cities represented a kind of "reserve army of potential citizens," to be exploited in emergencies. The military language is to be taken literally: Faced with existential crises like impending battles or sieges, the *poleis* sometimes offered the metic population citizenship en masse in exchange for staying and fighting – after all, a normal part of being a metic was freedom to leave the city at will.[177] The Athenians enfranchised metics on several occasions, including prior to the Battle of Arginusae in 406 and before Chaeronea in 338: In the aftermath of the latter event, the orator Lycurgus despaired that "the People had voted that foreigners be Athenians – a People that previously prided itself on being autochthonous and free."[178] Metics might prove useful in *stasis* too: In 410/9, the *dēmos* of Corcyra manumitted the slaves and enfranchised the resident foreigners in order to increase support for the democratic regime against oligarchic exiles.[179]

---

[173] Arist. *Pol.* 7.1326b20–21.   [174] Kapparis 2005.
[175] Dem. 57.18, 34–35 with Lape 2010: ch. 5. For the *diapsēphisis*, see Aeschin. 1.77 and Harp. *s.v. diapsēphisis* with Kapparis 2005: 92–95. For prejudice against metic working women, see Kennedy 2014: ch. 4.
[176] See Kasimis 2018, a profound exploration of the dialectic between metic and citizen.
[177] See further Oliver 2011: 359–60. Thasos offered honors to the children of metics who died in war, but to a lesser degree than to citizen orphans, in an act of unequal treatment Fournier and Hamon label "patent and deliberate": *SEG* 57.820b, ll. 9–11 with Fournier and Hamon 2007: 339.
[178] Lyc. 1.41. On these enfranchisements, see Diod. Sic. 13.97.1 (406); [Plut.] *Mor.* 849a (338).
[179] Diod. Sic. 13.48.7.

3.7 Dēmos and Others

The goal here was always greater *homonoia* ("unanimity"), and thus greater fighting resolve, as is expressly stated in a decree from beyond our period, during the Roman war against Mithridates of Pontus in the 80s BCE. In this instance the People of Ephesus free the slaves and make the *paroikoi* (their version of metics) citizens, so that "all undergo the danger [of war] being of one mind."[180] *Poleis* might also sell citizenship to metics to raise cash or enfranchise them to deal with depleted citizen numbers, but these sorts of actions were rare.[181] Finally, democratic antityranny legislation often contained incentives for metics to take part in resistance against tyrants or oligarchs. In the law from Ilium, from the first half of the third century, a foreigner who kills a usurper is awarded citizenship, and the antityranny law from Eretria likely contained a similar provision.[182] Democratic communities (indeed all Greek *polis* communities) were thus in a relationship of unequal bargaining power with metics, who provided the city with essential services and contributed to its economy but were also often desperate to obtain citizenship in their city of residence.[183] In democracies in particular the metic represented yet another group in comparison with which a poor citizen could feel superior, no matter the wealth of the foreigner – so long as one wasn't accused of being a metic oneself.

3.7.3 Enslaved People

We now come to the enslaved population of a democratic *polis*.[184] It is important to understand how, precisely, this cruel and inhumane practice made ancient Greek democracies possible, since popular audiences

---

[180] *Syll.*³ 742, ll. 24–25; cf. *OGIS* 338 (Pergamum in 133).
[181] See, e.g., Rizakis *Achaïe* III.3 (Dyme, third century); *SEG* 39.1155 (Ephesus, late fourth or early third century). In both cases citizenship was sold to free people born of free parents only; freedpeople and slaves need not apply. Aristotle notes that democracies cease to offer citizenship to those without full citizen parentage once they refill their numbers: *Pol.* 3.1278a26–34. On sale of citizenship and replenishment of the citizen body, see further Gauthier 1985: 199–202; Lonis 1992; Müller 2014.
[182] *I. Ilion* 25, ll. 28–31; Knoepfler 2001: 209–10. By contrast, the Athenians after 411 granted honors only to the legitimate children of citizen men who fought and died on behalf of democracy against oligarchy, not metics: OR 178, l. 4 with Stroud 1971: 286–87, 299–300. The Athenians did bury at public expense metics who fought alongside democrats in 403: Lys. 2.66.
[183] The fascinating inscriptions highlighted by Constantakopoulou 2012, in which citizens and noncitizen inhabitants jointly issue decrees, are very much the exception to the rule.
[184] I reserve for a footnote episodes similar to the mass enfranchisement of metics discussed above, in which the *dēmos* used the enticement of freedom or even citizenship to induce slaves to fight on its behalf: In addition to Athens in 406 and 338 (see above), the Rhodian People, under siege by Demetrius Poliorcetes, freed such slaves as proved themselves brave (Diod. Sic. 20.84.3), while the Abydenes likewise freed their slaves as Philip V of Macedon besieged them in 200, "so that they might have them as unhesitating partners in the ordeal" (Polyb. 16.31.2).

sometimes assume that the citizens of ancient Athens, for example, were completely freed from the need to work and therefore capable of participating in politics solely due to enslaved labor. In fact, many Athenian citizens would not have owned slaves at all, and enslaved people were always a minority of the total population of Attica. And while numerous citizen farmers and craftsmen labored alongside slaves in order to perpetuate their own households, enslaved people were mainly responsible for producing the surplus that granted the superelite within the citizenry the ability to live without working (and to enjoy numerous other luxuries in addition).

What slavery, as a system, did contribute to democratic ideology was the presence of a population completely without rights, legally owned by other human beings, compared with whom the poor citizen could be the equal of the wealthy solely on the basis of being free.[185] In other words, it is very likely that ancient Greek democracies required this kind of fundamentally dishonored out-group in order to render the divergent interests contained within the citizen body capable of achieving a unified identity and acting collectively.[186] As Robin Osborne has put it, "Citizens varied enormously in their wealth, but no one, however poor, lived entirely at the beck and call of, or under the thumb of, another citizen."[187] The stark dividing line between enslavement and freedom meant that every Athenian, no matter how poor, possessed privileges, such as freedom of speech and political participation, totally denied the slave.[188] "Don't you know that freedom of speech [*parrhēsia*] is the armor granted to a life of toil [*penia*]? If someone should lose this, he has thrown away the shield of his livelihood," says an unnamed character from a comedy by Nicostratus.[189] The philosopher Democritus, meanwhile, is credited with the maxim that "a life of toil [*penia* again] in a democracy is preferable to so-called happiness under overlords to the same degree that freedom [*eleutheria*] is preferable to

---

[185] Did it also matter that the free citizen poor were not "barbarian"? Did the racialization of enslaved groups contribute to a sense of the *dēmos* as a "naturally" free and therefore empowered group? This is a complex question; see recently Harrison 2020; Canevaro and Lewis forthcoming.

[186] Paulin Ismard (2017) has argued that slavery made democracy possible in another way, in that the technical expertise of public slaves [*dēmosioi*] was required if democratic institutions were to run smoothly and citizens were to be left free to be political amateurs. This is to some degree true, although I believe Ismard overestimates the number and influence of *dēmosioi*.

[187] Osborne 2010: 32. See also ch. 5 of the same volume. Aristotle articulates this ideology at *Pol.* 6.1317a40–b17.

[188] Claims that democracies were indulgent to slaves, like those claiming they haphazardly welcomed metics into the citizen rolls, are equally false: see, e.g., [Xen.] *Ath. Pol.* 1.10–12; Xen. *Hell.* 2.3.48; Plat. *Rep.* 8.563b.

[189] Fr. 30 Kassel-Austin.

slavery [*douleia*]."¹⁹⁰ The language of "slavery" could also prove productive for the citizen poor for the advancement of claims to greater rights and privileges, on the grounds that a life without them was tantamount to enslavement. In Plutarch's *Life of Dion*, for example, a demagogue of fourth-century Syracuse, Hippon, calls for a redistribution of land (*gēs anadasmos*), arguing in the assembly that "equality [*isotēs*] is the foundation of freedom [*eleutheria*], but a life of toil [*penia*] [is the foundation] of slavery [*douleia*] for those who possess nothing."¹⁹¹ In this regard Greek democrats, while not actually suffering the deprivations of the condition, might exploit the emotionally charged language of enslavement in order to conceptualize the freedom of the citizen no less than later theorists of "civic republicanism" in the Roman tradition like Cicero and Sallust.¹⁹²

*

In 405 BCE, Aristophanes in his *Frogs* could make the recently deceased tragedian Euripides claim, "[In my plays] the woman spoke and the slave no less, as would the master and maiden and crone," highlighting how his characters transgressed the pecking order of civic and social categories. "Then ought you not to have died for daring to do this?" demands Aeschylus. "No, by Apollo!" replies Euripides, "for these were democratic [*dēmokratikon*] things I did."¹⁹³

In the late fifth century, anxious elites could still worry that the empowerment of poor men under democracy would lead to the wholesale dissolution of all "natural" boundaries – between free and slave, man and woman, Greek and "barbarian."¹⁹⁴ In reality, ancient Greek democracies proved exceptionally efficient at perpetuating various forms of exclusion and inequality – these may in fact have constituted (but not exhausted) necessary conditions for democracy itself. It will therefore always strike the present author as somewhat ironic that the ancient historian Loren J. Samons, in a book entitled *What's Wrong with Democracy?*, charges democracy ancient and modern with undermining traditional devotion to God, family, and country (or gods, *oikos*, and *polis* in an ancient Greek context).¹⁹⁵ What I believe he neglects – which is much more apparent if one looks beyond Athens and beyond "Classical" periodization – is

---

¹⁹⁰ Democritus DK 68 B 251. One might speak here of poor citizens enjoying the "psychological wage" of not being like the enslaved, to adopt the language of W. E. B. du Bois (1935: 700–701) on poor white workers under segregation.
¹⁹¹ Plut. *Vit. Dio* 37.5. On this episode see Section 3.5.
¹⁹² On republicanism see the sources cited at Chapter 2.3.6. If anything, non-elite Greek democrats had much more to worry about in terms of being dominated than Roman *nobiles* like Cicero (on the latter see Kapust 2004).
¹⁹³ Ar. *Ran.* 950–52.   ¹⁹⁴ Jameson 2004.   ¹⁹⁵ Samons 2004.

that ancient Greek democracies represented a rough solution to the problem of class conflict within the citizenry, a solution that then allowed citizen men to unite around pursuing the traditional pieties and traditional hierarchies unimpeded for several centuries. These were – political equality between rich and poor citizen men very much notwithstanding – conservative societies. In addition, as I have sketched, they formed a kind of social pyramid, in which each stratum was constantly struggling to distinguish itself from that beneath it rather than working to eliminate stratification itself. In that regard, while comparison between ancient and modern democracy is always thought-provoking and fruitful, ancient Greek democracies are incapable of providing a model for a truly emancipatory politics.[196]

3.8 Looking Forward: The Rise of the Big Benefactors

As I bring this discussion of democracies in their heyday to a close, I must address a question that every historian of the Hellenistic period will surely be posing at this point: Where are the benefactors? An influential line of thought has viewed the Hellenistic *poleis* as undergoing a fundamental transformation, from constitutions governed by roughly equal citizen bodies to stratified societies dependent upon a small circle of more or less hereditary elites. These great patrons, who supposedly formed a distinct political class (the so-called *Honoratiorenschicht* or "stratum of notables"), financed the cities' various expenditures and met their needs in times of crisis using their extensive private wealth. In exchange, they predominated within the magistracies and were the recipients of fawning honors.[197] Perhaps as early as the late fourth century, this arrangement constituted a coherent political system of governance by benefaction, or what modern scholars call "euergetism" (from *euergetein*, "to benefit").[198] The special quality of this euergetism is not the fact that a community relies to some degree upon an elite of wealth and birth for political leadership and public finance – this had always been the case in ancient Greece – but instead that the class of notables now holds effective power to the exclusion of the remaining political community.[199] As the historian Paul Veyne put it,

---

[196] For an even more pessimistic assessment of ancient Greece's hierarchical structures, see Roubineau 2015; the author does not, in my opinion, give intra-citizen equality its due.
[197] *Honoratiorenschicht*: Quass 1993. See also the justly admired study of Veyne 1990.
[198] The term *euergetism* (*évergétisme* originally in French) was coined by Boulanger 1923. On the origins of euergetism in Athens see Domingo Gygax 2016.
[199] For a recent collection of studies on the relationship between gifts and honors throughout Greek antiquity see Domingo Gygax and Zuiderhoek 2021.

3.8 Looking Forward: The Rise of the Big Benefactors

"The Hellenistic ... cities, whether independent or autonomous, were governed by notables, by a class or order of rich and prestigious individuals who saw politics as a state duty rather than as a profession or vocation."[200]

There are some undeniable truths behind this picture. Inscribed honors for civic (as opposed to foreign) benefactors really do increase beginning in the third century. There clearly were ultrarich men in many communities who would step in on occasion to relieve the cities of their most pressing financial burdens. These figures acted not under the compulsion of liturgies but on seemingly voluntary grounds.[201] Even Athens, which had been stingy with honors for individual citizens after its heroization of Harmodius and Aristogeiton, began in the fourth century to award select politicians with the so-called highest honors (*megistai timai*): a bronze statue, dining rights (*sitesis*) in the Prytaneum, and a front-row seat in the theater (*prohedria*), among other privileges.[202] While there are a few instances, mainly based on military achievement, from earlier in the century, our epigraphic evidence for this phenomenon dates exclusively to the post-307 period (with the restoration of democracy after Demetrius of Phalerum's regime) and later. But are such practices evidence for the decline or even eclipse of democracy?

It seems instead that rewarding civic benefactors was, first, a relatively rare occurrence during the fourth, third, and early second centuries and, second, a necessity if ancient Greek polities, all of them smaller and poorer than Athens at the time of its empire, were to keep their elites loyal to the democratic status quo. In other words, if the Athens of the fifth-century high empire could dispense with conspicuously honoring its own citizens and with memorializing those honors on stone, that is because its exceptional wealth and power granted it exceptional elite buy-in and thus internal stability – other *poleis* were not so fortunate. Even still, it is not as though fifth-century Athens did not witness personal expenditure by civic benefactors and personal honors resulting therefrom. The fifth-century

---

[200] Veyne 1990: 42. See also 43, on the notables' monopoly of power: "[A] regime of notables has as its *formal* condition free access to politics for all citizens, and as its material condition, the wealth of some citizens, who *alone engage in politics*" (emphasis added).

[201] See, e.g., Boulagoras of Samos (*IG* XII.6 11, discussed below) and Protogenes of Olbia (*Syll.*³ 495), both from the later third century. For city finances during our period see Migeotte 2014; for Athens in particular, see Fawcett 2024. Liturgies, as obligatory expenditures levied on the wealthiest private citizens, remained the most progressive form of taxation, even as voluntary contributions by magistrates expanded. Contrast Sarrazanas 2021, who sees the Athenian magistracy of the *agonothesia* or "office of director of contests" as even more democratic than the festival liturgies of the earlier fifth and fourth centuries.

[202] Kralli 1999–2000.

sophist Gorgias of Leontini, looking back on the political career of Cimon the son of Miltiades, said that he "acquired money in order to use it, and he used it in order to be honored" – this is the basic logic of euergetism.[203] Cimon's name may not have appeared on any monuments, but his benefactions brought him personal glory and political support all the same. Later democracies made this type of exchange more institutionalized, in the process setting clearer and more explicit expectations for its elite, whose fidelity to democracy might otherwise waver during times of crisis.

Thus – as Philippe Gauthier convincingly argued almost forty years ago now – until the later second century, honors for civic benefactors tended to be rare, relatively modest, and always awarded for exceptional concrete actions, usually linked to the holding of formal political office.[204] Elites could not expect praise simply for belonging to a certain family or for holding multiple magistracies – they had to perform in an exemplary way in extraordinary circumstances. Honors might be bestowed by the People on elites for achievements in war, serving on embassies (an act that often entailed great personal risk in the ancient Mediterranean), or making personal monetary contributions (whether gifts or interest-free loans) in times of crisis. Consider the career of Boulagoras of Samos, who flourished in the latter half of the third century: As an inscription tells us, he served as ambassador to a Seleucid king, was elected advocate for the city by the People numerous times, was chosen overseer of the gymnasium, was sacred ambassador to the court of Ptolemy III in Alexandria (paying for numerous expenditures in the process), and lent money to the city during grain shortages. For these acts he received rather simple rewards: the announcement of a golden crown at the local Dionysia festival and the writing up of the decree praising him.[205] The situation does not differ greatly from that of the famous Athenian statesman Lycurgus of Butadae, whose honors were voted posthumously in 307/6.[206] The so-called hortatory clause of the decree establishing these honors, which explains the practical intent behind their ratification and inscription, states, "so that all know that those who choose to conduct their political life justly on behalf of democracy and freedom are held in the highest regard during life and are given eternal

---

[203] Plut. *Vit. Cim.* 10.5 (= DK 82 B 20); see further Domingo Gygax 2016: ch. 4, for additional fifth-century Athenian benefactors.
[204] Gauthier 1985. For more recent understandings of euergetism and its chronology along these lines see Migeotte 1997; Brélaz 2009; Forster 2018.
[205] *IG* XII.6 11.   [206] [Plut.] *Mor.* 851f ff. with Lambert 2015.

3.8 Looking Forward: The Rise of the Big Benefactors

thanks in death, with good fortune be it decreed by the People," and so forth.[207]

Similar statements are made in the posthumous rewards for Demosthenes and his nephew Demochares, likewise preserved in the pseudo-Plutarchan *Lives of the Ten Orators*.[208] Descriptions of the honorand as "having conducted his political life in the best manner for freedom and democracy out of all of his contemporaries" in the former case or as "being the only person out of the Athenians who engaged in political affairs during the time who didn't think to alter his fatherland to a constitution other than democracy" in the latter are not merely intended to score points against rivals (although they do that too). The language of the decrees incentivizes potential benefactors to compete for who can be most devoted not just to the polity but to democracy in particular.[209] If this was now a necessity for the Athenian democracy, all the more so did it apply to other democracies as well.[210] The honorands of these decrees were therefore not "patrons" or "masters" of their cities; to adopt Gauthier's perspective once again, they were a version of the *prostatai tou dēmou* or "champions of the People," known to us from Thucydides and other fifth-century sources.[211] If this description holds for the fourth, third, and earlier second centuries, changes were nevertheless on the horizon.

---

[207] [Plut.] *Mor.* 852d.   [208] [Plut.] *Mor.* 850f–51f.
[209] See Lambert 2011: 196–97; Miller 2016; Iacoviello 2025. For the use of the motivation clauses of these decrees and others in constructing an idealized version of the past, see Section 3.6.
[210] Here we should remember the words of Anaximenes of Lampsacus, who considered such a system of benefaction and reward a stabilizing mechanism for democracy: "One might [implant in the rich a sense of rivalrous zeal for spending money on the community's public services] in the following way, if there are certain honors specified by the laws for the owners of property in exchange for their expenditures for the community" (discussed in Section 3.3).
[211] Gauthier 1985: 69. For the term *prostatēs tou dēmou*, see Chapter 2.3.3. To be sure, however, the honorands from these decrees are represented as much more moderate figures than *prostatai tou dēmou* in their capacity as violent "demagogues."

CHAPTER 4

(D)evolutions of Democracy, 146 BCE to Late Antiquity

4.1 Introduction

Consider the following text from Greek antiquity. An author is discussing the proper conduct of a "statesman" (*politikos*). The question is how to stand one's ground in the face of a demanding multitude. The author, who elsewhere has described *dēmokratia* as "the finest and most law-abiding of constitutions," concedes that "the People has the power of a slave-owner [*despotikē exousia*]" over its politicians, but the true statesman will refuse to admit he is a slave. Instead, the author claims, the statesman will declare his intentions thus:

> Should I need to serve as a judge [*dikazein*], I will carry out my judicial duty favoring neither the wealthy man because of his resources nor the poor man out of pity for his misfortune.... And should I serve as councilor [*bouleuō*], I will introduce proposals that benefit the whole community, even if they are not to the audience's liking. And should I participate in the assembly [*ekklēsiazō*], I will leave flattering orations to others and make use of salutary and beneficial ones, chastising, admonishing, and moderating, having trained myself not in maddened and deranged arrogance but in sober frank speech [*parrhēsia*].

Here we have a classic statement of the workings of an ancient Greek democracy. The constitution comprises popular courts, a council, and an active assembly. Furthermore, the preponderant power of the *dēmos* in these institutions means that popular opinion can always be brought to bear on recalcitrant speakers, encouraging them to say what the audience wants to hear. The duty of the (semi)professional politician, almost certainly a member of the elite, is to withstand the criticism of the masses and to speak his mind freely, offering the assembled People what he considers his best advice.

The text reads like one of the passages of Attic oratory Josiah Ober analyzed in his 1989 work *Mass and Elite in Democratic Athens*, which established that the People exercised hegemonic power over its political class during the period of the fifth- and fourth-century democracy. But the work is not by Pericles or Demosthenes. It is by Philo, a Hellenizing Jewish scholar and Platonic philosopher who lived in the cosmopolitan city of Alexandria in the first century CE.[1] Philo's excursus on statesmanship is in fact part of a commentary on the biblical story of Joseph, who for Philo represents the ideal *politikos*.[2] Philo expected his audience to see in democratic institutions the typical locus for the display of statesmanlike qualities. Clearly, democracy had become part of the package, so to speak, of cultural Hellenism, to be exploited for diverse ends by writers and speakers socialized into Greek *paideia* or "education." But does the normative nature of democracy in Philo, apparent elsewhere in his oeuvre and in other writers of the later Hellenistic and Imperial periods, reflect the persistence of democratic institutions in the Greek cities after 146 BCE? Or are these so many classicizing tropes and clichés that conceal a much more oligarchic reality?

The answer, it seems, is both. In this final chapter I will attempt to chart the life (or better, lives) of Greek *dēmokratia* during what we can call Roman times (146 BCE–ca. 500 CE). Necessarily, the treatment must remain incomplete, since I will be covering almost six centuries' worth of history in a brief overview. Nevertheless, certain patterns emerge from a study of the evidence that will be explored in what follows. To summarize in advance: Despite the occasional direct intervention of the Romans on behalf of census-based regimes, most *poleis* retained their formally democratic institutions beyond the "heyday." But more than that – there was only rarely a return to the exclusionary and authoritarian style of oligarchy known from the fifth through third centuries BCE. The People had established a foothold in political life in the form of an active assembly culture that did not cease until (arguably) the fourth century CE. While the magistracies were increasingly monopolized by local elites, it was only with great difficulty that they ever established airtight agenda control over the assembly's workings. There was still breathing room for "demagogic" politicians willing to best their elite rivals by appealing in a more blatantly populist way to the People. In rare instances, this dynamic might even result in a popular uprising and a revolt against the Roman authorities, almost inevitably quashed. In other words, the *ekklēsia* was no demoralized appendage during this period, resigned to rubber-stamping the policies of the notables (to use the most common metaphor). Nor were the *politai* of these citizen bodies palpably exploited to the degree we might expect if

---

[1] On Philo's cultural and civic milieux see Sandelin 2014; Seland 2014.
[2] Philo *de Joseph*. 67. "Finest and most law-abiding of constitutions": *de spec. leg.* 4.237.

a truly unaccountable oligarchy were in place. The *polis* appears to have continued to provide privileges and securities to those fortunate enough to number among the *dēmos*, even if wealth inequality undeniably increased.

At the same time, these "citizen-states" underwent indisputable mutations. With a few exceptions, sortitive offices disappear. Popular law courts are less and less apparent – and certainly, the popular classes cease to apply the harsh discipline against leading elites that once characterized Athens and numerous other democracies. While membership on the council does not, in most instances, become a position for life, it was nevertheless the redoubt of the elite *politeuomenoi* or "political class," which certainly included the "big benefactors" discussed in Chapter 3.8, as well as less spectacularly wealthy citizens. We will trace rhetorical and institutional changes in the ways the cities dealt with these *euergetai* later in this chapter. In language and in iconography, the council and the assembly increasingly came to be represented as distinct in their composition and even in their respective interests. The *boulē* was thus no longer a representative sample of the citizen body but the characteristic organ of the upper classes. With the foreign policy remit of the *poleis* progressively curtailed by the *Imperium Populi Romani*, they contented themselves more and more with celebrating their civic benefactors through honorific statues, the decision increasingly conveyed by dedicatory inscriptions rather than formal decrees. To be sure, the cities continued to govern their own local affairs, often with substantive input from the People, but the changed treatment of local notables – in such areas as honorific titles, public funerals, and acclamations – bespeaks a much more elitist mentality. Still, no one likely could have anticipated, as late as the middle of the third century CE, that the familiar world of Greek civic politics, with an institutional setup (council, assembly, magistrates) known for almost one thousand years, would virtually disappear within a century. Following on the triumph of Constantinople and Christianity across the fourth and fifth centuries CE, a whole constellation of political concepts and traditions, on which democracy had left an indelible mark, faded from view.

4.2 Greek Cities under Roman Rule

The Roman encroachment into the Greek Mediterranean surveyed in the previous chapter continued unabated after the conclusion of the Achaean War in 146.[3] Central and southern mainland Greece became a protectorate in

---

[3] For a political history of the period that bridges the late Hellenistic and Imperial eras, see Chaniotis 2018, esp. chs. 8–12.

that year. "Asia" (western Anatolia) was reduced to provincial status following the death of the last Attalid king of Pergamum in 133 and the defeat of the pretender Aristonicus in 129. Other Greek *poleis* in Asia Minor came under Roman control as Pompey the Great (106–48 BCE) acquired what became the provinces of Bithynia-Pontus, Cilicia, Pisidia, Pamphylia, and Syria during his campaign of the 60s against King Mithridates VI of Pontus. Greeks slowly learned to live with a Roman governor and Roman taxes, although not without occasional resistance against their imperial overlords. While civic life – and, crucially, involvement by the popular masses – continued, the inscriptional record appears to register a decline in the inter*polis* institutions that had characterized the peer–polity interaction of the prior period: The sending of foreign judges, establishment of proxenies, and resort to *isopoliteia* agreements all fell into obsolescence under the *pax Romana*.[4] Within the cities themselves, the institution of the ephebate, previously so crucial for socializing and training young male citizens (at least those from the middling and upper ranks of society), became under Roman rule much more elitist; a telltale sign of change is the admission of wealthy noncitizens into the ranks of the ephebes.[5] The gymnasiarchy or magistracy in charge of the gymnasium became the preserve of the big benefactors (see Section 4.3), as the cities could no longer afford to provide costly olive oil for exercising; the "office" was basically a liturgy, and inscribed lists of ephebes decline in the later Imperial period.

Across the board, inscribed decrees in the *poleis* gradually give way to much more succinct honorific inscriptions, usually found on statue bases, in which the relevant civic institutions (*boulē*, *dēmos*) literally "dedicate" or "erect" the honorand. These cursory statements belie, however, rather more complex decisions undertaken during meetings of the assembly.[6] In tandem with a decline in the epigraphic recording of *psēphismata*, mentions of "democracy" in inscriptions of all kinds largely disappear as well: From a peak in the first half of the second century (about fifteen separate attestations), "*dēmokratia*" barely registers in the first centuries BCE and CE and completely disappears thereafter.[7] This process occurred even as democracy became a standard part of the package of Hellenic culture, as we have just seen in the case of Philo of Alexandria, and perhaps

---

[4] See Mack 2015: ch. 5. Cities continued to award proxenies (Dio Chrys. 38.22), but much more infrequently, and the practice of inscribing these honors basically disappears.
[5] Kennell 2009; Wiemer 2011; de Lisle 2020: 45–60.
[6] McLean 2002: 236–39. For the "grammar of honors" employed by these honorific inscriptions (*tituli honorarii*) and what they might tell us about the politics of bestowing honors, see Ma 2013: ch. 1.
[7] See Appendix.

serves as something of a corrective to the literary sources, which we will explore in greater detail.

The establishment of Roman rule was an uneven and contingent process, and imperial expansion advanced simultaneously with the internecine struggles at Rome itself that characterize the Late Republic. Navigating this tumultuous period, which eventually resulted in the ascendancy of Gaius Julius Caesar Octavianus (Octavian) as the first emperor Augustus in 27 BCE, presented great difficulties to the Greek *poleis*, but it also kept alive opportunities for extraordinary political leadership. The aforementioned Aristonicus War is a particularly illustrative period. A decree from the Ionian city of Metropolis, for example, enacted by the council and the People, praises an ideal(ized) citizen, Apollonius the son of Attalus, who previously in his political career had "shunned neither danger nor distress, whence it resulted that the People arrived at a much better state of affairs."[8] The decree then gives its own, ideologically charged account of the death of the last Attalid king in 133: "When the Romans, the common benefactors and saviors,[9] were returning freedom [*eleutheria*], as they had decreed, to all those previously subject to the kingship of Attalus, Aristonicus arrived and wished to take away the freedom returned to us by the Senate."[10] In these circumstances Apollonius led a contingent of young men to the camp of the Roman commanders in the region in preparation for combat with the forces of Aristonicus. On the eve of battle, "he exhorted those on campaign with him, as was appropriate for that man and our *polis*, and he considered it noble, struggling on behalf of the fatherland and citizens and the freedom bestowed, to have as his burial shroud the repute and honor that would accrue to him"; he duly died in the subsequent engagement.[11] For these undoubtedly heroic actions, the People of Metropolis initially decreed him a bronze statue on an inscribed marble base in the most conspicuous location within the agora. But then we read a striking addendum: Apollonius' sons Attalus and Agesandrus are granted the option of constructing a *hērōon* or hero shrine to Apollonius on their private property. In other words, Apollonius represents a well-known figure from the fifth through earlier second centuries, the local patriot awarded honors by his community in death, but with the rather novel developments added of intense devotion to the Romans and the worship of the protagonist, literally heroized, after death.[12]

---

[8] *I. Metropolis* 1a, ll. 4–5. [9] For these titles, see Chapter 3.2, with Erksine 1994.
[10] ll. 13–17. We will see more of this kind of propaganda on behalf of the Roman Empire.
[11] ll. 31–33. Recall the language of "struggling" discussed in Chapter 3.6.
[12] For another evocative example of a local honorand from the period of the Aristonicus War, see *SEG* 39.1244, an inscription from Claros near Colophon awarding honors to one Menippus.

This dynamic gradually became the rule as leading Greek statesmen negotiated with (or resisted) various rival elites during the Roman Civil Wars of the first century BCE. Successful politicians included those who, often out of blind luck, sided with ascendant Romans long enough to secure their cities' freedom. Communities also sometimes honored statesmen who negotiated a peaceful surrender to the Romans after choosing the *wrong* side. The city of Himera in Sicily, for example, was spared by Pompey the Great when its leading "demagogue," Sthenis, convinced the Roman commander that he had been the cause of his city's defection to the side of the Marian faction during the civil wars of the Sullan era. The decision was not, however, an autocratic one, as Sthenis makes clear: He had convinced his friends and forced his enemies to follow his lead, exercising the informal power of *rhētōr* within the city's popular assembly.[13]

As time goes on, these politicians' allegiances become apparent from the Latin praenomen and nomen that precede their Greek name, a sign of the patron who bestowed Roman citizenship on them.[14] Thus we find Gnaeus Pompeius Theophanes of Mytilene, a historian of Pompey's Mithridatic campaigns, who gained freedom for his native city and was honored posthumously as a hero.[15] Gaius Julius Artemidorus of Cnidus, who wrung benefits for his *polis* from Caesar after the Battle of Pharsalus in 48, was granted godlike honors and a festival in his name, the Artemidoreia, even while still alive.[16] A separate set of honors for his family members proclaims that through their efforts "the People was saved and conducts its political life in unanimity [*homonoia*] and democracy."[17] Gaius Julius Zoilus of Aphrodisias, a freedman of Augustus, became a major patron of his city and was honored in death with a monumental tomb, one sculpted frieze of which shows him honored by personified Demos and Polis.[18] Finally, Gaius Julius Hybreas was one of two illustrious "demagogues," as Strabo calls them, of Mylasa in Caria during the first century BCE, along with his fellow citizen Euthydemus. Hybreas resisted the Roman rebel Quintus Labienus, who attacked the empire with Parthian aid in the period after the murder of Julius Caesar. For his achievements and good relations with Rome, Hybreas was heroized by the Mylasans after his death.[19] In all these cases, the honors awarded by the politicians' home communities were anything but perfunctory: They celebrated acts performed during existential crises for the *poleis* in

---

[13] Plut. *Vit. Pomp.* 10.5.   [14] For many of the figures who follow, see Strubbe 2004; Heller 2011.
[15] Robert 1969.   [16] *I. Knidos* 59.   [17] *I. Knidos* 51–55.
[18] Robert 1966 (note Robert's statement, "a Gaius Julius is always interesting," p. 408); Smith 1993.
[19] For Hybreas see Strabo 14.2.24 and the overview of his career provided by Delrieux and Ferriès 2004. We will return to his title of "demagogue."

question, undertaken on the plane of intense international relations; the documents also sometimes cast these honors in explicitly democratic terms.[20] And yet the intensity of the individualistic honors, and the cities' dependence on Rome, also point to a changed world when it comes to civic elites and benefactors.[21] To those figures we now turn in greater detail.

4.3 The Big Benefactors of a New Era

The historian Louis Robert – whom we encountered several times in the notes of the preceding section – spent a lifetime studying the Greek inscriptions of the Hellenistic and Imperial eras. In 1960, already thirty-six years into a long career, he observed the following about Greek society in the period after 150 BCE, which he called the "late Hellenistic period" ("*basse époque hellénistique*"):

> More and more, the evolution of society removes the affairs of the cities from the sovereign action of the assembly of the people and democracy and places them in the hands of a minority of notables, more or less hereditary, who provide many of the essential services of the city through their wealth and receive in return ever more numerous and dazzling honors.[22]

Today, many scholars continue to uphold Robert's distinction between a "high" or early Hellenistic period, in which Greek democracies functioned much as they had in the fifth and fourth centuries, and a "late" one of hereditary notables and aristocratic rule (a true "euergetism": see Chapter 3.8).[23] The present study largely conforms to this picture, although as we will see, significant space and power remained for the assembly of the People even in later Imperial times. Where Robert remains absolutely convincing is in his highlighting of the explosion of honors for the civic elite. This section focuses on these changes, in order better to situate the reader in the elitist culture of the period in preparation for the institutional and social analysis that follows. For while there is no doubt that popular participation and "assembly politics" continued even through the fourth

---

[20] But see also Section 4.5 for *poleis* that rebelled from the Romans on self-professed democratic grounds.
[21] On the changing nature of these honors in light of the deification of the Roman emperors, see Kuhn 2017, esp. 202–204, discussing *I. Kyme* 19. Roman-era *poleis* frequently awarded their biggest benefactors intramural burial rights, as we will see.
[22] Robert 1960: 325, translated from the French.
[23] See, e.g., Gauthier 1985 and the contributions to Fröhlich and Müller 2005. On the other hand, Habicht 1995 argues that the main features of Greek politics (mass decision-making and elite leadership) remained largely unchanged from the Classical through Imperial periods.

4.3 *The Big Benefactors of a New Era*

century CE, it transpired in societies seemingly addicted to reinforcing, at every level and through numerous media, the sociopolitical distance between the few and the many.

In Chapter 3.8, we observed that there was nothing inherently antidemocratic about a community honoring its benefactors – in fact, this basic "compact," encouraged by Anaximenes of Lampsacus in his *Rhetoric to Alexander*, aided in keeping otherwise oligarchically minded elites loyal to democratic regimes. Down to the mid second century BCE, such honors tended to be modest: praise, a crown, a proclamation in the theater, a statue. They were rewards for individuals *qua* members of the broader civic community of equals who performed outstanding services for the *polis*. In the same vein, the motivation clauses of the decrees granting these honors usually make clear that the actions in question came either during the course of a regular magistracy (but performed in a manner over and above the norm) or during periods of extreme danger, for instance war or *stasis*. In some instances, as with the reward of the "highest honors" or *megistai timai* at Athens, the award comes at the end of the long and distinguished career of a *prostatēs tou dēmou* ("champion of the People") such as that of Lycurgus of Boutadai. Occasionally the decrees speak of the honorands' ancestors – Lycurgus "inherited from his ancestors their long-standing hereditary goodwill towards the People" – but this was a matter of the ancestors' concrete good deeds creating great expectations for their progeny, which the latter then had to match or exceed through their own efforts.[24]

After the mid second century, we see a markedly different approach to benefactors develop. Consider the opening of the motivation clause from a decree of Priene in Ionia from around 120 BCE:

> Whereas Moschion son of Cydimus, having been, since his earliest youth, a man of gentlemanly qualities, and having lived a life of piety towards the gods and of reverence towards his parents and towards those living with him in familiarity and intimacy and towards all the remaining citizens, and having behaved justly and honorably towards his fatherland in a manner worthy of the excellence and repute of his ancestors, having acquired as a witness [of his qualities] the favor of the gods throughout his life, etc.[25]

---

[24] Lycurgus: [Plut.] *Mor.* 852a.
[25] *I. Priene* B-M 64, ll. 14–21. For this decree as evidence for the decline of democracy see also Thonemann 2016: 130.

The description is of a hereditary aristocrat with "intrinsic" gentlemanly qualities (*kalokagathia*), one patently favored by the gods.[26] The decree goes on to recount a lifetime of benefactions, after more than three hundred lines finally enumerating Moschion's honors, which included a public funeral accompanied by a civic procession. If this feels excessive, consider the dossier of inscribed documents from Rhodiapolis in Lycia honoring one Opramoas, which carries on for approximately two thousand lines.[27] Numerous other such figures known from inscriptions – Diodorus Pasparus of Pergamum, Archippe of Aeolian Cyme (one of several female benefactors attested during the period), Niceratus of Olbia – are bywords for this development in honor-granting among the late Hellenistic and Imperial *poleis*.[28]

These new-style "big benefactors" not only assisted their *poleis* in times of crisis or through positions of political leadership; they increasingly served as a major source of revenue for the cities' expenditures. Many magistracies were transformed into liturgies: Upon accession to a position – for example, that of gymnasiarch – the *euergetēs* in question was expected to spend from his own pockets to keep the main institutions of the city functioning. The wealthiest euergetists could drop thousands of drachmas at once on spectacular gifts and endowments, but these kinds of benefaction were rarer.[29] To return to Priene, one Aulus Aemilius Zosimus, when serving as gymnasiarch, provided olive oil at his own expense to those exercising in the gymnasium from sunrise to sunset, in addition to furnishing punching bags, balls, hoops, and weapons to the ephebes.[30] The biggest benefactors also tended to cycle through all of the major magistracies, which by now might include the extremely prestigious and exclusive priesthood of the Imperial cult. We know of figures of this type from sources other than epigraphy: For example, the benefactor Nicolaus of Damascus in Syria, an acquaintance of Augustus and Herod the Great who moonlighted as

---

[26] The collocation *progonikē aretē* or "hereditary excellence" increases during this period: e.g., *IG* VII 4148; *I. Délos* 1512; *SEG* 48.1472; *TAM* II 838. Nevertheless, Anna Heller (2021: 316) has recently shown that only a small minority of honorands from Asia Minor (around 10 percent) boast a lineage of at least three generations. She wonders whether, *pace* Zuiderhoek (2009: 133–40), this fact is not due primarily to constant turnover among the narrow elite that monopolized offices but instead indicates that some officeholders remained of rather modest means.

[27] *TAM* II 905 (mid second century CE).

[28] *IG* IV 292–94; *SEG* 33.1035–41; *Syll.*³ 730. See further Gauthier 1985: 57–75. For female benefactors see van Bremen 1996. There is considerable overlap in social profile and in the nature of honors between these figures and the pro-Roman politicians surveyed earlier in this chapter: See again Strubbe 2004. For the honor of intramural burial in particular, see Fröhlich 2013.

[29] Again, the classic accounts are Veyne 1990, esp. 131–56; Quass 1993: 270–352. For the Imperial period in particular see Zuiderhoek 2009. For a massive second-century CE endowment in Oenoanda in Lycia, see Wörrle 1988.

[30] *I. Priene* B-M 68, ll. 58–62, 73–75, with Fröhlich 2009.

4.3 *The Big Benefactors of a New Era*

a historian, tells us in his autobiography that his father, Antipater, "was outstanding in his skill at speaking ... and benefited thousands of people, not just in a public capacity, but numerous townspeople [privately] also ... he was entrusted with the greatest number of embassies and acts of arbitration, and he worked his way through all the local offices [*archai epichorioi*]."[31]

In exchange for all these benefactions, the assembly of the People might award individuals titles such as "nourisher" (*tropheus*), "founder" (*ktistēs*), "paragon" (*aristeus*), and "savior" (*sōtēr*), many of which had previously been voted to the Hellenistic kings and were still bestowed upon Roman emperors.[32] In certain instances, when the People felt a person had not been properly honored through a proposal of the council (now an aristocratic redoubt, as we will see), they might register their desire through public acclamations in order to put pressure on the authorities.[33] For example, the "*polis* of Tlos" (meaning the *dēmos*) "shouted [*epeboēsato*] in the electoral assembly that the priest of the emperors [a local official] was to draft a *probouleuma* so that Lalla [a major female benefactor] be named 'mother of the *polis*.'"[34] In the writer Chariton of Aphrodias' novel *Callirhoe* (probably dating to the first century CE), there is a depiction of the ostensibly fifth-century BCE Syracusan assembly in action, albeit with Imperial-era coloring. At one point, a speaker in the *ekklēsia* proposes citizenship for certain mercenaries: In response, "the People shouted [*epeboēsen*], 'They are worthy to be our fellow citizens! Let these things be voted on by show of hands!'" The proposal was duly drafted (presumably by the Council) and ratified by the *dēmos*, in what is likely a faithful picture of contemporary, first-century CE practice.[35] Such interventions sometimes transpired at the time of the benefactor's death, when the common people requested that he or she receive

---

[31] Nic. Dam. *BNJ* 90 F 131. Intriguingly, Nicolaus, who of course inherited his father's role as public benefactor, presents himself in his autobiography as a populist who spent much of his time among the common people (*dēmotikoi*), on the grounds that there were many more respectable people (*epieikesteroi*) among them than among the wealthy (F 138). It is a rare self-portrait, along with those of Dio Chrysostom and Aelius Aristides, of a major benefactor of the period, who might otherwise be known only through inscriptions: See on this text Toher 2017.

[32] See Dio Chrys. 48.10 with, e.g., *I. Didyma* 84 (second/third century CE); *SEG* 53.1597 (Pednelissus, second century CE). For a systematic quantitative study of such titles, see Heller 2020.

[33] On acclamations see Roueché 1984; Fernoux 2011: 133–50; Kuhn 2013. We will return to their political function and relationship to traditional democratic *thorubos*.

[34] *SEG* 23.938 (mid second century CE). Incidentally, this inscription indicates another important kind of title that circulated during this period, that of "son," "father," or "mother" of the *dēmos/boulē/polis*: see Giannakopoulos 2008. Although in this case the People encourages the magistrates to do something they were not already planning to do, we should note that they do so on behalf of a member of the elite, in a way that arguably reinforces the hierarchical division in society between benefactors and common citizens. See also the case from Cnidus later in this chapter.

[35] Char. 8.8.13–14 with Lalanne 2017: 169–70, 175; Oppeneer 2018: 229–32.

a public funeral and intramural burial. In Cnidus around 100 CE, when a female benefactor's funeral cortege was conducted outdoors by her household, "the People, assembling with total enthusiasm in the theater ... gained possession of her body and collectively demanded that she be buried in the city and shouted [*epeboaseto*] on her behalf so that she might obtain worthy honors."[36] We should not interpret these episodes cynically, as mere pretexts for the common people to demand festive events from officeholders: They reveal extensive public esteem for the benefactors – bordering on worship in some cases – and serve as encouragement to future *euergetai*.

Two things are especially worth noting here before we move on to the formal civic institutions in which these benefactors operated. The first is that, despite the undeniable increase in social and political inequality of the period, of which these elites were the chief beneficiaries, they do not appear to have dominated or exploited their fellow citizens to the degree one might expect.[37] On the political plane, a community might accuse one of them of aiming at tyrannical power, but there is little evidence that they ever succeeded in reducing poorer *politai* to the status of serfs or even personal clients.[38] Although elites increasingly bestowed benefactions on noncitizen groups, including foreigners, rural communities, and even slaves, the citizen in-group/noncitizen out-group binary remained the primary dividing line in Greek society.[39] The members of the *dēmos* retained crucial social and political privileges outright denied to those unfortunate enough not to be enrolled among the citizenry. As unequal as this civic body may have become, it paid to be a *politēs*, and the primary victims of exploitation continued to be enslaved people and, to a lesser but

---

[36] *SEG* 50.1112 with C. P. Jones 1999 for additional "interrupted funerals." The Athenian super-benefactor Herodes Atticus' corpse was seized and publicly buried in a similar way: Philost. *VS* 2 pp. 565–66 Kayser with Rife 2008. The orator Dio of Prusa's ancestors received public burials: 44.4. In an inscription from Aeolian Cyme for Archippe, a female benefactor, we learn that there was a spot in the city "where the other benefactors of the *polis* have been buried" (*SEG* 33.1039, ll. 49–50).

[37] Contrast Gauthier 1985: 72, who speaks of the benefactors post 150 BCE as "dominating their fellow citizens." If he means that the elite had preponderant power within the constitution, I agree; but the evidence for "domination" in the sense of actively subjecting *politai* to unwanted behavior is basically nonexistent.

[38] For charges of tyranny, see, e.g., Strabo 14.2.19 (Nicias of Cos, first century BCE); Dio Chrys. 43.11, 47.18 (Dio of Prusa, ca. 100 CE); Philost. *VS* 2 p. 559 Kayser (Herodes Atticus of Athens, mid second century CE) with Kennell 1997. On the relative lack of exploitation during the Imperial period see Zuiderhoek 2009: 146–50. The particular Marxist model employed by de Ste. Croix 1981 would seem to predict an increase in intercitizen economic exploitation over time as *dēmokratia* dwindles, but the author is unable to produce much if any evidence of this for the Greek cities before the third century CE (pp. 453–62). I believe the gains won by the common people during the heyday of Greek democracies had a longer shelf life than de Ste. Croix would allow.

[39] For benefactions to those outside the citizen body, see Zuiderhoek 2017.

still considerable extent, nonenslaved but noncitizen inhabitants of the countryside, particularly in the Greek East.

Second, just as the citizenry was not disempowered, the benefactors could not rest on their laurels. Although some honors must have been routine – there are simply too many inscriptions for this not to be the case – the most ambitious *euergetai* worked tirelessly, perhaps even obsessively, to deliver ever greater outlays in anticipation of ever greater civic rewards, of which the *dēmos* continued to be the ultimate arbiter and issuing authority. The elite's privileged standing, as the proverbial goose that laid the golden eggs for the cities, meant that its members were unlikely to be severely disciplined, let alone put to death, by the community, in contrast to earlier democratic practice. But by the same token, the cities' greater reliance on the *euergetai* increased the chances that they might exhaust their ancestral wealth through constant liturgies and benefactions. While we should not shed a tear for the big benefactors, who numbered among the most privileged individuals of the Roman Empire, we must nevertheless acknowledge the intense stress and unceasing activity the role entailed. As one scholar has put it, these people were (as portrayed in civic discourse, anyway) "deliberate and rigorous *polis*-fanatics."[40] We can now turn to the institutional setup they navigated in the later Hellenistic and Imperial periods.

4.4 Mutations of Civic Institutions, Second Century BCE and Later

As always, the operative word here is "evolution," not "rupture." No particular date, be it 338, 188, or 146, signals the death once and for all of democracy in the Greek world. Even after the defeat of the Achaean League at the hands of the Romans in 146, many communities continued to understand themselves in democratic terms. In Athens, for example, a decree of the Council of 103/2 BCE orders, in quite traditional popular terminology, that a document be written up "since it is essential and expedient for the People to have the decree inscribed, so that it shall be easily followed by those who wish [*hoi boulomenoi*]."[41] Nevertheless, we see an undeniable overall shift in a more oligarchic direction beginning in the second century BCE, sometimes actively encouraged or imposed by the Romans.[42] Already in the aftermath of the Second Macedonian War, in

---

[40] Wörrle 1995: 244 ("bewußte und rigorose Polisfanatiker").
[41] Papazarkadas 2017: 328 (Papazarkadas' translation).
[42] For what follows see esp. Ferrary 2017: 21–34.

194 BCE, T. Quinctius Flamininus had imposed a monetary census on the council and judiciary of Thessaly.[43] Similar treatment followed for the cities of Euboea and Boeotia after 168.[44] As we saw in the previous chapter, the Roman commander Mummius dissolved democracies and required magistracies "based on property assessments," *apo timēmatōn*, after 146.[45] One particular mark of Roman influence was the appearance of a board of officials called *synedroi* in place of the more traditional *boulē* or council in some of the cities, especially on the mainland; this was likely no mere change in nomenclature but the creation of an oligarchic office based on property requirements.[46] The Romans counted on the wealthier citizens of the Greek *poleis* to guide their cities prudently and to keep the unruly masses in line with Roman policy.

Still, there was no blanket imposition of oligarchic institutions across the Greek-speaking world, nor did the Romans take the trouble to create Senate-like bodies in miniature, modeled on the specifically Roman conception of orders. The one Greek province that underwent such a transformation was Bithynia-Pontus along the coast of the Black Sea, where a *lex Pompeia* ("Pompeian law"), handed down by Pompey the Great, drew up a constitution featuring a council composed of ex-officeholders, perhaps selected by Roman-style censors called *timētai* in Greek.[47] But as we will see, not even this effort could prevent Greek city politics in Bithynia-Pontus from continuing along more traditional democratic lines, particularly when it came to the activity of the assembly. Elsewhere in Asia Minor *poleis* were largely left free by their imperial overlords to conduct their political life as before, albeit now with the ever-present shadow of the Roman governor looming over and disciplining local affairs.

Even if the Romans maintained a light touch, however, the internal dynamics of the cities were already undergoing more hierarchical developments. This was nowhere more apparent than in the case of the council.[48]

---

[43] Livy 34.51.6. [44] Knoepfler 1990. [45] Paus. 7.16.9.
[46] Heller 2009: 346; Ferrary 2017: 33. Still, the *synedroi* appear not to have been councilors for life on the Roman senatorial model (see later in this chapter), since an inscription mentions *synedroi* "from all years": *IG* VII 190, ll. 29–30 (first century BCE).
[47] Fernoux 2004: 142–46, examining the evidence of Pliny the Younger (*Ep.* 10.79, 112). *Timētai*: see, e.g., *SEG* 63.1147 (Nicomedia, late second/early third century CE). Officials called *boulographoi* or "council enrollers" almost certainly played this role elsewhere, e.g., at Ancyra (*OGIS* 549); see further Dmitriev 2005: 200–204.
[48] Quass 1993: 382–94; Müller 1995; Hamon 2005; Heller 2009. A list from Carystus on Euboea dating to the time of the emperor Hadrian declares that certain men obtained the position of *bouleutēs* or councilor by lottery (*SEG* 51.2217). However, we see that this institution is divided into sections of *probouloi*, a traditionally oligarchic office headed by an *archeproboulos* (see further Treheux 1989). The use of the lottery should therefore not deceive us: Classical-era oligarchies had also used lotteries

4.4 Mutations of Civic Institutions, Second Century BCE and Later

Even where cities did not impose formal property requirements for recruitment to the *boulē*, as the cities of mainland Greece likely did for the *synedroi*, the position of *bouleutēs* gradually became the preserve of the elite.[49] The council was no longer a microcosm of the civic body as a whole but developed its own distinct (and privileged) identity and interests.[50] A general cleavage emerged between average citizens and the bouleutic class, as is made apparent by numerous sources in various genres. Certain inscriptions draw a distinction, for example, between "offices belonging to the councilors" (*bouleutikai archai*) on the one hand and "offices belonging to the commoners" (*dēmotikai archai*) on the other; others divide the male citizenry among *bouleutai* and *dēmotai*.[51] We have already seen that the cities gradually ceased to issue inscribed decrees and relied more extensively on honorific statue bases. As one historian has shown statistically, these honorific inscriptions (already the product of a less democratic *polis*) shifted over time, from ones issued by the People alone to a later style in which the People and the council feature jointly.[52] I would interpret this as a result of the members of the council, who felt themselves separate from the *dēmos*, needing to register publicly their institution's involvement in granting honors.

The People and the council also began to honor *each other* with dedicatory statues. They sometimes appear as separate entities on civic coinage during the Imperial period as well. A few coin types show the personified Demos and Boulē shaking hands with *homonoia* or "unanimity" proclaimed between them; this makes little sense except as evidence that the

---

(see [Arist.] *Rhet. ad Alex.* 1424a40–b3), and the councilors from Carystus were likely limited to those satisfying a property requirement.

[49] Exceptionally, Rhodes appears to have continued to appoint councilors from the masses, with pay, at least down to the time of Cicero: *Rep.* 3.35.48. The "Letter to Caesar" attributed to Sallust says that the Rhodians of its time appointed poor men to the law courts by lot as well: 7.12. As late as the second century CE, a decree of Chersonesus on the Black Sea describes the city's difficulties with filling out its panels of judges due to "loss of manpower" (*oligandria*); officials are then enjoined to empanel *dikastai* – remarkably – by lottery: Kantor 2012. This democratic judicial method is very much the exception to the rule, however, where the evidence is not totally lacking.

[50] Part of the issue was that heavy expenditures were now expected of councilors. As Sviatoslav Dmitriev (2005: 140–57) has shown, however, there was no systematic imposition of councilors' fees in the Greek world, as there was for the *summa honoraria* of the Latin West.

[51] *TAM* II 301 (Xanthos, late second/early third century CE); *TAM* II 176 (Sidyma, reign of Commodus); *SEG* 48.592, ll. 2–3 (Delphi, later second century CE – a public division of land in which elites receive more than commoners). On these documents, see Quass 1993: 289–90; Heller 2009: 350. Of course, the presence of "offices belonging to the commoners" shows that some participation in magistracies was still formally available to the non-elite. We also see the emergence of a social stratum called the "councilors' rank" (*bouleutikon tagma*) in many Eastern Greek cities during the Imperial period: Dmitriev 2005: 318.

[52] Heller 2020: 105–107.

two bodies were made up of different socioeconomic classes and might be at odds with each other.[53] Beyond this growing disarticulation of *boulē* from *dēmos*, moreover, there developed even further political gradations and hierarchies *within* the council itself, membership in which merely marked one out as relatively prosperous but not necessarily one of the superelite.[54] In sum, although councilors were probably still elected by the People, and although in many *poleis* membership on the *boulē* was not yet a lifetime appointment (at least in the earlier Imperial period),[55] acquiring bouleutic status was a privilege limited to the relatively wealthy and a first step for going on to obtain ever greater magistracies and honors.

4.5 The Persistence of Popular Politics: *Dēmos* and Demagoguery in Roman-era *Poleis*

> And so the present [politicians] are thoughtless popularity-hunters [*anoētoi kai doxokopoi*], their mouths agape [*kechēnotes*] at the roar of the masses [*thorubos tou plēthos*], and they say nothing intelligent, based on no sound opinion, but as though making their way in the dark they are borne along [*pherontai*] constantly according to the clapping [*krotos*] and shouting [*boē*].

As with the quotation from Philo of Alexandria that opened this chapter, this passage reads like a Classical-era Athenian text critical of democracy. In fact, it bears more than a passing resemblance to a famous passage in Plato's *Republic*, where Socrates describes the effects of the crowd on a young, aspiring *rhētōr*:

> Whenever the assembled masses [*polloi*] sit together in meetings of the assembly ... some of the things said and done they castigate with a great hubbub [*thorubos*], others they praise, both excessively, shouting and

---

[53] See the coins classified as Waddington, *Recueil general des monnaies grecques d'Asie Mineure* nos. 710 (Nicaea, reign of Gordian III) and 95 (Nicomedia, reign of Marcus Aurelius), discussed by Fernoux 2011: 59n117; cf. Sheppard 1984–86. For divisions between council and People see, e.g., Dio Chrys. 34.16.

[54] Nawotka 1999: 192–208, for example, studies the emergence of the *boularchos* or "head of the council" within the *boulē* of Miletus beginning in the reign of Hadrian; note also the appearance of such offices as *prōtarchōn* ("first magistrate") and *archiprytanis* ("chief presiding officer"). Heller 2015 shows that being a councilor per se was not particularly prestigious.

[55] The sons of councilors would of course have been expected to match their father's position. Beginning in the second century CE there develops the title *patroboulos*, or "hereditary councilor": see Dmitriev 2005: 170, 318–19. Such titles, while they bespeak a greater emphasis on patrilineal, "aristocratic" qualities, conferred no special legal status. Giannakopoulos (2017: 240) argues that hereditary priesthoods voted to benefactors by the cities, which were quite small in number and therefore highly competitive, represent "perhaps as far as a Greek city could go to allow for the emergence of a truly hereditary aristocracy of office." On these priesthoods see further Muñiz Grijalvo 2005; Frija 2012; Camia 2014.

4.5 *The Persistence of Popular Politics*

clapping [*ekboōntes kai krotountes*] ... as for the young man, what sort of personal training and education of his will resist, which will not go borne off [*pheromenēn*], overwhelmed by such praise and blame, down the stream where this bears it?[56]

But again, this is no fifth- or fourth-century BCE source. It comes from a speech delivered around 100 CE to the assembly of Tarsus in Cilicia (birthplace of St. Paul) by the orator Cocceianus Dio of Prusa, often called "Chrysostom" or "the Golden-Mouthed."[57] The language is so close to that of Plato that we must ask once more whether it reflects the reality of contemporary assembly politics or is instead a brilliant (but perhaps misleading) example of the author's classicizing erudition. As with Philo, the answer appears to be both. As we will see, our Imperial-era sources, while showing off their traditional *paideia*, nevertheless reveal a "world of the *ekklēsia*" not radically different from antecedent democratic practice. If the other political institutions of the *poleis* had undoubtedly changed in all the ways outlined in the previous section, the assembly of the People remained, despite some important changes, the central site of popular action and the place, as Homer put it, "where men win glory."[58]

A glance at the evidence, both literary and epigraphic, makes obvious the continued presence and participation of an entity called "the *dēmos*" in the *poleis* of the later second century BCE and beyond. Decrees and honorific inscriptions continued to be issued in the name of the council and the People, for example. But was this *dēmos* of the same sociological profile – the "masses," the "poor," the "common mob" – as before? A few pieces of evidence from select cities suggest that certain mutations could trend in a more exclusionary direction. From the same speech of Dio Chrysostom for the Tarsians, for example, we learn that a group of resident linen workers were "outside the constitution [*politeia*]" and did not possess citizenship rights at Tarsus, although they seem to have been able to attend the assembly

---

[56] Plat. *Rep.* 6.492c. The later author draws upon the language of clapping, shouting, and being swept away but adds the idea of "gaping," usually predicated of the *dēmos* in fifth-century BCE comic sources but here applied to the speaker himself: cf. Ar. *Eq.* 956.

[57] Dio Chrys. 34.31. For Dio as evidence for Imperial-era assembly politics, see, e.g., Jones 1978; Salmeri 2000; Ma 2000b; Oppeneer 2020.

[58] Hom. *Il.* 1.490. The study of later Hellenistic and Imperial "popular politics" has undergone a transformation in recent decades akin to that effected by Gauthier in the 1970s and 1980s concerning earlier Hellenistic democracies. See esp. Zuiderhoek 2009; Fernoux 2011; Brélaz 2013a, 2021. While I am not as ready as some historians to see genuine "democracy" in these communities, I find their arguments more accurate overall than the pessimistic assessments of Jones 1940 and de Ste. Croix 1981. An intriguing recent development, basing itself in part on this revisionist literature, has been the interest on the part of scholars of biblical history in the early Christian church as a kind of assembly: see, e.g., Park 2015; Welborn 2019.

as onlookers. If they can provide the sum of five hundred drachmas, however, an official will "enroll them as citizens" (*politographein*) and they will be on equal footing with the other Tarsians.[59] Citizenship could obviously be purchased in this city, but it is unclear if all traditional Tarsian residents had to pay what was essentially a property qualification to enjoy full rights (thus making the constitution a timocratic oligarchy), or if this was the case only for admitting outsiders.[60] In a few Imperial-era inscriptions from Asia Minor we read of a civic group called "*ekklēsiastai*," seemingly "members of the assembly," separate from the mass of regular *politai*.[61] Here there may have been gradations among the citizen body, with a privileged group, picked out by age, wealth, or competence, exclusively capable of attending meetings of the *ekklēsia*.[62] Outside these rare instances, however, the evidence for property requirements for participation in the assembly is basically nonexistent, and our literary sources continue to speak of assembly goers in familiar terms, as "the mob," a "mass full of disorder and uproar," and so on.[63] To the extent that assemblies (the *dēmos*) continued to make binding civic decisions in the Greek cities, they were assemblies on the whole composed of a genuinely popular element.

But what did this assembly do? Simply assent, when they were allowed, to the *probouleumata* of their "social betters," thus providing a façade of democracy while spelling its practical demise? In reality, political life was much less manufactured than that. Cities still had genuine choices to make in numerous areas of civic concern, including the selection of officials (who competed for popular favor), managing and dispensing funds, keeping up public buildings, sending embassies, honoring benefactors, and maintaining good relations with the gods. In all cases the sources speak of the opinion of the *dēmos* as being considerable.[64] We have already seen that the common people might, through public acclamations, request that the magistrates formulate a *probouleuma* for their consideration.[65] Dio of Prusa, for his part, tells an assembled crowd in Alexandria, Egypt, that the People is like a power

---

[59] Dio Chrys. 34.21–23.   [60] See the discussion at Fernoux 2011: 88–90.
[61] *IGR* III 409 (Pogla in Pisidia), 800 (Sillyon in Pamphylia).   [62] Fernoux 2011: 87–88.
[63] Artemid. 3.42; Dio Chrys. 32.11.
[64] What follows, while in greater agreement overall with Fernoux 2011, is different more in degree than in kind from the more pessimistic arguments of Quass 1993: While the latter claims that the assembly of the People played a "bit part" ("Statistenrolle": 404) in city politics compared to the Council and magistrates, he goes on to show, with frequent recourse to the evidence of Dio and Plutarch, how such a statement is "not entirely complete" (405).
[65] *SEG* 23.938. See Fernoux 2011: 197–99 for further examples. Much less frequent in this period are instances of private citizens approaching the council with requests, but see Gauthier 2005 for a few examples.

4.5 The Persistence of Popular Politics

holder (*dunastēs*), which with any luck will tolerate the frank speech (*parrhēsia*) of its advisors.[66] It was still the case too that a hostile gathering could shout down a point of view using the traditional means of "raising a ruckus" or *thorubos*.[67] (Such indiscriminate shouting should, however, be distinguished from verbal acclamations.[68]) Popular audiences, by the same token, expected numerous points of view to be put forward by *rhētores*. A fascinating passage by Plutarch (early second century CE) gives a good indication of the dynamics of Imperial-era assembly politics.[69] In democracies, he says in a pamphlet entitled *Precepts of Statecraft*, the People become suspicious if proposals are introduced by the authorities unanimously, without debate, on the grounds that the political class is conspiring against them. Therefore, says the Chaeronean philosopher and politician, the *politeuomenoi* should stage a phony argument among themselves before the assembly, eventually winning over the "holdouts."[70] The passage reveals that the *dēmos* considered vigorous debate and disagreement among its leaders to be a matter of course. On the other hand, the ability of politicians to coordinate in advance to create a scripted discussion indicates the potential for a social and political cohesion among officeholders that is absent from earlier democracies (and that validates the People's propensity, according to Plutarch, to suspect conspiratorial practices).[71]

On the other hand, the age-old spirit of rivalry among the elite meant that such cohesion was not usually forthcoming. The *euergetai* and *politeuomenoi* of the Greek *poleis* continued to vie with each other on the public stage in order to attract greater popularity and honors. Thus backbiting and conflict, not conspiratorial unity, were the norm.[72]

---

[66] Dio Chrys. 32.25–27. Cf. Philo *de Joseph.* 67, cited previously, on the People possessing "the power of a master." The imagery goes back to the fifth century BCE and to the image of the People as unaccountable tyrant or slave master: see Landauer 2019 and Chapter 2.4.6. On the use of *parrhēsia* in the city politics of the Imperial era, see Fields 2020: ch. 4.

[67] See, e.g., Dio Chrys. 32.11, 46.10 with Quass 1993: 405–18. What was now lacking, it seems, was *isēgoria*, or the ability of the average citizen, regardless of their status as magistrate or not, to be acknowledged by the chairman and address the assembly. There is, however, an interesting scene in Chariton's Imperial-era novel *Callirhoe* in which the assembly of Syracuse hears the evidence of a simple fisherman, spoken from the floor: 3.4.11 with Alvares 2001–2002: 130.

[68] The age-old democratic tactic of *thorubos* expresses popular disapproval of a particular proposal in an attempt to change the speaker's tune or encourage another speaker to offer another, superior proposal. Acclamations, as we will see in the case of Oxyrhynchus, usually reinforced the status quo and brought glory to the magistrate who solicited them.

[69] On Greek city politics in Plutarch's milieu (Imperial-era Boeotia), see Jones 1971.

[70] Plut. *Mor.* 813a–b.   [71] On this passage, see further Quass 1993: 404; Fernoux 2011: 395.

[72] The persistent divisions among the elite in Imperial times constitute an additional reason to view these regimes as qualitatively different from earlier oligarchies, where internal quarrelling usually spelled doom for the ruling class in the form of a change in constitution toward democracy.

Plutarch tells the addressee of the *Precepts*, an aspiring young politician from Sardis, that he will need to know how to handle malicious retorts in the *ekklēsia*.[73] Dio reveals that his enemies labeled him a tyrant for the liberties he supposedly took with private property while working on a public building project, and in fact a letter of Pliny the Younger, Roman governor of Bithynia-Pontus, to the emperor Trajan sees Dio being fiercely attacked by opponents on precisely this subject.[74] It is therefore not surprising when Plutarch says that the chief task left to the statesman of his day is to instill friendship and "unanimity" (*homonoia*) – that constant watchword of the period – and to remove strife and division from among the political class.[75]

Sometimes, however, *homonoia* proved impossible, whether it was between cities, between politicians, between social classes, or even between Greek subjects and the Roman Empire – and occasionally all at once. Shortly after the passage just cited, Plutarch advises his addressee, Menemachus of Sardis, to consider the case of his fellow citizen Pardalas, whose feud with another member of the elite, Tyrrhenus, metastasized from "trifling private causes" to "revolt and war."[76] Earlier in the treatise we had already read that Pardalas "forgot his limits" (demarcated for him by the proverbial shoe of the Roman governor poised above his head) and incurred severe penalties as a result.[77] It seems that Pardalas, in order to best his political rival, stirred up the common people to the point of sparking an uprising against Roman rule, since Plutarch immediately goes on to chastise "the officials in the cities who raise up the masses, thoughtlessly calling on them to imitate the deeds of their ancestors, as well as thoughts and actions all out of step with present conditions."[78] In other words, the Greek *poleis* still faced the possibility of demagoguery and *stasis*.[79] The point is worth emphasizing, because *dēmagōgia* (in the charged

---

[73] Plut. *Mor.* 810e.   [74] Dio Chrys. 40.8, 47.18; Plin. *Ep.* 10.81.

[75] Plut. *Mor.* 824d. On *homonoia* (and its flip side, contestation) see also Dio Chrys. speeches 39–40; Ael. Arist. *Or.* 23 with Sheppard 1984–86; Sartre-Fauriat and Sartre 2000; Fernoux 2011: 395–402. The cities, led by ambitious elites, also frequently competed with their neighbors: Robert 1977; Heller 2006.

[76] Plut. *Mor.* 825d.

[77] *Mor.* 813e–f. Jones 1971: Appendix 11 shows that the *kaltioi* mentioned at 813e are Roman shoes, not soldiers' boots.

[78] *Mor.* 814a. Compare the quotation of Dio that begins this section.

[79] For the pairing, see the fascinating statue base from Epidaurus that celebrates the historian Philippus of Pergamum, who likely recorded the events of the Late Republican Civil Wars from a Greek perspective. In a passage on the base spoken in the first person, Philippus aims to inform his readers "how many evils are produced by courting the mob [*dēmokopia*, largely synonymous with *dēmagōgia* during this period: Urso 2019], boundless greed, internecine *stasis*, and perfidy" (*IG* IV² 1 687, ll. 11–14 = *BNJ* 95 F 1). Despite the recent arguments of Jones 2020, I follow Goukowsky 1995 in dating Philippus to the late first century BCE.

sense of "populist leadership") is a sign, if not of the continuity of robustly democratic institutions, then at least of the fact that there were still occasions when the People might defy their superiors, both civic and Roman. As in earlier periods, the temptation on the part of certain renegade members of the elite to one-up their competitors by tapping the power of the popular assembly sometimes proved irresistible, thereby opening up avenues for extraordinary collective action.[80]

There are numerous instances of this phenomenon beyond that of Pardalas, almost of all them displaying the same pattern of politicians riling up the *dēmos* based on a memory of, or desire for, a better, more democratic state of affairs than the status quo. The Romans nearly always intervened to reestablish control and in some cases installed oligarchic regimes in retaliation. The Mithridatic Wars and Civil Wars of the first century BCE provided the backdrop for such uprisings within numerous cities. In the famous and quite hostile account of the historian Posidonius of Apamea, a peripatetic philosopher named Athenion, said by Posidonius to be of servile origins and a fraudulently enrolled citizen of Athens, convinced the Athenians in 88 BCE that if they revolted against Rome and took the side of King Mithridates VI of Pontus, they would "recover their *dēmokratia*," apparently suspended by the Roman authorities, and "live in *homonoia*."[81] The civil war and rebellion at Athens that followed resulted in Sulla's sacking of the city in 86. In 74, when the Romans sent tax collectors to the city of Heraclea Pontica on the Black Sea, the "boldest man of those in the city" (*thrasutatos*, an adjective often predicated of "demagogues") persuaded his fellow citizens to murder the publicans and hide the bodies.[82] After the assassination of Julius Caesar in 44, the Rhodians refused to come over to the side of the tyrannicide Cassius, as the politicians Mnaseas and Alexander "played the demagogue" to the

---

[80] Now more than ever the common people had to watch for significant divisions among the political class if they hoped to advance a "politics from below." I say this not to insist on an elitist, "great man" model of political change but only to note that the *dēmos* was not irrational, given the circumstances: In a Roman Imperial context, reactionary punishment could be brutal. The question of the Greek masses' attitude toward the Romans is vexed: see, e.g., Briscoe 1967 (a nuanced picture of class struggle); Deininger 1971 (there was no more constitutional conflict, but the "ruling class" and "underclass" could have opposing interests); Bernhardt 1985 (no clear divisions between mass and elite on the question of Rome). I personally find Briscoe (and after him de Ste. Croix 1981) convincing on the point that, allowing for some nuance, *dēmoi* and democracies regarded the oligarchic Romans with skepticism if not hostility.

[81] *BNJ* 87 F 36. On this episode see Badian 1976; Gray 2018; Simonton 2022: 64–67. Athenion's uprising might be the historical context for an Athenian inscription (*SEG* 30.80) that mentions democracy and magistracies selected by lot.

[82] Memnon *BNJ* 434 F 27.6. Yarrow (2006: 140, 290) detects an almost boastful tone in the local historian Memnon's account of the murder.

masses and reminded them of their earlier victories over Demetrius Poliorcetes (see previous chapter) and Mithridates.[83]

Finally, we have precious evidence for the creation of the province of Lycia under the emperor Claudius somewhat later, in 45/46 CE, in the form of an enormous inscribed pillar called the *Stadiasmus Patarensis* ("mile marker from Patara"). We already knew from the third-century CE historian Cassius Dio that the formerly free Lycian *koinon* was reduced to provincial status after its citizens fell into *stasis* with each other and killed certain Roman citizens.[84] The *Stadiasmus*, erected in Claudius' honor after this event, is dedicated by the "Roman-loving and Caesar-loving Lycians, faithful allies, who have been freed from *stasis*, lawlessness, and brigandage through [Claudius'] divine care." Furthermore, they have "recovered *homonoia*, an equitable system of justice, and their ancestral laws, seeing that the constitution [*politeia*] has been taken away from the undiscerning masses [*akriton plēthos*] and entrusted to councilors [*bouleutai*] handpicked from among the best men [*aristoi*]."[85] This remarkable document appears to show continuing constitutional struggle between democrats and oligarchs as late as the first century CE, with a change from a more participatory *politeia* directed by the People to one determined by property requirements. The caustic description of the Lycian masses as "undiscerning," uncharacteristic of the vast majority of public documents from the Imperial period, points to the hostile feelings still being nursed by the "Roman- and Caesar-loving Lycians" now in power. What exactly happened prior to the creation of the province must remain a mystery, but many scholars have suspected a popular uprising against the local elite and their Roman backers.[86]

The *Stadiasmus Patarensis*, falling in the middle of the first century after Christ, serves as a bridge between the city politics of the age of the Civil Wars and the testimony of Plutarch and Dio Chrysostom at the turn of the second century CE; it suggests that we should not dismiss the literary sources' numerous mentions of demagoguery as so much anachronism. While never as cataclysmic or consequential as in the case of the Lycian *koinon*, the "populism" attested and criticized by these authors remained a potential source of civic instability.[87] Even in the later second century,

---

[83] App. *B Civ.* 4.9.66.   [84] Cass. Dio 60.17.3. Cf. Suet. *Claud.* 25.9.   [85] *SEG* 51.1832, ll. 13–30.
[86] Thornton 2001; Spawforth 2011: 37–39.
[87] On complaints about demagogues, see Plut. *Mor.* 801a–b, 802d–e; Dio Chrys. 34.37, 38.2. Dio in one treatise says that many demagogues "do not hesitate to introduce into the assembly [*dēmos*] decrees that have not been deliberated on in advance by the council [*aprobouleuta psēphismata*]" (56.10). If this indeed happened during his time, it would represent a lack of complete agenda control on the part of the elite.

4.5 The Persistence of Popular Politics

divisions within the Roman Imperial elite afforded opportunities to the Greek cities to enjoy, if not true autonomy, then at least a choice between alternatives.[88] The revolt of Avidius Cassius against the emperor Marcus Aurelius in 175 saw several *poleis*, including Antioch, take his side; the fact that Marcus subsequently deprived the Antiochenes "of their public gatherings and every form of meeting" strongly suggests that the decision to back Cassius had come from the *ekklēsia* and its politicians.[89] About twenty years later, numerous cities threw their weight behind Pescennius Niger against Septimius Severus, the result of what the historian Herodian called *stasis*, "that age-old misfortune [*archaion pathos*] of the Greeks, who, by always engaging in civil strife against each another and wishing to destroy those who appear to be prominent, ground down Hellas."[90] While his language is ambiguous, Herodian seems to mean that competition between the elite of the Greek *poleis* of the East encouraged the picking of favorites among rival *Imperatores*; there is no good reason not to think successful politicians carried their policies via approval in the assembly.

Although not on the same level of political import, we receive notice of the persistence of demagoguery in a source as unlikely as the *Oneirocritica*, or "Interpretation of Dreams," by Artemidorus of Ephesus, who probably saw his zenith in the early third century CE.[91] Among numerous other dreams, Artemidorus notes several that portend good fortune for "demagogues" or "leaders of the mob [*ochlos*]." These include walking on the sea, seeing a flock of sheep, and having sex with one's own mother (but only if it is face-to-face intercourse and she is alive, not dead).[92] Peter Thonemann has recently stated that Artemidorus' use of the term *dēmagōgos* "carries none of the negative connotations of the modern 'demagogue,'" but the imagery associated with Artemidorus' demagogues, some of it traceable to Aristophanes in the fifth century BCE and perhaps earlier, indicates (to my mind, anyway) that the Ephesian was familiar with a highly populist style of political leadership.[93] Certainly, his handbook presupposes

---

[88] It is important to note, however, that after the *Stadiasmus Patarensis*, we have no evidence for constitutional struggle (besides the occasional bout of tyranny) in the Greek-speaking world.
[89] *HA* Marcus 25.9.
[90] Hdn. 3.2.7–8. The leveling impulse attributed to the Greeks by Herodian can be found as early as Heraclitus, as we saw (Chapter 1.4).
[91] On his date, see Thonemann 2020: 9. This fascinating author has finally begun to receive the attention he deserves in recent years: See, in addition to Thonemann, Kirbihler 2014 on Artemidorus' social and political milieu.
[92] Artemid. 3.16, 2.12, 1.79, respectively. Puzzlingly, Sigmund Freud knew Artemidorus' text but seems never to have discussed the ancient author's account of incest dreams.
[93] Thonemann 2020: 113. For the People as sea, discussed also in Chapter 3.5, see, e.g., Dem. 19.136; Polyb. 21.31.9–13; Dio Chrys. 32.22–24. For dreaming about sex with one's mother as the mark of an

a continuing prominent role for the assembly in Ephesus and the other cities of Asia Minor.

Before moving on to look at the decline of assembly politics in the later Imperial period, it is worthwhile to pause and assess the constitutional nature of the communities we have been examining. Do they still qualify as "democracies"? Some of them could call themselves that on occasion. We have seen that the Rhodians had undeniably democratic institutions in the time of Cicero; about two hundred years later, they still maintained, at least in words, their devotion to popular government. The "Speech to the Rhodians on Concord" by the sophist Aelius Aristides, delivered perhaps in the 140s CE, contains the striking line, "you so praise democracy that you would not agree to become immortal unless someone will allow you to remain in this form of constitution."[94] Even in the late third century, the sophist Menander of Laodicea ("Menander Rhetor"), instructing readers on how to compose encomia of cities, can say that "it is necessary ... if a city is governed by mob rule, to praise it [*sc.* euphemistically] as being governed by a democracy."[95]

Such statements are exceptional, however. More generally, the first several centuries CE saw a decline in public devotion to *dēmokratia*, whether in inscriptions and coins or as an object of cult. That decrease is in keeping with the consolidation (not without hiccups) of the Roman empire under the Principate and the advance of social and political inequality. When we speak of an undeniable "oligarchization" of the cities, however, we must be careful about what we mean by that word. Except in certain cases like those of Bithynia-Pontus or Lycia, where a *lex provinciae* ("law of the province") imposed by Rome mandated formally census-based regimes, the *poleis* underwent a de facto rather than formal process of the monopolization of offices by the civic elite. But if Aristotle was correct that the chief quality of the (male) citizen was participation in magistracies and judicial decisions (*archē* and *krisis*), then we must acknowledge that the Greek cities of Roman Imperial times failed to guarantee these rights to a broad swath of their *politai*.[96] Even supposing that payment for office (*misthos*) and sortition are not necessary conditions for democracy, as was

---

ambitious politician, see Hdt. 6.107.1 (the Athenian ex-tyrant Hippias); Plut. *Vit. Caes.* 32.9 (Julius Caesar before crossing the Rubicon).

[94] 24.22 with Franco 2008.

[95] P. 359, ll. 28–31. On the other hand, some sources claim democracy has disappeared: The literary treatise "On the Sublime" attributed to Longinus, probably of the first century CE, contains a passage suggesting that the loss of *dēmokratia* means that great literature is no longer produced ([Long.] *de sublim.* 44.2).

[96] On this definition see Chapter 3.3 and 3.7.

argued in the previous chapter, we should note that the average citizen appears to have lacked *isēgoria*, the right to address the assembly from the speaker's platform, and that there were far fewer occasions for *ho boulomenos*, "whichever citizen that wishes," to initiate political and judicial procedures. Thus I cannot fully agree with Cédric Brélaz, who, in an illuminating and otherwise largely convincing overview of the period, has recently argued that "it would not have been impossible to use the word 'democracy' to describe the constitution of the Greek cities under Roman rule."[97]

The period is best understood as a hodgepodge of often contradictory attitudes and practices. On a more ideological level, the praise lavished on the notables, which increasingly drew attention to their ancestral virtue and glory, would seem to violate a genuinely democratic spirit of civic equality. On the other hand, the *ekklēsia* continued to possess considerable power, with thoroughgoing participation by average citizens and fierce competition for prominence among the elite themselves. In inscriptions and public discourse, "the *dēmos*," as one historian has put it, "in its double dimension, political and institutional, continue[d] ... to embody the city in its communitarian dimension."[98] The perpetuation of "assembly politics" (undeniable developments and changes notwithstanding) represented the legacy of earlier democratic achievements and practices, a legacy that has not always been sufficiently acknowledged in histories of ancient Greek politics. But *dēmokratia* was over.

4.6 The End of Popular Assemblies

Still in the third quarter of the third century CE, down to the reign of the emperor Gallienus (252–268), there is plenty of evidence to suggest that the traditional civic institutions of the Greek cities of the mainland and Asia Minor continued to meet regularly, even in small *poleis*.[99] The personified council and Demos are depicted on numerous coins, and decrees, although

---

[97] Brélaz 2021: 74.
[98] Fernoux 2011: 21 ("le *dēmos* ... dans sa double dimension politique et institutionnelle, continue ... d'incarner la cité dans sa dimension communautaire"). Contrast the position of Quass (1993: 421), who suggests that with a growing division between the People (understood as the "lower social strata") and the magistrates, "the awareness that the *dēmos* represented the citizenry as the members of the state was apparently no longer fully intact" ("Anscheinend war das Bewusstsein davon, dass der Demos die Bürgerschaft als Staatsvolk darstellte, nicht mehr ohne Einschränkung intakt").
[99] See Pont 2020: 218: "The original institutional triptych of the city [People, council, magistrates] is still detectable and active" ("le triptyque institutionnel originel de la cité est encore repérable et actif").

much rarer, could still be issued.[100] One fragmentary source even speaks of an arrogant equestrian named Palmatius, a citizen of Caesarea in Cappadocia during the reign of Valerian (253–260), who "was the leader of a faction opposed to the People," whatever that might mean in this historical context![101] Appropriately for the era, saints' lives and martyrologies now constitute an important part of the evidence base. The *Martyrdom of Pionios*, which, judging from its rich detail about the agora of Smyrna, corroborated by numismatics and archaeology (see Figure 4.1), can be dated to the reign of Decius (249–251), describes a scene where "the People wanted to hold an assembly in the theater so that they might hear more there [about the Christian presbyter Pionius' case]." The magistrates decide against it, on the ground that the *dēmos* might cause a disturbance (*thorubos*), but it appears that on other occasions an extraordinary assembly might be granted in response to a direct request by the masses.[102] As late as the 280s, during the reign of Carus and his sons, an inscription records a decision (*dogma*) of the *boulē* and *dēmos* of Termessus to honor one M. Aurelius Kiliortes.[103]

It turned out, however, that the institutional life of the *poleis* was anything but stable. The turn of the fourth century witnessed a precipitous decline in all inscribed public documents, including decrees (already on their way out) but also honorific titles. As Anna Heller has shown using quantitative data, from a high point around 200 CE the practice of inscribing honors in Asia Minor basically disappeared by the time of the Tetrarchy (293 and after).[104] As is often pointed out, the absence of material evidence for honors does not mean that assemblies had ceased to grant them: we may simply be seeing a change in the Greek cities' culture of inscribing. The literary evidence, however, while offering no positive proof that assemblies were outlawed or otherwise fell into disuse in the fourth century, is conspicuously silent about *ekklēsiai*. They were apparently no longer the venue where cities received itinerant sophists and *rhētores*, for example, as they had been in the time of Philostratus in the mid third century.[105] In the late 380s, a different "Golden-Mouth" from Dio of

---

[100] For the evidence of coins, see Fernoux 2011: 70–79; Pont 2020: 190–93.
[101] Hesychius *BNJ* 390 F 6. I owe this reference to Pont 2020: 88. Such an "oligarchic faction," if that is what the source means, is unparalleled in the later Imperial period, but note that it appears to assume that the *dēmos* of Caesarea was hegemonic, i.e., the city was governed by a "democracy."
[102] *Vit. S. Pionii* 7 with Robert 1994. The author of the *Martyrdom* adds that if there were to be a "disturbance," it would be about the grain supply.
[103] *SEG* 51.1813–14.   [104] Heller 2020: 129 with figs. 3.1–2.
[105] See La Rocca 2019: 31–34, reviewing Libanius, Themistius, Julian, Eunapius, and other fourth- and fifth-century authors. The Cappadocian Fathers – Basil of Caesarea, Gregory of Nyssa, and Gregory of Nazianzus – while evincing continued interest in *polis* citizenship (Langley 2020), do

4.6 The End of Popular Assemblies

Figure 4.1 Smyrnaean agora. (Photo: uskarp / Alamy).

Prusa, this time Ioannes the bishop of Antioch (St. John Chrysostom), could paint a vivid picture of a civic benefactor being honored in the theater in terms strikingly redolent of the earlier age of pagan *euergetai*; the crowd here addresses their patron as "Nile" and "Ocean" (that is, bounteous in his gifts).[106] Despite the similarities between John Chrysostom's tableau and the evidence of Plutarch and Dio, however, his imagined gathering likely represents a moment at the games and not an institutionalized meeting of the *ekklēsia*, which probably did not exist in his time.[107]

What had happened to popular assemblies? It would be wrong to say they totally disappeared. We have scattered evidence for their existence from well-established cities like Athens, Ephesus, Miletus, and Aphrodisias as late as the fifth century, as a search of the useful Last Statues of

---

not, to my knowledge, mention assemblies of their own time (but Gregory of Nyssa knows that they occurred in the preceding third century, in the time of his biographical subject Gregory Thaumaturgus: vol. 46, p. 908 Migne, *en koinois sullogois*, "in their collective meetings").

[106] Ioann. Chrys. *De inani gloria* = SC 188, 74–78. Compare the titles listed by Dio Chrys. 48.10, corroborated by inscriptions, and see *P. Oxy.* 1. 41, a papyrus from Oxyrhynchus ca. 300 CE, in which the president of the council Dioscorus is acclaimed as "Ocean." Acclamations of officials like this can be found as late as the sixth century (Roueché 1984) and, as we have seen, normally served to reinforce the status quo, although they might occasionally serve as a vehicle for popular demands.

[107] See further Oppeneer 2018: 237–41.

172   4 (D)evolutions of Democracy, 146 BCE to Late Antiquity

Antiquities database reveals.[108] A remarkable set of documents from fifth-century Stratonicea in Caria gives a possible clue as to the reason for the assembly's overall decline, however. The inscriptions are all in verse and record honors for the local magistrate Maximus, who in one inscription is described as having "twice held all the offices of the city."[109] So far, so typical of the Imperial period. But the inscription is covered with no fewer than five crosses and the heading "Chi – Mu – Gamma" (an abbreviation for "Christ was born to Mary"). Three out of the four total inscriptions for Maximus found thus far feature Christian iconography and language. But they are also innovative in their issuing authorities. The one just mentioned was awarded, quite traditionally, by the council and the People. Another was dedicated by the *dēmos* alone.[110] The remaining two, however, feature an unprecedented actor, the body of *akteanoi poliētai* or "citizens without property."[111] In one instance these people actually join with the *boulē* in honoring Maximus. Are they synonymous with the *dēmos* or a separate group?[112] In any case, the documents show a community seemingly between two worlds. The collocation "council and People" points to the Greek city of the pagan past, while the appearance of the *akteanoi polietai* reflects Christian concern for the poor in particular, rather than the citizenry as a whole (although the presence of the word *polietai* shows that the concept of citizenship is not totally obsolete).[113] Outside of Stratonicea, a place that appears to have clung tenaciously (but rather exceptionally) to old-style civic traditions, the Christian conceptualization of the community as the bishop and his flock had long since largely won out over the poliadic vision of the privileged (male) citizen body of equals.[114] In the new dispensation, there was less need to register the opinion of the legally demarcated *dēmos*, gathered officially for the purpose, than to minister to the spiritual health of the congregational community, regardless of status.[115]

---

[108] *IG* II² 13274 (Athens, late fourth century), 13281 (Athens ca. 400); *I. Ephesos* 1320 (late fourth to fifth century); *Milet* VI, 3, no. 1129 (later fifth century, inscribed with a Christian cross); Roueché 1989: no. 22 (Aphrodisias, ca. 360). For the database, see http://laststatues.classics.ox.ac.uk.
[109] *SEG* 38.1163, ll. 3–5. On these texts see Jones 2009.   [110] *SEG* 58.1252.
[111] *SEG* 58.1254; *I. Stratonikeia* 1204. In one of the inscriptions Maximus is thanked for his actions on behalf of the *penētes* or poor.
[112] Brown 2002: 72, writing apparently without knowledge of *SEG* 38.1163, thought that the *akteanoi* had taken the place of the *dēmos*, but we now see that that is not necessarily true.
[113] For the persistence during the Imperial period of the ideological viewpoint (largely fictional) that the citizen body was homogeneous rather than divided into rich and poor, see Brélaz 2013b.
[114] The word *ekklēsia* in this period comes primarily to mean "church," as reflected to this day in, e.g., Spanish *iglesia*.
[115] See Brown 1992, 2002; Rapp 2005. I do not mean to suggest that enslaved people did not remain exploited.

4.6 The End of Popular Assemblies

In fact, even before Christianity first became the religion of an emperor under Constantine the Great in 312, it had played an important role, in concert with a number of other factors, in undermining the traditional forms of civic politics. As Anne-Valérie Pont has shown, in a work on the "end of the Greek city," the late third and early fourth centuries saw simultaneously a series of civil conflicts or *staseis* in the *poleis*, as pagan authorities persecuted Christian minorities, and the centralization of Imperial control under the Tetrarchy and Constantine, with a concurrent diminution of local authority.[116] With fewer civic matters to administer, and with communities deeply divided along religious lines, assemblies became much less likely to honor local benefactors or otherwise pass decrees.

This is not to say that *cities* disappeared. Large walled conurbations with traditional civic infrastructure – baths, theaters, colonnades, hippodromes – persisted, based on a similar political economy to what had come before. The cities basically traded one combination of administration and civic ideology for another.[117] But with the end, by and large, of assembly politics, a way of life that had characterized Greek-speaking communities in the Mediterranean since at least the seventh century BCE passed out of existence. Contemporaries in the fourth, fifth, and sixth centuries (and beyond) still spoke of the People, but not as the legally authorized voice of the community. The *dēmos* was now instead a dangerous social force that might riot, loot, and in some cases murder public officials, as it no longer possessed the traditional institutional outlet for expressing its concerns.[118] One scholar has even referred to late antiquity as "the age of crowds."[119] The old world of citizen debate in the *ekklēsia* disappeared, although the memory of it survived in Byzantine authors trained in the *paideia* of the pagan classics. Agathias, for example, the continuator of the better-known historian Procopius of Caesarea (both later sixth century CE), places a Thucydidean–style debate scene (almost certainly invented out of whole cloth) among the Laz people of the Caucasus. In it, a fiery *rhētōr* "leapt into the middle of the crowd and addressed them in a speech [*edēmēgorei*] as though he were in a democratic

---

[116] Pont 2020. [117] Whittow 1996: 56–68; Liebeschuetz 2001.
[118] Note the description of the *dēmos* of fifth-century CE Alexandria by the church historian Evagrius (late sixth century), which contains many classicizing *topoi*: "The People is a thing easily kindled toward anger, which takes whatever chance pretext as the fuel for commotions [*thoruboi*]. . . . They say it is possible for anyone who wishes, by aggravating the situation, to make the city break out in a Bacchic frenzy of popular strife [*dēmotikē stasis*]" (Book 2, p. 55). Nevertheless, while the *dēmos* does murder a patriarch in this particular episode, it acts entirely in informal, nonassembly settings.
[119] Magalhães de Oliveira 2020.

council-chamber [*dēmokratikon bouleutērion*]."[120] In this new world, a scholar like Agathias eager to show off his knowledge of Thucydides had to imagine popular assemblies among "barbarian" peoples, since the Greek cities had long since ceased to host them. Byzantium, the Roman Empire of the East, might still have possessed "republican" elements, as one scholar has provocatively argued, but with the loss of an assembly of the People, the last threads connecting the *poleis* to the democracies of earlier times had been severed.[121] *Extra ecclesiam nulla civitas popularis.*[122]

---

[120] Agathias 3.8.8. [121] Kaldellis 2015.
[122] That is, "outside of an assembly there is no popular government." I riff on the saying of the early Christian church fathers that *extra ecclesiam nulla salus*: "Outside of the *church* [according to the new Christian meaning of *ekklēsia*] there is no salvation."

Appendix: Instances of "Democracy" on Stone

The present list was current, to the best of my knowledge, as of December 2023. I have divided centuries into halves, so that "C4a" means "first half of the fourth century BCE," and so forth. "CE1a" and the like refer to the Common Era. I have sought out *dēmokratia/damokratia* and related words, including the participle *dēmokratoumenē* predicated of a *polis*, a "democratically governed city." Understandably, Athenian examples make up a large number of the total. I have therefore created two concluding graphs, one that includes Athenian examples and another that excludes them. The results are striking: Even when controlling for Athens, we see general growth across the third century BCE, with a peak (in the Athens-excluding record) in the first half of the second century BCE. Thereafter both lines fall significantly and never recover. There is no known instance of the word *dēmokratia* on stone after the later first century CE. I have been able, thanks to the specificities of the dates, to chart eighty-three of the ninety-two examples (unused examples are marked with an asterisk, *); the reader should bear in mind that future study could result in altered dates for some of these inscriptions (though probably not radically altered). I indicate where multiple instances of *dēmokratia*-related words occur in the same inscription, but I have not counted those instances multiple times toward the total. I am of course not necessarily endorsing the democratic bona fides of the cities in question here; the point is to give the reader a gestalt picture of *dēmokratia*-related words on stone over time.

Athens

1. *SEG* 28.46: Athens. C5b. *dēmokratia*.
2. *IG* II² 448: Athens. 318/17 (C4b). *dēmokratia* (2x).
3. *IG* II² 1604: Athens. 377/6 (C4a). *dēmokratia*.
4. *IG* II² 1606: Athens. 374/3 (C4a). *dēmokratia*.

5. *IG* II² 1607: Athens. 373/2 (C4a). *dēmokratia*.
6. *IG* II² 1611: Athens. 357/6 (C4a). *dēmokratia*.
7. *IG* II³ 1, 320: Athens. 337/6 (C4b). *dēmokratia*.
8. *IG* II² 1496: Athens. 331/0 (C4b). *dēmokratia* (2x).
9. *IG* II² 1623: Athens. 334/3 (C4b). *dēmokratia*.
10. *SEG* 21.679: Athens. 333/2 (C4b). *dēmokratia*.
11. *IG* II² 1628: Athens. 326/5 (C4b). *dēmokratia*.
12. *IG* II² 1629: Athens. 325/4 (C4b). *dēmokratia* (2x).
13. *IG* II² 1631: Athens. 323/2 (C4b). *dēmokratia*.
14. *SEG* 31.80: Athens. 307–301 (C4b). *dēmokratia* (restored).
15. *Hesperia* 1936: Athens. 305/4 (C4b). *dēmokratia*.
16. *SEG* 36.164: Athens. 304/3 (C4b). *dēmokratia*.
17. *SEG* 25.149: Athens. 303/2? (C4b). *dēmokratia* (2x).
18. *IG* II² 1620: Athens. C4b. *dēmokratia*.
19. *IG* II² 509: Athens. Likely C4b. *dēmokratia*.
20. *IG* II² 559: Athens. Likely C4b. *dēmokratia*.
21. *IG* II³ 1, 853: Athens. 295/4 (C3a). *dēmokratia*.
22. *IG* II³ 1, 877: Athens. 283/2 (C3a). *dēmokratia*.
23. *IG* II³ 1, 884: Athens. 280/79 (C3a). *dēmokratia* (1x), *dēmoukratoumenē* (1x).
24. *SEG* 28.60: Athens. 270/69 (C3a). *dēmokratia*.
25. *IG* II³ 1, 985: Athens. 259/8 (C3a). *dēmokratoumenē*.
26. *IG* II³ 1, 928: Athens. C3a. *dēmokratia*.
27. *IG* II³ 1, 933: Athens. C3a. *dēmokratia*.
28. *SEG* 29.116: Athens. 214/13 (C3b). *dēmokratia* (cf. *IG* II³ 1, 1166).
29. *IG* II² 1167: Athens. C3 (unspecified). *dēmokratia*.*
30. *IG* II³ 1, 1288: Athens. 185/4 (C2a). *dēmokratoumenē*.
31. *IG* II² 971: Athens. 140/39 (C2b). *dēmokratia*.
32. *IG* II² 1011: Athens. 106/5 (C2b). *dēmokratia*.
33. *IG* II² 1062: Athens. Mid C1 (so either C1a or C1b). *dēmokratikos*.*
34. *IG* II² 4992: Athens. 89/8 (C1a). *dēmokratia*.
35. *SEG* 26.120: Athens. Ca. 86 BCE (C1a). *dēmokratia*.

The Rest

36. *SEG* 51.1096: Thasos. C4a. *dēmokratia*.
37. RO 85: Mytilene. Ca. 340–330 (C4b). *damokratia*.
38. RO 84: Chios. 334 (C4b). *dēmokratia*.
39. *IG* XII.4. 1 129: Cos. 306–301 (C4b). *dēmokratia*.

40. *IG* XII.9 192: Eretria. 308/7 (C4b). *dēmokratia*.
41. *IG* XII.4 1.132: Telos. Ca. 300 (C4b). *damokratia* (3x).
42. *IosPE* I² 402: Chersonesus. C3a. *dēmokratia*.
43. *IG* XII.4 1.296: Cos. Ca. 296 (C3a). *damokratia*.
44. *IG* XII.4 1.68: Cos. 278 (C3a). *damokratia*.
45. *SEG* 50.1195: Cyme. Ca. 270 (C3a). *damokratia*.
46. *IG* XII.5 444: Paros. 263/2 BCE (C3a). *dēmokratia*.
47. *Milet* I 3, 123: Miletus. 259 BCE (C3a). *dēmokratia*.
48. *I. Erythrai* 29: Erythrae. C3a. *dēmokratia* (cf. *Syll.*³ 442).
49. *I. Ilion* 45: Ilium. C3a. *dēmokratia*.
50. *I. Ilion* 25: Ilium. Ca. 281 (C3a). *dēmokratia* (8x).
51. *SEG* 59.1407: Cyme. Ca. 275–250 (C3a). *damokratia*.
52. *I. Erythrai* 504: Ionian League. 268/62 (C3a). *dēmokratoumenē*.
53. *IG* XI.4 566: Delos. 300–250 (C3a). *politeiai dēmokratoumenai*.
54. *I. Labraunda* 3: Mylasa. Ca. 240 (C3b). *dēmokratia*.
55. *I. Labraunda* 3b: Mylasa. C3b. *dēmokratia*.
56. *I. Smyrna* 573. 1: Smyrna. 245? (C3b). *dēmokratia*.
57. *I. Labraunda* 8b: Mylasa. Ca. 235 (C3b). *dēmokratoumenē*.
58. *SEG* 58.1220: Mylasa. Ca. 220 (C3b). *dēmokratia*.
59. *IG* XII.4 1.152: Cos. Ca. 208 (C3b). *damokratia* (2x).
60. *SEG* 23.547: Olous. 201/1 (C3b). *dēmokratia* (1x); *damokratia* (1x).
61. *OGIS* 234: Antiocheia: 201 (C3b). *damokratia*.
62. *SEG* 41.1104: Teos. Ca. 196 (C2a). *dēmokratia*.
63. *Syll.*³ 613a: Delphi. Ca. 186 (C2a). Delphi. *dēmokratia* (1x); *demokratoumenai*.
64. *IC* I viii 9*: Cnossus. After 196 (C2a). *damokratia*.
65. *I. Iasos* 4: Iasos. 195/190 (C2a). *dēmokratia*.
66. *Syll.*³ 591: Lampsacus. 196/195 (C2a). *dēmokratia*.
67. *Syll.*³ 633: Miletus. Ca. 180 (C2a). *dēmokratia*; *dēmokratoumenē*.
68. *Syll.*³ 665: Arbitration between Achaean League and Sparta. Post 164 BCE. (C2a). *damokratoumenoi*.
69. *IC* IV 176: Gortyn. Ca. 184 (C2a). *damokratia*.
70. Meier, *Kibyra in hellenistischer Zeit* 2019, no. 2: Kibyra. C2a. *dēmokratia*.
71. *I. Didyma* 358: Miletus. C2a. *dēmokratia*.
72. *IC* III iii 3: Hierapytna. C2a. *damokratia*.
73. *I. Stratonikeia* 14: Stratonicea. C2a. *dēmokratoumenē*.
74. *SEG* 39.1244: Colophon. C2b. *dēmokratia*.
75. *OGIS* 337: Pergamum. Ca. 133 (C2b). *dēmokratia*.
76. *Syll.*³ 694: Pergamum. 129 (C2b). *dēmokratia*.

178 Appendix: Instances of "Democracy" on Stone

77. *SEG* 50.1211: Pergamum. C2b. *dēmokratia*.
78. *IG* XII.4 1.314: Cos. Ca. 150–100 (C2b). *damokratia*.
79. *TAM* II 582: Tlos. Pre 100 (C2b). *dēmokratia*.
80. *IG* XII Suppl. 270: Andros. "Second century" (so C2a or C2b). *dēmokratia*.*
81. *I. Iasos* 244: Iasos. "Middle second" (so C2a or C2b). *dēmokratia*.*
82. *I. Labraunda* 47: Mylasa. "Second century" (so C2a or C2b). *dēmokratia* (restored).*
83. *I. Priene B-M* 119: Priene. C2a or C2b. *dēmokratia*.
84. *TAM* III.1.2: Termessus. C2? *dēmokrateia* [*sic*].*
85. *IC* I xxiv 2: Priansos. C2? *damokratia*.*
86. *SEG* 28.953: Cyzicus. C1a. *dēmokratikōtaton*.
87. *IG* XIV 986: Lycian *koinon*. Post 86. (C1a). *dēmokratia*.
88. *OGIS* 449: Pergamum. 46–44 BCE. (C1b). *dēmokratia*.
89. *I. Knidos* I 51–55: C1b. *damokratia* (x3); *damokratoumenai* (x1).
90. *Syll.*³ 810: 55 CE (CE1b). *dēmokratia*.
91. *I. Tralles* 31: No date (CE1?) *demokratikōs*.*
92. *IG* XII.2 59: Mytilene. No date. *damokratia*.*

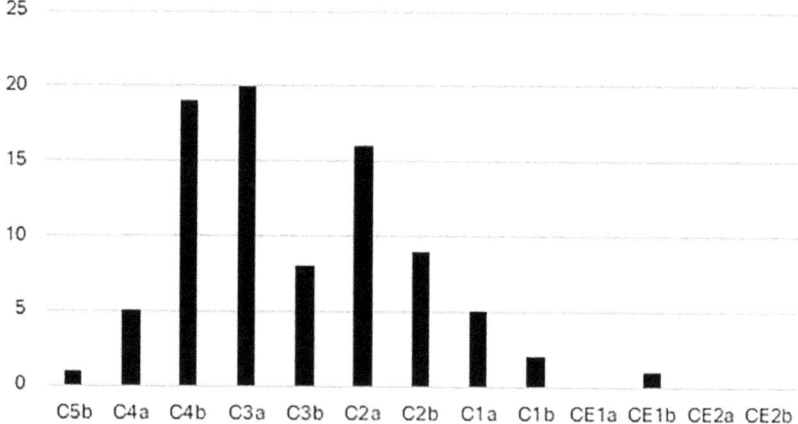

Figure A1 Instances of "democracy" words on stone, including Athenian examples.

Appendix: Instances of "Democracy" on Stone

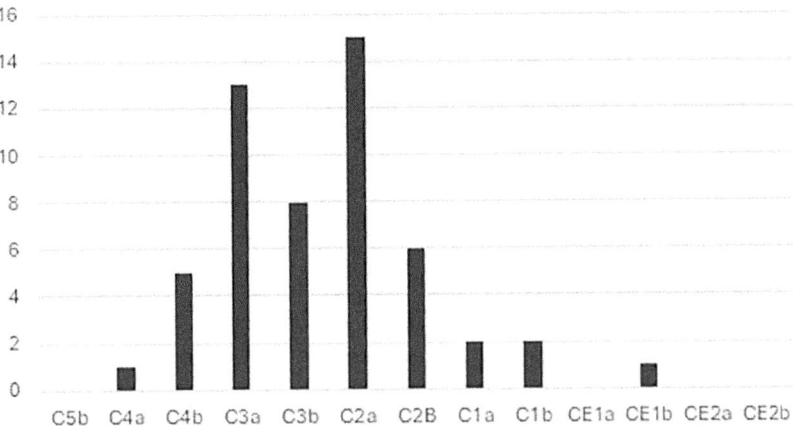

Figure A2 Instances of "democracy" words on stone, excluding Athenian examples.

Bibliographical Essay

The bibliography on ancient Greek democracy is vast, although recent trends suggest it may have peaked, at least for now. What follows is necessarily selective. When it comes to overviews of ancient Greek politics and society, for scope, ambition, vivacity, and theoretical sophistication, it is difficult to top de Ste. Croix 1981, a towering life's work. Everyone should read it, even if only to disagree with it. In a similar vein is Cartledge 2018, focused on democracy specifically. It reaches different conclusions from the ones offered here, in particular regarding the Hellenistic period, but is forceful and engaging. Meier 1990 remains excellent on Greek politics in general. Davies 1993 and O'Neil 1995 are overviews of ancient Greek democracy concentrating on the Classical period. Ma 2024 appeared only after the present manuscript was completed. While I have not been able to incorporate references to this impressive achievement throughout the text, the reader should be aware that it is one of the strongest arguments yet for seeing genuinely democratic practices down through the period of the high Empire (second century CE and beyond).

For Archaic Greece, Morris 1996 and Raaflaub and Wallace 2007 provide good overviews of the egalitarian trends of the period, citing political, military, archaeological, and ideological developments. Bernhardt and Canevaro 2022 contains essays addressing the state of the question on numerous important aspects of Archaic history. Several recent works have revealed the danger of anachronism in importing terms like "aristocracy" and "oligarchy" into the Archaic period: see, for example, Fisher and van Wees 2015 and Meister 2020. Duplouy (2006, 2019) offers a revisionist picture of the Archaic city as Durkheimian, organicist, and focused on the performance of elite status; while convincing in numerous respects, this position swings too hard in the other direction from institutional and class-based understandings of Archaic politics. Contrast Rose 2012, a sophisticated Marxist reading of Archaic Greece. A similar revisionist spirit to that of Duplouy permeates Brock and Duplouy 2018, which makes many scholars' work available to Anglophone readers for the first time. For the role of the *dēmos* in Archaic Greece, see Werlings 2010. Robinson 1997 detects numerous democracies emerging during the period, although I myself do not see any that predate the late sixth century.

There are, unsurprisingly, numerous works on ancient Athenian democracy. For political, demographic, archaeological, and other developments of Archaic Attica down to Cleisthenes' reforms, we now have Osborne 2023. Ostwald 1986 traces fifth-century political and legal transformations, while Hansen 1999 is a classic treatment of the institutions and ideology of the "age of Demosthenes" in the later fourth century. Carugati 2019 provides an analysis informed by social science on the constitutional changes of the late fifth century. No study of Athens is complete without the trilogy of Ober – 1989, 1998, 2008 – which subtly shifts over time from discourse analysis to the study of problems of common knowledge and collective action. Anderson 2018 applies postcolonial theories to construct a unique "ontological history" of Athens. Blok 2017 is one of the most important and original studies of Athenian citizenship in decades, focusing on the parity of male and female citizen roles in civic cult, in contrast to an Aristotelian understanding of *politeia*. For political leadership see Mann 2007 and Azoulay 2014; Lafargue 2022 defends the "demagogues." Parker 2005 and Evans 2010 study the intertwining of religion, politics, and society. Taylor 2017 analyzes the distribution of wealth and the experience of poverty within the Athenian democracy. For Athens' reliance on enslaved labor, see Ismard 2017, Lewis 2018, and Forsdyke 2021. Kasimis 2018 is an exploration of metic status from the perspective of political theory. Studies of individual institutions include Rhodes 1972 on the Council (an early entry by one of the true experts on Athenian history of the twentieth and early twenty-first centuries), Forsdyke 2005 on ostracism, Loraux 1986 (with Pritchard 2024) on the funeral oration, and Liddel 2020 on decree culture. Building projects are covered by Paga 2020 (late Archaic period) and Shear 2016 (on the "Periclean" building program). The oligarchies of the later fifth century receive treatment from Shear 2011 (also very full on political and archaeological developments at the turn of the fourth century) and Caire 2016; Azoulay and Ismard 2020 focuses on the aftermath of civil war in 403. Roberts 1994 is unsurpassed as a history of the reception of the Athenian democracy; on this topic see also Piovan and Giorgini 2020.

For events and ideas of the Classical period more generally, Cartledge 1987, while nominally devoted to a Spartan king, is a classic of political history; the same author's 2009 study examines Greek political thought in practice. De Ste. Croix 1972 seeks to explain the outbreak of the Peloponnesian War between Athens and Sparta and much more besides. Robinson 2011 expertly covers the other democracies of the period, establishing their bona fides. Commentary on important epigraphical documents of the period, in reverse chronological order, can be found in Rhodes and Osborne 2003 (RO) and Osborne and Rhodes 2017 (OR). Mackil 2013 explores the political, ritual, and economic networks of federations (*koina*) during this and later periods. Gehrke 1985 is the standard treatment of Classical *stasis* between democrats and oligarchs, while Gray 2015 explores exile and reconciliation down through the early Hellenistic period. Simonton 2017 takes up Classical oligarchies, and Teegarden 2013 elucidates the strategic logic behind antityranny legislation. Greek notions of freedom in the late Archaic and Classical periods are the subject of Raaflaub 2004. Patterson's 1991 study of slavery in the making of freedom complements de Dijn's (2020) recent intervention on freedom as a collective enterprise. Balot 2006 covers freedom and other aspects of Greek political thought, including justice, equality, and imperialism; the same author's 2014 focuses on courage in democratic Athens. Finally, there is no denying the profound impact of Sir Moses Finley on our understanding of ancient Greek politics: his 2019 and 1983 volumes stand out as especially important.

Two massive and beautifully written books of 1990 – those of Green and Veyne – have long colored our view of the Hellenistic period. A more optimistic reading of politics and democracy, at least for the earlier Hellenistic period, was developed by Gauthier (see, e.g., his 1984, 1985), following the lead of his teacher Louis Robert; see also the essays in Rhodes with Lewis 1997 and Ma 1999. Now the tide has fully turned, and "Hellenistic democracy" is the new orthodoxy: see Carlsson 2010 and Grieb 2008, with review by Hamon 2009. The essays in Canevaro and Gray 2018 study democratic Athens' influence on Hellenistic politics. Some of the contributors to Mann and Scholz 2012, however, provide good grounds for remaining skeptical. Thonemann 2016 is a succinct and successful overview of the whole Hellenistic world. Habicht 1997 represents the culmination of a life's work on Hellenistic Athens, while Worthington 2020 is a worthy update continuing to the reign of Hadrian. Börm 2019 applies Gehrke's elite-focused understanding of *stasis* to the Hellenistic period, and Börm and Luraghi 2018 contains numerous useful essays on the politics of the period. For individual institutions there is Fröhlich 2004 on audit procedures for officeholders, Mack 2015 on *proxenies*, and Saba 2020 on *isopoliteia*; all of these practices tellingly decline in the later Hellenistic and Imperial eras.

Speaking of which, historians of the later Hellenistic and Imperial periods, but also all students of history, will benefit from the brilliance contained in the selected essays of Robert 2007. Important edited volumes continuing in this tradition are Wörrle and Zanker 1995 and Fröhlich and Müller 2005. For the Greek cities' archaizing and nostalgic culture under Roman rule see Swain 1996. Ma 2013 explicates the politics of honorific statue-granting. Dmitriev 2005 is a useful handbook of Greek magistracies and political bodies under Roman rule. Zuiderhoek 2009, meanwhile, reinjects politics into the system of later *euergetism*; see also van Nijf and Alston 2011 on political culture in the Imperial period. Quass 1993, continuing the thesis of Veyne 1990, is a massive account of the "class of the notables," supposedly the rulers of their *poleis* already in the early Hellenistic period. By contrast, recent work has been doing for the Imperial period what Robert and Gauthier did for the politics of the early Hellenistic period, namely calling rumors of its death greatly exaggerated. Fernoux 2011 rehabilitates the *dēmos* in the Greek cities under Roman rule, while Brélaz (2013a, 2021) explores whether the same *poleis* can be considered democracies. Heller 2020 quantifies the honorific titles of Imperial-era elites, showing that political activity was not confined to a tiny caste; see further the essays in Heller and van Nijf 2017. While not as sanguine about popular politics, Jones 1940 remains a good overview of the Greek cities down to the sixth century CE. Pont 2020, finally, is a dense and rewarding account of the "end of the Greek city" following the Tetrarchic period (beginning 293 CE), after which time the traditional trio of assembly-council-magistracies largely disappears.

Bibliography

Abbreviations

BE	*Bulletin épigraphique.* Published annually in *Revue des études grecques.*
BNJ	I. Worthington, ed. *Brill's New Jacoby.* Leiden 2007–.
FGrH	F. Jacoby, S. Schorn, H.-J. Gehrke, et al., eds. *Die Fragmente der Griechischen Historiker.* Leiden 1923–.
ML	R. Meiggs and D. M. Lewis, eds. *A Selection of Greek Historical Inscriptions to the End of the Fifth Century BC.* Revised edition. Oxford 1988.
OR	R. Osborne and P. J. Rhodes, eds. *Greek Historical Inscriptions 478–404 BC.* Oxford 2017.
RO	P. J. Rhodes and R. Osborne, eds. *Greek Historical Inscriptions 404–323 BC.* Oxford 2003.
SEG	*Supplementum Epigraphicum Graecum.* Leiden.
*Syll.*³	W. Dittenberger, ed. *Sylloge Inscriptionum Graecarum.* Third edition. Leipzig 1917–1920.

Works Cited

Ackermann, D. 2018. *Une microhistoire d'Athènes: Le dème d'Aixônè dans l'Antiquité.* Athens.

Adak, M. and P. Thonemann. 2022. *Teos and Abdera: Two Cities in Peace and War.* Oxford.

Ager, S. 1996. *Interstate Arbitrations in the Greek World, 337–90 BC.* Berkeley, CA.

Akrigg, B. 2019. *Population and Economy in Classical Athens.* Cambridge.

Allen, D. 2000. *The World of Prometheus: The Politics of Punishing in Democratic Athens.* Oxford.

Alvares, J. 2001–2002. "Some Political and Ideological Dimensions of Chariton's *Chaereas and Callirhoe*." *CJ* 97: 113–44.

Anderson, G. 2018. *The Realness of Things Past: Ancient Greece and Ontological History.* Oxford.

Andrewes, A. 1954. *Probouleusis: Sparta's Contribution to the Technique of Government (Inaugural Lecture)*. Oxford.
Aperghis, G. 2013. "Athenian Mines, Coins and Triremes." *Historia* 62: 1–24.
Arcenas, S. L. 2020. "The Silence of Thucydides." *TAPA* 150: 299–332.
Arendt, H. 1958. *The Human Condition*. Chicago, IL.
Arrington, N. 2015. *Ashes, Images, and Memories: The Presence of the War Dead in Fifth-Century Athens*. Oxford.
Asmonti, L. 2006. "The Arginusae Trial, the Changing Role of the *Strategoi* and the Relationship between *Demos* and Military Leadership in Late-Fifth Century Athens." *BICS* 49: 1–21.
Azoulay, V. 2009. "La gloire et l'outrage: Heurs et malheurs des statues honorifiques de Démétrios de Phalère." *Annales HSS* 64: 301–40.
  2014a. *Pericles of Athens*. Princeton, NJ.
  2014b. "Rethinking the Political in Ancient Greece." *Annales HSS* 69: 385–408.
  2017. *The Tyrant-Slayers of Ancient Athens: A Tale of Two Statues*. Oxford.
Azoulay, V. and P. Ismard. 2020. *Athènes 403: Une histoire chorale*. Paris.
Badian, E. 1976. "Rome, Athens and Mithridates." *AJAH* 1: 105–28.
  1993. *From Plataea to Potidaea: Studies in the History and Historiography of the Pentecontaetia*. Baltimore, MD.
Balot, R. K. 2006. *Greek Political Thought*. Malden, MA.
  2014. *Courage in the Democratic Polis: Ideology and Critique in Classical Athens*. Oxford.
Baltes, E. P. 2020. "A Monumental Stepped Statue Base in the Athenian Agora." *Hesperia* 89: 339–77.
Barbato, M. 2020. *The Ideology of Democratic Athens: Institutions, Orators and the Mythical Past*. Edinburgh.
  2021. "'For Themistocles of Phrearrhioi, on Account of Honour': Ostracism, Honour and the Nature of Athenian Politics." *CQ* 71: 500–19.
  2023. "Elite Politicians or Ordinary Citizens? Decree Making and Political Friendship in Fifth-Century Athens." *Klio* 105: 403–48.
Beck, H. and P. Funke, eds. 2015. *Federalism in Greek Antiquity*. Cambridge.
Berger, S. 1992. *Revolution and Society in Greek Sicily and Southern Italy*. Stuttgart.
Berlin, I. 2003. "Two Concepts of Liberty" (1958). Repr. in *Liberty: Incorporating Four Essays on Liberty*. Oxford: 166–217.
Bernhardt, J. C. and M. Canevaro, eds. 2022. *From Homer to Solon: Continuity and Change in Archaic Greece*. Leiden.
Bernhardt, R. 1985. *Polis und römische Herrschaft in der späten Republik (149–31 v. Chr.)*. Berlin.
Bernini, J. 2023. *"Plaise au peuple": Pratiques et lieux de la decision démocratique en Ionie et en Carie hellénistiques*. Bordeaux.
Bers, V. 1985. "Dikastic *Thorubos*." In P. A. Cartledge and F. D. Harvey, eds., *CRUX*. Exeter: 1–15.
Blanshard, A. 2004. "Depicting Democracy: An Exploration of Art and Text in the Law of Eukrates." *JHS* 124: 1–15.

Blok, J. H. 2005. "Becoming Citizens: Some Notes on the Semantics of 'Citizen' in Archaic Greece and Classical Athens." *Klio* 87: 7–40.
   2009. "Perikles' Citizenship Law: A New Perspective." *Historia* 58: 141–70.
   2013. "Citizenship, the Citizen Body, and Its Assemblies." In H. Beck, ed., *A Companion to Ancient Greek Government*. Malden, MA: 162–75.
   2015. "The *Diōbelia*: On the Political Economy of an Athenian State Fund." *ZPE* 193: 87–102.
   2017. *Citizenship in Classical Athens*. Cambridge.
Blok, J. H. and E. van 't Wout. 2018. "Table Arrangements: Sitesis as a Polis Institution (IG I3 131)." In F. van den Eijnde, J. H. Blok, and R. Strootman, eds., *Feasting and Polis Institutions*. Leiden: 181–204.
Bolmarcich, S. 2005. "Thucydides 1.19.1 and the Peloponnesian League." *GRBS* 45: 5–34.
Börm, H. 2019. *Mordende Mitbürger: Stasis und Bürgerkrieg in griechischen Poleis des Hellenismus*. Stuttgart.
Börm, H. and N. Luraghi, eds. 2018. *The Polis in the Hellenistic World*. Stuttgart.
Boulanger, A. 1923. *Aelius Aristide et la sophistique dans la province d'Asie au IIe siècle de notre ère*. Paris.
Boulay, T. 2014. *Arès dans la cité: Les poleis et la guerre dans l'Asie Mineure hellénistique*. Pisa.
Brélaz, C. 2009. "Les bienfaiteurs, 'sauveurs' et 'fossoyeurs' de la cité hellénistique? Une approche historiographique de l'évergétisme." In O. Curty, ed., *L'huile et l'argent: Gymnasiarchie et évergétisme dans la Grèce hellénistique*. Fribourg: 37–56.
   2013a. "La vie démocratique dans les cités grecques à l'époque impériale," *Topoi* 18: 367–99.
   2013b. "Les 'pauvres' comme composante du corps civique dans les *poleis* des époques hellénistique et impériale." *Ktèma* 38: 67–87.
   2021. "Democracy, Citizenship(s), and 'Patriotism': Civic Practices and Discourses in the Greek Cities under Roman Rule." In C. Brélaz and E. Rose, eds., *Civic Identity and Civic Participation in Late Antiquity and the Early Middle Ages*. Turnhout: 65–90.
Brenne, S. 2018. *Die Ostraka vom Kerameikos*. Wiesbaden.
Briscoe, J. 1967. "Rome and the Class Struggle in the Greek States 200–146 BC." *P&P* 36: 3–20.
Brock, R. 1989. "Athenian Oligarchs: The Numbers Game." *JHS* 109: 160–64.
   2009. "Did the Athenian Empire Promote Democracy?" In J. Ma, N. Papazarkadas, and R. Parker, eds., *Interpreting the Athenian Empire*. London: 149–66.
Brock, R. and A. Duplouy, eds. 2018. *Defining Citizenship in Archaic Greece*. Oxford.
Brown, P. 1992. *Power and Persuasion in Late Antiquity*. Madison, WI.
   2002. *Poverty and Leadership in the Later Roman Empire*. Hanover.
Buckley, W. F. 1963. *Rumbles Left and Right: A Book about Troublesome People and Ideas*. New York.

Burckhardt, J. 2013 [1898]. *History of Greek Culture*. Mineola, NY.
Burke, E. 1986 [1790]. *Reflections on the Revolution in France*. New York.
Burton, P. 2019. *Roman Imperialism*. Leiden.
Byrne, S. G. 2010. "The Athenian *Damnatio Memoriae* of the Antigonids in 200 BC." In A. M. Tamis, C. J. Mackie, and S. G. Byrne, eds., *Philathenaios: Studies in Honour of Michael J. Osborne*. Athens: 155–77.
Caire, E. 2016. *Penser l'oligarchie à Athènes aux Ve et IVe siècles: Aspects d'une idéologie*. Paris.
  2019. "Aux origines de la démagogie: Naissance et manipulations d'un concept." *IncAnt* 17: 137–67.
Cairns, D., M. Canevaro, and K. Manzouranis. 2022. "Recognition and Retribution in Aristotle's Account of Stasis." *Polis* 39: 1–34.
Camia, F. 2014. "Political Elite and Priestly Posts in Athens during the Roman Imperial Period: Some Considerations." *ZPE* 188: 139–48.
Cammack, D. 2021. "Representation in Ancient Greek Democracy." *History of Political Thought* 42: 567–601.
Campa, N. T. 2024. *Freedom and Power in Classical Athens*. Cambridge.
Canevaro, M. 2013. *The Documents in the Democratic Orators: Laws and Decrees in the Public Speeches of the Demosthenic Corpus*. Oxford.
  2017a. "The Rule of Law as the Measure of Political Legitimacy in the Greek City States." *Hague Journal on the Rule of Law* 9: 211–36.
  2017b. "The Popular Culture of the Athenian Institutions: 'Authorized' Popular Culture and 'Unauthorized' Elite Culture in Classical Athens." In L. Grig, ed., *Popular Culture in the Ancient World*. Cambridge: 39–65.
  2018a. "The Public Charge for *Hubris* against Slaves: The Honour of the Victim and the Honour of the *Hubristēs*." *JHS* 138: 100–26.
  2018b. "Majority Rule vs. Consensus: The Practice of Democratic Deliberation in the Greek Poleis." In M. Canevaro, A. Erskine, B. Gray, and J. Ober, eds., *Ancient Greek History and Contemporary Social Science*. Edinburgh: 101–56.
  2019. "La délibération démocratique à l'Assemblée athénienne: Procédures et stratégies de légitimation." *Annales HSS* 74: 339–81.
  2022. "Social Mobility vs. Societal Stability: Once Again on the Aims and Meaning of Solon's Reforms." In Bernhardt and Canevaro 2022: 363–413.
  2024. "L'hybris degli oppressi: Onore e controllo sociale nel mondo greco (e nel nostro)." *RFIC* 152: 15–66.
  forthcoming. "Nativism vs. Class Denigration: Athenian Autochthony between Inclusion and Exclusion." In M. Bellomo, A. M. Cimino, V. Saldutti, and E. Zucchetti, eds., *Class and Classics: Subalterns and the Production of Classical Culture*. Berlin.
Canevaro, M. and A. Esu. 2018. "Extreme Democracy and Mixed Constitution in Theory and Practice: *Nomophylakia* and Fourth-Century *Nomothesia* in the Aristotelian *Athenaion Politeia*." In C. Bearzot, M. Canevaro, T. Gargiulo, and E. Poddighe, eds., *Athenaion Politeiai tra storia, politica e sociologia: Aristotele e Pseudo-Senofonte*. Milan: 105–45.

Canevaro, M. and B. Gray, eds. 2018. *The Hellenistic Reception of Classical Athenian Democracy and Political Thought.* Oxford.
Canevaro, M. and E. M. Harris. 2012. "The Documents in Andocides' *On the Mysteries.*" *CQ* 62: 98–129.
Canevaro, M. and D. M. Lewis. 2024. "Between 'The Character of the Athenian Empire' and *The Origins of the Peloponnesian War* (and Beyond)." *Polis* 41: 176–202.
  forthcoming. "Poverty, Race, and Ethnicity." In C. Taylor, ed., *A Cultural History of Poverty in Antiquity (500 BCE–500 CE).* London.
Carawan, E. 2020. *Control of the Laws in the Ancient Democracy at Athens.* Baltimore, MD.
Cargill, J. 1981. *The Second Athenian League: Empire or Free Alliance?* Berkeley, CA.
Carlsson, S. 2010. *Hellenistic Democracies: Freedom, Independence and Political Procedure in Some East Greek City-States.* Stuttgart.
Carter, L. B. 1986. *The Quiet Athenian.* Oxford.
Carter, D. 2004a. "Was Attic Tragedy Democratic?" *Polis* 21: 1–25.
  2004b. "Citizen Attribute, Negative Right: A Conceptual Difference between Ancient and Modern Ideas for Freedom of Speech." In I. Sluiter and R. M. Rosen, eds., *Free Speech in Classical Antiquity.* Leiden: 197–220.
Cartledge, P. A. 1987. *Agesilaos and the Crisis of Sparta.* London.
  2009. Ancient Greek Political Thought in Practice. Cambridge.
  2018. Democracy: A Life. New edition. Oxford.
  2020. "Afterword: The Boy from Cydathenaeum: Some Concluding Reflections." In R. M. Rosen and H. Foley, eds., *Aristophanes and Politics: New Studies.* Leiden: 273–78.
Carugati, F. 2019. *Creating a Constitution: Law, Democracy, and Growth in Ancient Athens.* Princeton, NJ.
Carugati, F., B. Weingast, and R. Calvert. 2023. "Judicial Review by the People Themselves: Democracy and the Rule of Law in Ancient Athens." *Journal of Law, Economics, and Organization* 39: 1–26.
Cawkwell, G. 1997. *Thucydides and the Peloponnesian War.* London.
Chaniotis, A. 1995. "Sich selbst feiern? Städtische Feste des Hellenismus im Spannungsfeld von Religion und Politik." In Wörrle and Zanker 1995: 147–72.
  2005. War in the Hellenistic World: A Social and Cultural History. Oxford.
  2010. "Illusions of Democracy in the Hellenistic World." *Athens Dialogues.* www.athensdialogues.org
  2018. Age of Conquests: The Greek World from Alexander to Hadrian. Cambridge, MA.
Chankowski, A. S. 2010. *L'Éphébie hellénistique: Étude d'une institution civique dans les cités grecques des îles de la Mer Égée et de l'Asie Mineure.* Paris.
Christ, M. R. 1998. *The Litigious Athenian.* Baltimore, MD.
  2001. "Conscription of Hoplites in Classical Athens." *CQ* 51: 398–422.
  2006a. Review of Herman 2006. *BMCR* 2007.07.37.

2006b. *The Bad Citizen in Classical Athens.* Cambridge.

2007. "The Evolution of the *Eisphora* in Classical Athens." *CQ* 57: 53–69.

Christesen, P. 2012. "Athletics and Social Order in Sparta in the Classical Period." *ClAnt* 31: 193–255.

Christesen, P., G. Lentini, S. Murray, and M. Simonton. 2024. "Chios, Lesbos, Samos." In P. Christesen and P. A. Cartledge, eds., *The Oxford History of the Archaic Greek World.* Oxford: 245–487.

Clairmont, C. 1983. *Patrios Nomos: Public Burial in Athens during the Fifth and Fourth Centuries BC.* Oxford.

Clements, J. 2021. "The Gift of Identity: (Re)presenting Autochthony in Classical Athens." *Ramus* 50: 189–209.

Connelly, J. B. 2014. *The Parthenon Enigma: A New Understanding of the West's Most Iconic Building and the People Who Made It.* New York.

Connor, W. R. 1992. *The New Politicians of Fifth-Century Athens.* Indianapolis, IN.

Constant, B. 1988. *Political Writings.* Cambridge.

Constantakopoulou, C. 2012. "Beyond the Polis: Island *Koina* and Other Non-Polis Entities in the Aegean." *REA* 114: 301–21.

Conwell, D. 2008. *Connecting a City to the Sea: A History of the Athenian Long Walls.* Leiden.

Crowther, C. 1992. "The Decline of Greek Democracy?" *JAC* 7: 13–48.

Culasso Gastaldi, E. 2003. "Abbattere la stele: Riscrittura epigrafica e revisione storica ad Atene." *CCG* 14: 241–62.

Davies, J. K. 1977. "Athenian Citizenship: The Descent Group and the Alternatives." *CJ* 73: 105–21.

1993. *Democracy and Classical Greece*, 2nd edition. Cambridge, MA.

2003. "Democracy without Theory." In P. Derow and R. Parker, eds., *Herodotus and His World: Essays from a Conference in Memory of George Forrest.* Oxford: 319–35.

Davies, P. A. 2017. "Articulating Status in Ancient Greece: Status (In)consistency as a New Approach." *CCJ* 63: 29–52.

de Dijn, A. 2020. *Freedom: An Unruly History.* Cambridge, MA.

de Laix, R. A. 1973. *Probouleusis at Athens: A Study of Political Decision-Making.* Berkeley, CA.

de Lisle, C. 2020. "The Ephebate in Roman Athens: Outline and Catalogue of Inscriptions." *AIO Papers*, no. 12.

2021. *Agathokles of Syracuse: Sicilian Tyrant and Hellenistic King.* Oxford.

de Ste. Croix, G. E. M. 1954. "The Character of the Athenian Empire." *Historia* 3: 1–41.

1972. *The Origins of the Peloponnesian War.* London.

1975. "Political Pay Outside Athens." *CQ* 25: 48–52.

1981. *The Class Struggle in the Ancient Greek World: From the Archaic Age to the Arab Conquests.* [Corr. reimpr. 1983.] London.

Deininger, J. 1971. *Der politische Widerstand gegen Rom in Griechenland (217–86 v. Chr.).* Berlin.

Delrieux, F. and M.-C. Ferriès. 2004. "Euthydème, Hybréas et Mylasa: Une cité grecque de Carie dans les conflits romains de la fin du Ier siècle a.C. (première et deuxième partie)." *REA* 106: 49–71, 499–515.
Deneen, P. 2018. *Why Liberalism Failed*. New Haven, CT.
Diggle, J. 2004. *Theophrastus: Characters*. Cambridge.
Dmitriev, S. 2005. *City Government in Hellenistic and Roman Asia Minor*. Oxford.
Domingo Gygax, M. 2016. *Benefaction and Rewards in the Ancient Greek City: The Origins of Euergetism*. New York.
Domingo Gygax, M. and A. Zuiderhoek, eds. 2021. *Benefactors and the Polis: The Public Gift in the Greek Cities from the Homeric World to Late Antiquity*. New York.
Donlan, W. 1999. *The Aristocratic Ideal and Selected Papers*. Wauconda, IL.
Dössel, A. 2003. *Die Beilegung innerstaatlicher Konflikte in den griechischen Poleis vom 5.-3. Jahrhundert v. Chr.* New York.
Dreher, M. 2013. "Die Herausbildung eines politischen Instruments: Die Amnestie bis zum Ende der klassischen Zeit." In K. Harter-Uibopuu and F. Mitthof, eds., *Vergeben und Vergessen? Amnestie in der Antike*. Vienna: 71–94.
Driscoll, E. 2016. "Stasis and Reconciliation: Politics and Law in Fourth-Century Greece." *Chiron* 46: 119–55.
——— 2018. *The Making and Meaning of the Athenian Empire*. Dissertation, Berkeley, CA.
Droysen, J. G. 1836–43. *Geschichte des Hellenismus*. 3 vols. Munich.
Du Bois, W. E. B. 1935. *Black Reconstruction in America*. New York.
Duplouy, A. 2006. *Le prestige des élites: Recherches sur les modes de reconnaissance sociale en Grèce entre les Xe et Ve siècles avant J.-C.* Paris.
——— 2019. *Construire la cité: Essai de sociologie historique sur les communautés de l'archaïsme grec*. Paris.
Ebner-Landy, K. and R. de Nicolay. 2023. "Theophrastus' 'Oligarch' and the Political Intention of the *Characters*." *CCJ* 69: 1–21.
Edge, M. 2009. "Athens and the Spectrum of Liberty." *History of Political Thought* 30: 1–45.
Elsner, J. 2015. "Visual Culture and Ancient History: Issues of Empiricism and Ideology in the Samos Stele at Athens." *ClAnt* 34: 33–73.
Errington, R. M. 2020. *Die Verträge der griechisch-römischen Welt von ca. 200 v. Chr. bis zum Beginn der Kaiserzeit. Die Staatsverträge des Altertums, 4*. Munich.
Erskine, A. 1994. "The Romans as Common Benefactors." *Historia* 43: 70–87.
Esu, A. 2024. *Divided Power in Ancient Greece: Decision-Making and Institutions in the Classical and Hellenistic Polis*. Oxford.
Evans, N. 2010. *Civic Rites: Democracy and Religion in Ancient Athens*. Berkeley, CA.
Fabiani, R. 2012. "*Dedochthai tei boulei kai toi demoi*: Protagonisti e prassi della procedura deliberativa a Iasos." In Mann and Scholz 2012: 109–65.
——— 2015. *I decreti di Iasos: Cronologia e storia*. Munich.

Fachard, S. 2012. *La défense du territoire: Étude de la "chōra" érétrienne et de ses fortifications.* Athens.

2019. "Common Denominators? The Emergence of Territorial Organization in Athens and Eretria." In O. Palagia and E. P. Sioumpara, eds., *From Hippias to Kallias: Greek Art in Athens and Beyond, 528–449 BC.* Athens: 172–81.

Faraguna, M. 2017. "Documents, Public Information and the Historian: Perspectives on Fifth-Century Athens." *Historika* 7: 23–52.

Farioli, M. 2020. "*Les liaisons dangereuses.* Postmodernismo e femminismo mainstream in alcune tendenze attuali della storia antica." *IncAnt* 18: 15–78.

Fawcett, P. 2016. "'When I Squeeze You with *Eisphorai*': Taxes and Tax Policy in Classical Athens." *Hesperia* 85: 153–99.

2024. "Athenian Taxes in the Hellenistic Period." *Hesperia* 93: 29–82.

Fernoux, H. 2004. *Notables et élites des cités de Bithynie aux époques hellénistique et romaine, IIIe siècle av. J.-C.-IIIe siècle ap. J.-C.: Essai d'histoire sociale.* Lyon.

2011. *Le Demos et la cité: Communautés et assemblées populaires en Asie Mineure à l'époque impériale.* Rennes.

Ferrary, J.-L. 2017. *Rome et le monde grec: Choix d'écrits.* Paris.

Feyel, C. 2009. ΔΟΚΙΜΑΣΙΑ: *La place et le rôle de l'examen préliminaire dans les institutions des cités grecques.* Paris.

Fields, D. 2021. *Frankness, Greek Culture, and the Roman Empire.* Abingdon.

Filonik, J. 2019. "'Living as One Wishes' in Athens: The (Anti-)Democratic Polemics." *CPh* 114: 1–24.

Finley, M. I. 1981. *Economy and Society in Ancient Greece.* London.

1983. *Politics in the Ancient World.* Cambridge.

2019. *Democracy Ancient and Modern.* Reprint edition. New Brunswick, NJ.

Fisher, N. R. E. 2000. "Hybris, Revenge and Stasis in the Greek City-States." In H. van Wees, ed., *War and Violence in Ancient Greece.* Swansea: 83–123.

Fisher, N. R. E. and H. van Wees, eds. 2015. *"Aristocracy" in Antiquity: Redefining Greek and Roman Elites.* Swansea.

Flower, H. I. 2006. *The Art of Forgetting: Disgrace and Oblivion in Roman Political Culture.* Chapel Hill, NC.

Forsdyke, S. 2005. *Exile, Ostracism, and Democracy: The Politics of Expulsion in Ancient Greece.* Princeton, NJ.

2021. *Slaves and Slavery in Ancient Greece.* Cambridge.

Forster, F. R. 2018. *Die Polis im Wandel: Ehrendekrete für eigene Bürger im Kontext der hellenistischen Polisgesellschaft.* Gottingen.

Foucault, M. 2019. *Discourse & Truth and Parrēsia.* Chicago, IL.

Fournier, J. and P. Hamon. 2007. "Les orphelins de guerre de Thasos: Un nouveau fragment de la stèle des Braves (ca 360–350 av. J.-C.)." *BCH* 131: 039–81.

Franco, C. 2008. "Aelius Aristides and Rhodes: Concord and Consolation." In W. V. Harris and B. Holmes, eds., *Aelius Aristides between Greece, Rome, and the Gods.* Leiden: 217–49.

Friend, J. L. 2019. *The Athenian Ephebeia in the Fourth Century BCE.* Leiden.

Frija, G. 2012. *Les prêtres des empereurs: Le culte impériale civique dans la province romaine d'Asie*. Rennes.

Fröhlich, P. 2004. *Les cités grecques et le contrôle des magistrats (IVe–Ier siècle avant J.-C.)*. Geneva.

—— 2009. "Les activités évergétiques des gymnasiarques à l'époque hellénistique tardive: La fourniture de l'huile." In O. Curty, ed., *L'huile et l'argent: Gymnasiarchie et évergétisme dans la Grèce hellénistique*. Fribourg: 57–94.

—— 2013. "Funérailles publiques et tombeaux monumentaux Intramuros dans les cités grecques à l'époque hellénistique." In M.-C. Ferriès, M. P. Castiglioni, F. Létoublon, eds., *Forgerons, élites et voyageurs d'Homère à nos jours*. Grenoble: 227–309.

—— 2016. "La citoyenneté grecque entre Aristote et les modernes." *CCG* 27: 91–136.

—— 2019. "Institutions des cités d'Éolide à l'époque hellénistique: Décrets honorifiques et proximités institutionelles entre cités." *Chiron* 49: 45–68.

—— 2021. "Les prytanes d'Iasos, l'*épitropos* et la question du remplacement des magistrats en poste dans les cités hellénistiques." In K. Harter-Uibopuu and W. Riess, eds., *Symposion 2019*. Vienna: 289–328.

—— forthcoming a. "The Nature of Hellenistic Democracies." In V. Arena and E. W. Robinson, eds., *The Cambridge History of Democracy Vol. I*.

—— forthcoming b. "The Rise and Fall of Hellenistic Democracies." In V. Arena and E. W. Robinson, eds., *The Cambridge History of Democracy Vol. I*.

Fröhlich, P. and C. Müller, eds. 2005. *Citoyenneté et participation à la basse époque hellénistique: Actes de la table ronde des 22 et 23 mai 2004, Paris BNF*. Geneva.

Frullini, S. 2021. "Politics and Landscape in the Argive Plain after the Battle of Sepeia." *JHS* 141: 110–35.

—— 2023. *Democracy in the Peloponnese, c. 550–146 BCE*. Dissertation, Cambridge.

Gabrielsen, V. 1994. *Financing the Athenian Fleet: Public Taxation and Social Relations*. Baltimore, MD.

Gagarin, M. 2020. *Democratic Law in Classical Athens*. Austin, TX.

Gauthier, P. 1982. "Notes sur trois décrets honorant des citoyens bienfaiteurs." *RPh* 108: 215–31.

—— 1984. "Les cités hellénistiques: Épigraphie et histoire des institutions et des régimes politiques." In A. G. Kalogeropoulou, ed., *Actes du VIIIe Congr. int. épigr. 1982*. Athens: 82–107. Reprinted in Gauthier 2011: 315–50.

—— 1985. *Les cités grecques et leurs bienfaiteurs (IVe–Ier siècle avant J.-C.): Contribution à l'histoire des institutions*. Athens.

—— 1993. "Les cités hellénistiques." In M. H. Hansen, ed., *The Ancient Greek City-State*. Copenhagen: 211–31. Reprinted in Gauthier 2011: 351–74.

—— 2005. "Trois exemples méconnus d'intervenants dans des décrets de la basse époque hellénistique." In Fröhlich and Müller 2005: 79–93.

—— 2011. *Études d'histoire et d'institutions grecques: Choix d'écrits*. D. Rousset, ed. Geneva.

Geddes, A. 2007. "Ion of Chios and Politics." In V. Jennings and A. Katsaros, eds., *The World of Ion of Chios*. Leiden: 110–38.

Gehrke, H.-J. 1985. *Stasis. Untersuchungen zu den inneren Kriegen in den griechischen Staaten des 5. und 4. Jahrhunderts v. Chr.* Munich.

　1986. *Jenseits Athen und Sparta: Das Dritte Griechenland und seine Staatenwelt.* Munich.

Giannadaki, I. 2020. *A Commentary on Demosthenes'* Against Androtion. Oxford.

Giannakopoulos, N. 2008. "Remarks on the Honorary titles ΥΙΟΣ ΒΟΥΛΗΣ, ΥΙΟΣ ΔΗΜΟΥ and ΥΙΟΣ ΠΟΛΕΩΣ in Roman Asia Minor." In A. D. Rizakis and F. Camia, eds., *Pathways to Power: Civic Elites in the Eastern Part of the Roman Empire.* Athens: 251–68.

　2017. "Decrees Awarding Offices for Life and by Hereditary Right as Honours." In Heller and van Nijf 2017: 220–42.

Glowacki, K. 2003. "A Personification of Demos on a New Attic Document Relief." *Hesperia* 72: 447–66.

Goldhill, S. 1987. "The Great Dionysia and Civic Ideology." *JHS* 108: 58–76.

Gottesman, A. 2021a. "What Is Below? The Case of the Athenian Riot of 508/7 BC." In C. Courrier and J. C. Magalhães de Oliveira, eds., *Ancient History from Below: Subaltern Experiences and Actions in Context.* Abingdon: 216–36.

　2021b. "The Concept of *Isēgoria*." *Polis* 38: 175–98.

Goukowsky, P. 1995. "Philippe de Pergame et l'histoire des guerres civiles." In *Hellènika symmikta* 2. Paris: 39–53.

Gourevitch, A. 2015. *From Slavery to the Cooperative Commonwealth: Labor and Republican Liberty in the Nineteenth Century.* Cambridge.

Gray, B. 2015. Stasis *and Stability: Exile, the Polis, and Political Thought, c. 404–146 BC.* Oxford.

　2018. "A Later Hellenistic Debate about the Value of Classical Athenian Civic Ideals? The Evidence of Epigraphy, Historiography, and Philosophy." In Canevaro and Gray 2018: 139–76.

Green, P. 1990. *Alexander to Actium: The Historical Evolution of the Hellenistic Age.* Berkeley, CA.

Grieb, V. 2008. *Hellenistische Demokratie: Politische Organisation und Struktur in freien griechischen Poleis nach Alexander dem Grossen.* Stuttgart.

　2013. "Polybios' *Wahre* Demokratie und die *politeia* von Poleis und Koina in den Historien." In V. Grieb and C. Koehn, eds., *Polybios und seine Historien.* Stuttgart: 183–218.

Grote, G. 1849. *A History of Greece: Vol. 1.* Second edition. London.

Habicht, C. 1995. "Ist ein 'Honoratiorenregime' das Kennzeichen der Stadt im späteren Hellenismus?" In Wörrle and Zanker 1995: 87–92.

　1997. *Athens from Alexander to Antony.* Cambridge, MA.

Hamilton, A., J. Madison, and J. Jay. 2014. *The Federalist Papers.* Mineola, NY.

Hamilton, C. D. 1979. *Sparta's Bitter Victories: Politics and Diplomacy in the Corinthian War.* Ithaca, NY.

Hammer, D. 2004. "Ideology, the Symposium, and Archaic Politics." *AJPh* 125: 479–512.

Hamon, P. 2001. "À propos de l'institution du Conseil dans les cités grecques de l'époque hellénistique." *REG* 114: xvi–xxi.

2005. "Le conseil et la participation des citoyens: Les mutations de la basse époque hellénistique." In Fröhlich and Müller 2005: 121–44.

2008. "Kymè d'Éolide, cité libre et démocratique, et le pouvoir des stratèges." *Chiron* 38: 63–106.

2009. "Démocraties grecques après Alexandre: À propos de trois ouvrages récents." *Topoi* 16: 347–82.

2012. "Mander des juges dans cité: Notes sur l'organisation des missions judiciaires à l'époque hellénistique." *CCG* 23: 195–22.

2018. "Tout l'or et l'argent de Téos: Au sujet d'une nouvelle edition des décrets sur les pirates et l'emprunt pour la liberation des otages." *Chiron* 48: 333–74.

Hansen, M. H. 1980. "Seven Hundred *Archai* in Classical Athens." *GRBS* 21: 151–73.

1983. *The Athenian Ecclesia: A Collection of Articles, 1976–83*. Copenhagen.

1989. *The Athenian Ecclesia II: A Collection of Articles, 1983–89*. Copenhagen.

1999. *The Athenian Democracy in the Age of Demosthenes: Structure, Principles, and Ideology*, Revised edition. Norman, OK.

2010. "Greek Freedom and the Concept of Freedom in Plato and Aristotle." *GRBS* 50: 1–27.

Hansen, M. H. and T. H. Nielsen, eds. 2004. *An Inventory of Archaic and Classical Poleis*. Oxford.

Harris, E. M. and D. M. Lewis. 2022. "What Are Early Greek Laws About? Substance and Procedure in Archaic Statutes, c. 650–450 BC." In Bernhardt and Canevaro 2022: 227–62.

Harrison, A. R. W. 1968–71. *The Law of Athens*. 2 vols. New York.

Harrison, T. 2020. "Reinventing the Barbarian." *CP* 115: 139–63.

Harvey, D., J. Wilkins, and K. J. Dover, eds. 2000. *The Rivals of Aristophanes: Studies in Athenian Old Comedy*. London.

Hedrick, Jr., C. W. 1999. "Democracy and the Athenian Epigraphical Habit." *Hesperia* 68: 387–439.

Heller, A. 2006. *'Les bêtises des Grecs': Conflits et rivalités entre cités d'Asie et de Bithynie à l'époque romaine: 129 a.C.-235 p.C.* Bordeaux.

2009. "La cité grecque d'époque impériale: Vers une société d'ordres?" *Annales HSS* 64: 341–73.

2011. "Des Grecs au service des imperatores romains, ou comment rester Grec tout en devenant Romain." In J.-C. Couvenhes, S. Crouzet, and S. Péré-Noguès, eds., *Pratiques et identités culturelles des armées hellénistiques du monde méditerranéen*. Bordeaux: 227–44.

2015. "Membership of the *Boulē* in the Inscriptions of Asia Minor: A Mark of Elevated Social Status?" In A. B. Kuhn, ed., *Social Status and Prestige in the Graeco-Roman World*. Stuttgart: 247–67.

2020. *L'âge d'or des bienfaiteurs: Titres honorifiques et sociétés civiques dans l'Asie Mineure d'époque romaine: Ier s. av. J.-C. -IIIe s. apr. J.-C.* Geneva.

2021. "Des dynasties de notables? La mise en scène du prestige familial dans les inscriptions honorifiques d'Asie Mineure à l'époque impériale." *Pallas* 115: 289–318.

Heller, A. and O. M. van Nijf. 2017. *The Politics of Honour in the Greek Cities of the Roman Empire*. Leiden.
Henderson, T. R. 2020. *The Springtime of the People: The Athenian Ephebeia and Citizen Training from Lykourgos to Augustus*. Leiden.
Herman, G. 1987. *Ritualised Friendship and the Greek City*. Cambridge.
  2006. *Morality and Behaviour in Democratic Athens: A Social History*. Cambridge.
Hesk, J. 2000. *Deception and Democracy in Classical Athens*. Cambridge.
Hill, C. 1965. "The Many-Headed Monster in Late Tudor and Early Stuart Political Thinking." In C. H. Carter, ed., *From the Renaissance to the Counter-Reformation: Essays in Honor of Garrett Mattingly*. New York: 296–324.
Hin, S. 2007. "Class and Society in the Cities of the Greek East: Education during the Ephebeia." *Anc Soc* 37: 141–66.
Höcker, C. 2006. "Parthenon." In H. Cancik and H. Schneider, eds., *Brill's New Pauly*. Leiden.
Hodkinson, S. 2000. *Property and Wealth in Classical Sparta*. Swansea.
Hölkeskamp, K.-J. 2010. *Reconstructing the Roman Republic: An Ancient Political Culture and Modern Research*. Princeton, NJ.
Horky, P. 2016. "*Empedocles Democraticus*: Hellenistic Biography at the Intersection of Philosophy and Politics." In M. Bonazzi and S. Schorn, eds., *Bios Philosophos: Philosophy in Ancient Greek Biography*. Leuven: 37–71.
Hornblower, S. 1991. *A Commentary on Thucydides. Volume I: Books I–III*. Oxford.
  2004. *Thucydides and Pindar: Historical Narrative and the World of Epinician Poetry*. Oxford.
  2011. *The Greek World 479–323 BC*. Fourth edition. London.
Hunter, V. 2000. "Policing Public Debtors in Classical Athens." *Phoenix* 54: 21–38.
Hurwit, J. M. 1999. *The Athenian Acropolis: History, Mythology, and Archaeology from the Neolithic Era to the Present*. Cambridge.
Iacoviello, A. 2025. "The history and rationale of the Athenian highest honours." *Chiron* 55: 141–87.
Ismard, P. 2017. *Democracy's Slaves: A Political History of Ancient Greece*. Cambridge, MA.
Jacoby, F. 1947. "Some Remarks on Ion of Chios." *CQ* 41: 1–17.
James, C. L. R. 1956. "Every Cook Can Govern: A Study of Democracy in Ancient Greece. Its Meaning for Today." www.marxists.org/archive/james-clr/works/1956/06/every-cook.htm
Jameson, M. H. 2004. "Women and Democracy in Fourth-Century Athens." Reprinted in E. W. Robinson, ed., *Ancient Greek Democracy: Readings and Sources*. Malden, MA: 282–92.
Jones, A. H. M. 1940. *The Greek City from Alexander to Justinian*. Oxford.
Jones, C. P. 1971. *Plutarch and Rome*. Oxford.
  1978. *The Roman World of Dio Chrysostom*. Cambridge, MA.
  1999. "Interrupted Funerals." *Proceedings of the American Philosophical Society* 143: 588–600.

2009. "New Late Antique Epigrams from Stratonicea in Caria." *EA* 42: 145–51.
2020. "The Historian Philip of Pergamon." *JHS* 140: 120–27.
Jones, N. 1999. *The Associations of Classical Athens: The Response to Democracy*. Oxford.
2004. *Rural Athens under the Democracy*. Philadelphia, PA.
Kaldellis, A. 2015. *The Byzantine Republic: People and Power in New Rome*. Cambridge, MA.
Kallet, L. 2003. "*Dēmos Tyrannos*: Wealth, Power, and Economic Patronage." In K. A. Morgan, ed., *Popular Tyranny: Sovereignty and Its Discontents in Ancient Greece*. Austin, TX: 117–53.
2008. "Money Talks: Rhetor, Demos, and the Resources of the Athenian Empire." In P. Low, ed., *The Athenian Empire*. Edinburgh: 185–210.
2013. "The Origins of the Athenian Economic *Archē*." *JHS* 133: 43–60.
Kallet, L. and J. H. Kroll. 2020. *The Athenian Empire: Using Coins as Sources*. Cambridge.
Kamen, D. 2013. *Status in Classical Athens*. Princeton, NJ.
Kantor, G. 2012. "Local Courts of Chersonesus Taurica in the Roman Age." In P. Martzavou and N. Papazarkadas, eds., *Epigraphical Approaches to the Post-Classical Polis*. Oxford: 69–86.
Kapparis, K. 2005. "Immigration and Citizenship Procedures in Athenian Law." *Revue internationale des droits de l'antiquité* 52: 71–113.
2018. *Athenian Law and Society*. Abingdon.
Kapust, D. 2004. "Skinner, Pettit and Livy: The Conflict of the Orders and the Ambiguity of Republican Liberty." *History of Political Thought* 25: 377–401.
Kasimis, D. 2018. *The Perpetual Immigrant and the Limits of Athenian Democracy*. Cambridge.
Kavaddias, G. and A. P. Matthaiou. 2014. "A New Attic Inscription of the Fifth Century BC from the East Slope of the Acropolis." In A. P. Matthaiou and R. K. Pitt, eds., Ἀθηναίων ἐπίσκοπος: *Studies in Honour of Harold B. Mattingly*. Athens: 51–72.
Keaney, J. J. and A. Szegedy-Maszak. 1976. "Theophrastus' *de elegendis magistratibus*: Vat. Gr. 2306, Fragment B." *TAPA* 106: 227–40.
Keim, B. 2018. "Xenophon's *Hipparchikos* and the Athenian Embrace of Citizen *Philotimia*." *Polis* 35: 499–522.
Kellogg, D. 2013. *Marathon Fighters and Men of Maple: Ancient Acharnai*. Oxford.
Forthcoming. "Call the Witnesses: Athenian Citizenship Practice at the Crossroads of Memory, Ritual, and Identity." In V. Panoussi and W. Hutton, eds., *Memory, Ritual, and Identity in Ancient Greece and Rome*. Berlin.
Kennedy, R. F. 2014. *Immigrant Women in Athens: Gender, Ethnicity, and Citizenship in the Classical City*. Abingdon.
Kennell, N. M. 1997. "Herodes Atticus and the Rhetoric of Tyranny." *CPh* 92: 346–62.
2009. "The Greek Ephebate in the Roman Period." *International Journal of the History of Sport* 26: 323–42.

Kierstead, J. 2014. "Grote's Athens: The Character of Democracy." In K. N. Demetriou, ed., *Brill's Companion to George Grote and the Classical Tradition*. Leiden: 161–210.

———. 2019. "Incentives and Information in Athenian Citizenship Procedures." *Historia* 68: 26–49.

Kirbihler, F. 2014. "Artémidore d'Éphese, témoin des sociétés éphésienne et romaine du IIe siècle." In C. Chandezon and J. Dubouchet, eds., *Artémidore de Daldis et l'interprétation des rêves*. Paris: 53–103.

Knoepfler, D. 1990. "Contributions à l'épigraphie de Chalcis. III. Décrets fédéraux et décrets municipaux au IIe siècle av. J-.C." *BCH* 114: 473–98.

———. 2001. "Loi d'Érétrie contre la tyrannie et l'oligarchie (première partie)." *BCH* 125: 195–238.

———. 2008. "Une cité au coeur du monde méditerranéen antique. Érétrie et son territoire, histoire et institutions." *Annuaire du Collège de France* 108: 593–616.

———. 2018. "Amarynthos trente ans après: L'épigraphie a tranché, Strabon n'aura pas à plaider coupable." *CRAI* 162: 883–953.

———. 2019. "Des honneurs suprêmes à la damnatio memoriae. Athènes au temps des derniers Antigonides (261–199 av. J.-C.): Nouvelles interprétations et restitutions épigraphiques." *Mediterraneo Antico* 19: 113–53.

Knoepfler, D. and G. Ackermann. 2013. "*Phulè Admètis*: Un nouveau document sur les institutions et les cultes d l'Érétriade trouvé dans les fouilles de l'École Suisse d'Archéologie en Grèce." *CRAI* 156: 905–49.

Knox, R. M. 1985. "'So Mischievous a Beaste'? The Athenian *Demos* and Its Treatment of Its Politicians." *G&R* 32: 132–61.

Koerner, R. 1993. *Inschriftliche Gesetzestexte der frühen griechischen Polis*. K. Hallof, ed. Cologne.

Kosmin, P. J. 2015. "A Phenomenology of Democracy: Ostracism as Political Ritual." *ClAnt* 34: 121–62.

Kralli, I. 1999–2000. "Athens and Her Leading Citizens in the Early Hellenistic Period (338–261 BC): The Evidence of the Decrees Awarding Highest Honours." *Archaiognosia* 10: 133–61.

Kritzas, C. 2006. "Nouvelles inscriptions d'Argos: Les archives des comptes du trésor sacré (IVe s. av. J.-C.)." *CRAI* 150: 397–434.

Kron, G. 2011. "The Distribution of Wealth at Athens in Comparative Perspective." *ZPE* 179: 129–38.

Kuhn, C. T. 2013. "Emotionality in the Political Culture of the Graeco-Roman East: The Role of Acclamations." In A. Chaniotis, ed., *Unveiling Emotions: Sources and Methods for the Study of Emotions in the Greek World*. Stuttgart: 295–316.

———. 2017. "The Refusal of the Highest Honours by Members of the Urban Elite in Roman Asia Minor." In Heller and van Nijf 2017: 199–219.

Kurke, L. 1991. *The Traffic in Praise: Pindar and the Poetics of Social Economy*. Ithaca, NY.

1999. *Coins, Bodies, Games, and Gold: The Politics of Meaning in Archaic Greece.* Princeton, NJ.

2007. "Visualizing the Choral: Epichoric Poetry, Ritual, and Elite Negotiation in Fifth-Century Thebes." In C. Kraus, S. Goldhill, H. Foley, and J. Elsner, eds., *Visualizing the Tragic: Drama, Myth, and Ritual in Greek Art and Literature.* Oxford: 63–101.

La Rocca, A. 2019. "Quando sono scomparse le assemblee popolari delle città greche?" *Scienze dell'Antichità* 25: 25–38.

Lafargue, P. 2013. *Cléon, Le guerrier d'Athéna.* Bordeaux.

2022. *Fiers d'être démagogues! Ce que nous pouvons apprendre de la démocratie athénienne.* Paris.

Lalanne, S. 2017. "Le témoignage de Chariton d'Aphrodisias sur la pratique civique des honneurs." In Heller and van Nijf 2017: 147–81.

Lambert, S. D. 1993. *The Phratries of Attica.* Ann Arbor, MI.

2011. "What Was the Point of Inscribed Honorific Decrees in Classical Athens?" In S. D. Lambert, ed., *Sociable Man: Studies in Ancient Greek Social Behaviour in Honour of Nick Fisher.* Swansea: 193–214.

2012. "Inscribing the Past in Fourth-Century Athens." In J. Marincola, L. Llewellyn-Jones, and C. Maciver, eds., *Greek Notions of the Past in the Archaic and Classical Eras: History without Historians.* Edinburgh: 253–75.

2015. "The Inscribed Version of the Decree Honouring Lykourgos of Boutadai (*IG* II^2 457 and 3207)." *AIO Papers* 6.

2017. *Inscribed Athenian Laws and Decrees in the Age of Demosthenes: Historical Essays.* Leiden.

Lamont, J. 2023. *In Blood and Ashes: Curse Tablets and Binding Spells in Ancient Greece.* Oxford.

Landauer, M. 2019. *Dangerous Counsel: Accountability and Advice in Ancient Greece.* Chicago, IL.

Landemore, H. 2020. *Open Democracy: Reinventing Popular Rule for the Twenty-First Century.* Princeton, NJ.

Lane Fox, R. 1997. "Theophrastus' *Characters* and the Historian." *PCPhS* 42: 127–70.

Langley, T. R. 2020. "Local and Universal Citizenship in Works of the Cappadocian Fathers." *Al-Masâq* 32: 34–53.

Lanni, A. 2006. *Law and Justice in the Courts of Classical Athens.* Cambridge.

2016. *Law and Order in Ancient Athens.* Cambridge.

Lape, S. 2010. *Race and Citizen Identity in the Classical Athenian Democracy.* Cambridge.

Larsen, J. A. O. 1954. "The Judgment of Antiquity on Democracy." *CPh* 49: 1–14.

Lawton, C. 1995. *Attic Document Reliefs: Art and Politics in Ancient Athens.* Oxford.

Lazar, L. 2024. *Athenian Power in the Fifth Century BC.* Oxford.

Lebow, R. N. 2012. "International Relations and Thucydides." In K. Harloe and N. Morley, eds., *Thucydides and the Modern World: Reception, Reinterpretation and Influence from the Renaissance to the Present.* Cambridge: 197–211.

Lendon, J. E. 2010. *Song of Wrath: The Peloponnesian War Begins*. New York.
Lenfant, D. 2017. *Pseudo-Xénophon: Constitution des Athéniens*. Paris.
Lewis, D. M. 1963. "Cleisthenes and Attica." *Historia* 12: 22–40.
  1997. "Democratic Institutions and Their Diffusion." In P. J. Rhodes ed., *Selected Papers in Greek and Near Eastern History*. Cambridge: 51–59.
  2018. *Greek Slave Systems in Their Eastern Mediterranean Context, c. 800–146 BC*. Oxford.
Lewis, S. 2004. "Καὶ σαφῶς τύραννος ἦν: Xenophon's Account of Euphron of Sicyon." *JHS* 124: 65–74.
Liddel, P. 2007. *Civic Obligation and Individual Liberty in Ancient Athens*. Oxford.
  2010. "Epigraphy, Legislation, and Power within the Athenian Empire." *BICS* 53: 99–128.
  2020. *Decrees of Fourth-Century Athens (403/2–322/1 BC)*. 2 vols. Cambridge.
Liebeschuetz, J. H. W. G. 2001. *The Decline and Fall of the Roman City*. Oxford.
Lintott, A. 1982. *Violence, Civil Strife and Revolution in the Classical City*. Baltimore, MD.
Loening, T. C. 1987. *The Reconciliation Agreement of 403/402 BC: Its Content and Application*. Stuttgart.
Lonis, R. 1992. "L'*anaplērōsis* ou la reconstitution du corps civique avec des étrangers à l'époque hellénistique." In R. Lonis, ed., *L'Étranger dans le monde grec*. Nancy: 245–70.
Loraux, N. 1986. *The Invention of Athens: The Funeral Oration in the Classical City*. Cambridge, MA.
  2000. *Born of the Earth: Myth and Politics in Athens*. Ithaca, NY.
  2002. *The Divided City: On Memory and Forgetting in Ancient Athens*. New York.
Low, P. 2003. "Remembering War in Fifth-Century Greece: Ideologies, Societies, and Commemoration beyond Athens." *World Archaeology* 35: 98–111.
  2008. *The Athenian Empire*. Edinburgh.
Luraghi, N. 2008. *The Ancient Messenians: Constructions of Ethnicity and Memory*. Cambridge.
  2010. "The Demos as Narrator: Public Honors and the Construction of Future and Past." In L. Foxhall, H.-J. Gehrke, and N. Luraghi, eds., *Intentional History: Spinning Time in Ancient Greece*. Stuttgart: 247–63.
  2019. "Memory and Community in Early Hellenistic Athens." In W. Pohl and V. Wieser, eds., *Historiography and Identity I: Ancient and Early Christian Narratives of Community*. Turnhout: 107–31.
Ma, J. 1999. *Antiochos III and the Cities of Western Asia Minor*. Oxford.
  2000a. "Fighting Poleis of the Hellenistic World." In H. van Wees, *War and Violence in Ancient Greece*. Swansea: 337–76.
  2000b. "Public Speech and Community in the *Euboicus*." In S. Swain, ed., *Dio Chrysostom: Politics, Letters, and Philosophy*. Oxford: 108–24.
  2003. "Peer Polity Interaction in the Hellenistic Age." *P&P* 180: 9–39.
  2006. "A Gilt Statue for Konon at Erythrai?" *ZPE* 157: 124–26.

2013. *Statues and Cities: Honorific Portraits and Civic Identity in the Hellenistic World.* Oxford.

2014. Review of Siewert and Taeuber 2013. *BMCR* 2014.06.18.

2018. "Whatever Happened to Athens? Thoughts on the Great Convergence and Beyond." In Canevaro and Gray 2018: 277–98.

2024. *Polis: A New History of the Ancient Greek City-State from the Early Iron Age to the End of Antiquity.* Princeton, NJ.

Ma, J., N. Papazarkadas, and R. Parker, eds. 2009. *Interpreting the Athenian Empire.* London.

MacDowell, D. M. 1978. *The Law in Classical Athens.* Ithaca, NY.

Mack, W. 2015. *Proxeny and Polis: Institutional Networks in the Ancient Greek World.* Oxford.

Mackil, E. 2013. *Creating a Common Polity: Religion, Economy, and Politics in the Making of the Greek Koinon.* Berkeley, CA.

Madson, L. and A. Smith. 2024. "*Oligarchia* Revisited." *Klio* 106: 58–99.

Magalhães de Oliveira, J. C. 2020. "Late Antiquity: The Age of Crowds?" *P&P* 249: 3–52.

Magnetto, A. 2016. "Interstate Arbitration and Foreign Judges." In E. M. Harris and M. Canevaro, eds., *The Oxford Handbook of Ancient Greek Law.* Oxford: 192–215.

Malkin, I. and J. Blok. 2024. *Drawing Lots: From Egalitarianism to Democracy in Ancient Greece.* Oxford.

Manent, P. 2013. *Metamorphoses of the City: On the Western Dynamic.* Cambridge, MA.

Manin, B. 1997. *The Principles of Representative Government.* Cambridge.

Mann, C. 2007. *Die Demagogen und das Volk: Zur politischen Kommunikation im Athen des 5. Jahrhunderts v. Chr.* Berlin.

2012. "Gleichheiten und Ungleichheiten in der hellenistischen Polis: Überlegungen zum Stand der Forschung." In Mann and Scholz 2012: 11–27.

Mann, C. and P. Scholz, eds. 2012. *"Demokratie" im Hellenismus: Von der Herrschaft des Volkes zur Herrschaft der Honoratioren?* Mainz.

Mann, M. 1986. *The Sources of Social Power. Vol. 1: A History of Power from the Beginning to AD 1760.* Cambridge.

Martin, T. R. 2016. *Pericles: A Biography in Context.* Cambridge.

Matthaiou, A. P. 2010. *The Athenian Empire on Stone Revisited.* Athens.

2011. *Ta en tēi stēlēi gegrammena: Six Greek Historical Inscriptions of the Fifth Century BC.* Athens.

McLean, B. 2002. *An Introduction to Greek Epigraphy of the Hellenistic and Roman Periods from Alexander the Great down to the Reign of Constantine (323 BC–AD 337).* Ann Arbor, MI.

Meier, C. 1990. *The Greek Discovery of Politics.* Cambridge, MA.

Meier, L. 2019. *Kibyra in hellenistischer Zeit: Neue Staatsverträge und Ehreninschriften.* Vienna.

Meiggs, R. 1972. *The Athenian Empire.* Oxford.

Meister, J. B. 2020. *"Adel" und gesellschaftliche Differenzierung im archaischen und frühklassischen Griechenland.* Stuttgart.
Mencken, H. L. 1916. *A Little Book in C Major.* New York.
Meritt, B. D., H. T. Wade-Gery, and M. F. McGregor. 1939–49. *The Athenian Tribute Lists.* 4 vols. Princeton, NJ.
Meyer, E. A. 2013. "Inscriptions as Honors and the Athenian Epigraphic Habit." *Historia* 62: 453–505.
Migeotte, L. 1997. "L'évergétisme des citoyens aux périodes classique et hellénistique." In M. Christol and O. Masson, eds., *Actes du Xe Congrès international d'épigraphie grecque et latine.* Paris: 183–96.
   2014. *Les finances des cités grecques: Aux périodes classique et hellénistique.* Paris.
Millar, F. 1986. "The Political Character of the Classical Roman Republic, 200–151 BC." *JRS* 74: 1–19.
Miller, J. 2016. "Euergetism, Agonism, and Democracy: The Hortatory Intention in Late Classical and Early Hellenistic Athenian Honorific Decrees." *Hesperia* 85: 385–435.
Millett, P. 2007. *Theophrastus and His World.* Cambridge.
Missiou, A. 2011. *Literacy and Democracy in Fifth-Century Athens.* Cambridge.
Morris, I. 1996. "The Strong Principle of Equality and the Archaic Origins of Greek Democracy." In J. Ober and C. Hedrick, eds., *Dēmokratia: A Conversation on Democracies, Ancient and Modern.* Princeton, NJ: 19–48.
Muldoon, J. 2022. "A Socialist Republican Theory of Freedom and Government." *European Journal of Political Theory* 21: 47–67.
Müller, H. 1976. *Milesische Volksbeschlüsse.* Gottingen.
   1995. "Bemerkungen zu Funktion und Bedeutung des Rats in den hellenistischen Städten." In Wörrle and Zanker 1995: 41–54.
Müller, C. 2014. "(De)constructing *Politeia*: Reflections on Citizenship and the Bestowal of Privileges upon Foreigners in Hellenistic Democracies." *Annales HSS* 69: 533–54.
   2016. "Le prestige peut-il s'acheter? Réflexions sur la vente de la citoyenneté et des honneurs dans les cités grecques aux époques hellénistique et romain." In R. Baudry and F. Hurliet, eds., *Le prestige à Rome à la fin de la République et au début du Principate.* Paris: 281–94.
Muñiz Grijalvo, E. 2005. "Elites and Religious Change in Roman Athens." *Numen* 52: 255–82.
Nawotka, K. 1999. *Boule and Demos in Miletus and Its Pontic Colonies from Classical Age until Third Century AD.* Wroclaw.
Neils, J. 2001. *The Parthenon Frieze.* Cambridge.
Nietzsche, F. 1974. *The Gay Science.* Trans. Walter Kaufmann. New York.
Nyquist, M. 2013. *Arbitrary Rule: Slavery, Tyranny, and the Power of Life and Death.* Chicago, IL.
O'Neil, J. 1984–86. "The Political Elites of the Achaian and Aitolian Leagues." *Anc Soc* 15/17: 33–61.
   1995. *The Origins and Development of Ancient Greek Democracy.* Lanham, MD.
O'Shea, T. 2020. "Socialist Republicanism." *Political Theory* 48: 548–72.

Ober, J. 1989. *Mass and Elite in Democratic Athens: Rhetoric, Ideology, and the Power of the People.* Princeton, NJ.
  1996. "The Athenian Revolution of 508/7 BC: Violence, Authority, and the Origins of Democracy." In J. Ober, ed., *The Athenian Revolution.* Princeton, NJ: 32–52.
  1998. *Political Dissent in Democratic Athens: Intellectual Critics of Popular Rule.* Princeton, NJ.
  2003. "Tyrant Killing as Therapeutic *Stasis*: A Political Debate in Images and Texts." In K. Morgan, ed., *Popular Tyranny: Sovereignty and Its Discontents in Ancient Greece.* Austin, TX: 215–50.
  2007. "'I Besieged That Man': Democracy's Revolutionary Start." In K. A. Raaflaub, J. Ober, and R. W. Wallace, eds., *Origins of Democracy in Ancient Greece.* Berkeley, CA: 83–104.
  2008. *Democracy and Knowledge: Innovation and Learning in Classical Athens.* Princeton, NJ.
  2010. "Wealthy Hellas." *TAPA* 140: 241–86.
  2012. "Democracy's Dignity." *American Political Science Review* 106: 827–46.
Oliver, G. 2011. "Mobility, Society, and Economy in the Hellenistic Period." In Z. H. Archibald, J. K. Davies, and V. Gabrielsen, eds., *The Economies of Hellenistic Societies, Third to First Centuries BC.* Oxford: 345–67.
Oppeneer, T. 2018. "Assembly Politics and the Rhetoric of Honour in Chariton, Dio of Prusa and John Chrysostom." *Historia* 67: 223–43.
  2020. "Grain Crisis at Prusa: Persuading the People in the Imperial Period." *Mnemosyne* 73: 975–98.
Oranges, A. 2021. *Euthyna: Il rendiconto dei magistrati nella democrazia ateniese (V–IV secolo a.C.).* Milan.
Osborne, R. 1985. *Demos: The Discovery of Classical Attika.* Cambridge.
  2010. *Athens and Athenian Democracy.* Cambridge.
  2023. *The Oxford History of the Archaic Greek World. Volume II: Athens and Attica.* Oxford.
Ostwald, M. 1986. *From Popular Sovereignty to the Sovereignty of Law: Law, Society, and Politics in Fifth-Century Athens.* Berkeley, CA.
  1988. "The Reform of the Athenian State by Cleisthenes." In J. Boardman, N. G. L. Hammond, D. M. Lewis, and M. Ostwald, eds., *The Cambridge Ancient History Vol. 4.* Cambridge: 303–46.
Paga, J. 2020. *Building Democracy in Late Archaic Athens.* Oxford.
Papakonstantinou, Z. 2021. *Cursing for Justice: Magic, Disputes, and the Lawcourts in Classical Athens.* Stuttgart.
Papazarkadas, N. 2009. "Epigraphy and the Athenian Empire: Reshuffling the Chronological Cards." In Ma, Papazarkadas, and Parker 2009: 67–88.
  2017. "Judicial and Financial Administration in Late Hellenistic Athens: A New Decree of the Athenian Council." *Hesperia* 86: 325–57.
  2021. "Courts, Magistrates and Allotment Procedures: A New Kleroterion from Hellenistic Athens." In K. Harter-Uibopuu and W. Riess, eds., *Symposion 2019.* Vienna: 105–204.

2022. "Wastias: The Lion of Thebes." *JHS* 142: 298–316.
Papazarkadas, N. and D. Sourlas. 2012. "The Funerary Monument for the Argives Who Fell at Tanagra (*IG* I³1149): A New Fragment." *Hesperia* 81: 585–617.
Park, Y.-H. 2015. *Paul's Ekklesia as a Civic Assembly: Understanding the People of God in Their Political-Social World*. Tubingen.
Parker, R. 2005. *Polytheism and Society at Athens*. Oxford.
Patterson, O. 1991. *Freedom Vol. 1: Freedom in the Making of Western Culture*. New York.
Pébarthe, C. 2006. *Cité, démocratie et écriture : Histoire d'alphabétisation d'Athènes à l'époque classique*. Paris.
Perrin-Saminadayar, E. 2007. *Éducation, culture et société à Athènes: Les acteurs de la vie culturelle athénienne (229–88)*. Paris.
Pettit, P. 1997. *Republicanism: A Theory of Freedom and Government*. Oxford.
Phillips, D. 2013. *The Law of Ancient Athens*. Ann Arbor, MI.
Piepenbrink, K. 2021. "Die Rhetorica ad Alexandrum und die attischen Redner: Politische Differenzierung und praktische Rhetorik im Griechenland des 4. Jhd. V. Chr." *Klio* 103: 436–62.
Piérart, M. 2020. "Ἀργείων πολιτεία." In O. Curty, ed., *Kluton Argos: Histoire, société et institutions d'Argos. Choix d'articles de Michel Piérart*. Bordeaux: 113–27.
Piovan, D. and G. Giorgini, eds. 2020. *Brill's Companion to the Reception of Athenian Democracy*. Leiden.
Pont, A.-V. 2020. *La fin de la cité grecque: Metamorphoses et disparition d'un modèle politique et institutionnel local en Asie Mineure*. Geneva.
Pownall, F. 2020. "Politics and the Pamphlet of Stesimbrotus of Thasos." *Mouseion* 17 Suppl. 1: 125–49.
Price, J. 2001. *Thucydides and Internal War*. Cambridge.
Pritchard, D. 2015. *Public Spending and Democracy in Classical Athens*. Austin, TX.
Pritchard, D., ed. 2024. *The Athenian Funeral Oration: After Nicole Loraux*. Cambridge.
Quass, F. 1993. *Die Honoratiorenschicht in den Städten des griechischen Ostens: Untersuchungen zur politischen und sozialen Entwicklung in hellenistischer und römischer Zeit*. Stuttgart.
Raaflaub, K. A. 1983. "Democracy, Oligarchy, and the Concept of the 'Free Citizen' in Late Fifth-Century Athens." *Political Theory* 11: 517–44.
  1996. "Equalities and Inequalities in Athenian Democracy." In J. Ober and C. Hedrick, eds., *Dēmokratia: A Conversation on Democracies, Ancient and Modern*. Princeton, NJ: 139–74.
  2003. "Stick and Glue: The Function of Tyranny in Fifth-Century Athenian Democracy." In K. A. Morgan, ed., *Popular Tyranny: Sovereignty and Its Discontents in Ancient Greece*. Austin, TX: 59–94.
  2004. *The Discovery of Freedom in Ancient Greece*. Chicago, IL.
  2006. "Athenian and Spartan *Eunomia*, or: What to Do with Solon's Timocracy?" In J. Blok and A. Lardinois, eds., *Solon of Athens: New Historical and Philological Approaches*. Leiden: 390–428.

2007. "The Breakthrough of *Dēmokratia* in Mid-Fifth-Century Athens." In K. A. Raaflaub, J. Ober, and R. W. Wallace, eds., *Origins of Democracy in Ancient Greece*. Berkeley, CA: 105–54.

Raaflaub, K. A. and R. W. Wallace. 2007. "'People's Power' and Egalitarian Trends in Archaic Greece." In K. A. Raaflaub, J. Ober, and R. W. Wallace, eds., *Origins of Democracy in Ancient Greece*. Berkeley, CA: 22–48.

Rapp, C. 2005. *Holy Bishops in Late Antiquity: The Nature of Christian Leadership in an Age of Transition*. Berkeley, CA.

Raubitschek, A. E. 1962. "Demokratia." *Hesperia* 31: 238–43.

Rhodes, P. J. 1972. *The Athenian Boule*. Oxford.

1991. "The Athenian Code of Laws, 410–399 BC." *JHS* 111: 87–100.

2000. "Oligarchs in Athens." In R. Brock and S. Hodkinson, eds., *Alternatives to Athens*. Oxford: 119–36.

2001. "Public Documents in the Greek States: Archives and Inscriptions, Parts 1 and 2." *G&R* 48: 33–44, 136–53.

2003. "Nothing to Do with Democracy: Athenian Drama and the Polis." *JHS* 123: 104–19.

2008. "After the Three-Bar Sigma Controversy: The History of Athenian Imperialism Reassessed." *CQ* 58: 501–6.

2016. "Demagogues and *Demos* in Athens." *Polis* 33: 243–64.

Rhodes, P. J. with D. M. Lewis. 1997. *Decrees of the Greek States*. Oxford.

Rife, J. L. 2008. "The Burial of Herodes Atticus: Élite Identity, Urban Society, and Public Memory in Roman Greece." *JHS* 128: 92–127.

Robert, L. 1960. "Recherches épigraphiques." *REA* 62: 276–361.

1966. "Inscriptions d'Aphrodisias." *AC* 35: 401–32. Reprinted in Robert 2007: 623–45.

1969. "Théophane de Mytilène à Constantinople." *CRAI* 113: 42–64. Reprinted in Robert 2007: 603–21.

1973. "Les juges étrangers dans la cité grecque." In E. von Caemmerer, J.-H. Kaiser, G. Kegel, W. Müller-Freienfels, and H.-J. Wolff, eds., *Xenion: Festschrift für Pan. J. Zepos*. Athens: 765–82. Reprinted in Robert 2007: 299–314.

1977. "La titulature de Nicée et de Nicomédie : La gloire et la haine." *HSCP* 81: 1–39. Reprinted in Robert 2007: 673–703.

1994. *Le Martyre de Pionios, prêtre de Smyrne*. G. W. Bowersock, C. P. Jones, A. Vaillant, eds. Washington, DC.

2007. *Choix d'Écrits*. D. Rousset, ed. Paris.

Roberts, J. T. 1982. *Accountability in Athenian Government*. Madison, WI.

1994. *Athens on Trial: The Antidemocratic Tradition in Western Thought*. Princeton, NJ.

2017. *The Plague of War: Athens, Sparta, and the Struggle for Ancient Greece*. Oxford.

Robinson, E. W. 1997. *The First Democracies: Early Popular Government outside Athens*. Stuttgart.

2006. "Thucydides and Democratic Peace." *Journal of Military Ethics* 5: 243–53.

2011. *Democracy beyond Athens: Popular Government in the Greek Classical Age*. Cambridge.
Rosanvallon, P. 2006. *Democracy Past and Future*. New York.
Rose, P. W. 2012. *Class in Archaic Greece*. Cambridge.
Roselli, D. K. 2011. *Theater of the People: Spectators and Society in Ancient Athens*. Austin, TX.
Rosen, R. W. and H. P. Foley. 2020. *Aristophanes and Politics: New Studies*. Leiden.
Rosenbloom, D. 2004. "*Ponēroi* vs. *Chrēstoi*: The Ostracism of Hyperbolos and the Struggle for Hegemony in Athens after the Death of Perikles, pts. 1 and 2." *TAPA* 134: 55–105, 323–58.
Rosivach, V. 1987. "Autochthony and the Athenians." *CQ* 37: 294–306.
Roubineau, J.-M. 2015. *Les cités grecques (Vie–Iie siècle avant J.-C.): Essai d'histoire sociale*. Paris.
Roueché, C. 1984. "Acclamations in the Later Roman Empire: New Evidence from Aphrodisias." *JRS* 74: 181–99.
Roueché, C., ed. 1989. *Aphrodisias in Late Antiquity*. London.
Rousseau, J.-J. 1973. *The Social Contract and Discourses*. London.
Roy, J. 2000. "Problems of Democracy in the Arcadian Confederacy 370–362 B C." In R. Brock and S. Hodkinson, eds., *Alternatives to Athens*. Oxford: 308–26.
Rubinstein, L. 2000. *Litigation and Cooperation: Supporting Speakers in the Courts of Classical Athens*. Stuttgart.
Ruschenbusch, E. 1995. "Zur Verfassungsgeschichte Griechenlands." In K. Kinzl, ed., *Demokratia: Der Weg zur Demokratie bei den Griechen*. Darmstadt.
Ruzé, F. 2017. "The Empire of the Spartans (404–371)." In A. Powell, ed., *A Companion to Sparta*. Hoboken, NJ: 320–53.
Saba, S. 2020. *Isopoliteia in Hellenistic Times*. Leiden.
Saldutti, V. 2014. *Cleone: Un politico ateniese*. Bari.
2015. "Sul demagogo e la demagogia in età classica: Una sintesi critica." *IncAnt* 13: 81–110.
Salmeri, G. 2000. "Dio, Rome, and the Civic Life of Asia Minor." In S. Swain, ed., *Dio Chrysostom: Politics, Letters, and Philosophy*. Oxford: 53–92.
Samons, L. J. 2004. *What's Wrong with Democracy? From Athenian Practice to American Worship*. Berkeley, CA.
2016. *Pericles and the Conquest of History: A Political Biography*. Cambridge.
Sandelin, K.-G. 2014. "Philo as a Jew." In T. Seland, ed., *Reading Philo: A Handbook to Philo of Alexandria*. Grand Rapids, MI: 19–46.
Sarrazanas, C. 2021. *La cité des spectacles permanents: Organisation et organisateurs des concours civiques dans l'Athènes hellénistique et impériale*. Bordeaux.
Sartre-Fauriat, A. and M. Sartre. 2000. "Notables en conflit dans le monde grec sous le Haut-Empire." *Cahiers d'histoire* 45: 507–32.
Savalli-Lestrade, I. 2009. "Usages civiques et usages dynastiques de la damnatio memoriae dans le monde hellénistique." In S. Benoist, A. Daguet-Gagey, C. Hoët-Cauwenberghe, eds., *Mémoires partagées, mémoires disputées: Écriture et réécriture de l'histoire*. Metz: 127–58.

Saxonhouse, A. 2005. *Free Speech and Democracy in Ancient Athens*. Cambridge.
Scafuro, A. 1994. "Witnessing and False Witnessing: Proving Citizenship and Kin Identity in Fourth-Century Athens." In A. L. Boegehold and A. Scafuro, eds., *Athenian Identity and Civic Ideology*. Baltimore, MD: 156–98.
Schaps, D. 1998. "What Was Free about a Free Athenian Woman?" *TAPA* 128: 161–88.
Schmitt, H. H. 1969. *Die Staatsverträge des Altertums*. Vol. 3. Munich.
Scholz, P. 2012. "'Demokratie in hellenistischer Zeit' im Licht der literarischen Überlieferung." In Mann and Scholz 2012: 28–55.
Schubert, C. 2021. *Isonomia: Entwicklung und Geschichte*. Berlin.
Schwartzberg, M. 2014. *Counting the Many: The Origins and Limits of Supermajority Rule*. Cambridge.
Sebillotte-Cuchet, V. 2017. "*Gender Studies* et domination masculine: Les citoyennes de l'Athènes classique, un défi pour l'historien des institutions." *CCG* 28: 7–30.
Seland, T. 2014. "Philo as a Citizen: *Homo Politicus*." In T. Seland, ed., *Reading Philo: A Handbook to Philo of Alexandria*. Grand Rapids, MI: 47–74.
Shear, J. L. 2011. *Polis and Revolution: Responding to Oligarchy in Classical Athens*. Cambridge.
  2021. *Serving Athena: The Festival of the Panathenaia and the Construction of Athenian Identities*. Cambridge.
Shear, Jr., T. L. 2016. *Trophies of Victory: Public Building in Periklean Athens*. Princeton, NJ.
Sheppard, A. R. R. 1984–1986. "*Homonoia* in the Greek Cities of the Roman Empire." *Anc Soc* 15/17: 229–52.
Shipley, G. 2000. *The Greek World after Alexander, 323–30 BC*. London.
Sickinger, J. P. 1999. *Public Records and Archives in Classical Athens*. Chapel Hill.
  2009. "Nothing to Do with Democracy: 'Formulae of Disclosure' and the Athenian Epigraphic Habit." In L. Mitchell and L. Rubinstein, eds., *Greek History and Epigraphy: Essays in Honour of P. J. Rhodes*. Swansea: 87–102.
  2017. "New Ostraka from the Athenian Agora." *Hesperia* 86: 443–508.
Siewert, P. and H. Taeuber. 2013. *Neue Inschriften von Olympia: die ab 1896 veröffentlichten Texte*. Vienna.
Simonton, M. 2015. "The Cry from the Herald's Stone: The Revolutionary Logic behind the Rhodian Democratic Uprising of 395 BCE." *TAPA* 145: 281–324.
  2017. *Classical Greek Oligarchy: A Political History*. Princeton, NJ.
  2018a. "The Local History of Hippias of Erythrai: Politics, Place, Memory, and Monumentality." *Hesperia* 87: 497–543.
  2018b. "The Burial of Brasidas and the Politics of Commemoration in the Classical Period." *AJPh* 139: 1–30.
  2018c. "Who Made Athens Great? Three Recent Books on Pericles and Athenian Politics." *Polis* 35: 220–35.
  2019. "The Telos Reconciliation Dossier (*IG* XII.4.132): Democracy, Demagogues and Stasis in an Early Hellenistic Polis." *JHS* 139: 187–209.

2020. "Teisamenos the Son of Mechanion: New Evidence for an Athenian Demagogue." *TAPA* 150: 1–38.

2021. "Representing the Demos: Adapting Insights from the Constructivist Turn in Political Representation." *Ramus* 50: 129–44.

2022. "Demagogues and Demagoguery in Hellenistic Greece." *Polis* 39: 35–76.

2024. "Civil Strife and the Persistence of 'Populism' in Hellenistic Greece: Democracy, Demagogues, and Contemporary Theories of Populism." In C. Riedweg, R. Schmid, and A. V. Walser, eds., *Demokratie und Populismus in der griechischen Antike und heute*. Berlin: 367–91.

2025. "'Ambition for Office' and the Nature of Election in Ancient Greek Democracies." *Journal of Sortition* 1: 109–36.

Simpson, P. 2011. "A Corruption of Oligarchs." In D. Tabachnick and T. Koivukoski, eds., *On Oligarchy: Ancient Lessons for Global Politics*. Toronto: 70–89.

Sinclair, R. K. 1991. *Participation and Democracy at Athens*. Cambridge.

Sintomer, Y. 2023. *The Government of Chance: Sortition and Democracy from Athens to the Present*. Cambridge.

Skinner, Q. 1998. *Liberty before Liberalism*. Cambridge.

Smith, R. R. R. 1993. *The Monument of C. Julius Zoilos*. Mainz.

Sobak, R. 2015. "Sokrates among the Shoemakers." *Hesperia* 84: 669–712.

Sommerstein, A. H. 1996. "How to Avoid Being a *Komoidoumenos*." *CQ* 46: 327–56.

Spawforth, A. 2011. *Greece and the Augustan Cultural Revolution*. Cambridge.

Stefanaki, V. A. 2008. "The Coinage of Telos in the Late Classical and Early Hellenistic Periods." *NC* 168: 21–32.

Steinbock, B. 2013. *Social Memory in Athenian Public Discourse: Uses and Meanings of the Past*. Ann Arbor, MI.

Stovall, T. 2021. *White Freedom: The Racial History of an Idea*. Princeton, NJ.

Strauss, B. 1996. "The Athenian Trireme, School of Democracy." In J. Ober and C. Hedrick, eds., *Dēmokratia: A Conversation on Democracies, Ancient and Modern*. Princeton, NJ: 313–25.

Stroud, R. S. 1971. "Greek Inscriptions: Theozotides and the Athenian Orphans." *Hesperia* 40: 280–301.

2006. *The Athenian Empire on Stone*. Athens.

Strubbe, J. H. M. 2004. "Cultic Honours for Benefactors in the Cities of Asia Minor." In L. de Ligt, E. Hemelrijk, and J. H. Singor, eds., *Roman Rule and Civic Life: Local and Regional Perspectives*. Amsterdam: 315–29.

Swain, S. 1996. *Hellenism and Empire: Language, Classicism, and Power in the Greek World, AD 50–250*. Oxford.

Tacon, J. 2001. "Ecclesiastic *Thorubos*: Interventions, Interruptions, and Popular Involvement in the Athenian Assembly." *G&R* 48: 173–92.

Tamiolaki, M. 2013. "A Citizen as a Slave of the State? Oligarchic Perceptions of Democracy in Xenophon." *GRBS* 53: 31–50.

Taylor, C. 2007. "From the Whole Citizen Body? The Sociology of Election and Lot in the Athenian Democracy." *Hesperia* 76: 323–45.

2017. *Poverty, Wealth, and Well-Being: Experiencing Penia in Democratic Athens.* Oxford.
Teegarden, D. 2013. *Death to Tyrants! Ancient Greek Democracy and the Struggle against Tyranny.* Princeton, NJ.
Theocharaki, A. M. 2019. *The Ancient Circuit Walls of Athens.* Berlin.
Thériault, G. 1996. *Le culte d'*Homonoia *dans les cités grecques.* Lyons.
Thomsen, C. 2020. *Politics of Association in Hellenistic Rhodes.* Edinburgh.
Thonemann, P. 2016. *The Hellenistic Age.* Oxford.
 2020. *An Ancient Dream Manual: Artemidorus'* The Interpretation of Dreams. Oxford.
Thornton, J. 2001. "Gli aristoi, l'*akriton plēthos* e la provincializzazione della Licia." *Mediterraneo Antico* 4: 427–46.
 2019. "Istituzioni democratiche e tensioni sociali: Dalla *polis* ellenistica alla città imperiale." In N. Andrade, C. Marcaccini, G. Marconi, D. Violante, eds., *Roman Imperial Cities in the East and Central-Southern Italy.* Rome: 55–90.
Todd, S. C. 1993. *The Shape of Athenian Law.* Oxford.
Toher, M. 2017. *Nicolaus of Damascus:* The Life of Augustus *and* The Autobiography. Cambridge.
Traill, J. S. 1975. *The Political Organization of Attica: A Study of the Demes, Trittyes, Phylai, and Their Representation in the Athenian Council.* Hesperia Supplement 14. Princeton, NJ.
Treheux, J. 1989. "Sur les *probouloi* en Grèce." *BCH* 113: 241–47.
Urso, G. 2019. "Δημαγωγοί e δημαγωγία nella storiografia greca d'età romana." *Erga-Logoi* 7: 83–116.
van Bremen, R. 1996. *The Limits of Participation: Women and Civic Life in the Greek East in the Hellenistic and Roman Periods.* Leiden.
van Nijf, O. M. and R. Alston, eds. 2011. *Popular Culture in the Greek City after the Classical Age.* Leuven.
Vassallo, C. 2013. "Ein vergessenes Fragment eines sokratischen Dialogs: *PSI* xi 1215." *ZPE* 187: 77–80.
Veyne, P. 1990. *Bread and Circuses: Historical Sociology and Political Pluralism.* London.
Villacèque, N. 2013a. "θόρυβος τῶν πολλῶν: Le spectre du spectacle démocratique." In A. Macé, ed., *Le savoir public: Savoirs collectifs et figures publiques du savoir en Grèce Ancienne.* Besancon: 287–312.
 2013b. *Specateurs de paroles! Délibération démocratique et théâtre à Athènes à l'époque classique.* Rennes.
Vlassopoulos, K. 2007. "Free Spaces: Identity, Experience and Democracy in Classical Athens." *CQ* 57: 33–52.
Vlastos, G. 1953. "Isonomia." *AJPh* 74: 337–66.
Walbank, F. W. 1995. "Polybius' Perception of the One and the Many." In I. Malkin and Z. W. Rubinsohn, eds., *Leaders and Masses in the Roman World.* Leiden: 201–222.
Wallace, R. W. 2015. *Reconstructing Damon: Music, Wisdom Teaching, and Politics in Perikles' Athens.* Oxford.

Wallace, S. 2014. "History and Hindsight: The Importance of Euphron of Sikyon for the Athenian Democracy in 318/7." In H. Hauben and A. Meeus, eds., *The Age of the Successors and the Creation of the Hellenistic Kingdoms (323–276 BC)*. Studia Hellenistica 53. Leuven: 599–629.

Walser, A. V. 2012. "ΔΙΚΑΣΤΗΡΙΑ: Rechtsprechung und Demokratie in den hellenistischen Poleis." In Mann and Scholz 2012: 75–108.

Waxman, W. and A. McCulloch. 2022. *The Democracy Manifesto: A Dialogue on Why Elections Need to Be Replaced with Sortition*. Lanham, MD.

Wecowski, M. 2023. *Athenian Ostracism and Its Original Purpose: A Prisoner's Dilemma*. Oxford.

Welborn, L. L. 2019. "How 'Democratic' Was the Pauline *Ekklēsia*? An Assessment with Special Reference to the Christ Groups of Roman Corinth." *NTS* 65: 289–309.

Werlings, M.-J. 2010. *Le dèmos avant la démocratie: Mots, concepts, réalités historiques*. Paris.

Whitehead, D. 1977. *The Ideology of the Athenian Metic*. Cambridge.

　　1983. "Competitive Outlay and Community Profit: *Philotimia* in Democratic Athens." *C&M* 34: 55–74.

　　1986. *The Demes of Attica, 508/7-ca.250 B.C. A Political and Social Study*. Princeton, NJ.

Whittow, M. 1996. *The Making of Byzantium, 600–1025*. Berkeley, CA.

Wiemer, U. 2011. "Von der Bürgerschule zum aristokratischen Klub? Die athenische Ephebie in der römischen Kaizerzeit." *Chiron* 41: 487–538.

Wijma, S. M. 2014. *Embracing the Immigrant: The Participation of Metics in Athenian Polis Religion (5th–4th Century BC)*. Stuttgart.

Williamson, C. G. 2013. "As God Is My Witness: Civic Oaths in Ritual Space as a Means towards Rational Cooperation in the Hellenistic Poleis." In R. Alston, O. M. van Nijf, and C. G. Williamson, eds., *Cults, Creeds and Identities in the Greek City after the Classical Age*. Leuven: 119–74.

Wilson, P. J. 1992. "Demosthenes 21 (*Against Meidias*): Democratic Abuse." *PCPhS* 37: 164–95.

　　2000. *The Athenian Institution of the* Khoregia: *The Chorus, the City and the Stage*. Cambridge.

　　2009. "Tragic Honours and Democracy: Neglected Evidence for the Politics of the Athenian Dionysia." *CQ* 59: 8–29.

Winkler, J. J. and F. Zeitlin, eds. 1990. *Nothing to Do with Dionysos? Athenian Drama in Its Social Context*. Princeton, NJ.

Wohl, V. 2002. *Love Among the Ruins: The Erotics of Democracy in Classical Athens*. Princeton, NJ.

Wolpert, A. 2002. *Remembering Defeat: Civil War and Civic Memory in Ancient Athens*. Baltimore, MD.

Wörrle, M. 1988. *Stadt und Fest im kaiserzeitlichen Kleinasien: Studien zu einer agonistischen Stiftung aus Oinoanda*. Munich.

1995. "Vom tugendsamen Jüngling zum gestressten Euergeten. Überlegungen zum Bürgerbild hellenistischer Ehrendekrete." In Wörrle and Zanker 1995: 241–50.

Wörrle, M. and P. Zanker, eds. 1995. *Stadtbild und Bürgerbild im Hellenismus.* Munich.

Worthington, I. 2020. *Athens after Empire: A History from Alexander the Great to the Emperor Hadrian.* Oxford.

Yarrow, L. M. 2006. *Historiography at the End of the Republic: Provincial Perspectives on Roman Rule.* Oxford.

Yunis, H. 1996. *Taming Democracy: Models of Political Rhetoric in Classical Athens.* Ithaca, NY.

Zaccarini, M. 2017. *The Lame Hegemony: Cimon of Athens and the Failure of Panhellenism, ca. 478–450 BC.* Bologna.

2018. "The Fate of the Lawgiver: The Invention of the Reforms of Ephialtes and the 'Patrios Politeia.'" *Historia* 67: 495–512.

Zuiderhoek, A. 2009. *The Politics of Munificence in the Roman Empire: Citizens, Elites and Benefactors in Asia Minor.* Cambridge.

2017. "Un-civic Benefactions? Gifts to Non-citizens and Civic Honours in the Greek Cities of the Roman East." In Heller and van Nijf 2017: 182–98.

Index Locorum

Literary Texts
Aelius Aristides
  Orations
  23: 164
  24.22: 168
Aeneas Tacticus
  11.7: 54
  11.7–10: 113, 118
  11.10b: 54, 113
  11.13–15: 113, 118
  11.15: 54
  17.2–4: 113
Aeschines
  1.23: 50
  1.77: 138
  3.190: 88
  3.220: 51
Aeschylus
  Suppliants
  604: 35
Agatharchides (ed. Müller)
  Fr. 18: 121
Agathias
  3.8.8: 174
Alcaeus (ed. Liberman)
  Fr. 130b.18: 12
Andocides
  1.96–98: 89, 117
  Fr. 5 Dalmeyda: 71
Antiphon
  5.69–70: 81
  Fr. 1a Nicole: 53
Appian
  B Civ.
  4.9.66: 166
  Samn.
  16: 121
  Syr.
  65: 127
Archilochus (ed. West)
  Fr. 242: 34

Aristophanes
  Acharnians
  45: 51
  530: 53
  Aves
  1022: 61
  Ecclesiazusae
  128: 50
  130: 51
  176–77: 84
  473–75: 55
  Equites
  Passim: 54, 94
  42–43: 58
  51: 78
  66: 121
  214: 121
  280–81: 67
  692: 121
  956: 161
  1017: 84
  1352: 78
  Nubes
  588–89: 55
  Pax
  632–48: 45
  684: 84
  1183–84: 56
  Ranae
  950–52: 141
  1422–25: 94
  Thesmophoriazusae
  295–351: 50
  Vespae
  Passim: 67
  488–99: 50
  835–42: 84
Aristotle
  Politics
  3.1275a22–23: 104, 134
  3.1275b5–7: 104

Aristotle (cont.)
  3.1275b35-37: 137
  3.1275b35-37: 15
  3.1277b13-16: 22
  3.1278a26-34: 139
  3.1278a27-29: 48
  3.1279a17-21: 82
  3.1280a24-25: 73
  3.1286b20-22: 16, 104
  4.1289b4-5: 104
  4.1292a12-23: 94
  4.1292a13-15: 38
  4.1292a15-30: 105
  4.1292a23-25: 82
  4.1294b7-9: 64
  4.1296a9-10: 16
  4.1296a13-16: 16
  4.1296a22-23: 104
  4.1298a28-31: 23
  4.1300a32: 105
  5.1301a28-30: 73
  5.1301a31-33: 73
  5.1301b35-40: 73
  5.1302a8-11: 104
  5.1302b23-24: 120
  5.1302b27-30: 19, 38
  5.1303a6-8: 18
  5.1304a27-29: 62
  5.1304b19-1305a7: 105
  5.1304b20-24: 109
  5.1304b25-31: 120
  5.1305a5-7: 109
  5.1305a26-27: 94
  5.1305a28-32: 64
  5.1305b18-19: 6
  5.1306a35-36: 6, 17
  5.1306b39-1307a1: 11
  5.1308a14-16: 63
  5.1310a9-10: 92, 115
  5.1310a25-36: 75
  5.1310a30-31: 74
  5.1310b30-31: 94
  6.1317a40-b13: 75
  6.1317a40-b17: 140
  6.1317b1-7: 105
  6.1317b17-1318a10: 22, 105
  6.1317b28-30: 23
  6.1319b23-27: 31
  6.1320a4-6: 109, 120
  6.1320b11-14: 102
  6.1320b18-20: 22
  7.1326b20-21: 138
  Rhetoric
  1.1354a16-21: 66
  1.1358b6-28: 66
  1.1365b32: 62
Fragments (ed. Rose)
  Fr. 592: 19
  Fr. 611.40: 17
[*Rhetorica ad Alexandrum*]
  1424a13-38: 105
  1424a40-b3: 159
[*Constitution of the Athenians*]
  8.4: 62
  9.1: 67
  13.4: 31
  13.5: 25
  15.2: 6, 17
  18: 28
  20: 6
  20–22: 13
  20.1: 14
  20.2: 29
  20.4: 15
  20.6: 31
  21.6: 26
  22: 68
  22.4–8: 68
  24.3: 21, 61, 66
  25.1–2: 13
  26.3: 48
  27.3–4: 22
  27.4: 78
  28.1–3: 53
  28.2: 35
  28.3: 54, 78
  28.4: 55
  35.2: 67, 128
  39: 46
  40.1–2: 89
  40.3: 82
  41.2: 13, 82
  41.3: 111
  42.1: 48
  42.2–5: 49
  43.5: 68
  44.1: 63
  44.2–3: 51
  45.4: 63, 121
  48.3–5: 79
  49.4: 56
  53.2–6: 71
  55: 79
  61.1: 64
  62.2: 63, 67
  62.3: 21
  63–69: 66
Arrian
  Anab.
  1.17.11: 128

Index Locorum 213

Artemidorus
  1.79: 167
  2.12: 167
  3.16: 167
  3.42: 162
Athenaeus
  13.604d: 37
  15.695a-b: 28

Bacchylides
  13.149: 35

Cassius Dio
  60.17.3: 166
Charax, *BNJ* 103
  F 19: 118
Chariton
  3.4.11: 163
  8.8.13–14: 155
Cicero
  Republic
  3.35.48: 108, 159
Comica Adespota (ed. Kassel and Austin)
  Fr. 700: 92
Cratinus (ed. Kassel and Austin)
  Fr. 73: 86
Critias (DK 88)
  A 13: 94, 123

Democritus (DK 68)
  B 251: 141
Demosthenes
  9.60: 118
  15.1: 77
  18.91: 123
  18.170: 51
  19.70: 50
  19.136: 121, 167
  19.256: 55
  20.16: 74
  22: 63
  25.40: 84
  57.18: 138
  57.34–35: 138
  60: 59
Dio Chrysostom
  32.11: 162, 163
  32.22–24: 167
  32.25–27: 163
  34.16: 160
  34.21–23: 162
  34.31: 52, 161
  34.37: 166
  38.2: 166
  38.22: 149
  39–40: 164
  40.8: 164
  43.11: 156
  44.4: 156
  46.10: 163
  47.18: 156, 164
  48.10: 155, 171
  56.10: 63, 121, 166
Diodorus Siculus
  11.72.2: 89
  11.87.3: 71
  11.87.3–6: 71
  11.87.5: 54, 67
  13.34.6: 54, 62, 81
  13.48.7: 138
  13.95: 94
  13.97.1: 138
  15.57.3–58: 54, 92
  15.81.5: 119
  15.95.3: 118
  18.18.4: 108
  18.74.3: 108
  19.6: 119
  20.79.3: 108
  20.84.3: 111, 139
  20.93.6–7: 130
Diogenes Laertius
  1.87: 34
  5.77: 129
Dionysius of Halicarnassus
  Ant. Rom.
  19.4–5: 121
  19.7.2: 121
Dissoi Logoi (DK 90)
  B 7: 61, 62, 91

Eupolis (ed. Kassel and Austin)
  Fr. 102: 53
  Fr. 245: 67
Euripides
  Suppliants
  243: 84
  412–16: 58
Evagrius
  2 p. 55: 173

Gorgias (DK 82)
  B 6: 59
  B 20: 144
Gregory of Nyssa
  Vol. 46, p. 908 Migne: 171

Harpocration
  Aixōnēsin: 72
  Diapsēphisis: 138

Harpocration (cont.)
  Potamos: 72
Hellenica Oxyrhynchia (ed. Chambers)
  18.1–3: 95
Heniochus (ed. Kassel and Austin)
  Fr. 5: 123
Heraclitus (DK 22)
  B 104: 34
  B 121: 25, 69
Herodian
  3.2.7–8: 167
Herodotus
  1.59.3: 31
  3.80.6: 20, 23, 62, 74, 79
  3.81.2: 94
  3.82.4: 84
  4.137.2: 5
  5.30–37: 14
  5.37.2: 19
  5.55–57: 28
  5.66: 6
  5.66.2: 14, 26
  5.66–78: 13
  5.70.1: 15
  5.72.1–2: 15
  5.77–78: 16
  5.78: 74
  5.99.1: 17
  6.43.3: 19
  6.83: 18
  6.88–91: 14
  6.107.1: 168
  6.109.2: 61
  6.131.1: 13
  7.155.2: 6
Hesiod
  Theogony
    902: 11
Hesychius, *BNJ* 390
  F 6: 170
Hippias of Erythrae, *BNJ* 421
  F 1: 114
Historia Augusta
  Marcus
    25.9: 167
Homer
  Iliad
    1.490: 161
    2.204–205: 38
    7.234: 38
  Odyssey
    17.487: 11
  Homeric Hymns
    30.11: 11

Hyperides
  6: 59
Idomeneus, *BNJ* 338
  F 2: 55
  FF 11–15: 55
Ioannes Chrysostomus
  SC 188: 171
Ion of Chios, *BNJ* 392
  F 6: 37
  F 13: 36
  F 14: 36
  F 15: 36
Isocrates
  7.20: 74, 76
  7.26: 62
  8.14: 77
  8.82: 57
  8.88: 137
Istros, *BNJ* 334
  F 16: 50

Justin
  16.4.1–10: 119

Livy
  31.44.3: 130
  31.44.4: 129
  34.51.6: 158
  43.4.8–13: 124
[Longinus]
  de sublim.
    44.2: 168
Lycurgus
  1.41: 138
  1.79: 116
  1.122–27: 89
Lysias
  2: 59
  2.66: 139
  13.12: 55
  16: 79
  24: 56
  26: 79
  31: 79

Memnon, *BNJ* 434
  F 27.6: 165
Menander Rhetor
  P. 359: 168

Nepos
  Dio
    6.4: 38
Nicolaus of Damascus, *BNJ* 90

Index Locorum

F 60: 12
F 131: 155
F 138: 155
Nicostratus (ed. Kassel and Austin)
   Fr. 30: 140

Pausanias
   1.3.3: 123
   7.2.10: 127
   7.16.9: 103, 108, 158
Phaenias of Eresus, *BNJ* 1012
   F 4: 94
Philippus of Pergamum, *BNJ* 95
   F 1: 164
Philo
   de Joseph.
   67: 147, 163
   de spec. leg.
   4.237: 147
Philochorus, *BNJ* 328
   F 30: 68
   F 37: 86 [change from 327 to 328]
   F 64: 109
   F 121: 86, 87
   F 181: 128
Philostratus
   VS
   2 pp. 565–66 Kayser: 156
   2 p. 559 Kayser: 156
Pindar
   Nemeans
   10: 34
   Olympians
   3: 34
   5: 34
   Pythians
   2.86–87: 33
   Fragments (ed. Snell and Maehler)
   Fr. 52a: 35
Plato
   Apology
   36d: 67
   Gorgias
   455e: 86
   481e: 52
   519a: 86
   Laws
   8.832c: 34
   Menexenus
   59
   Protagoras
   319d: 51
   Republic
   1.338e: 82
   6.492c: 52, 161

   6.493a-b: 92
   8.551b: 61
   8.557a: 62
   8.557b: 75
   8.560e-61a: 76
   8.561e: 74
   8.563b: 140
   9.588c: 91
Plato Comicus (ed. Kassel and Austin)
   Fr. 203: 71
Pliny the Elder
   NH
   35.137: 123
   35.69: 123
Pliny the Younger
   Epistles
   10.79: 158
   10.81: 164
   10.112: 158
Plutarch
   Moralia
   68a-b: 88
   349f: 126
   801a-b: 166
   802d-e: 166
   810e: 164
   813a-b: 163
   813e-f: 164
   814a: 164
   824d: 164
   825d: 164
   842a: 136
   849a: 138
   850f-51f: 145
   851f: 144
   852a: 153
   852d: 145
   Vit. Alc.
   13.3–5: 70
   Vit. Arat.
   34.4: 114
   49.2–3: 118
   53.4: 127
   Vit. Arist.
   7.1–2: 69
   7.2: 25
   7.5–6: 68
   26.3: 81
   Vit. Caes.
   32.9: 168
   Vit. Cim.
   4.5: 36
   9.1: 36
   10.5: 144
   16.8: 36

Plutarch (cont.)
  17.3–4: 86
  Vit. Dem.
  8.4: 78
  Vit. Dio
  37.3: 120
  37.5: 141
  53.1: 114
  53.2–3: 119
  53.4: 13
  Vit. Lyc.
  6: 10
  Vit. Lys.
  19.2: 92
  21.4: 92
  Vit. Nic.
  11.3–4: 70
  Vit. Per.
  5.3: 36
  13.5: 86
  16.3: 53
  Vit. Pomp.
  10.5: 151
  Vit. Pyrrh.
  13.2: 102, 110
  13.2–5: 121
  Vit. Tim.
  22.1–3: 129
Pollux, *Onomasticon*
  8.19: 68
Polybius
  2.38.7: 112
  3.11.7: 38
  4.31.2: 118
  5.88.5–8: 123
  5.104.10: 102
  6.57.9: 113
  7.10.1: 118
  15.21.1–2: 119
  16.31.1–5: 111, 136
  16.31.2: 139
  21.31.9–13: 121, 167
  23.12.8: 120
  29.11.2: 110
  38.12.4–5: 109, 112
Posidonius, *BNJ* 87
  F 36: 165

[Sallust]
  Letter to Caesar
  7.12: 159
Scholia to Aeschines
  3.4: 21, 64
Scholia to Aristophanes
  Eq.
  855: 71
Simonides (ed. West)
  Fr. 86: 35
Solon (ed. West)
  Fr. 4.32: 11
  Fr. 5.1: 11
  Fr. 34.9: 11
Stesimbrotus of Thasos, *BNJ* 107
  F 4: 36
Strabo
  6.3.4: 102
  9.1.12: 86
  14.1.21: 109
  14.2.19: 156
  14.2.24: 151
Suetonius
  Claudius
  25.9: 166

Theophrastus
  Characters
  26.2: 38, 63
  26.3: 80
  26.4: 37
  26.5: 56, 67
  28.6: 76
  29.2–5: 84
Theopompus, *BNJ* 115
  FF 85–100: 55
  F 96a: 70
  F 100: 126
  F 233: 102, 126
Thucydides
  1.1.2: 44
  1.23.6: 44
  1.89–93: 85
  1.89.1: 43
  1.93.4: 86
  1.102.3: 43
  1.107.1: 85
  1.107.4: 37, 86
  1.108.3: 19
  1.110: 43
  1.122.3: 94
  2.8.4–5: 44
  2.13.5: 87
  2.34.1: 59
  2.34.6: 59
  2.35–46: 59
  2.37.2: 75
  2.65.8–9: 54
  2.65.9: 53
  2.65.10–11: 53
  3.62.3: 74

3.70.3: 54
3.82.8: 74
3.98.5: 81
4.28.5: 90
4.46.4: 54
4.48.5: 92
4.66.3: 54
4.74.3: 55
5.16.1: 54
5.31.6: 93
5.43.2: 52
5.47.1: 65
5.60.6: 81
5.81.2: 113
6.15.4: 94
6.35.2: 54
6.38.5: 74
6.54–58: 28
6.54.5: 16
6.89.5: 84
6.89.6: 90
7.55.2: 93
7.69.2: 75
8.53: 45
8.48: 24
8.48.1: 56
8.63.4: 56
8.64: 24
8.64.1: 44
8.65.2: 55
8.65.3: 88
8.66.1: 61
8.67–69: 45
8.73.3: 55, 70
8.86.8: 93
8.95–96: 24

Vita Sancti Pionii
7: 170

Xenophon
Hellenica
1.1.27–31: 81
1.7: 81
2.2.3: 44
2.2.6: 93
2.2.20: 37
2.2.23: 44
2.3.12: 67
2.3.48: 140
2.4.1: 46
2.4.38: 46
3.2.27: 54
3.4.7: 44
3.4.9: 95

5.2.1–10: 47
5.2.6: 92, 93
5.2.7: 54
5.3.10–25: 47
5.3.13: 67
5.4.1–12: 47
6.4.3–16: 47
6.5.7: 14
7.1.43: 93
7.1.44: 93
7.1.44–46: 94
7.3.12: 89, 128
7.4.3: 55
7.5.14–27: 47
Memorabilia
1.2.9: 61
1.2.40–46: 33, 82
1.2.58–59: 38
3.6.1: 52
3.7.5–6: 52
4.6.12: 20
[*Constitution of the Athenians*]
1.3: 64
1.4: 82, 84
1.5: 91
1.6–8: 82
1.9: 91
1.10–12: 136, 140
1.12: 74
1.13: 57, 67
1.14: 44
1.16–18: 67
2.9–10: 57, 126
3.2: 57, 126
3.11: 19, 38, 92
3.12–13: 82
3.13: 20

Epigraphical Texts
(For full bibliographic references, see https://aiegl.org/grepiabbr.html)
I. Délos
1512: 154
I. Didyma
84: 155
I. Ephesos
1320: 172
1470: 109
I. Labraunda
8: 114
47: 117
I. Rhamnous
404: 115
I. Stratonikeia
1204: 172

I. Didyma
  358: 127
I. Erythrai
  21: 114
  28: 110
  29: 115
  503: 129
I. Ilion
  25: 117, 139
  45: 117
I. Knidos
  51–55: 151
  59: 151
I. Kyme
  19: 152
I. Metropolis
  Ia: 150
I. Priene B-M
  6: 127, 132
  16–19: 127
  27: 128
  28: 135
  64: 153
  68: 154
  119: 122
  132: 127
I. Sinope
  1: 117
I. Thasos
  III.1: 93
  III.5: 111
IG
  I³ 1: 23
  I³ 14: 117
  I³ 229: 128
  I³ 1147: 59
  II² 448: 131
  II² 457: 132
  II² 1163: 110
  II² 13274: 172
  II² 13281: 172
  II³ 1 378: 131
  II³ 1 877: 127
  II³ 1 910: 129
  II³ 1 911: 100, 132
  II³ 1 918: 114
  II³ 1 985: 115
  IV 292–94: 154
  IV² 1 687: 164
  VII 190: 158
  VII 4148: 154
  XII.4 68: 115
  XII.4 132: 116, 120
  XII.4 152: 116
  XII.6 11: 143, 144
  XII.7 3: 92
  XII.9 192: 114, 127
  XII *Suppl.* 549: 24
IGCyr
  010800: 108
IGR
  III 409: 162
  III 800: 162
IosPE I²
  401: 117
  402: 117

Milet
  VI, 3 1129: 172
ML
  8: 12
  15: 16
  35: 59
  94: 128

Nomima
  I.78: 12
  I.100: 6

OGIS
  229: 117
  338: 139
  549: 158
OR
  111: 59
  121: 19, 21, 61
  122: 19
  126: 18, 24
  133: 24
  135: 87
  143: 19
  150: 51
  162: 51
  175: 25
  178: 88, 139
  191: 93

Rizakis, *Achaïe*
  III.3: 139
RO
  2: 94
  8: 46
  22: 47
  25: 57
  39: 92, 128
  41: 94, 117
  56: 47
  73: 127
  79: 117
  83B: 114

85: 92, 115
88: 116
99: 111

SEG
21.679: 123
23.938: 155, 162
24.1095: 110
25.847: 117
28.45: 88
28.46: 112
29.361: 59
30.80: 165
33.1035–41: 154
33.1039: 156
38.1163: 172
39.1155: 139
39.1244: 150
46.80: 69
47.1563: 117
48.592: 159
48.1472: 154
50.1112: 156
51.1075: 92
51.1105a: 108, 112
51.1105b: 114, 115, 117
51.1813–1814: 170
51.1832: 166
51.2217: 158
53.1597: 155
57.576: 92
57.820b: 111, 138
57.1409: 116
58.1220: 124, 127
58.1252: 172
58.1254: 172
59.1407: 115, 132
62.50: 89
63.645: 132
63.1147: 158
64.30: 117
67.792: 136

Syll.^{3}
353: 109
363: 127
495: 143
526: 115
589: 108, 135
591: 118
633: 101, 108
647: 110
683: 110
694: 125
730: 154
742: 139

TAM
II 176: 159
II 301: 159
II 905: 154
III.1 2: 117

General Index

Abdera/Abderites, 25, 124
Abydus/Abydenes, 110, 136, 139
acclamations, 155–56, 162–63, 171
accountability, 79–81
Achaea/Achaeans, 93, 94, 113, 117
Achaean League, 101, 103, 108, 112, 157
Achaean War, 98, 108, 148
Acragas/Acragantines, 34, 89
acropolis (high point of the city at Athens and elsewhere), 15, 26, 28, 32, 43, 47, 80, 86, 113, 114, 116, 129, 130, 132
Aegina/Aeginetans, 14, 35
Aelius Aristides, 155, 168
Aeneas Tacticus, 113
Aeschines, 40, 88
Aeschylus, 35, 44, 141
Aetolia, 81, 102, 121
Agathocles of Istria, 110
Agathocles of Syracuse, 119
agora (marketplace of a city), 9, 12, 17, 26–27, 28, 35, 37, 49, 52, 56, 59, 63, 68, 80, 87, 88, 89, 106, 113, 116, 123, 124, 128, 129, 130, 132, 150
agoranomoi (commissioners of the market), 63
Agyrrhius of Athens, 55
Aixone (Athenian deme), 72
Alcaeus of Mytilene, 12
Alcibiades of Athens, 52, 70, 82, 90
Alexander "the Great" of Macedon, 1, 5, 96, 97, 99, 112, 113, 128, 130
Alexander of Rhodes, 165
Alexandria Troas, 122
Alexandria/Alexandrians, 144, 147, 162, 173
amateurism, 78, 140
anarchy, 38, 76, 85
Anaximenes of Lampsacus, 103, 106, 107, 108, 109, 111, 119, 121, 145, 153
Andocides, 40, 71
Androcles of Athens, 55, 88

Antigonus Monophthalmus, 99, 100, 130
Antioch/Antiochenes, 167, 171
Antiochus II, 127
Antiochus III, 102
Antipater, 130
Antiphon, 40
antityranny legislation, 97, 108, 112, 114, 117, 129, 139, 182, *see also* tyrant/tyranny
Apatouria festival, 48
Aphrodisias, 151, 172
Apollo, 26, 115, 141
Apollonius of Metropolis, 150
Aratus of Sicyon, 101, 127
arbitrators, 71, 101, 120, 155
Arcadian League, 47, 55, 93
Arcesine on Amorgos, 92
archai. see magistrates/magistracies (*archai*)
Archilochus, 34
Archinus of Athens, 89
Archippe of Cyme, 154, 156
Arendt, Hannah, 78
Areopagus, 128
Argos/Argives, 6, 14, 18, 19, 24, 34, 41, 46, 54, 59, 63, 64–65, 71, 80, 81, 89, 92, 93, 113, 118, 120
Aristagoras of Miletus, 14, 19
Aristides of Athens, 68
Aristogeiton. *see* Harmodius and Aristogeiton
aristokratia, personification of, 123
Aristolaus (artist), 123
Aristonicus, 149, 150
Aristophanes, 40, 45, 50, 54, 58, 67, 121, 123, 141, 167
Aristotle, 6, 7, 9, 13, 15, 16–19, 22, 31, 37, 38, 48, 58, 63, 64, 66, 73, 75, 91, 94, 97, 103, 104–5, 106, 107, 108, 109, 113, 115, 119–21, 134, 137, 138, 139, 140, 168, 181
Artemidorus of Ephesus, 167,
Artemidorus, Gaius Julius of Cnidus, 151
Artemis, 114, 126
Assassin's Creed Odyssey (video game), 54

220

General Index

assembly (*ekklēsia*), 5, 9–13, 20, 21, 22–24, 25, 26, 31, 33, 35, 37, 42, 49–52, 53, 61, 62, 63, 64, 65, 66, 68, 71, 74–75, 76, 77, 79, 84, 89, 91, 97, 105, 107, 108, 109, 110–11, 117, 119, 121, 130, 132, 136, 141, 146, 147, 148, 149, 151, 152, 155, 158, 160–63, 167, 168, 169–74, 183
Astias of Thebes, 38
astu (city center), 28, 29, 37, 38, 72, 85, 113
astynomoi (commissioners of the city), 63
Athena, 64, 86, 131
Athenagoras of Syracuse, 74
Athenian Amnesty, 46
Athenian Empire, 7, 14, 19, 21, 35, 36, 37, 40, 41, 43, 45, 48, 56, 57, 61, 79, 81, 85, 86, 87, 90, 137, 143
Athenion of Athens, 165
Athens/Athenians, 6, 8, 10, 11, 13–16, 17, 21, 22, 27–28, 32, 40, 45, 53, 54, 56, 59, 73, 75, 78, 80, 83, 95, 99, 100, 110, 111–13, 117, 118, 123, 125–27, 128, 129–31, 134–35, 136–37, 139–40, 143–45, 157, 165, 175–76, 181–82
Augustus (Gaius Julius Caesar Octavianus), 5, 150, 151, 154
autochthony, 48, 60, 75, 137, 138
Avidius Cassius, 167

Bacchylides, 34
"barbarians" (non-Greeks), 110, 135, 141, 174
Battle of Aegospotami, 405 BCE, 93
Battle of Arginusae, 406 BCE, 81, 138
Battle of Chaeronea, 338 BCE, 99, 138
Battle of Cnidus, 394 BCE, 46, 88
Battle of Cynoscephalae, 197 BCE, 102
Battle of Leuctra, 371 BCE, 47
Battle of Mantinea, 362 BCE, 47, 98
Battle of Munychia, 403 BCE, 94
Battle of Pharsalus, 48 BCE, 151
Battle of Pydna, 168 BCE, 102
Battle of Tanagra, 457 BCE, 18
benefactors (*euergetēs/euergetai*), 80, 98, 111, 124, 127, 129, 132, 133, 142–45, 148, 149, 152–57, 162, 171, 173
Bias of Priene, 34
Bithynia-Pontus, 149, 158, 164, 168
Blok, Josine, 134–35
Boeotia, 6, 16, 19, 38, 93, 158
Boeotian League, 93
Boulagoras of Samos, 144
boulē. *see* council (*boulē*)
bouleutērion (Council House), 26, 80, 174
Brélaz, Cédric, 169
Buckley, William F., Jr., 77
building projects, 26, 27, 40, 43, 85, 86–87, 89, 122, 124, 162, 164, 181
Burckhardt, Jacob, 54

burial
in the *agora* or intramurally, 89, 127, 128, 130, 152, 156
of the war dead, 18, 59, 106, 107, 112
Burke, Edmund, 82
Byzantium, Byzantines, 123

Caesar, Gaius Julius, 151, 159, 165, 168
Caesarea/Caesareans, 170
Callias of Sphettus, 129
Callistratus of Athens, 55
Calymna/Calymnians, 116
Camarina, 34
Carthage/Carthaginians, 102
Carus (Emperor), 170
Carystus/Carystians, 158
casualty lists, 59
census. *see* property requirements
Cephalus of Athens, 55
Cephalus of Syracuse, 137
Chabrias of Athens, 88
Chalcis/Chalcidians, 16
Chariton of Aphrodias, 155
Chersonesus/Chersonesitans, 71, 116, 159
children/childhood, 47–49, 59, 60, 75, 88, 106, 111–12, 135–36, 138, 139
Chios/Chians, 12, 24, 35, 43, 92, 99, 114
Chremonidean War, 100
Christianity/Christians, 148, 161, 170, 172, 173
Cibyra, 117
Cicero, Marcus Tullius, 108, 141, 159, 168
Cimon of Athens, 37, 144
citizens (*politēs/politai*), 1, 3, 4, 7, 9, 10, 11, 14, 15, 16, 18, 19, 21, 22, 39, 104, 136, 137, 147, 156, 162, 168
City Dionysia, 57
Cius/Cianians, 119
civic subdivisions, 12, 15, 21, 26, 32, 80
class conflict, 9, 13, 15, 83, 90, 95, 119, 120, 121, 142, 160, 164
Claudius (Emperor), 166
Clearchus of Heraclea Pontica, 119
Cleisthenes of Athens, 16, 18, 20, 23, 25, 32, 68, 137, 181
Cleomenes, king of Sparta, 15, 19
Cleon of Athens, 54, 58, 67, 84, 90, 121
Cleophon of Athens, 54, 55, 84
Clitarchus of Eretria, 126
Cnidus/Cnidians, 46, 88, 120, 125, 151, 156
coins/coinage, 2, 35, 87, 120, 122, 125–26, 159, 160, 168, 169, 170
comedy, 54, 56, 58, 140
Conon of Athens, 46, 88
Constant, Benjamin, 69
Constantine (Emperor), 173

General Index

Corcyra/Corcyreans, 54, 92, 113, 118, 138
Corinth/Corinthians, 6, 12, 21, 46, 65, 93, 98, 99
Corinthian War, 46, 65, 93
Cos/Coans, 72, 115, 116, 120, 126, 156
council (*boulē*), 9, 11, 12, 22, 23–24, 25, 26, 31, 45, 49, 50–51, 56, 63, 64, 91, 100, 107, 109, 118, 121, 127, 146, 148, 149, 150, 155, 157, 158, 161, 169, 170, 171, 172, 181, 183
  evolution of in "late Hellenistic period," 160
countryside, 135
Cratinus, 54
Critias of Athens, 94, 123
cult, 9, 26, 31, 32, 48, 57–58, 86, 89, 115, 122, 123, 125–26, 154, 168, 181
curses, 25, 66
Cyme/Cymaeans, 97, 115, 132, 154, 156
Cyrene/Cyreneans, 71, 108
Cyriac of Ancona, 114
Cyzicus/Cyzicenes, 87

Damon of Athens, 78
Darius III of Persia, 99
de Ste. Croix, G. E. M., 180
debt, cancellation of, 115
decarchy, 46
Decelea (Athenian deme), 45
Decius (Emperor), 170
decree (*psēphisma*), 8, 12, 22, 23–25, 40, 46, 49, 61, 79, 82, 88, 89, 107, 109, 112, 114, 115, 116, 120, 121, 123, 124, 126, 127, 128, 129, 130–33, 135, 136, 139, 144–45, 148, 149, 150, 154, 157, 159, 161, 169, 173, 181
defixiones (binding spells), 66
Delos/Delians, 43, 126
Delphi/Delphians, 26, 115, 159
demagogues/demagoguery, 4, 37, 42, 45, 53–55, 58, 65, 71, 74, 84, 88, 92, 94, 97, 105, 106, 107, 108, 109, 113, 119–22, 125, 141, 147, 151, 160–69, 181
demes
  of Attica, 28–31, 45, 46, 48–49, 53, 63, 64, 68, 69, 71–72, 86, 130
  of Cos, 72
  of Eretria, 32
Demeter, 127
Demetrius I Poliorcetes, 100, 111, 130, 139, 166
Demetrius of Phalerum, 109, 129, 130, 132, 143
Demochares of Athens, 145
Democritus, 140
dēmokratia, 2, 8, 10, 16, 20, 23, 35, 123, 125, 135, 147, 149, 165, 169, 175
  personification of, 123, 125, 146
dēmos ("the People"), 8, 9, 10, 12, 14, 15, 20, 22, 24, 35, 38, 49, 64, 73, 75, 76, 77, 79, 81, 92, 105, 107, 112, 133, 135, 139, 157, 160–74

  personification of, 58, 89, 123, 126, 131, 132, 151, 159, 169
Demosthenes of Athens, 40, 66, 77, 78, 81, 118, 121, 123, 145, 147, 181
Diagoras of Eretria, 17–18, 31–32
Dicaea/Dicaeopolitans, 92
Dio Chrysostom, 109, 155, 161, 166
diōbelia (welfare fund at Athens), 56
Diocles of Syracuse, 62, 81
Diodorus Pasparus of Pergamum, 154
Dion of Syracuse, 114, 118, 120
Dionysius I of Syracuse, 88, 94, 119
Dionysius II of Syracuse, 102, 114, 129
Dionysus, 44, 114, 125, 127
disability, 56
Dissoi Logoi, 62, 90, 106
distribution of wealth, 33, 73, 136, 143, 155, 181
document reliefs, 123, 131, 132
dokimasia, 79
domination, 83
Droysen, J. G., 97
du Bois, W. E. B., 141

Egypt, 43, 44, 45, 162
Eighty (board of magistrates at Argos), 65
ekklēsia. see assembly (*ekklēsia*)
election, 11, 53, 61–62, 63–64, 65, 77, 105, 106, 108, 110, 111, 115, 144, 155, 160
Elis/Eleans, 6, 14, 18, 19, 37, 54, 55, 93, 94, 117, 118
emotions, 66, 132, 141
Empedocles, 34
Emperor, Roman and Imperial Family, 150, 155, 164, 166, 167, 169
Epaminondas of Thebes, 47, 98
ephebes/ephebate, 49, 101, 116, 149, 154
Ephesus/Ephesians, 19, 25, 34, 69, 109, 128, 139, 167, 168
Ephialtes of Athens, 13, 128
Epicrates of Athens, 55
Epidaurus/Epidaurians, 164
epiklētoi (oligarchic office at Ephesus), 109
epitaphios logos (funeral oration at Athens), 58–60, 75
Eponymous Heroes of Attica, 26, 56
equality, 1, 3, 11, 12, 14, 33, 39, 42, 73–75, 77, 81, 85–89, 105, 117, 134, 137, 140, 141, 142, 153, 169, 172, 182
Erechtheion, 86
Eresus, 114
Eretria/Eretrians, 6, 8, 9, 14, 17–18, 24, 31–32, 72, 85, 97, 99, 108, 112, 113, 114, 117, 122, 126, 127, 139
Erythrae/Erythraeans, 6, 19, 21, 41, 46, 47, 61, 114, 115, 117, 126, 129
Euboea, 6, 31, 32, 43, 99, 118, 126, 158

General Index

euergetēs, euergetai. see benefactors (*euergetēs/euergetai*)
euergetism, 142–45, 152
eunomia ("good order"), 9–13, 24, 33, 35, 66, 91
Euphraeus of Oreus, 118
Euphranor (artist), 123
Euphron of Sicyon the elder, 89, 94, 128, 130
Euphron of Sicyon the younger, 130–32
Eupolis, 54
Euripides, 44, 58, 141
Euthydemus of Mylasa, 151
euthynai (audits of outgoing officials), 79
Evagoras of Salamis, 88

Fabiani, Roberta, 109
festivals, 16, 28, 34, 48, 56, 57–58, 72, 87, 89, 113, 114, 122, 124, 126–29, 144, 151
finance, 21, 32, 56, 65, 142, 143
fines, 57, 67, 79
Flamininus, Titus Quinctius, 102, 158
fleet. see navy/fleet
foreign judges, 101, 121, 149, see also judges (*dikastai*)
Foucault, Michel, 76
Four Hundred (oligarchic regime at Athens), 45, 79, 88, 93, 112
Framers of the United States Constitution, 50
freedom, 73–75, 85, 89, 101, 103, 105, 114, 115, 122, 124, 126, 127, 137, 138, 139, 140, 141, 144, 145, 150, 151, 166, 182
"true," 76
neo-republican notion of, 83, 141
of speech, 76–77, 140, see *parrhēsia* ("frank speaking," "freedom of speech")
personal, 75–76
Freud, Sigmund, 167
funerals, 58, 59, 60, 75, 148, 154, 156, 181

Gallienus (Emperor), 169
gamoroi ("land-sharers") of Syracuse, 6
garrison, 100, 114, 118, 126, 127, 130
Gauthier, Philippe, 101, 132, 144, 145, 182, 183
gender, 3, 7, 9, 14, 26, 33, 39, 42, 47–49, 57, 87, 125, 133, 134–36, 141, 156, 172, 181, see also men, see also women
generals, 21, 46, 47, 48, 51, 53, 70, 81, 88, 97, 98, 101, 115, 130
Gorgias of Leontini, 144
Graces, 126
Great Rhetra of Sparta, 10
Grote, George, 54, 96
gymnasiarch/gymnasiarchy, 149, 154

Hadrian (Emperor), 158, 160, 182
Hagnonides of Athens, 130

Halasarna (deme of Cos), 72
Hamilcar Barca, 38
Hannibal Barca, 38
Harmodius and Aristogeiton, 17, 27, 29, 35, 88, 143
Hegel, G. W. F., 104
Hellenotamiae, 81
Heller, Anna, 154, 170, 183
helots, 43, 47
Heraclea Pontica/Heracleotes, 54, 113, 119, 165
Heraclea under Latmus, 101, 108, 117
Heraclides of Syracuse, 114, 119, 120
Heraclitus of Ephesus, 25, 34, 69, 167
herald of the assembly, 50, 51, 135
hero cult, 89, 128, 130, 143, 150, 151
Herod the Great, 154
Herodes Atticus, 156
Herodotus, 7, 13, 18, 19, 20, 23, 62, 79, 106
Heropythus of Ephesus, 128
Hiero II of Syracuse, 102, 123
Hiero of Priene, 127
Hiero of Syracuse, 33
Hieronymus of Syracuse, 102
Hipparchus of Athens (son of Pisistratus), 27
Hipparchus the son of Charmus of Athens, 68
hippeis ("horsemen," Eretrian regime), 6, 17, 18
Hippias of Athens, 27
Hippon of Syracuse, 120, 141
Histiaeus of Miletus, 6
ho boulomenos. see volunteer (*ho boulomenos*)
Homer, 10, 26, 38, 56, 161
homonoia (unanimity), 75, 111, 115, 139, 151, 159, 164, 165, 166
honors, 11, 17, 18, 28, 35, 46, 57, 69, 80, 83, 88, 89, 99, 102, 105–7, 111–12, 114, 127, 128, 129, 130–31, 132, 133, 138, 139, 142–45, 148, 149, 150–57, 159–60, 161, 162, 163, 166, 170–72, 173
hoplites, 4, 44, 56, 137
Hortensius, Lucas, 124
hubris, 44, 67, 80, 92, 94
Hybreas, Gaius Julius of Mylasa, 152
Hyperbolus of Athens, 54, 55, 71, 84

Iasos/Iasians, 109, 111
Ilium/Ilians, 117, 129, 139
inscribing of political decisions, 8, 23, 80, 89, 92, 100, 107, 123, 125, 128, 149, 157, 159, 170
Ion of Chios, 35, 37
Iphicrates of Athens, 64, 88
isēgoria (equality of public/political address), 51, 74, 137, 163, 169
Isocrates, 77
isonomia ("equal distribution" of political power), 11–12, 19, 20, 28, 33, 73–74, 117

isopoliteia (bilateral offer to grant citizenship between the citizens of two different poleis), 101, 108, 149, 182
Istria/Istrians, 110
Itanos/Itanians, 115
Iulis on Ceos, 128

James, C. L. R., 78
John Chrysostom, 171
judges (*dikastai*), 9, 65–67, 105, 107, 116, 122, 146, 149, 159, *see also* foreign judges
justice, 25, 58, 65–67, 73, 78, 80, 82, 83–84, 116, 121–22, 146, 159, 166, 182

Kerameikos, 59, 69
King's Peace, 47
Koiratadas of Thebes, 38

Labienus, Quintus, 151
Lalla of Tlos, 155
Lamian War, 100, 130
Lampsacus/Lampsacenes, 103, 145, 153, *see also* Anaximenes of Lampsacus
Larsen, J. A. O., 1
law (*nomos*), 33, 72, 74, 108
  rule of, 82
law courts (*dikastērion/dikastēria*), 26, 65–67, 76, 84, 107, 110, 120, 129, 146, 148, 159
Law of Eucrates, 117, 123, 124
Lenaea festival, 58
Leon of Athens, 121
Lesbos, 43, 114
limitations on office holding, 21, 63, 64
literacy, 68, 80
liturgy/liturgies, 56, 73, 143, 149, 154, 157
logographos (speechwriter), 66
Long Walls of Athens, 37, 44–45, 85, 86
lottery/sortition, 21, 62, 78, 110, 159
Lycia, 154, 167, 168
Lycurgus of Athens, 116, 132, 136, 138, 144, 153
Lysander of Sparta, 44, 46, 92
Lysias, 40, 59
Lysicles of Athens, 54
Lysimachus, 68, 109

Macedon/Macedonians, 97, 100, 102, 110, 118, 124, 126, 131
magic, 66, 70
magistrates/magistracies (*archai*), 10, 12, 16, 22, 61–65, 105, 107–9, 111, 143, 146, 148, 155, 160, 162, 163, 169, 170
Magnesia on the Maeander, 108
Magnesia under Sipylus, 116

Mantinea/Mantineans, 18, 19, 47, 54, 89, 92, 93, *see also* Battle of Mantinea, 362 BCE
Marcus Aurelius (Emperor), 167
marriage, politics of, 17
Marx/Marxism, 72, 91, 156, 180
Massalia/Massaliotes, 118
Medeon, 110
Megalopolis/Megalopolitans, 47, 89
Megara/Megarians, 71, 93, 118
memory, 59, 89, 131
men, 41, 47–49, 51, 53, 57, 64, 65, 72, 74, 87, 89, 101, 104, 110, 133, 134–36, 149, 159, 168, 172, *see also* gender, *see also* women
Mencken, H. L., 55
Menemachus of Sardis, 164
Messene/Messenians, 19, 47, 110, 118
Metapontum/Metapontines, 125
metics (foreign residents), 56, 57, 112, 134, 136–39, 140, 181
Metropolis/Metropolitans, 150
Miletus/Milesians, 6, 19, 92, 108, 109, 110, 127, 135, 160
Miltiades of Athens, 36
misthos (payment, often for office holding), 22, 63, 65, 78–79, 107, 108, 168
Mithridates of Pontus, 139, 149, 165
Mnaseas of Rhodes, 165
Molpagoras of Cius, 119
Moschion of Priene, 153–54
Mummius, Lucius, 98, 103, 158
murder/assassination, 55, 70, 120, 151, 165, 173
Mylasa/Mylasans, 114, 123, 127, 151–52
Mytilene/Mytilenaeans, 12, 75, 115, 151

navy/fleet, 37, 44, 46, 56, 57, 85, 93, 106, 137, *see also* trireme
Naxos/Naxians, 43, 71
Nicaea/Nicaeans, 160
Niceratus of Olbia, 154
Nicias of Athens, 70, 75
Nicodromus of Aegina, 14
Nicolaus of Damascus, 154, 155
Nicomedia/Nicomedians, 158, 160
Nietzsche, Friedrich, 78
nomophylakes (guardians of the law), 108–9
nomothesia (passing of laws), 82

oaths, 88, 89, 91–92, 93, 100, 115–17
Ober, Josiah, 146
Odeion, 86
Odysseus, 38
Old Oligarch (pseudo-Xenophon), 20, 38, 57, 64, 82, 84, 91, 106, 126, 137

General Index

oligarchy/oligarchs, 4, 11, 13, 16, 20, 34, 42, 45–47, 54–55, 61, 62, 67, 73–74, 75–76, 82, 88, 90–95, 98–100, 103, 104, 107–9, 111–16, 117–20, 123, 126, 128–29, 131, 139, 148, 157–58, 162, 163, 166, 168, 169, 181, 182
  personification of, 37, 80
Olympichus, 114, 124, 127
onomastics (the study of names), 38
Opramoas of Rhodiapolis, 154
orator. *see rhētōr* (orator)
orphans, 59, 88, 107, 111, 117, 138
Osborne, Robin, 140, 181, 182
ostracism, 25, 68–71
Oxyrhynchus, 171

Paches of Athens, 81
Palmatius of Caesarea, 170
Panathenaea Festival of Athens, 16, 87
Paralus (Athenian state galley), 44
Pardalas of Sardis, 164–65
parents/parentage, 47–49, 73, 133, 139, 160
Parrhasius (artist), 123
parrhēsia ("frank speaking," "freedom of speech"), 76–77, 120, 140, 146, 163
Parthenon, 26, 43, 86
Pausanias (*periegete*), 7
Pausanias King of Sparta, 86–87
Pelopidas of Thebes, 47
Peloponnesian War (431–404 BCE), 1, 7, 18, 19, 35, 37, 40, 43, 44, 46, 55, 59, 93, 94, 182
Pergamum/Pergamenes, 125
Pericles of Athens, 22, 48, 53, 59
Pericles' Citizenship Law of 451/0, 22, 47–49, 75
Perinthus/Perinthians, 123
peristiarchos, 50
Perseus of Macedon, 102, 110
Persia/Persians, 17, 19, 25, 36, 44, 45, 46–47, 50, 86, 99
Persian Wars (490 and 480–79 BCE), 8, 13, 17, 19, 25, 28, 43, 85, 99
Pescennius Niger, 167
petalism (form of ostracism at Syracuse), 71
Phalerum (Athenian harbor), 37
Phanes of Erythrae, 114
Phidias, 86
Philip II of Macedon, 96, 98
Philip V of Macedon, 100, 102, 110, 136, 139
Philippus of Pergamum, 164
Philites of Erythrae, 129
Philo of Alexandria, 146–47
Philoxenus ("demagogic" tyrant), 94, 119
Phlius/Phliasians, 47, 67, 94, 117
phratries, 31, 48, 80
Pidasa/Pidasans, 117, 136
Pindar, 7, 33, 35

Pionios of Smyrna, 170
Piraeus (Athenian harbor), 37, 43–45, 85
Pisistratids of Athens, 16, 27
Pisistratus of Athens, 15, 68
plague of Athens, 45, 53
Plato, 2, 40, 51, 52, 59, 61, 70, 86, 160
Plato Comicus, 54
Pliny the Elder, 123
Pliny the Younger, 164
Plutarch, 7, 8, 12, 141, 162, 163–65, 166
Pnyx Hill of Athens, 25, 26, 35, 50, 89
polemarchs, 65
politeia (constitution/citizenship), 20, 29, 33, 93, 100, 103, 104, 114, 134–35, 166, 181
politeuma, 61, 116
Polybius, 2, 102, 110, 112–13, 120, 121, 129
Pompey the Great (Gnaeus Pompeius Magnus), 149, 151, 158
Pont, Anne-Valérie, 173
Posidonius of Apamea, 166
poverty, 181
Priene/Prienians, 127, 153
probouleuma, 11, 51, 155, 162
probouleusis (advance deliberation), 10–11, 23, 24, 63
probouloi (oligarchic magistracy), 12, 108, 109, 158
property requirements, 20–21, 34, 61, 64, 102, 103, 107, 108, 109, 121, 137, 158, 159, 162, 166, *see also* wealth/wealthy
Propylaea, 86
prostatēs ("champion," usually of the People), 15, 118, 119, 137, 145, 153
proxeny, 101, 128
prytaneis ("presidents" at Athens and elsewhere), 31, 51, 109
prytany (tenth of the political year at Athens), 31, 63, 68, 71
Ptolemy III, 144
punishment
  corporal, 57
  legal, 67, 81, 136, 165
Pyrrhus of Epirus, 102

race/racialization, 140, 141
reconciliation, 115, 182, *see also* Athenian Amnesty
recordkeeping/bureaucracy, 65, 69, 80
redistribution
  of land, 15, 24, 31, 82, 106, 115, 119–20, 141
  through confiscation, 24, 73
  through taxation, 56, 73, 137, 143
representative democracy, 4
rhētōr (orator), 53–54, 63, 77, 84, 119, 121, 151, 160–61, 163, 170, 174
Rhodes, P. J., 51, 182

Rhodes/Rodians, 94, 99, 108, 110, 111, 120, 123, 130, 139, 159, 165, 168, 181
Robert, Louis, 152–53, 182, 183
Robinson, Eric, 89, 97, 181, 182
Rome/Roman Empire, 75, 102, 150, 151, 157, 165, 168
Rousseau, Jean-Jacques, 55

sacrifices, 4, 50, 86, 115, 125–27
Sallust (Gaius Sallustius Crispus), 141, 159
Samons, Loren J., Jr., 141
Samos/Samians, 43, 70, 93
Sardis/Sardians, 163–64
Second Athenian League, 47
Second Macedonian War, 100, 157
Second Punic War, 102
Seleucus I, 99
Senate of Rome, 63, 102, 150
Septimius Severus (Emperor), 167
Sicily, 6, 45
Sicyon/Sicyonians, 89, 127, 130, 132
Sidyma, 159
Simonides, 35
Sinope/Sinopeans, 117
skytalismos (clubbing) of Argos, 92
slaves/slavery, 3, 4, 18, 38, 43, 48, 54, 56, 57, 58, 71, 73, 75, 76, 83, 91, 134, 135, 137, 138, 139–42, 157, 181, 182
Smyrna/Smyrnaeans, 117, 170
Social War, 99
Socrates, 20, 51–52, 61, 66, 86, 161
Solon, 11–12
Solonian census classes, 11, 61
Sophocles, 36, 44
sortition. *see* lottery/sortition
Sotas of Priene, 135
Soteria Festival, 127
Sparta/Spartans, 9, 10–11, 16, 18, 19, 21, 23, 28, 36, 37, 42, 43, 44–47, 49, 62, 81, 91, 92, 93, 94, 97, 109, 110, 182
stasis (civil strife), 20, 34, 37, 41, 45, 90–91, 92, 93, 105, 113, 119, 138, 153, 164, 166, 167, 173, 182
statues, 18, 28, 35, 46, 56, 86, 87–89, 123–25, 127–30, 143, 148, 149, 150, 153, 159, 164, 183
Stesimbrotus of Thasos, 36
Sthenis of Himera, 151
Stiris, 110
Stoa Basileios of Athens, 123
Stovall, Tyler, 3
Strabo, 7
Stratonicea/Stratoniceans, 172
Styra, 32
Sulla, 165

sykophants, 67, 71
sympoliteia, 110, 116, 117, 135
synedroi, 158
synoecism, 9, 18
Syracuse/Syracusans, 6, 41, 62, 71, 74, 81, 89, 93, 94, 102, 108, 120, 123, 129, 141, 163

Tarentum/Tarentines, 102, 121, 126
Tarsus/Tarsians, 161–62
Teegarden, David, 117, 182
Tegea/Tegeans, 19
Telos/Telians, 109, 116, 117, 120, 126
Teos/Teans, 26, 124, 125, 136
term of office, 21, 79, 107
Termessus/Termessians, 118, 170
Thasos/Thasians, 36, 41, 43, 92, 111, 138
Thebes/Thebans, 6, 19, 35, 38, 46, 47, 74, 93, 95, 98, 99
Themistocles of Athens, 8, 36, 68, 69, 85, 86
Theophanes, Gnaeus Pompeius of Mytilene, 151
Theophrastus, 37, 63, 64, 67, 80, 83, 84
Theopompus of Chios, 126
Theozotides of Athens, 88
Theseus, 123
Thessaly, 158
Third Macedonian War, 124
Thirty Tyrants (Athenian oligarchic regime), 45–46, 67, 79, 82, 88, 113, 123, 126, 128
Thirty Years' Peace, 43
Thonemann, Peter, 167, 182
thorubos (raising a ruckus), 51–52, 109, 160–61, 163, 170
Thrasybulus of Athens, 46, 88, 126
Thucydides, 2, 8, 16, 37, 40, 43, 44, 53, 54, 55, 58, 59, 65, 70, 74, 86, 90, 92, 113, 145, 174
Thurii/Thurians, 71
Timaeus of Tauromenium, 102
timētai (Roman-style censors), 158
Timoleon of Syracuse, 129
Timotheus of Athens, 88
Tiryns, 12
titles, 148, 155, 160, 170, 171
Tlos/Tloeis, 155
tragedy, 58
Tribute-Quota Lists, 43
trireme, 56, *see also* navy/fleet
trittys/trittyes (thirds), 28
tyrant/tyranny, 6–7, 11, 14, 15, 16, 17, 18, 27–28, 32–35, 46, 54, 55, 68, 77, 82, 88, 89, 95, 97, 98–99, 102, 104, 112, 113–19, 126–30, 139, 164, *see also* antityranny legislation
Tyrrhenus of Sardis, 164

United States of America, 50, 60
urbanization, 8, 16, 45

Valerian (Emperor), 170
veto, 10, 23, 49, 51, 109
Veyne, Paul, 142, 182, 183
virtue, 34, 76, 77, 169
volunteer (*ho boulomenos*), 67, 169

walls, 37, 44, 85–86, 114
war/warfare, *see also* individual wars, 3, 4, 15, 19, 44, 47, 131
wealth/wealthy, 6, 20, 33, 36, 53, 56–57, 58, 67, 73, 74, 86, 90, 103, 105–7, 119, 137, 140, 142, 146, 148, 149, 152–57, 158, 160, *see also* oligarchy/oligarchs
women, 58, 136, 138, 154, 155, 156, *see also* men, *see also* gender

Xanthippus of Athens, 48, 68
xenia (guest friendship), 15
Xenophon, 2, 20, 41, 44, 47, 52, 82, 89, 108, 128

Zeus, 8
Zoilus, Gaius Julius of Aphrodisias, 151
Zosimus, Aulus Aemilius of Priene, 154

For EU product safety concerns, contact us at Calle de José Abascal, 56–1º,
28003 Madrid, Spain or eugpsr@cambridge.org.

www.ingramcontent.com/pod-product-compliance
Ingram Content Group UK Ltd.
Pitfield, Milton Keynes, MK11 3LW, UK
UKHW022317240426
470365UK00021B/665